Latin American Economic Development

T0293214

Latin America is one of the most intriguing parts of the world. The region's illustrious history, culture, and geography are famous internationally, but in terms of economics, Latin America has been generally associated with problems. For many, the combination of a resource-rich region and poor economic conditions has been a puzzle.

This extensively revised and updated third edition of *Latin American Economic Development* continues to provide the most up-to-date exploration of why the continent can be considered to have underperformed, how the various Latin American economies function, and the future prospects for the region. The book addresses the economic problems of Latin America theme by theme.

Changes and new features in this new edition include:

- a new chapter on economic growth that reflects the new understanding of slow growth in the region;
- two new appendices on basic microeconomics and macroeconomics;
- expanded coverage on new commodities such as lithium and quinoa;
- a number of new boxes and updates to existing boxes.

The book provides a comprehensive text for undergraduate economics courses on Latin America and is also suitable for use by students in other disciplines looking for a wide-ranging guide to the region. This book will continue to be an invaluable resource for undergraduates looking at Latin American economics, growth, and development.

Javier A. Reyes is Professor of Economics and the Milan Puskar Dean of the John Chambers College of Business and Economics, University of West Virginia, US.

W. Charles Sawyer is the Hal Wright Professor of Latin American Economics, Texas Christian University, US.

Routledge Textbooks in Development Economics

African Economic Development
Steven Langdon, Archibald R. M. Ritter and Yiagadeesen Samy

Development Economics
A Critical Introduction
Shahrukh Khan

Latin American Economic Development, 3e
Javier A. Reyes and W. Charles Sawyer

For more information about this series, please visit: www.routledge.com/Routledge-Textbooks-in-Development-Economics/book-series/RTDE

Latin American Economic Development

Third edition

Javier A. Reyes and W. Charles Sawyer

LONDON AND NEW YORK

Third edition published 2020
by Routledge
2 Park Square, Milton Park, Abingdon, Oxon OX14 4RN

and by Routledge
52 Vanderbilt Avenue, New York, NY 10017

Routledge is an imprint of the Taylor & Francis Group, an informa business

© 2020 Javier A. Reyes and W. Charles Sawyer

First edition published by Routledge 2011
Second edition published by Routledge 2016

British Library Cataloguing-in-Publication Data
A catalogue record for this book is available from the British Library

Library of Congress Cataloging-in-Publication Data
A catalog record has been requested for this book

ISBN: 978-1-138-38840-6 (hbk)
ISBN: 978-1-138-38841-3 (pbk)
ISBN: 978-0-429-42556-1 (ebk)

Typeset in Times New Roman
by Newgen Publishing UK

Contents

Figures

Tables

Boxes

Acknowledgments

Books don't appear out of a vacuum. Like coffee, this one has been brewing for a number of years. The frustrations of trying to teach the economics of Latin America led to many conversations over the years about just how to do this. As a result, the "contributors" to the process that culminated in this book are literally too numerous to mention. This is especially true of the main contributors to this process: our students. The years of reading exams and papers do a brutally efficient job of telling one what works and what doesn't, what's possible and what's not. More subtle, but just as revealing, are the excitement generated in a class when something works and the blank faces telling one when something doesn't. An area study class such as Latin American economics offers one further check on the material. This is the "now I understand why something happens in my country" look. Few things in a classroom are more rewarding and instructive. We would also like to thank a different class of students who have contributed to the approach used in the book. A class of good MBA students can really help one focus on what the point of a course is. Knowledge for the sake of knowledge is a valuable thing. However, knowledge that can be usefully applied can be of even greater value. In this regard, bright students with work experience can be very effective teachers.

A few more specific thanks are in order. We would like to thank Tom Fullerton for first planting the idea of writing this book. At the time, his suggestion was not taken seriously. A subsequent suggestion by Robert Langham was. His editorial work was absolutely critical in the development of this book. His support and especially his patience are deeply appreciated. Robert's support of this book was been taken up by Emily Kinleysides in the first and second edition. For this edition, Lisa Lavelle patiently helped us through the process. Without her support, the third edition would not have been possible. We would also like to thank Juan José Miranda for his valuable suggestions on climate change. Luisa Blanco, Isabel Ruiz, and Rossitza Wooster have helped give us a better understanding of foreign direct investment (FDI) in Latin America. In a more general sense, we have benefited from conversations with César Rodriguez and Alejandro Velez. For this edition, we would like to thank Susan Ramirez for valuable insights on colonial Latin America. Alejandro Murillo Segura provided outstanding research work on this edition. Finally, between this draft being written and the book you are reading is a morass of tedious detail that most readers, fortunately, will never experience. Thankfully, the authors didn't bear the brunt of it. If the authors are lucky, there is someone with an infinite reservoir of competence, patience, and good cheer who accomplishes this. For this edition, we were lucky enough to have Liz Hudson and Kelly Winter turning the very rough draft into a "book." Finally, we would like to thank the University of West Virginia and Texas Christian University for providing the environment and resources for us to write this book.

Preface

Trying to teach the economics of Latin America to undergraduate students can be a frustrating task. Attempting to cover 500 years of economic history inevitably involves a difficult set of trade-offs. Spend too much time on history, and the Lost Decade may end up being "lost." Allocate too much time to the late twentieth century, and it is all too easy to neglect colonial Latin America and its lingering effects in the twenty-first century. There are countless other examples. A region that is large and diverse, and has a long history, creates many such trade-offs. From the start, it has to be realized that one cannot cover *everything* in one semester. The problem then becomes one of deciding what is included in the course and what is not. While this solves the main problem, the question of how much emphasis to put on each topic is still on the table. The objective is to narrow the material to a manageable amount for the typical one-semester course. This is particularly the case in an area where there is no established "template." We have tried to do this in three ways, listed below.

In trying to narrow and balance the material in the book, we have consistently relied on a concrete decision rule that focuses on the students enrolled in the course. For the vast majority of students, this course will be their only exposure to the economics of Latin America. One can assume that, for whatever reason, they have an inherent interest in the area. It may be purely personal or involve their professional goals. Normally, this interest won't stop after the semester is over. Most of the students will continue to follow developments in the region throughout their careers. It is also safe to assume that very few will follow developments in Latin America by reading academic journals. Their main sources of information will probably be reading material in publications such as *The Economist*, the *Financial Times*, or the host of other sources of information that assume readers have a post-secondary degree. This situation sets up the primary decision rule for this book. Our objective is to equip students leaving this course with the minimum amount of information necessary for them to easily understand virtually anything about the economics of Latin America that they are likely to encounter in their careers. In modern parlance, we are attempting to help students become the proverbial "intelligent layman" with respect to the economics of the region. A simple thought exercise illustrates what the book is trying to accomplish. At the start of the course, most students might find reading an article on economics in "The Americas" section of *The Economist* to be relatively difficult. In many cases, these articles are assuming that the reader has a certain background level of knowledge that most students don't have. The purpose of this book is to provide just this sort of information.

History and institutions

Historically, Latin American economics has been taught with an emphasis on history and institutions. Both of these are important approaches to the subject. Modern Latin America was born of an invasion from Europe, and the subsequent 500 years have been characterized by conditions that were not always conducive to economic growth. Further, in any economy or region, institutions matter for economic development. As a result, the book includes a substantial amount of historical and institutional material. However, one cannot possibly cover all of this material. Again, in this regard, there is a decision rule. Most of the historical and institutional information covered is that which still affects Latin America in the twenty-first century. This serves to make the material both more manageable and more relevant to the lives of the students taking the course. An example of this approach is the box on "Two Wars" in Chapter 2. While these conflicts occurred over 100 years ago, they still affect a number of the countries in the region.

Major themes in Latin American economic development

While history and institutions are critical in understanding the economies of the region, they are only some of the tools that are necessary for understanding the contemporary economic situation in the region. The next task is to reduce the material students need to know to a manageable collection of common themes. The book is organized around the major themes listed below.

Growth: The most serious problem of modern Latin America has been that economic growth has been slow relative to much of the rest of the world.

Commodities: Many countries in Latin America are major producers and exporters of commodities, and this has had a substantial influence on the economic development of the region.

Import substitution industrialization (ISI): In the second half of the twentieth century, many countries in Latin America attempted to create industries designed to replace imports from developed countries. ISI has had very important implications for economic development in the region.

Trade policy: From the 1930s, Latin America has pursued trade policies that tended to make the markets of the region relatively closed to foreign competition. This overall policy had a tendency to make Latin America less integrated into the world economy.

Exchange-rate policy: Countries have a choice between managing their exchange rate and allowing it to float. In Latin America, these choices at times have had serious implications in terms of economic growth.

Debt: A recurring theme in Latin American economic history has been the tendency for governments in the region to borrow heavily from banks and other financial institutions.

Macroeconomic instability: On average, gross domestic product (GDP) growth, inflation, and unemployment have been somewhat unstable in many countries of Latin America. Unfortunately, this instability has been so pervasive that for many it is one of the defining characteristics of the region. Explaining this instability is one of the major tasks of this book.

Poverty and inequality: GDP per capita in Latin America is low relative to the high-income countries. In addition, Latin America has one of the most unequal distributions of income in the world.

Obviously, this is not an exhaustive list of all the economic issues of the region. However, in keeping with the discussion above, it represents a minimum list of subjects necessary for a student to be able to understand the current and future state of the region. Even with this minimum list of themes, covering this material in one semester could be difficult. In order to keep the amount of material manageable, the book has been written with an assumption about the students. The basic assumption is that students using this book will have had at least a one-semester survey of economics course, or perhaps a two-semester principles sequence. In accordance with this assumption, all the tools of analysis used throughout the book are those used in principles of economics. We have found that this frees the instructor from attempting to teach *both* the materials and new tools of analysis. Conveying the basic themes given above can be done with principles-level tools. In turn, this frees up more time to spend on more material related to the region. However, we do not assume that students perfectly recall what they learned in principles. In most cases, the basic tools of analysis are briefly reviewed in order to ensure that students are prepared to use the tools to analyze economic issues in the region.

Analysis of economic policy in Latin America

To further narrow the scope of the course, we have avoided the sometimes acrimonious debates over economic policy in the region. To a large extent, the countries of the region are operating under the general umbrella of "democratic capitalism." Policy in the region is now set by freely elected governments. No economist can perfectly predict the outcome of various policies or perfectly prescribe policies for any particular country. However, economists have learned over the years that certain policies tend to have particular outcomes. For example, large government budget deficits financed by printing money tend to lead to inflation. Unfortunately, Latin America has been a proving ground for such major policy mistakes. Thus, the analysis of policy in the book focuses on what actually occurred in the past and the effects of recent changes in policy in much of the region. Our focus is on applying standard economic analysis to economic history and the current situation. We consciously avoid discussing what *should* have happened in the past or *should* occur in the future. The former is usually obvious, and the latter is the prerogative of the citizens of the region. This allows the instructor to focus on analyzing policies, the results of past policies, and the potential outcome of current policies. Our focus is on equipping students with the tools of analysis to be able to analyze policy. Students with good tools of analysis can understand policy on a somewhat higher level than their more unfortunate contemporaries without such tools.

In summary, our hope is that this book will be of use to instructors attempting to teach an inherently difficult course. In this case, the difficulty is one of the sheer breadth of the material. What we have attempted to do is reduce the material to an amount that balances student needs with the realities of the limited time available in a one-semester course. We've attempted to do this by using a limited number of important themes and by balancing history and institutions and standard economic analysis. Finally, for several reasons, we have tried to produce a book that, to the greatest extent possible, relies on economic analysis for guidance on questions of economic policy. As will be shown at many points in the book, ideology mixed with policy without economic analysis can lead to unfortunate outcomes.

1 Latin America and the world economy

Introduction

Since you are reading this book, it is safe to assume that you have an interest in Latin America. That's understandable. Latin America is a very interesting region of the world for any number of reasons. In terms of world history, language, literature, music, and, more currently, sports, Latin America is a very influential part of the world. While this is common knowledge, the place of Latin America in the world economy usually is less well understood. If you were asked to write a paragraph about Latin America in the world economy, what would you write? For many, the answer would be "not much." The first objective of this chapter is to provide you with some useful background information on the region. The focus of the chapter is to provide basic economic data for Latin America and then to put this information into a global context. In this way, we can learn something about the economies of the region and also learn how Latin America fits into the larger mosaic of the world economy. A second objective of the chapter is to introduce a number of recurring themes concerning the economies of Latin America. All of the world's regions are distinctive in some ways. However, no region of the world, such as Europe, Asia, Africa, or Latin America, is completely homogeneous. Latin America is no different in this regard. There are several recurring themes that are common to most of the economies of Latin America. These major themes form a sort of roadmap for understanding both how the economies of Latin America are distinctive and why the economic performance of the region in the past century has been less than perhaps could have been possible. This introduction to these themes then allows us to consider some major economic policy debates that are common in the region. Economic growth in Latin America has spawned a healthy debate over various economic policy options for the region. Over the past century, several types of economic policies have been proposed and implemented. The relative merits of these policies have been vigorously debated for a long time. These policy debates are such an important part of the story of the economies of Latin America that the final part of the chapter provides a brief introduction to these different debates.

Latin America and the world

It's a reasonably safe assumption that any person in the world who has completed primary school could find Latin America on a map. Latin America comprises 14 percent of the world's land mass. In the Western Hemisphere, it accounts for 50 percent of the total area. However, the picture changes somewhat if one considers population.

The population of Latin America is approximately 644 million, or 8.6 percent of the population of the world. However, Latin America makes up 64 percent of the population of the Western Hemisphere. Relative to much of the world, Latin America is not a particularly crowded place. There are exceptions, such as El Salvador, but in general the view of much of Latin America, outside the major cities, is more like the US or Australia than Europe or some parts of Asia. With nearly 10 percent of the population of the world, Latin America is obviously an important place. However, this percentage perhaps paints too limited a picture of the importance of the population of Latin America. Part of this importance can be traced to the movements of people over the centuries. Countless millions have immigrated to Latin America in search of a better life. This immigration has created one of the most fascinatingly diverse regions of the world. The culture of Latin America is diversity in action. The indigenous culture of the area is overlaid with immigration from Europe, Africa, Asia, and the Middle East. Immigrants from Latin America to North America, Europe, and most recently Asia have in both small and large ways changed the character of these regions. The importance of Latin America in the world extends beyond its borders, as millions of people living outside the region have, in some measure, a connection to it.

Latin America has also made more general contributions to the world at large. Nearly 500 million people in the world speak Spanish, making it the world's second most used language after Mandarin. Another 200 million people speak Portuguese. This linguistic influence spreads beyond the borders of Latin America to the rest of the world. Spanish and Portuguese terms have crept into many of the world's languages through books, poetry, music, and films. Spanish words and phrases are now part of the language of the world. In the modern world, images from Buenos Aires, Rio de Janeiro, or Mexico City are as familiar as those from London, Paris, or Sydney. A similar story exists with respect to history. The pre-Columbian civilizations of Mexico, Central America, and South America are well-known parts of the cultural heritage of the world. The literature of the region has been recognized by Nobel Prizes. Many forms of music, dance, or art are immediately recognizable outside the region as being "Latin American." It would take too long to discuss Latin America and sports. It is difficult to imagine football (the real one), tennis, boxing, American baseball, or track and field without teams and individual athletes from Latin America. All of this is just a way of expressing the importance of Latin America to the world at large. However, this book has a more specific purpose. In order to get a complete view of the importance of Latin America to the world, the study of the economics of Latin America is critical. In the next section, we'll begin our study of the economy of Latin America.

The economic output of Latin America

In economics, it is usual to express the economic output of a country using the term GDP (gross domestic product). GDP represents the output of all final goods and services produced in an economy during a year. Nominal GDP is GDP expressed in terms of current prices. In many of our discussions, we will focus on a related term, real GDP. Real GDP is GDP that has been adjusted for changes in the price level. This adjustment allows us to compare the output of the economy over time by factoring out price-level changes. The basic data on GDP in Latin America is given in Table 1.1. The GDP of the countries of Latin America is shown in the table, along with some global data for comparison. The columns of the table give data on population, total GDP,

Table 1.1 Population, GDP, and GDP per capita for Latin America, low-, middle-, and high-income countries, and the world (2017)

	Population (millons)	GDP (billons)	GDP per capita
Argentina	44.3	637.4	14,398.4
Bolivia	11.1	37.5	3,394
Brazil	209.3	2,053.6	9,812.3
Chile	18.1	277.1	15,346.4
Colombia	49.1	314.5	6,408.9
Costa Rica	4.9	57.3	11,677.3
Ecuador	16.6	104.3	6,273.5
El Salvador	6.4	24.8	3,889.3
Guatemala	16.9	75.6	4,471
Honduras	9.3	23	2,480.1
Mexico	129.2	1,150.9	8,910.3
Nicaragua	6.2	13.8	2,221.8
Panama	4.1	62.3	15,196.4
Paraguay	6.8	39.7	5,823.8
Peru	32.2	211.4	6,571.9
Uruguay	3.5	56.2	16,245.6
Venezuela, RB	32	482.4	15,692.4
Latin America	644.1	5,972.1	9,271.6
Low income	732.4	576.9	787.7
Middle income	5,548.8	28,758.6	5,182.8
High income	1,248.4	51,625.9	41,352.4
World	7,529.7	80,934.8	10,748.7

Source: World Bank (2019).

Notes: Venezuela GDP, GDP per capita from 2014. Data in current US dollars.

and GDP per capita. GDP per capita is simply total GDP divided by the population. In addition to information on Latin America, Table 1.1 contains information on the world economy and various subcomponents for comparison purposes. The World Bank divides the world into roughly three different types of economies: low-, middle-, and high-income economies.[1] Using the world and these three different types of economies provides the reference points necessary to give one a picture of Latin America's place in the world economy.

Note from the bottom row of Table 1.1 that the economic output of the world is approximately $81 trillion. The output of Latin America is nearly $6 trillion, or about 7 percent of the economic output of the world. Among the countries of the region, GDP is highly concentrated. The GDP of Brazil and Mexico is over $1 trillion. From there, a substantial drop occurs to GDP of over $300 billion for Argentina, Colombia, and Venezuela.[2] Only three other countries in the region have a GDP of over $100 billion: Chile, Ecuador, and Peru. The next largest economy (Guatemala) is noticeably smaller. The other countries of the region are in a relatively tight cluster of GDP between $23 billion and $62 billion. As a result, there is a large variance in the absolute size of the economies of the region. Two of the countries are now in the trillion-dollar club in the world economy. Argentina, Colombia, and Venezuela occupy a space between these two and the group of countries with a GDP of at least $100 billion. In summary, the economies of the region run the gamut from five relatively large economies to a collection of medium to small economies in terms of GDP.

For some, the information on Latin America as a part of the world economy may be surprising. Obviously, Latin America is an important part of the world economy. However, its economic status does not quite seem to match what one would expect. This apparent disconnect is a theme we will return to many times as we move through the book. Latin America's relatively small place in the world economy is not something that occurred overnight; it is the result of decades of economic growth in Latin America that was slow by international standards. In 1960, Latin America comprised 5.9 percent of the world economy. By 2017, it comprised 7 percent. This means that, collectively, the economies of Latin America have grown only slightly faster than the world economy overall. Relative to the world and other developing countries, economic growth in Latin America has been slow. One of the primary purposes of this book is to shed some light on the relatively poor economic performance of the region. As we will see, there is no single explanation of this problem. The answers lie in many areas of economics and quite possibly some of the other social sciences. As we move through the book, we will try to cover the economic problems of the region that are "common knowledge." Ultimately, low growth of the economies of the region leads to another problem. Combining GDP with population yields GDP per capita. If the former is growing slowly, then the latter is as well. In the next section, we cover GDP per capita in Latin America.

GDP per capita in Latin America

Combining a population of 644 million and total GDP of $5.9 trillion, GDP per capita in Latin America is approximately $9,271. This simple statistic contains both good news and bad news. The good news is that most of Latin America is solidly middle-income by global standards. Indeed, the average GDP per capita is in the upper realm of the world middle class. For the most part, modern Latin America is a far cry from the grinding poverty of the low-income countries of sub-Saharan Africa or parts of Asia. On the other hand, it is also far from the easy affluence that characterizes North America or the high-income countries in general. Within the region, there are substantial differences in GDP per capita. Seven of the seventeen countries of the region have GDP per capita in the vicinity of $10,000 or more. The range for the rest of the region is from a low of $2,221 to $6,572. At the lower end of this range, life is not easy. Food, housing, health care, and some other basic amenities of life cannot be taken for granted. As we will see in Chapter 13 a troublingly large percentage of the population of the region are still struggling to maintain the basics of life. Moreover, keep in mind that the average numbers for Latin American countries are masking a substantial amount of intracountry differences in standards of living. Incomes in rural areas are frequently far less than those of the urban middle class. These differences occur for a variety of reasons, but this is a theme that we will return to on several occasions.

The situation we described in the previous section has an impact on the growth of GDP per capita in Latin America. Since the rate of growth of GDP has been slow relative to the world and other developing countries, GDP per capita growth has been relatively slow. In addition, population growth in Latin America during the latter part of the twentieth century was relatively fast by global standards. Putting the two factors together means that GDP per capita growth during the past century has not been particularly fast. It has been fast enough to put much of Latin America into the global middle class, but not fast enough to bring many of the residents of the region a more comfortable standard of living. This problem is the primary focus of this book. Again, there are no quick and easy answers to this problem. However, part of the problem has been a pattern of international trade that has been badly skewed by policy choices made by many governments in the region. Because of the importance of trade, the next section introduces the basic data on Latin America's trade with the rest of the world.

Box 1.1 The Human Development Index

In the previous section, the data for GDP per capita in Latin America was presented and discussed. Embedded in this discussion was an unstated assumption. This assumption is that human welfare is very highly correlated with GDP per capita. For the most part, this is the case. Everything else being equal, a higher GDP per capita is preferred to a lower one. However, there is obviously more to life than money. A large number of factors could cause a divergence between welfare and GDP per capita. To attempt to correct for this, the United Nations (UN) Development Programme publishes an annual ranking of the countries of the world by the Human Development Index shown in Table 1.2. The index has three components with equal weights. The first is the usual GDP per capita. The second component is life expectancy at birth. Obviously, a longer life span is associated with human welfare. A final component is education. Adult literacy makes up a third of this component; the other two-thirds comprises the ratio of students enrolled in primary, secondary, and tertiary schools as a percentage of the population of school age. The resulting index number varies from 0 to 1. Globally, the

Table 1.2 The Human Development Index in Latin America (2017)

	Human Development Index
Argentina	0.825
Bolivia	0.693
Brazil	0.759
Chile	0.843
Colombia	0.747
Costa Rica	0.794
Ecuador	0.752
El Salvador	0.674
Guatemala	0.650
Honduras	0.617
Mexico	0.774
Nicaragua	0.658
Panama	0.789
Paraguay	0.702
Peru	0.750
Uruguay	0.804
Venezuela, RB	0.761
Latin America	0.758
Portugal	0.847
Spain	0.891
Canada	0.926
United States	0.924

Source: United Nations Development Programme (2019).

highest and lowest scores are 0.944 for Norway and 0.337 for Niger. The regional average for Latin America is 0.758. The index ranges from 0.617 for Nicaragua to 0.843 for Chile. All of the countries in the region fall into the high to medium categories for the index. Latin America performs better on this index than for GDP per capita. In no country of the region is life expectancy less than seventy years, and adult literacy rates are high. However, note also that there is a gap between much of Latin America and the four high-income countries in the table. These differences are driven primarily by differences in GDP per capita and the gross enrollment ratio.

Latin America and international trade

As we will see at a number of points in the book, international trade has always been an important part of the economies of Latin America. Table 1.3 shows the basic data on Latin America's trade with the rest of the world. Imports and exports of goods, services, and the total are shown in the table for Latin America, the high-, middle-, and low-income economies, and the world. Virtually everyone is used to thinking about trade in goods. However, thinking about trade in services is not as common. International trade in services comprises items such as transportation, tourism, business services, and royalties and license fees. World trade in goods amounts to nearly $18 trillion, while world trade in services is almost $5.4 trillion. The data for Latin America is shown in the first row. Latin America's exports of goods and services to the world are nearly $1.1 trillion and $189 billion, respectively. This yields total exports of almost $1.3 trillion, accounting for 5.3 percent of world exports. A similar story emerges on the import side. Latin American imports of goods and services are $1 trillion and $239 billion, respectively. Total imports for the region are $1.3 trillion. Again, imports in Latin America are about 5.6 percent of world imports. In 2017, Latin America as a whole imported slightly more than it exported. A small trade surplus in goods was offset by a deficit in services. Note from the data that this is a normal pattern of trade for the middle-income countries as a whole.

At this point, recall that Latin America comprises 6 percent of the world economy. However, in international trade it accounts for less than 5 percent. Superficially, this doesn't seem to be a large difference. However, looking at the data differently yields another way of thinking about international trade and Latin America. The final column shows the importance of international trade to Latin America. The degree to which an economy is open to international trade can be measured by the ratio of exports plus imports $(X + M)$ to GDP (Y). The higher this ratio, the more "open" an economy is to the rest of the world. Conversely, the lower this ratio, the more "closed" the economy is. Looking at the data in this way shows how different Latin America is from much of the rest of the world. The ratio for Latin America is 0.44. The global average is much higher, at 0.58, and is very similar to the average for the high- and middle-income countries. The conclusion is that Latin America does not trade as much as most other high- and middle-income countries. Normally, it is true that a more open an economy is to international trade, the faster the rate of economic growth.[3] This is one of the reasons why this measure of openness is considered important. In a Latin American context, we will see that a number of policies pursued by many countries in Latin America during the

Table 1.3 Latin America and international trade (2017)

	Exports (billions of current US dollars)			Imports (billions of current US dollars)			Trade openness
	Goods	Services	Total	Goods	Services	Total	X + M/GDP
Latin America	1,094.1	189.3	1,283.0	1,050.8	238.5	1,289.2	0.44
High income	11,747.3	4,336.0	16,083.2	11,661.8	3,774.3	15,436.1	0.61
Middle income	5,694.7	1,067.2	6,761.8	5,312.8	1,324.3	6,637.2	0.49
Low income	80.8	35.2	115.5	151.6	40.6	192.0	0.57
World	17,534.0	5,439.5	22,972.6	17,119.8	5,139.3	22,258.9	0.58

Source: World Bank (2019).

twentieth century had a tendency to reduce the degree of openness. We will return to this theme on a number of occasions as we move through the book. However, international trade in goods and services is only part of the inflows and outflows of money in an economy as it interacts with the rest of the world. Trade flows are critically important, but they are only part of the picture. In the next section, we will consider other types of transactions between Latin America and the rest of the world.

Capital flows and Latin America

As we will see in a later chapter, the mirror image of trade in goods and services (along with a few other items) has to be matched in some way by capital flows. In a simple sense, any imbalance in trade in goods and services must be offset by capital flows. Like trade flows, capital can flow either into a country (inflows) or out (outflows). To some extent, most of us are vaguely familiar with capital flows, but the general knowledge about these flows is usually sketchy. In the case of Latin America, these flows have been critically important. Since shortly after the wave of independence movements in the first part of the nineteenth century, capital flows into Latin America have been both a blessing and a curse. All developing countries need capital flows in order to attain the maximum amount of economic growth. As we will see later in the book, the amount of capital a country has relative to its labor force is a critical determinant of economic growth. Poorer countries can normally utilize an amount of capital in excess of what can be generated by domestic savings alone. Developing countries frequently cannot generate enough domestic savings to produce an optimum amount of investment in new production facilities. However, these beneficial flows of capital do not always occur in a smooth or orderly fashion. Latin American economic history is marked by periods of rapid inflows of foreign capital coupled with sometimes disastrous outflows. In this section, we will provide a brief overview of these flows for Latin America.

Capital flows come in various types. With globalized financial markets, an important type of capital flow for developing countries is the flow of *portfolio capital*. Portfolio capital is money that crosses borders in order to buy financial assets such as stocks or bonds. At times, this type of capital flow can be critically important, because financial markets in developing countries are typically rather small. In such a case, large inflows or outflows of portfolio capital can cause significant volatility in these markets. Conversely, large outflows can be devastating to equity prices in local markets. As we

Table 1.4 Capital flows in Latin America (2017)

	FDI	
	Billions of USD	*% of the world*
Latin America	235.9	12.10
High income	1,412.2	72.44
Middle income	522.1	26.78
Low income	15.2	0.78
World	1,949.6	–

Source: World Bank (2019).

will explain later in the book, large inflows and outflows also have large effects on trade flows and the exchange rate. Another important form of capital flow is *foreign direct investment* (FDI). FDI is the purchase of real assets, such as production facilities, in a foreign country. In this case, the augmentation of domestic investment by FDI is a critical part of the process of economic development.

Flows of portfolio capital can be extremely volatile. As a result, we will cover these flows in Chapter 10 At this point, our discussion will be restricted to the FDI data given in Table 1.4. The first column contains data on FDI flows for Latin America, the high-, middle-, and low-income countries, and the world. The second column reports FDI as a percentage of the world total. In 2017, Latin America received $236 billion in FDI. This amounts to 12.1 percent of world FDI. In a relative sense, this is a bright spot for the region. Latin America's percentage of world FDI is double its percentage of world output. By contrast, the middle-income countries have 26.8 percent of world FDI and 36.0 percent of world GDP. Since the 1990s, Latin America's inflows have been increasing relative to the historical norm for the region. As we will see in a later chapter, these inflows are critical as a means of increasing economic growth.

Latin America and world resources

There are few areas in which Latin America is more important than the production of commodities. A *commodity* is the general term for a product made up of units that are indistinguishable from each other. For example, one bushel of wheat is indistinguishable from another. This leads to an interesting market structure for commodities. In general, the price of commodities is determined in a global market by the forces of supply and demand. Further, these markets are usually characterized by both inelastic supply and demand. In economics, "inelasticity" refers to the property of a supply or demand curve in which the quantity demanded or supplied does not change much in response to changes in price in the short run (i.e. both have a very steep slope). On the demand side, this occurs because many commodities are necessary for the production of other goods (oil) or they are a basic product frequently used by consumers (rice). On the supply side, the production of most commodities cannot be easily changed in the short run in response to even a large change in price. The result of these technical conditions is that the prices of commodities are subject to a substantial amount of volatility. For Latin America, large fluctuations in the price of oil, copper, and agricultural commodities are simply a part of the economic life of the region.

From the start of the colonial period in 1492, much of the interest in Latin America as a region stemmed from the relatively plentiful supply of some important commodities. The activities of the Spanish government in the extraction of gold and silver in Latin America from the sixteenth to the early nineteenth century is a part of world history that almost everyone is familiar with. Less well known is the importance of Latin America in the production of other important minerals such as oil, copper, tin, and, more recently, lithium. Latin America is also an important supplier of agricultural commodities. A short list of these commodities includes sugar, coffee, bananas, soybeans, wheat, and beef. What this means is that the production and export of commodities are even today an important part of the economic landscape of Latin America. It also makes land a critically important resource. Recall that when economists use the term "land," they are not just speaking of some geometric area such as a hectare. They are also referring to any resources that the land contains or the potential use of the land to produce commodities. Thus, in Latin America, the ownership of land and the distribution of the ownership of land is an important public-policy issue. Of course, this is true in any country, but it becomes even more critical in an area with a natural abundance of commodities.

Unfortunately, for a country or a region the possession or production of commodities can be both a blessing and a curse. In one sense, commodities are a stroke of luck for a country. The production of commodities may earn large amounts of money combined with low production costs. If used wisely, this windfall can be used to develop the country as a whole faster than would otherwise be the case. It might also allow the development of downstream industries based on the use of these commodities. The downside of the possession of commodities is less obvious. However, start out with a simple thought question. Of the countries of the world that produce large amounts of primary commodities, how many of these countries have used this windfall to become high-income countries? The ratio of the countries that have managed to do this to the countries that have failed is depressingly low. New Zealand and Australia are almost the exceptions that prove the rule. Unfortunately, Latin America falls into the denominator in this ratio. The region is very well endowed with commodities but has failed to turn this into higher GDP growth. The reasons for this are numerous, and Latin America is hardly alone in this regard. An egregious example is that Saudi Arabia is still a *middle-income* country. However, commodities and economic development are one of the major themes of the economics of Latin America that we will encounter as we move through the book. In the next section, we start to look at the overall economic problem of Latin America.

Latin America and the world: a summary

Two somewhat conflicting issues emerge from the material we've covered so far. First, in a broad sense, Latin America is an important part of the world. Its vivid history, its large geographic area, the relatively large population of the region, the effects of the region on the culture of the world at large, and its economic impact on the world make Latin America important. On the other hand, there is frequently a sense of something missing or something slightly wrong with this picture. This feeling is not misplaced: There is something a bit amiss. Despite all the above, Latin America is not what it *could* have been. Let's put this problem into more precise terms. One of the major, if not the most important, themes of this book is that economic growth in Latin America over the past century has been low relative to other parts of the world economy at a similar stage of economic development. Countries and sometimes regions grow at different rates: some faster, some more slowly. Unfortunately, Latin America tends to fall into the latter category. A commonplace comparison is the economic growth of Latin America relative to the rapid growth rates that have been common for decades in certain parts of Asia, particularly East Asia. In the second half of the twentieth century, many countries in East Asia transformed themselves from low-income countries to middle-income countries and in some cases high-income countries. These "growth miracles" are not accomplished overnight. A combination of the rule of seventy and relatively fast growth makes the difference. As you will recall, the rule of seventy is simply a way of roughly calculating the number of years it takes some variable to double in size. When applied to economic growth, the results can be startling. An economy growing at 10 percent per year doubles in size every seven years. If the growth rate drops to 4 percent, it now takes nearly eighteen years for the economy to double in size. Economic growth in Latin America is much like the latter example. There has been economic growth in the region, but it has been relatively slow. The result of this is that Latin America today is a smaller part of the world economy than it could have been. To illustrate the problem, refer to Figure 1.1. In the figure, the lowest line is the average GDP per capita for Latin America from 1960 to 2012 measured in constant (2005) dollars. Measured in this way, GDP per capita in the region has doubled over the past fifty years. However, two other lines are included in the figure. The next highest line shows what GDP per capita could have been if growth had been as fast as in the fastest-growing economy of the region, Chile. In the early 1980s, GDP per capita in Chile started to grow faster than the Latin American average. If Latin America as a whole had been able to achieve this growth rate, GDP per capita in the region would have been substantially higher than it is now. Unfortunately, while Chile has been a fast-growing economy in Latin America, it has not grown as fast as some of the economies of Asia. However, these economies have grown so fast over the past fifty years that this comparison may not be completely relevant. Many of these economies started this period as low-income economies, whose growth can naturally be much faster.[4] As a result, in Figure 1.1 we show a final comparison of growth in Latin America with an Asian country with some characteristics similar to Latin America. Indonesia is a large country that is a major commodity exporter. Further, the country has had a long history of authoritarian government, coupled with some internal instability. As we move through the book, it will become clearer why Indonesia may be more useful as a comparison than Hong Kong, Singapore, South Korea, or Taiwan. The highest line shows what GDP per capita in Latin America *could* have been if economic growth in the region had been as fast as it was in one of the more slowly growing economies of Asia with some of the same problems as Latin America. This line, compared with the actual collective GDP of the region, is at the heart of the economic problem of Latin America. There has been reasonable economic growth. However, it could have been much better. It should have been possible for the region to do as well as Chile or Indonesia. Over time, such differences produce startling variations in GDP per capita. While the arithmetic exercise is interesting, one needs to keep in mind that this lost GDP would have made a tremendous difference to the standard of living of the average person in Latin America.

A natural question at this point is what has caused economic growth in Latin America to be relatively slow. This is especially puzzling for a region at the center of the world economy, and one which is endowed with a large number of valuable natural resources.

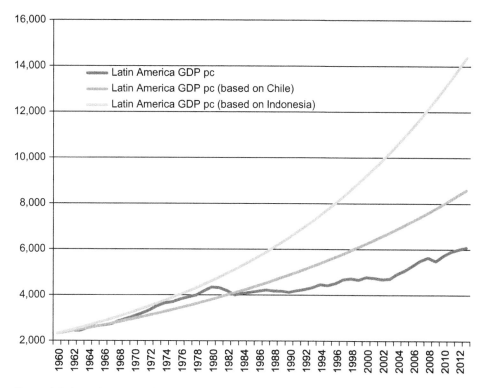

Figure 1.1 Actual vs. potential changes in GDP per capita in Latin America (constant 2005 US dollars).

Sadly, there is no simple or certain answer to that question. Economists have been studying the issue for a long time, and it is fair to say that no definitive answer has emerged from this research. However, it is also true that we now understand a substantial part of what went wrong. In general terms, a mixture of the history of the region, its natural endowments, and poor economic policy has tended to lower the economic growth of the region. The answers to the questions are not yet complete, but there are a number of recurring themes in Latin American economics that form a sort of "standard list" of issues that help to understand the relative economic underperformance of the region.

Box 1.2 Latin America and the US

I see where we are starting to pay some attention to our neighbors to the south. We could never understand why Mexico wasn't just crazy about us; for we have always had their good will, and oil and minerals, at heart.

(Will Rogers)

The focus of this book is the economic development of Latin America. As we have seen in this chapter, Latin America is intertwined with the rest of the world, and the development of the region is very much related to the world economy.

Table 1.5 The economic relationship between Latin America and the US (US$ billions)

Imports	617.2
Goods	504.6
Services	112.6
Exports	650.7
Goods	468.6
Services	182.1
Capital flows	146.1
FDI	63.48
Portfolio capital	82.59

Source: Bureau of Economic Analysis (2018).

However, the economies of Latin America are even more closely linked to the two high-income economies in the Western Hemisphere: the US and Canada. Here we will look more closely at the economic relationship between Latin America and the US. Much of the discussion can be extrapolated to Canada, but the Canadian economy is about 10 percent of the size of the US economy, so for the sake of brevity, we will focus on the former. The economic relationship between Latin America and the US is summarized in Table 1.5.

The first part of this relationship concerns GDP. The total GDP of the US is approximately $20 trillion. The GDP of Latin America is $6 trillion. At this point, the economy of the US is almost three times the size of the economy of Latin America. This sort of disparity means that economic events in the US tend to have an outsized effect on Latin America. Unfortunately, the reverse is not the case. None of the economies of Latin America is large enough for economic events there to have a large effect on the US economy. This disparity is exacerbated by trade and capital flows. Approximately 40 percent of Latin America's exports are accounted for by the US. Economic conditions in the US can have a substantial impact on Latin American exports. Also, Latin America is somewhat dependent on the US, as a similar percentage of imports originate there. A similar story emerges for FDI. A quarter of Latin America's FDI comes from the US. In addition, portfolio capital flows into and out of the region can be large. In 2017, they amounted to $83 billion. On the other hand, in some years there have been large flows out of the region. The above figures are conservative. They do not account for other flows, such as the remittances of workers from Latin America or flows of public and private aid into the region. For better or worse, the US and Latin America are locked into an economic relationship that is important for the US but much more important to Latin America. If the relationship between the two seems strained at times, the numbers above explain at least a part of that strain.

Recurring themes in Latin American economic development

In the process of explaining economic growth in Latin America, a number of themes keep cropping up. They appear with such regularity that they are just part of the "conventional wisdom" about the economies of Latin America. In this case, the conventional wisdom has become so because it is essentially correct. An important aspect of the economies of Latin America is their relative homogeneity. Each country in the region has its own distinctive characteristics. However, to a surprising extent, there are many important similarities. These common themes are sufficiently important that they will come up time and time again as we attempt to explain the economic characteristics and performance of the countries of Latin America. The following is a list of these themes and a short description of each one to help begin our study of the region.

History: One can rarely understand the current state of any economy or region without a basic understanding of economic history. This is particularly true with respect to Latin America.

Growth: The most serious problem of modern Latin America has been that economic growth has been slow relative to much of the rest of the world.

Commodities: As we have mentioned above, many countries in Latin America are major producers and exporters of commodities. As we will see, this can have a substantial influence on the economic development of a country.

Import substitution industrialization (ISI): In the second half of the twentieth century, many countries in Latin America attempted to create industries designed to replace imports from developed countries. ISI has had very important implications for economic development in the region.

Trade policy: From the 1930s, Latin America has pursued trade policies that tended to keep the markets of the region relatively closed to foreign competition. This overall policy tended to cause Latin America to be less integrated into the world economy. The results are reflected in the data in Table 1.3.

Exchange-rate policy: Countries have a choice of managing their exchange rate or allowing it to float. In Latin America, these choices at times have had serious implications in terms of economic growth.

Debt: A recurring theme in Latin American economic history has been the tendency for governments in the region to borrow heavily from banks and other financial institutions. As we will see, at times this borrowing has been a source of economic instability.

Macroeconomic instability: On average, GDP growth, inflation, and unemployment have been somewhat unstable in many countries of Latin America. Unfortunately, this instability has been so pervasive that for many it is one of the defining characteristics of the region. Explaining this instability is one of the major tasks of this book.

Poverty and inequality: As indicated earlier in the chapter, GDP per capita in Latin America is low relative to the high-income countries. In addition, this relative poverty is not a burden that is equally shared by all segments of the population of Latin America. In comparison to the rest of the world, Latin America has one of the most unequal distributions of income.

This list of major themes in Latin American economics is not exhaustive. However, it does cover much of what makes Latin America distinctive in an economic sense. To a large extent, the interplay of these themes will serve to explain both the economic history of the region and its current place in the world economy. Note that the majority of these themes are related to government policy. The actions of governments are rarely perfect, and in any country or region they can be the subject of debate. In the case of Latin America, the debate over government policy has been active. In the final chapter of the book, we will cover some of the major economic policy debates in the region. The reason for this is twofold. First, assessing economic policy requires a certain amount of basic economic knowledge. One of the major purposes of this book is to provide the reader with a sufficient knowledge of basic economics to understand different types of economic policy. Second, the focus of the book will be on the results of policies that were implemented in the past and have either succeeded or failed. Thus, the focus of the book is on what actually occurred. By learning the economic history of the region, one can gain a lot of insight into alternative economic policy going forward into the twenty-first century.

Key terms and concepts

commodity: a product one unit of which is indistinguishable from another.
exchange rate: the price of one currency in terms of another currency.
foreign direct investment (FDI): the purchase of real assets, such as production facilities, in a foreign country.
gross domestic product (GDP): the market value of all final goods and services produced in an economy in a year.
import substitution industrialization (ISI): a set of policies designed to replace imports of industrial products with domestic production.
portfolio capital: the purchase of financial assets, such as stocks and bonds, in a foreign country.
World Bank: a multilateral institution that makes loans to developing countries to enhance economic development.

Questions for review and discussion

1   Describe why Latin America is a relatively important region of the world. List some specific examples that were not given in the chapter.
2   In terms of GDP, how important is Latin America in the world economy?
3   Describe the economic position of Argentina, Brazil, and Mexico in relation to the rest of Latin America.
4   What is the average GDP per capita in Latin America, and what is the range around this average? Describe how GDP per capita in Latin America compares with the same number in low- and middle-income countries around the world.
5   Compare and contrast GDP per capita and the Human Development Index in terms of Latin America.
6   How important is Latin America in world trade in goods and services?
7   How does one measure how "open" or "closed" an economy is? Is Latin America on average more open or closed than the world economy at large?
8   What is the difference between movements of portfolio capital and FDI? How are commodities and the quote at the beginning of the chapter related?
9   Describe the economic growth of Latin America relative to East Asia. Why does this difference matter?
10 Describe the economic relationship between Latin America and the US.
11 List and describe some of the recurring themes in Latin American development.

Notes

1 The acronyms HIC, MIC, and LIC will be used in some tables to stand for high-, middle-, and low-income economies, respectively.
2 One occasionally sees the term "ABM" (Argentina, Brazil, and Mexico).
3 For the classic reference on trade and growth, see Edwards (1993).
4 Why this is true will be shown in the next chapter.

References

Edwards, Sebastian (1993) "Openness, Trade Liberalizations, and Growth in Developing Countries," *Journal of Economic Literature*, 31 (September): 1358–1393.

United Nations Development Programme (2019) *Human Development Report 2014*, Basingstoke: Palgrave Macmillan.

US Bureau of Economic Analysis (2018) *US Economic Accounts*, Washington, DC: US Bureau of Economic Analysis.

World Bank (2019) *World Development Indicators*, Washington, DC: World Bank.

Recommended reading

Weintraub, Sidney (2010) *Unequal Partners: The United States and Mexico*, Pittsburgh, Pa.: University of Pittsburgh Press.

2 Latin American economic history

Introduction

At the beginning of the book, a number of recurring themes in the economics of Latin America were introduced. Recall as well that the history of the region that is most relevant for our purposes begins at the end of the fifteenth century. Some of the economic themes that were introduced in the first chapter have their roots almost as far back as that. The discovery of the Americas was followed shortly by the discovery of gold and silver. In turn, this discovery may have set the region on a certain path of development. Gold and silver were just the first of many commodities that were and are important to the region. In a related vein, the exploitation of these commodities required enormous amounts of labor. Unfortunately, the labor market in colonial Latin America was not exactly the competitive market found in a labor economics text. In a similar way, the conquest of Latin America by the colonial powers produced a distribution of land that was in keeping with the way the land was acquired. The theft of the land from the indigenous population was followed by the distribution of much of it to a small population of Europeans. The initial distribution of the land and the labor-market conditions created a highly unequal distribution of income. In the economic history of Latin America, commodities, poverty, and inequality often have an uncomfortable relation to one another.

Other themes that were introduced earlier also have a long history in the region. Macroeconomic stability has rarely been a characteristic associated with Latin America. Although data limitations prevent much commentary on colonial economic performance, the data now available stretching back to the nineteenth century shows some of the same sort of instability that was associated with the region in the twentieth century. In short, macroeconomic stability seems to be a problem with historical roots. The same is true of debt. Many of the countries of Latin America became debtor nations upon independence. For some of the creditors, the loans were not a positive experience. Debt and its often painful aftermath are an integral part of the history of Latin America in the past 200 years. While the line between what is modern and what is history is indistinct, the origins of ISI go back to the early part of the twentieth century. Enough time has passed that this era is becoming more and more a part of the economic history of the region.

Because of the long historical roots of some of the major themes associated with economic development in the region, the purpose of this chapter is to provide a brief economic history of Latin America. Of necessity, this history can only be covered in the most cursory fashion. The main purpose is to introduce some historical context and some important events and concepts that are essential to understanding how the economy of Latin America came to be as it is. The chapter will proceed historically, beginning with the colonial period, which covers nearly half of the relevant history. The period from independence until the latter part of the nineteenth century is covered in the third section of the chapter. The next sections of the chapter cover a brief golden age of economic growth from the late nineteenth to the early twentieth century, the interwar years, the period of ISI, and the recovery from these policies.

The colonial period

> I come for gold, not to till the land like a peasant.
>
> (Hernán Cortés)

The economic history of Latin America begins with the discovery of the Americas by Christopher Columbus in 1492. The immediate discovery of gold set off a flurry of activity by Spain to acquire whatever gold and silver were available in the hemisphere. The early sixteenth century was ushered in by the conquest of both Mexico and Peru and the beginning of three centuries of Spanish colonial rule in Latin America. During this period, three economic themes developed that still influence the region. First, the goal of Spain was the plunder of gold and silver. This first commodity boom was just the first of many, and new booms appear periodically and continue in the twenty-first century. The gold and silver boom was followed by widespread investment in agricultural commodities. The production and export of these products has always been, and still is, an important part of the economy of the region. Even today, it is hard to imagine a Latin America that does not export commodities. As was true of all colonial powers, Spain imposed the policy of *mercantilism* on Latin America. The policy distorted trade and production patterns for hundreds of years and left a legacy everywhere it was imposed. Latin America is no different in this regard. Finally, the colonial history of Brazil is sufficiently different from the rest of Latin America that the section concludes with a consideration of these differences.

Gold and silver

Initially, the goal of the Spanish government was primarily the plunder of gold and silver. The sums involved were enormous. At the beginning of the conquest of the region, gold and silver flowed naturally back to Spain, as Spanish citizens wanted to repatriate their money. After the initial plunder, it became necessary to begin working the original mines used by the indigenous people. The focus now shifted from simple theft to actually having to produce the minerals. Governments at the time were not inclined to do this on their own, so another means had to be found to develop the resource. In Latin America, this involved the development of the *encomienda*. An encomienda was a large tract of land granted to a Spanish citizen to develop. Technically, the *encomenderos* did not own the land but were simply holding it in trusteeship for the indigenous population, and the land was to be eventually returned to the government. The indigenous workers were to be cared for by the encomenderos and given instruction in the Christian faith. Abuses of the system inevitably occurred through the use of debt or the simple reality that workers might not easily find employment elsewhere.

While the workers were supposedly free, the labor market did not approximate what one would call a free labor market. The Spanish government also employed the *mita* system, which had originally been developed in the Inca Empire. Under this system, workers were obliged to provide free labor to the government for infrastructure projects. In effect, this was a tax paid by the population in kind (labor). While the system worked well under the Incas, it was frequently abused in the colonial period, as workers were used in mining gold and silver. The interest of the Spanish government in the system was in the *repartida*. Landowners were granted land and access to cheap labor. In return, they owed the Spanish government a share of the output of the land. The repartida flowed back to Spain to be used for general government expenditures.

In a historical sense, the initial riches provided by gold were rather short-lived. By the mid sixteenth century, the production of gold was in decline. At this point, silver came to dominate the mining sector in Latin America. This was enhanced by technological change. A technique known as mercury amalgamation was discovered. This allowed the profitable extraction of silver from low-grade ore. This sort of silver mining required a much higher level of investment and commitment and was a major reason for an increasing Spanish presence in Latin America. In turn, the encomienda system expanded. This production of silver occurred primarily in the Andes and Mexico. In the former, the center of production was Potosí. In Mexico, most production occurred in the Zacatecas, Pachuca, and Sonora mines. The production of silver was so important to Spain that silver production affected the economic development of the whole region for nearly a century. The development of economic output in the rest of Latin America was based on supplying the needs of the mining regions. Development languished in other parts of the region without gold and silver or the resources necessary for their production. By the mid seventeenth century, the production of silver began to decline. The better grades of ore had been extracted, and output inevitably fell. The repartida had to be adjusted downward to account for the lower production, and some mines closed altogether. The closing of this era meant that the economy of Latin America was about to undergo significant changes. However, as we move through other periods and look into the twenty-first century, the marks left by this initial part of colonial Latin American history are not hard to find.[1]

A question that usually comes to mind at this point concerns just how much gold and silver was transferred from Latin America to Spain during the colonial period. Between 1520 and 1660, the answer is staggering. Officially during this period 200 *tons* of gold was shipped from the New World to Spain. Most of this transfer occurred early between 1520 and 1560 and fell rapidly afterwards. The amount of silver shipped was much larger and amounted to over 18,000 tons. As indicated above, the bulk of the silver was shipped after the middle of the sixteenth century. The data above is considered to be conservative by a minimum of 10 percent as gold and silver were sometimes smuggled to avoid taxes.[2] Unfortunately, this shower of money did little to enrich Spain. The country was almost perpetually in a state of war for much of the sixteenth and seventeenth centuries. The expenditures on these conflicts completely consumed the transfer of money from Latin America and necessitated borrowing from foreign bankers. In the middle of the sixteenth century, Spain's debts amounted to 60 percent of GDP. The inflow of gold and silver was not constant and was needed to make payments on this debt. The precarious public finances of Spain led to a number of defaults. The result of this inflow of money never really contributed to the economic development of the country. By the seventeenth century, Spain had already begun its long decline.[3] As we will see below, this decline was partially responsible for the end of colonial rule in Latin America.

Box 2.1 The long-run effects of the *mita* system

A theme that will crop up over and over in this chapter and others to follow is the negative effects of the colonial empires on economic outcomes, which have persisted over centuries. Much of the research makes a logical case for the existence of these effects. More recently, the research has become more empirical in order to validate the conceptual arguments. What is much rarer is research showing that a specific colonial institution has had such long-run effects. Dell (2010) has produced just this sort of empirical evidence with respect to the mita system mentioned above. To be more specific, the mita system was used in Bolivia and Peru between 1573 and 1812 to provide forced labor for mercury and silver mines. The system required over 200 indigenous communities to provide one-seventh of the adult male population to work in the mines, while all other communities in the region were exempt from the system. The implementation of the system allows the sort of "natural experiment" that can yield insights that are usually not available.

In general, the mita region still shows the effects of the system in the twenty-first century. Consumption in the region is 25 percent less and the incidence of stunted growth is 6 percent higher than in the non-mita region. This is strong evidence of the long-run effects of the system. As is the norm in empirical studies, the results are robust with respect to different specifications and data. However, the research goes further and details the channels by which these effects have drifted down through the centuries. First, the mita and non-mita regions developed different land-tenure systems. In the mita region, the government prohibited the development of large land holdings to minimize the competition for labor. Instead, the state promoted communal farming in the mita region. With the abolition of the mita system, the state banned communal farming but did not replace it with a system of enforceable property rights for small farmers. The result was the confiscation of peasant lands, peasant rebellions, and other problems with the rule of law that persisted into the twentieth century. With secure property rights, large landowners in the non-mita regions were able to obtain public goods such as roads. Second, even in the twenty-first century, residents of the mita region have less education and are less well integrated into the road system. Third, subsistence farming is still more prevalent in the mita region. These resulting effects, which can be traced back to the colonial period in a quantitative way, are important, as they allow us to be somewhat more confident in discussing the lingering negative effects of the colonial period on modern Latin America.

Agriculture

With the decline in silver production that was occurring in the mid sixteenth century, economic activity migrated toward the production of agricultural commodities. The age of exploration in the fifteenth century, and subsequent discoveries by European explorers and later colonists, had led to the introduction into Europe of commodities that quickly became goods for consumption that were in high demand. Some of these goods had trickled into Europe as early as the Roman Empire. However, distances and high transportation costs had kept prices for these products so high that they were prohibitively expensive for the merely well-off, much less the average consumer. The production of popular commodities in the Americas, coupled with relatively cheap transportation costs, lowered the prices of these commodities to the point where the number of European consumers who could afford some of this output was much larger.

The market was enhanced by the existence of triangular trade. The start of the process was the shipment of simple manufactured goods to the west coast of Africa. Goods were then exchanged for slaves. The slaves were then shipped to the Americas and sold at a major center of this activity, such as Havana or Cartagena. The need for these slaves was twofold. Recall the devastating drop in population that occurred in Latin America during the sixteenth century. As the production of agricultural products increased, there were labor shortages in many parts of Latin America. In many cases, these shortages were difficult to fill with immigrants from Europe. While the indigenous population of Latin America had little protection against European diseases, the reverse was also often the case: Europeans were susceptible to tropical diseases. The tragic solution was the importation of slaves from Africa, who were both better acclimated to the climate and less vulnerable to tropical diseases. The proceeds from the sale of slaves were used to purchase commodities, which were shipped to Europe and sold at a profit. The process could then be repeated. Unfortunately, the mere fact that certain forms of economic activity are immoral does not necessarily make them unprofitable.

The important commodities exported from Latin America during this period were sugar, cocoa, tobacco, hides, cotton, and indigo. Production of some of these commodities was associated with a succession of commodity booms centered in various parts of the region. The production of cocoa was originally centered in Venezuela in the early eighteenth century. The production of tobacco was centered in Cuba. Argentina prospered as a result of the production of hides needed for an expanding global leather market. European demand for sugar was especially high. Production was centered in the Caribbean but also took place in other parts of the region. Booms were also associated with less important commodities such as indigo and cochineal. Mexico passed through this period in a somewhat different manner. Silver production in the country slackened but never fell as precipitously as it did in the Andes. The fading importance of gold and silver and the establishment of agricultural production was the high-water mark of the interest of Spain in Latin America. Past the mid sixteenth century, revenue from Latin America would never be as high as in the previous century, and the country was distracted by events in Europe.

Landownership patterns

The colonial economy of Latin America turned from mining gold and silver during the sixteenth and seventeenth centuries to the production of agricultural commodities. The mining of gold and silver had led to a particular type of land use in the region. While the economic structure of the region changed, the land-use patterns did not. Recall that the Spanish government allocated large tracts of land to citizens for the mining of gold and silver. As the economy transferred to agriculture, the encomiendas discussed above continued. Several reforms of the system, designed to lessen its abuses, began in the early sixteenth century. However, no meaningful reforms were ever accomplished, and the system was officially abolished in 1720. What followed was hardly an improvement. The encomienda system was transformed into a collection of *latifundia*. Large tracts of land were formally held by a small group of landholders. Crops were grown primarily for export to Europe. Earnings from these exports were frequently repatriated. This meant that less of these earnings were reinvested in the region. Landowners had little interest in paying taxes for either schooling or the improvement of infrastructure. What investment there was in the latter was focused on transportation systems for getting crops to the ports and the ports themselves. With such poor infrastructure, many latifundia became *haciendas*.[4] These were almost feudal estates, with few ties even to other parts of the country, and were nearly self-sufficient. This had two effects that still can be seen in the twenty-first century. As we will see in the next chapter, public education is an economic-development problem in the region. This is not a new problem, and its roots go back to this period. Second, the transportation infrastructure of Latin America is poor. Again, this is a problem with long historical roots. For the masses without extensive landholdings, there was the prospect of some work on the latifundia. The more fortunate might hold a small plot of land for subsistence farming. These *minifundia* were a staple of the economy of colonial Latin America and are still a common form of land usage.

The extensive use of the encomienda system at the start of the colonial period set the region on an unfortunate path. Colonial Latin America was virtually born with an extremely unequal distribution of income. The transformation of the encomienda system into a collection of latifundia perpetuated the initial inequality. Further, large landowners had little interest in infrastructure beyond their holdings other than a minimal transportation system. Public education was unimportant, as the mass of workers performed agricultural labor, for which the *human capital* requirements were low. Because the possession of land would create income in future generations, the initial highly unequal distribution of land created a highly unequal distribution of income, which tended to persist. Economic development became difficult, as domestic markets were not well integrated due to poor transportation infrastructure. Human capital was not developed, as no one in charge of the system saw any reason to develop it. To be clear, these historical legacies are not the only sources of income inequality in Latin America. However, they are an important factor in understanding the distribution of income in the region. Note, too, that this situation did not come into existence because of market forces. Both the initial land distribution and the conditions under which much of the population labored were set by the state or landholders who had been given control of resources by the state.[5]

Box 2.2 Latifundia: a brief history

In the section above, the development of latifundia in Latin America was described. However, this pattern of land usage was not used for the first time by the Spanish in Latin America. The use of the term can be traced back to ancient Greece. While large holdings of land were not common in Greece itself, the term was used to describe large landholdings in Egypt and Syria that produced agricultural products for export. As with many things, the Roman Empire borrowed the term to describe a pattern of land use that should have a familiar ring. In the early second century BC, large landholdings cropped up as the spoils of war with the expansion of the empire. Conveniently, conquest also provided slave labor to work the land. As the Roman Empire expanded to the Mediterranean, the pattern of land use followed. Most importantly in our context, latifundia were common in southern Spain. Smaller landholdings were granted to Roman soldiers as a reward for service in the legions. The owners of the latifundia frequently became spectacularly wealthy, as productivity was very high and much of the output was exported. The owners of the land formed the backbone of the ruling class of the Roman Empire.

This pattern of land use reemerged with the retaking of Portugal and Spain from the Muslims. The *reconquista* provided the governments with large tracts of land for distribution. The government chose to allocate the land to the nobility, military allies, or the Catholic Church. In turn, the new owners established large agricultural operations producing commodities for both local consumption and export. It was a return to the Roman system minus the slavery. The concept was easily applied to Latin America because it was already common in Spain. Land gained by conquest was given by the government to nobility or others performing significant military or administrative duties. Formal slavery was not used in Spain or, initially, in Spanish Latin America. In Latin America, there was an adequate supply of now landless indigenous people to work the land. The main point is that in Latin America, latifundia was a concept with deep historical roots, which unfortunately was replanted in a region where conditions were almost ideal for its use.

Mercantilism

The crown had forbidden the manufacture of luxury goods in the colony to eliminate competition with European imports, a stricture that stirred subversives to dream about separation.

(John Ross)

Like most governments of the time, the Spanish government used the policy of mercantilism in administering colonial holdings. At the beginning, there was little need for a formal policy. The acquisition of gold and silver by the Spanish naturally created a backflow of this wealth back to Spain. Mercantilism was the predominant economic philosophy of the age. The focus of most governments was on maximizing the trade surplus using restrictive trade practices and attempting to lower the cost of exports. Spain was no different, although there were some country-specific variations on the general policy. First, all goods coming from Latin America and all goods going to the region had to pass through Spain. This had the effect of raising the prices colonists paid for goods and lowering the prices obtainable for exports. Neither of these effects is positive in terms of economic development. Those without large holdings were fortunate to be able to farm a minifundium for subsistence. Finally, Spain discouraged even the production of any goods in Latin America that would compete with production in Spain. This policy applied to both manufacturing and agriculture. In short, the mercantilist policies of the Spanish government were even more restrictive than was typical of the era.

The demise of Spanish mercantilist policy matched the decline of the country relative to the UK and, to a lesser extent, France.[6] The defeat of the Spanish Armada in 1588 was a highly visible sign of this demise. After this point, Spain found it increasingly difficult to enforce its mercantilist policies, and illicit trade between Latin America and the rest of Europe became increasingly common. The Treaty of Utrecht in 1713 ceded control of the slave trade to the UK and gave British ships a legitimate reason to enter ports in Latin America. Spain formally granted the colonies the ability to trade among themselves in 1778. After this point, mercantilism was only a slight impediment to the economic development of the region.

As has been mentioned earlier and will be touched on many times in the book, Latin America historically has been somewhat isolated from the world economy. Further, trade within the region today is still somewhat less than one might expect. Nearly 300 years of Spanish mercantilist policy had something to do with this. The policies of the Spanish government were even more restrictive with respect to international trade than was typical of the era. The *annual* fleets of ships bringing goods from Spain and returning to Spain with commodities are a stark example of the mindset of the Spanish government. Trade was for the benefit of Spain, with the economic welfare of Latin America a minor consideration. The suppression of any economic activity in Latin America in competition with Spanish production exacerbated the adverse effects of trade restrictions. Even worse, Spain regulated trade between ports in Latin America, which increased the economic isolation of each part of the region from the others. As with many economic policies, the direction of change is clear. These policies hindered the economic development of the region. The extent to which they did so is not clear. However, such a long history of relative isolation is not easily overcome.

Brazil: variations on a theme

The previous brief sketch of the economic history of colonial Latin America deliberately neglected the development of Brazil. The creation of what is now modern Brazil is an interesting example of accident and international diplomacy. Even before the Americas were discovered, the pope of the Catholic Church had granted all lands south of the Canary Islands to Portugal. Following the discovery of the New World, a subsequent Spanish-born pope decreed in 1493 essentially that most of the land in Latin America belonged to Spain. Understandably, Portugal was unhappy with this decision, and a solution was brokered between the two countries by the Vatican. The Treaty of Tordesillas, signed in 1494, provided Portugal with more land in Latin America. In modern terms, Portugal was entitled to land in Latin America along a north–south line slightly east of modern Rio de Janeiro.[7] Spain never effectively interfered with Portuguese expansion into the interior of South America. This expansion was much more gradual than in the Spanish colonies. There were no obvious deposits of precious metal to exploit. The original export of the colony was brazilwood, which was used to produce a popular dye in Europe. This success attracted French interest in the colony and set a pattern somewhat different from the rest of the region. Portugal had continuous problems defending the colony from the incursions of other, more powerful, European powers. As a result of French interest, Portugal began encouraging greater colonization efforts in the early sixteenth century.

This effort was encouraged by the Portuguese government granting large tracts of land for development. These *fazenda* estates were very similar to the latifundia of the

Spanish colonies. They were very quickly used to produce an important cash crop: sugar. By the mid seventeenth century, Brazil was the world's leading producer. Since the production of sugar is labor-intensive, the development of the industry required a large labor force that the colony did not possess. The solution was an event that changed the face of Brazil. Large numbers of slaves were imported from Africa beginning in the late sixteenth century. The combination of sugar and the labor to expand the industry created yet another commodity boom in the region. As is usually the case, the boom ended with the Dutch starting their own plantations in the Caribbean after a failed attempt to wrest control of Brazil from the Portuguese. Another boom followed shortly after, on the heels of the decline in the sugar market. In the late seventeenth century, gold was discovered in the southeastern region of Brazil (Minas Gerais). This was followed by the discovery of diamond deposits in the early eighteenth century. Exploitation of these two resources created a spectacular boom in the colony that lasted well into the second half of the eighteenth century.

In general, the colonization and development of Brazil occurred more slowly than in the rest of the region. This is logical, as the colony did not initially yield the massive wealth of the Spanish colonies. While Portugal imposed many of the same mercantilist policies as Spain, the regulations were looser and not enforced as rigorously. After the discovery of gold and diamonds, Portuguese interest in and control of the colony intensified. However, the importation of slaves made it virtually impossible to restrict trade to Portuguese ships only; the demand was simply too great. Mercantilist policies were further weakened by a treaty between Portugal and the UK that formally gave British ships access to Brazilian ports. In summary, the colonial development of Brazil differed from the Spanish colonies in three important ways. First, due to the absence of any initial discovery of mineral wealth, the early development of the colony was based on the production of agricultural commodities such as sugar and tobacco. Second, the mercantilist policies of the Portuguese government were never as thorough or rigorously enforced as was the case in the rest of Latin America. Finally, these policies ended much sooner because the natural trade relations of both the mother country and the colony were inextricably influenced by the world's rising economic power of the time, the UK.[8]

Box 2.3 Slavery in Latin America

In Chapter 1, we noted that Latin America is one of the most diverse regions of the world in many senses. Over the centuries, both larger and smaller migrations into the region have originated from all of the other regions of the world. One of the largest of these migrations was from Africa. Unfortunately, this migration was different. Unlike other migrations, this one involved forced migration, that is, slavery. As one might expect, the origins of this migration are complex. Slavery had been known in Europe since the time of the Greek and Roman Empires. During the Age of Discovery in the fifteenth century in Portugal, there had been a small migration of African slaves to both Portugal and Spain. Portuguese ties with West Africa grew substantially during this period and provided the foundations for a steady supply of slaves that could be transported to the Western Hemisphere. This supply was awaiting a demand in the region that quickly materialized. Developments in mining and, later, agriculture grew into an enormous demand for labor. This demand could not be fully supplied from the indigenous population. Neither colonial power decided to extend a formal system of slavery to this population; labor could be obtained without slavery in both Mexico and Peru, as there were initially large concentrations of workers where they were needed. However, as noted earlier, disease took a huge toll on this population. In other areas, particularly Brazil, the indigenous population of hunter/ gatherers was too small and difficult to control to provide satisfactory amounts of labor. Migration from Portugal and Spain was not an option. Portugal's small population at the time (1 million) made a large migration impossible. High wages in Spain, coupled with military operations in northern Europe, reduced migration from Spain to a low level.

The solution was large-scale importation of slaves from Africa. The numbers involved are truly staggering. Until the 1830s, more Africans than Europeans crossed the Atlantic. The total migration from all regions of the world from 1492 to the 1830s is estimated to be 6.6 million. Of these, 4.5 million were African slaves. Within Latin America, the major destination was Brazil. Other countries that received a substantial number of slaves were Colombia, Venezuela, Peru, and Mexico. This massive migration literally changed the face of Latin America. Today, somewhere between 100 and 150 million Latin Americans are descendants from this migration. The majority of this population is Brazilian. Nearly half of the population of Brazil is descended from African slaves. Data for other countries can be a problem, as census procedures vary from country to country. However, there are substantial populations in Colombia, Venezuela, and Peru. This forced migration changed the face of many of the countries of the region. Imagining modern Latin America without this part of the population would be a difficult task.[9]

Institutions and economic growth

The Spanish colonies, therefore, from the moment of their first establishment, attracted very much the attention of their mother country; while those of the other European nations were for a long time in a great measure neglected.

(Adam Smith)

A central theme of Latin American economics has been the relatively slow growth of the economies of the region. Over time, this has resulted in a large gap between GDP per capita in Latin America and in the developed countries. This gap is particularly striking between Latin America and the US and Canada. This has not always been the case. Maddison (2004) estimated that in 1700 GDP per capita in North and South America was roughly equivalent. The subsequent centuries have resulted in the gap shown in Table 1.1. Until recently, the standard explanation for this was that the fifty years of postcolonial turmoil outlined in the next section caused a large gap in GDP per capita that subsequently was never closed.[10] This explanation is difficult to reconcile with the historical record stretching back hundreds of years. There is little doubt that growth was inhibited by postcolonial turmoil. However, even accounting for that loss, the remaining gap is difficult to explain. The research on Latin America over the past two decades has developed into a compelling argument that a central economic problem of the region is poor institutions. Further, the existence of weak institutions can be traced back to the colonial period.

A first question in this regard is to determine why institutions in the region have historically been weak. The "new institutional economics" pioneered by North (1995) provides a general answer that seems applicable to Latin America.[11] Institutions may form to protect the interests of an elite. Elites with sufficient wealth or power frequently establish laws and institutions that will effectively protect their interests. In effect, institutions develop that are primarily concerned with maintaining the status quo. Another way of putting this is that institutions develop to prevent the process of "creative destruction." Unfortunately, laws and institutions designed to protect the status quo may not be related to higher productivity or even the social good. While the insights of North and others are important in a general way, it would be useful to take the basic idea and put it into a more specific framework that is applicable to Latin America. A more specific explanation for weak institutions was put forth in an influential paper by Engerman and Sokoloff (1997). To focus on the differences in outcomes, they look at the differences in the initial conditions found in the various colonies. They distinguish among three different types of colonies. The first were those where the climate and soil were suitable for the production of tropical crops such as sugar. In this case, production required large operations and the use of imported slaves due to a small indigenous population. The second was the existence of mineral wealth, which required much more capital. In this case, there was also the need for a large labor force, but it was available from the indigenous population. The third case was the situation where the climate and soil were best suited to the production of crops that did not need large amounts of either capital or labor. The first two cases can lead to unfortunate results: in this case, to the development of small elites that were able to extract a disproportionate share of the income produced by tropical crops or minerals. Interestingly, the consolidation of this power was aided by restrictions on immigration from Spain. The subsequent link to institutions is straightforward. The elites were able to establish a set of laws and institutions that would solidify the initial inequalities of income and political power. Thus, much of Latin America started with laws and a legal framework that were designed to protect the interests of a small elite at the expense of the interests of the vast majority of the population. As one can imagine, a system designed to maintain a status quo is not well suited to economic growth. An example can be drawn from landholdings in North America versus Latin America. In 1900, 75 percent of rural households in the US owned land. In Argentina in 1895, only 19 percent owned land. The story in Mexico is even more striking. In 1910, only 2.4 percent of rural households owned land.[12] Given disparities of this kind, the divergence of institutions is not surprising.

Subsequent research on the persistence of institutions has focused on more precisely defining the mechanisms that perpetuate institutions that inhibit growth. In a series of influential papers, Acemoglu and Robinson (2008a and 2008b) and Acemoglu et al. (2001) and his coauthors describe the mechanisms that make this possible and provide empirical results concerning their model.[13] They first assume that society is divided into two broad groups: the elite and the rest of the population. This is a good description of Latin America in the colonial period and, to a certain extent, still persists. Under colonial rule, the elite had both de-jure and de-facto power. Over time, institutions may evolve that transfer de-jure power away from the elites, such as the independence movements in the region in the early nineteenth century. Such a transfer of de-jure power may alter institutions.

However, it may not have as much effect on the de-facto distribution of power. In a sense, the post-independence balance of power in the region between the elites and the rest of the population may be an example of this at work. For example, the repression of labor using the encomienda, the mita system, or slavery did not end with the abolition of these institutions. The landed elites were able to accomplish similar outcomes by dominating the political landscape.[14] What this implies is that the initial path on which a colony began can be perpetuated for long periods of time. The effects on economic growth are predictable. Protection of the interests of the elite may lead to an institutional framework in which property rights and the rule of law become flexible instruments used to protect the existing economic order. Likewise, competition, either domestic or foreign, may be suppressed. The development of human capital through education or the improvement of infrastructure may be given a low priority, as they are less necessary in an economy focused on maintaining the existing structure. The initial conditions may produce institutions that perpetuate both inequality and lower levels of economic growth that can be independent of the political structure. This raises the possibility that economic development is a consequence of political development. Acemoglu and Robinson (2008b) take this one step further in a study of Latin America. If existing elites persist, then it would be useful to understand the composition of those elites. Drawing on extensive previous research, they show that elites going back to the colonial period have been quite successful in capturing leadership in countries that have moved to democratic regimes. In many cases, the elites are the direct descendants of the original Spanish elite. As summarized in the paper, case studies for Central America, Chile, Colombia, and Mexico provide examples of their argument. As a result, both the theory and some empirical evidence point to the difficulties involved in reducing the persistence of institutions that inhibit economic growth.

The research summarized above points to both the origins of institutions in the region that may inhibit growth and also to the limitations of the research. Improvements in the quality of institutions should lead to higher growth in the region, but this is hardly a guarantee. "Institutions" is a multifaceted term, and economists working in this area would find it difficult to precisely define the institutional changes that are most important for particular countries or even a region. As a result, one must be careful not to assume that institutional change will automatically produce higher economic growth. A second issue is that if North and others working on institutional change are right, then institutions will change when those with de-facto power feel it is in their best interests. If the institutions that support an older status quo no longer fulfill their purpose, then the prospects for changes in institutions will become more likely. In watching the ongoing changes in the institutions of the region, it is at least helpful to understand both how the existing institutions evolved and the forces that might change them.

Box 2.4 The Columbian exchange

The material above is an example of how we tend to think of the early relationship between Latin America and the rest of the world. The discovery of the region led to the transfer of European institutions and technology and more ominously new diseases to Latin America. Far less frequently do we consider the reverse. In reality the new relationship was not a one way transfer but in many ways an exchange. First, while European diseases were passed to the Americas, the venereal disease, syphilis, was passed back to Europe. The original disease was far more serious than is the case today and the effects on the Old World were initially more serious. Second, we literally eat the results of the exchange every day. Several classes of foods were involved. The introduction of potatoes, sweet potatoes, maize, and cassava improved the diets of the people of the world by providing cheap sources of calories. A second class of crops provided less in the way of calories but improved nutrition and taste. These foods include tomatoes, cacao, vanilla, and chili peppers. Finally, the Americas provided the world with a new source of previously untapped agricultural land. Crops such as sugar, soybeans, oranges, and bananas could now be grown in much larger quantities. In turn, this resulted in far greater supplies and lower prices. Finally, the Columbian exchange involved the introduction of tobacco and coca to the rest of the world with the resultant damage to world health. The main point is that the exchange of products between the Old and New Worlds was more balanced than is usually thought. A world without this transfer from Latin America is hard to imagine.[15]

Independence and postcolonial turmoil

From the brief sketch of the economic history of colonial Latin America, one can already see the seeds of the decline of Portuguese and Spanish rule. Recall that the production of gold and silver in the Spanish colonies declined after the middle of the seventeenth century. While the production of agricultural commodities increased, revenue to Spain from the colonies was difficult to maintain. There were periodic commodity booms, but nothing like the flow of money from gold and silver would ever return. In addition, things were not going well in Spain itself. The defeat of the Spanish Armada in 1588 marked the beginning of a long decline. Spain could never match the industrial output of the UK and increasingly needed goods that the country could not produce. This led to the continual loosening of the commercial ties to Spain, both formally by changes in law and treaties and informally (i.e. by smuggling). In effect, over 300 years the Spanish colonies of Latin America were slipping out of Spain's control.

Three factors in particular led to the independence movements of the late eighteenth and early nineteenth centuries. First, there was the issue of taxation. Taxes were being collected locally and then shipped to Spain. There were also still residual restraints on trade. These burdens were increasingly difficult to defend. Second, the top administrative positions in the colonies were always held by those born in Spain. After so long a time, much of the economic power of the region was held by those born and raised there. Invariably this led to tension, as the people of the region did not have the usual rights granted to citizens of Spain. Then there was the question of land. The initial distribution of land left much of the population landless and impoverished. With little possibility of redress from the Spanish government, the idea of independence gave some hope for the future. However, the end of Spanish rule was determined as much in Europe as in Latin America. French control of the Spanish government put the whole legitimacy of Spanish rule into question. It also put Spain in a situation where, as a result of political turmoil, it could not hold on to the colonies. In a decade of unrest between 1810 and 1825, most of Latin America had achieved independence from Spain. Under a somewhat different set of circumstances, Brazil became independent in 1822.[16]

While independence brought constitutions promising liberal democracy, this did not last long. The various wars of independence had left many countries badly in need of reconstruction. However, instead of reconstruction, independence brought boundary disputes among countries. This situation was compounded by groups seeking power not through voting but through violence. While Spanish rule (or misrule) had reduced economic growth in the region, what followed independence in many cases was worse in an economic sense.

Generally, economists have few positive things to say about wars and domestic conflict. In terms of the traditional theory of economic growth, growth is a function of increases in the labor force and the capital stock. War and domestic conflict diminish growth. The casualties of war translate into a smaller labor force and a lower GDP in the future. Similarly, war involves the destruction of a part of the capital stock. This is a particular problem in an area such as post-independence Latin America, where the stock of capital was not large to begin with. The combination of these two factors can result in lower economic growth following the end of a military conflict. Newer versions of growth theory emphasize the positive effects on growth of the accumulation of human capital. Wars and domestic conflict, at a minimum, can disrupt the educational process in a country. The loss of life can also mean a loss of human capital as well as just losing another worker. In an area where educational attainment was low to begin with, losing educated citizens to war can be particularly damaging. In short, the loss of labor, capital, and human capital that wars and domestic conflict cause usually reduces economic growth. If the conflicts are severe, the negative effects may last for decades.

The most recent research on economic growth focuses on the role of institutions. To review briefly, it has been shown that two of the critical preconditions for economic growth are property rights and the rule of law. Without these two critical preconditions, economic growth is difficult at best. For all its faults, the Spanish colonial government provided these two basic conditions. Property rights were established. They may have been initially arbitrary, but at least they were clear. As time passed, the initial inequities in the distribution of land ossified into a highly unequal distribution of this critical resource. While this is not a desirable situation, a situation in which property rights become uncertain is worse. If the government cannot protect land or other forms of property, then economic activity becomes difficult. During the wars of independence and subsequent conflicts, the protection of property rights in many parts of Latin America became problematical. The same is true for the rule of law. Colonial rule was far from perfect, but for hundreds of years there was law and a government to enforce the law. Laws made in Madrid and Lisbon may have been inappropriate for the region, but at least there was law and a consistent means of enforcing it. With independence, this system of law broke down in many parts of the region.

In any economy, the consequences of a breakdown in property rights and the rule of law are dire. As was mentioned earlier, this virtually defines the modern concept of a failed state. For several decades in postcolonial Latin America, many of the countries of the regions would have qualified as failed states for substantial periods of time. Under these conditions, economic growth was minimal. While the promise of liberal democracy was not realized, the vacuum left by the exit of Spanish colonial rule was worse. The result was that some sort of stability was essential. Neither property rights nor the rule of law is a binary variable. Stability in this sense means that the institutions of government are stable enough to provide sufficient day-to-day protection for the population that something like normal economic activity can occur. It took nearly three decades for this to occur in Latin America as a whole. The situation can be summarized by the frequent references to this period as the "lost decades."

By the 1850s, the worst of the wars and domestic conflict in Latin America was over. Without strong democratic institutions, political power may accrue to whatever group or groups have the strength to exercise power. Thus, the enforcement of property rights or the rule of law becomes arbitrary. Who owns what or the application of law becomes arbitrary depending on who happens to be in power at the moment. In Latin America, this frequently meant rule by some combination of landed elites and the military. Such combinations of power frequently prove to be unstable. This instability in government would continue to plague the region for more than 150 years. Many of the institutional weaknesses described in Chapter 4 have their roots in this era. Further, the legacies of Spanish rule remained. The region was deeply divided in terms of the distribution of wealth and income. Educational levels were generally low. Except in major agricultural areas and ports, infrastructure in the region was poor. The legacy of mercantilism lingered in that the region was still isolated from the global economy. Economic activity was still dominated by the production of commodities, and the manufacturing sector was small. With some exceptions in major cities, Latin America in the mid nineteenth century could be characterized as isolated and poor. However, the instability of the first decades after independence had subsided and enough stability had been achieved that the region would be able to benefit greatly from the last part of the nineteenth century.[17]

Box 2.5 Reversal of fortune

A fascinating application of the role of institutions is contained in the well-known paper by Acemoglu et al. (2001) on changes in the distribution of income in the world economy since 1500. Although data from this period is sparse, it draws on the established relationships between income and urbanization and population density. Intuitively, both variables are positively correlated with income. This is because only societies with high agricultural productivity and good transportation networks can create enough of a surplus to support large urban populations. In preindustrial societies, only high-income areas could support urbanization or high population densities.

This applies to Latin America, because at the time of the Spanish conquest, Peru, Mexico, and parts of Central America quite probably were among the high-income parts of the world. The same was true of parts of the Indian subcontinent.

If one compares the proxies for income in 1500 with GDP per capita today, an interesting pattern emerges. Areas that had high incomes in the past now have low GDP per capita. The explanation of this "reversal of fortune" is related to institutions. In the late fifteenth century, the European powers began their push into areas that eventually became colonies. This resulted in major changes to the institutions they encountered. The Europeans introduced extractive industries in areas where they did not previously exist or maintained the existing extractive institutions. Extractive industries were particularly profitable for the colonizers in areas that were urbanized or had high population densities. The indigenous populations could be forced to work in these industries or taxed to support their operation using the existing tax systems. The introduction of extractive institutions constituted an institutional reversal from the indigenous institutions. While the system worked for the European powers, this institutional reversal led to changes that were not consistent with economic growth in the long run. This is consistent with the timing of the reversal during the subsequent 500 years. The new institutions "worked" for a system based on mining and agriculture. For example, Brazil and Mexico were richer than the US as late as 1700. By the late eighteenth and early nineteenth centuries, the rest of the world had begun to industrialize, and GDP per capita in Europe and North America began to rise rapidly. Latin America, among other areas, missed the turn. Industrialization and income grew much more slowly in Latin America. The colonial institutions of Latin America and the turmoil of post-independence were ill suited to industrialization. Note in the material below that as the institutional environment of the region improved, the economic performance improved as well.

The golden age, 1870–1914

The decades following independence in Latin America eventually provided sufficient stability in much of the region for economic growth to commence as we will describe in the next chapter. Increases in the labor force, coupled with the accumulation of physical and human capital, began having their usual effects: GDP per capita began increasing. Indeed, the period from 1870 to 1914 marked something of a golden age of growth in the region.[18] As is usually the case, the rapid economic growth of the region during this period was a result of favorable internal developments within the region coupled with a favorable external environment. To summarize in advance, Latin America had become sufficiently stable in terms of property rights and the rule of law. In addition, the world economy was experiencing an unusually rapid period of growth. In this section, we will cover both the internal and external factors that contributed to this period of rapid economic growth. Since Latin America did not fare nearly so well in much of the rest of the twentieth century, it is important to understand what went right during this period to more fully appreciate what went wrong later.

In the first place, in the second half of the nineteenth century some measure of political stability had been achieved. For example, political turmoil ended in Argentina with the installation of the rule of an oligarchy in 1890. In Mexico, the *reforma* ended a period of political chaos and was followed by the *Porfiriato*. The liberal economic reforms and political stability created by the rule of Porfirio Diaz resulted in a golden age in Mexican economic history. Monarchical rule ended in Brazil, and the country peacefully transitioned to a republic. The story varies from country to country, but the common theme was that the turmoil that followed independence was dying down. Independence initially brought the promise of liberal democracy for the region. Unfortunately, that vision would not be fulfilled for another century and a half. Internal turmoil had been replaced by one version or another of authoritarian rule. As has been witnessed in more modern settings, authoritarian rule or rule by an oligarchy can be consistent with rapid economic growth. While political freedoms may have been suppressed, decades of turmoil in many countries make this outcome at least more comprehensible.

The return of something like internal stability to the region was matched by a relatively peaceful international environment. From the end of the Napoleonic Wars to the beginning of World War I, there were no major international conflicts. The influence of the former colonial powers, Portugal and Spain, had faded with uncharacteristic speed. Further, in 1823 the US declared the Western Hemisphere to be off limits to other potential colonial powers. With the notable exception of a French attempt to take over Mexico in the 1860s, the direct influence of colonial powers in Latin American affairs was negligible. Political influence was replaced by economic influence. The European country with the most active interest in the region was the UK. This was logical, as the UK was the world's most important economic power during the nineteenth century. During this period, economic ties between Latin America and the US strengthened. The end of post-independence turmoil helped usher in a wave of FDI from the UK and later from the US. Virtually nothing is more detrimental to FDI than domestic political instability or what is now referred to as "country risk." When the level of GDP per capita in a country is low, it is difficult for a country to grow rapidly. Since saving is a function of income, low GDP per capita usually translates into a low level of saving in a country. For a country in a state of *autarky*, it becomes difficult to generate enough savings to achieve a high level of investment. From our discussion in Chapter 3, this means that the production function for the economy does not increase as fast as it would if domestic investment were being augmented by FDI. The return of political stability to the region translated into an increase in FDI coupled with the increase in economic growth that one would expect.

Box 2.6 Two wars

Two major exceptions to the general tranquility of the region during the latter part of the nineteenth century were the War of the Triple Alliance and the War of the Pacific. Sadly, both of these conflicts have effects that still echo into the twenty-first century. The War of the Triple Alliance began when long-standing problems such as boundary disputes led Paraguay to invade Brazil in 1864. By 1865, Argentina, Brazil, and Uruguay formed the Triple Alliance and declared war on Paraguay. Paraguay was defeated by 1870, but the losses to the country are still difficult to comprehend. Paraguay lost 55,000 square miles of territory, or over a quarter of the country, to Argentina and Brazil. The human cost was staggering. The population dropped from 525,000 to 221,000 due to military losses, malnutrition, and disease. At the end, only 28,000 men were still alive in the country, a testament to the savage nature of the war. One cannot help but notice that Paraguay is one of the least developed countries in the region. To what extent the War of the Triple Alliance affected the long-run development of the country cannot be calculated. However, one should keep in mind that the country suffered a catastrophe on a scale not seen in the region since the Spanish conquest.

A lingering problem following independence along the coast of South America was the borders among Bolivia, Peru, and Chile, which led to the War of the Pacific. Bolivia and Chile had attempted to settle their disputes by treaty in 1866 and 1874. However, distrust of Chile was such that Bolivia and Peru formed a defensive alliance in 1873. The tensions were exacerbated by economic interests. The province of Antofogasta (then in Bolivia) is a high mountain desert rich in nitrates. In this period, these nitrates, in the form of saltpeter used to produce explosives and guano used for fertilizer, were extremely valuable. In addition, the region contains an incredible amount of copper. The resources were being exploited by British capital backing Chilean companies. Bolivia and Chile had reached agreement on the taxation of Chilean companies in 1874, but in 1878 Bolivia attempted to increase taxes beyond the previously agreed-upon rates. A counterthreat by Bolivia to confiscate Chilean property led to an invasion of the country in 1879. The defensive alliance immediately brought Peru into the war. In order to hold Antofagasta, it was necessary for Chile to control naval access to the province. In a series of battles, the Chilean navy gained this control, which led to a successful ground campaign. The military conflict ended in 1883. Chile had gained not only Antofagasta province but two provinces in Peru. Under the treaty, the status of these two Peruvian provinces was supposed to be determined by a plebiscite to be held in ten years. Disagreement over the terms of the plebiscite resulted in the dispute continuing until 1929. At this point, US mediation led to one of the provinces being returned to Peru. Peru lost a war and a province. Bolivia lost a war and its access to the sea, becoming a landlocked nation. Chile gained valuable territory at the expense of its two neighbors. For all the countries of the area, the ill will generated by this war lingers into the twenty-first century, partially because the region is still so important for its resources. While saltpeter and guano are part of economic history, substantial revenues accrue to Chile from copper and, more recently, lithium.

Growth in the region was assisted by rapid growth in the world economy. The period from 1850 to 1913 has sometimes been referred to as the "first era of globalization." Rapid growth in the world economy was powered by changes in technology. The spread of railroads and steamships dramatically lowered transportation costs both domestically and internationally.[19] For Latin America, this meant that commodities such as wheat could now be profitably exported. The refrigeration of meat allowed Argentina to begin large-scale exports of beef and mutton to Europe in the 1880s. The laying of transatlantic cable for the transmission of telegraph messages in the 1860s revolutionized communication around the world. This technology provided the basis for truly global financial markets to emerge. These developments changed the face of Latin America. For over 300 years, the region had been a relatively isolated backwater of the Spanish Empire. Fortunately, the return of political stability to the region occurred at about the same time as the world economy was changing as a result of new technology. The decrease in isolation brought the ability to trade and increases in investment to the region. The result was that Latin America was much more a part of the world economy at the end of the nineteenth century than it had been at the beginning.

These favorable developments in the world economy led to a large demand for commodities in the second half of the nineteenth century.[20] Improvements in transportation technology, the return of stability to the region, and the ability to produce large amounts of commodities at competitive prices created a very favorable environment for Latin American exports. Wool, wheat, hides, and meat poured out of Argentina in unprecedented volumes bound for Europe. Nitrates used in the production of explosives and fertilizers were exported in large quantities from Chile, Peru, and Bolivia. Coffee and bananas were exported from the countries of Central America. Increasing amounts of coffee and then rubber were produced and exported from Brazil. Booms sometimes turn into busts, which is in the nature of commodities.[21] Despite the punctuations of periodic busts, the overall economy of the region enjoyed an unprecedented period of economic growth. Political stability made it possible for purely domestic economic activity to resume its normal course. Stability also made it possible for foreign investors to augment domestic savings and increase the overall rates of investment. Increases in exports of commodities further fueled growth. Government finances stabilized to the point that public-sector investments could be made in ports and other parts of the transportation infrastructure. In modern terms, during this period much of Latin America was making the transition from low- to middle-income status. For some countries, the situation was even better. By the beginning of the twentieth century, Argentina and Australia were roughly equal. Immigrants from Europe flowed into Argentina on the reasonable assumption that the country was a better bet than the US. Immigrants also arrived from China, Japan, and the Middle East.[22] To an economist, this is one of the main indicators of economic success. The decision to immigrate, especially in the nineteenth century, was a serious business. People making such important choices are unlikely to move to an area where future economic prospects are not considered to be good. Immigrants do not only contribute labor; frequently they bring human capital as well. As we will see in the next chapter, the potential effects on economic growth can be large.[23] The interaction of all of these positive factors created an environment of rapid growth that the region has never been able to replicate. As we will see below, the largest problem for the economy of the region in the twentieth century has been the inability to regain the levels of growth that were obtained in the late nineteenth and early twentieth centuries.

Box 2.7 The Argentina paradox

There are four kinds of countries in the world: developed countries, undeveloped countries, Japan, and Argentina.

(Simon Kuznets)

The most golden country of the Golden Age was Argentina. A term used in economic development is "growth miracle." This refers to a relatively short period of time when a formerly poor country makes a dramatic leap upwards. The economies of East Asia were able to accomplish this in the second half of the twentieth century, and China is the best current example. The growth miracle of the late nineteenth century was Argentina. Before World War I, GDP per capita in Argentina was higher than in any country in Western Europe except the UK. It was as high as in other new countries such as Australia, Canada, and the US. It was still ranked number ten in the world in 1947. Then began a long decline. Table 1.1 shows that GDP per capita now is only slightly above 20 percent of the high-income country average. Argentina is now an important country for a perverse reason. It is the only country in the world that was once developed and is now a solidly developing country. It is an important country to study in order to understand what went wrong and how to prevent it from happening again.

There is little disagreement on how Argentina got rich. As noted above, the world economy in the second half of the nineteenth and the early years of the twentieth century was booming. Argentina had a wealth of products to sell in world markets, such as grain, meat, wool, and leather. The introduction of the steamship and refrigerated transport allowed the country to increase exports rapidly. The growth was enhanced by large inflows of physical, human, and financial capital. There is also agreement that things began to go wrong somewhere in the early twentieth century. Taylor (1992) argues that the change occurred in 1913. Using purely statistical techniques, Campos et al. (2012) estimate that growth slowed dramatically in 1922 and again in 1964. What went wrong is more contentious. The markets for Argentina's exports became more competitive over time, with a depressing effect on prices. It is also true that the economy became much more closed during the early twentieth century. The boom in Argentina was linked to large inflows of foreign capital that have rarely returned to those levels. Since the country traditionally had a low savings rate, capital investment has been low. In the twentieth century, macroeconomic instability has been a frequent problem. Fiscal deficits linked to money creation and inflation have periodically plagued the economy. These deficits are not surprising considering that the country has had a number of democratic regimes punctuated by military dictatorships. Under the circumstances, low institutional quality is not unexpected. The result is that economists cannot find one primary reason for Argentina's relative failure. Instead, it seems to be due to a host of adverse factors, both external and internal. Over the past century, almost everything that could go wrong in Argentina has gone wrong at one time or another. This is not a satisfactory answer, but it may help to explain why the country is unique in a negative way.[24]

Wars and depression

One of the oldest economic myths is that war is good for the economy. While it may be beneficial for certain industries, military conflicts are a poor substitute for production and trade under peaceful conditions. The start of World War I brought the boom in both Latin America and the world at large to a halt. The next thirty years would include two world wars and a global depression. In this sort of environment, it would be difficult for any country or region to do well. Latin America was no different. The rapid growth of the Golden Age came to an end. However, the economic story for the region during these years is a complicated mix of change on many fronts. Along with slower growth, the region was grappling with changes in world commodity markets. To make matters worse, the collapse of the international monetary system made things more difficult for both the world and Latin America. The economic focus of the world and Latin America also shifted during this period. The major economic power of the nineteenth century, the UK, gave way to the new rising economic power: the US. For Latin America, this change was more important than for much of the rest of the world. This period also saw the beginnings of modern industrialization in the region. The development of this sector became one of the most important economic issues in the region in the postwar era. As in the rest of the world, the Great Depression was a devastating economic event for the region. Finally, although World War II did not involve the region, the disruption of trade that it caused meant that neutral Latin America was not unaffected. As we will see, this period involves an important transition from the Golden Age to the next period of economic history in the region.

Box 2.8 The world economy: a brief history

When the term "economic growth" is used, almost invariably what is being discussed is a country's GDP growth rate. However, no country or region is an economic island. Since all countries or regions are to a greater or lesser extent integrated into the world economy, it is reasonable to think about world economic growth. If the world economy is growing at a faster or slower rate, then it will be, accordingly, easier or harder for a national economy to grow.

To get some idea of the rate of growth of the world economy, economic historians have been constructing estimates of past GDP growth in various countries and aggregating these estimates over the past several decades. In general terms, they have identified distinct periods of growth in the world economy over the past 150 years.[25] From 1850 to 1914, the world economy experienced a prolonged period of rapid economic growth. Rapid advances in transportation and communication helped fuel the growth of trade both domestically and internationally in many countries. It is no accident that Latin America's Golden Age coincided almost exactly with this period. A period of slow growth began with the start of World War I and ended in 1945 with the end of World War II. In addition to two world wars, this period included a global economic depression. As we saw above, this was also a difficult period for Latin America.

A prolonged period of rapid world economic growth began in 1945. The period from 1945 to 1973 was a golden age for the world economy, characterized by rapid increases in output and, especially, international trade. Growth in trade was partially a function of the dismantling of many of the trade barriers erected during the 1930s. Unfortunately, this period ended abruptly in 1973 with the rapid increase in oil prices. As we will see, Latin America did not fare as well during this second boom in the world economy. This is partly due to the set of policy choices discussed below. Unfortunately for the region, the end result of these policy choices occurred in the context of a world economy that was growing very slowly. The point is that economic outcomes for countries are not totally determined by internal factors. Good policy choices coupled with rapid world economic growth can produce sustained periods of rapid growth. As we will see, the reverse set of circumstances can produce very difficult economic conditions for a country or region.

During this period, commodity prices became unstable. The long period of rising commodity prices was followed by the instability in prices that has become the norm in the twentieth century. Further, declines in the demand for commodities can be doubly problematical. Not only does the volume of exports decline, but frequently there may be a concomitant decline in the prices of these commodities. As we will see in the next chapter, the supply and demand conditions in commodity markets frequently make these price declines severe. These problems were not universal in the region. The outbreak of war led to increases in the demand for oil and other strategic raw materials. Countries such as Mexico and Venezuela benefited from this. Other countries that were more dependent on commodities used for personal consumption fared less well. Brazil and coffee is a relevant example. The periodic collapse in the prices of some commodities led to severe economic problems in some countries. Nitrate prices fell sharply, causing serious economic problems in Chile. Coffee prices began a long fall, with serious consequences for Brazil. By World War I, Latin America's integration into the world economy carried risks as well as rewards. On the one hand, if economists know anything about international trade, it is that autarky does not work.[26] Everything else being equal, trade enhances prosperity. Prior to the Golden Age, one of the region's economic problems was its isolation from the world economy. Part of the rapid growth of the region during this period can be traced to its increasing integration into the world economy. While such integration enhances growth, there is a cost. To the extent that growth is dependent on exports, this growth can be threatened by relatively slow growth in the world economy. This contributed to the end of the Golden Age in Latin America. Global growth slowed and with it the exports of commodities that were an important component of the overall rapid growth in the region.

The period before and after World War I also saw a major change in the relationships among Europe, Latin America, and the US. The war disrupted trade relationships, as exports to the UK and France were encouraged and exports to Germany and its allies were discouraged. As the power of the UK in the world economy waned, so did its influence in Latin America. In many senses, World War I marked a change in the influence of the UK in the world economy. That influence was increasingly being replaced by the influence of the US. During the 1920s, the US had replaced the UK as the major source of trade and FDI for Latin America. Part of this was the normal pull of economic geography. Trade tends to be more intense between countries that are geographically closer. In this case, the relative health of the US economy, both during the war and after, led to a closer trade and investment relationship between Latin America and the US.

This period also marked the beginning of an increase in manufacturing in the region. While there had been some manufacturing output in Latin America for hundreds of years, the sector remained relatively small. In the main, industry was of the craft or "cottage industry" variety. However, the boom of the Golden Age led to an increase in small-scale manufacturing. As the economies of the region became wealthier and more urbanized, the demand for consumer goods increased. In addition, investments in infrastructure helped to make industrialization possible. From 1913 to 1929, manufacturing in the region grew at a 3 percent annual rate. This rate increased to 3.9 percent from 1929 to 1945. While this may sound modest at first, one must consider that this period was not exactly a perfect environment for industrial development in any part of the world. The reasons for this growth are not entirely clear, but some factors no doubt contributed to the solid growth in manufacturing that occurred during this period, which laid the groundwork for the much faster growth of industry that took place after World War II. One of the major factors involved was a breakdown in the international payments system. The war disrupted trade, FDI, and the flow of money in general to Latin America. The end of World War I brought some degree of stability to the international payments system. However, the advent of the Great Depression permanently shattered the old system. Instability in the payments system, coupled with unstable prices for the exports of commodities, meant that importing foreign goods was no longer a purely automatic process. In many countries, *exchange controls* were instituted. Exchange controls make the government or central bank the only legal buyer and seller of foreign exchange. In such a situation, one cannot just buy imports because one has enough domestic currency to do so. One must also obtain the requisite foreign exchange from the central bank. The effect was that imports were not as cheap or easy to obtain in all cases. As competition from imports fell, domestic manufacturing became relatively more attractive. Further, exchange rates became unstable. In most cases, the effect of the change was to make foreign goods more expensive. Of course, such a change makes domestic production more attractive relative to foreign production. Finally, there was both an implicit and an explicit increase in protection for domestic industry. Many *tariffs* in Latin America were *specific* tariffs.[27] As prices fell during the Great Depression, the level of protection with this sort of tariff increased. Of course, tariffs were frequently raised as a matter of trade policy as the world economy experienced a trade war started by the US in 1930. In any case, an increased level of protectionism encourages domestic manufacturing. The effects on manufacturing were important, but the region was starting from a very low base. By the end of the period, manufacturing in most countries was still less than 20 percent of GDP.

Summarizing the economic changes that occurred in Latin America between the start of World War I and the end of World War II is not a simple matter. One way to view the period is in terms of the region dealing with a succession of economic shocks. First, the export-driven growth model of the Golden Age did not end in 1914. However, the disruptions of the wars, coupled with the global slowdown in growth, reduced the importance of commodity exports as a driver of economic growth for the region. Some commodities, such as oil, did well, and countries such as Mexico prospered. But for most countries, booming commodity exports would never return as a reliable source of growth. The collapse of the global exchange-rate system injected a new source of instability for the world and the region.[28] It would be decades before Latin America fully adjusted to the new world of floating exchange rates. The two wars and the relative decline of the UK shifted the focus of Latin American trade and investment from the UK to the US. It takes time for any country or region to adjust to the establishment of new trade and investment relationships. The Great Depression was a watershed event for Latin America and the world. The decline in demand and real GDP, coupled with a global trade war, made increases in economic activity for the region difficult. Perhaps one way to summarize the period is to think in terms of restructuring. Latin America was being forced to change from a very successful model of economic growth based on exporting commodities to a booming world economy. The changes of this period meant that both the volume of these exports slowed and the prices received became much more unstable. As the parts of the economy connected to this export sector become relatively smaller, resources needed to move to another, faster-growing, part of the economy. Both domestic changes and changes in the world economy were acting to favor the small manufacturing sector in the region. The combination of these factors led to a noticeable increase in manufacturing relative to GDP in the region. However, there were both internal and external constraints on the growth of manufacturing. The result was that manufacturing could not possibly grow fast enough in this period to make up for the slowdown in commodity exports. As we will see in the next section, the base was established for more rapid growth in this sector after World War II.[29]

Import substitution

As we saw in the previous section, the manufacturing sector in Latin America began to grow somewhat faster in the early twentieth century than it had done previously. Initially, this was due to changes that were occurring outside the region. The changing nature of world commodity markets led to drops in export earnings for many of the countries of the region. These shortages prompted drops in imports of goods that could be replaced by local manufacturing.

The collapse of the world economy in the late 1920s brought about the collapse of the global system of fixed exchange rates. For Latin American countries, this frequently meant devaluations of the currency, which made imports more expensive. As a result of the global trade war that occurred during the Great Depression, tariffs on imports rose across the region. Obviously, both devaluations and greater protectionism would tend to stimulate the development of local manufacturing. In summary, the changes that occurred in the world and the region from 1914 to 1945 tended to favor the growth of manufacturing. Since much of the growth in manufacturing was related to domestic consumption, it is easy to characterize this growth as import substitution. From some-time in the early 1930s to the early 1970s, much of the growth of protected manufacturing in the region was geared toward production for the domestic market. However, in the early part of this process the increase was driven primarily by circumstances occurring outside the region, and a collection of policies could best be described as a reaction to a changing world economy.

After World War II, this ad-hoc collection of policies began to coalesce into something more akin to a plan for economic development. As was mentioned in Chapter 2, ISI emerged as the dominant postwar policy for economic development in the region. There are a number of reasons for this. First, it seemed apparent at the time that the commodity-driven boom of the Golden Age was unlikely to return. Second, in the postwar era, industrialization was taken as being more or less synonymous with economic development. Third, many economists in Latin America itself theorized that industrialization designed to replace imports was a potentially attractive development strategy within the region. In a sense, ISI was just a continuation of what was already occurring in the region. Industry had developed in the first half of the century primarily as a way to replace more expensive imports. Also, some of the tools of ISI, such as high tariffs, were already in place. Thus, in the postwar era, ISI was more a continuation and formalization of what was already occurring than a set of policies designed from scratch. Since the formalization of ISI occurred in the late 1940s, we will date the start of the next period from that time.[30]

What followed was an almost three-decade period of the development of industry in the region, primarily geared toward rapid industrialization based on the replacement of imports from the developed countries with production in the region. In one undeniable sense, the policy worked. During this period, GDP per capita rose rapidly.[31] Industry grew, and the agricultural sector shrank. This is not surprising, as the overall policy was pursued rather aggressively in many countries. As we will see in Chapter 8, tariffs rose to astonishingly high levels. Frequently, these tariffs were supplemented by the use of import "quotas". These industries were also supported by even more active policies. Private-sector producers were frequently offered subsidized credit, tax relief, and other forms of government assistance. When possible, FDI was channeled into production for the domestic market. If no domestic or foreign firms could be induced to produce for the domestic market, then the government might set up a *state-owned enterprise (SOE)* if the production was deemed to be critical to the overall success of ISI in a country.[32] Usually exchange rates were maintained at artificially low levels so that firms could purchase inputs at lower prices. As one would expect, this collection of policies led to a boom in the manufacturing sector in the region that lasted for several decades. In the beginning, ISI seemed superficially successful. GDP per capita was growing and agriculture was declining, which were both associated at the time with successful development. Because industry was frequently geographically concentrated in a few urban areas, many of the major cities in the region were growing rapidly. Understandably, higher incomes, a larger industrial sector, and increasing urbanization created the sense that ISI was working.

Unfortunately, under this veneer of success all was not well. ISI began to lead to a number of distortions in the economies of the region that eventually led to its demise. First, the agricultural sector in the region was usually neglected. This was unfortunate, as a substantial percentage of the population of Latin America resides in the country-side. One result of this neglect could be seen in the migration of workers to the industrial centers even in the face of high unemployment. These migrants were not being irrational. The wage gap between the rural and urban areas had become so large that a worker could still improve their standard of living through migration even if employment opportunities were limited. It is not accidental that the large "informal" sector in Latin America grew apace with the success of ISI. Second, in many countries, government support of ISI led to ruinous macroeconomic policies. Government subsidies and support of SOEs meant that the national governments were running chronic budget deficits. With no private market for government debt, the alternative in many cases was simply printing money to cover the deficit. The effect on national inflation rates was what one would expect. ISI was contributing to macroeconomic instability. Inflation and the periodic attempts to reduce it were making the growth rate of real GDP unstable for many countries in the region. In addition, the policy was leading to chronic imbalances in international trade. Exchange rates were being held at too low a level to make imported inputs into manufacturing less expensive. Such a policy also encouraged other imports and, perhaps more importantly, discouraged exports. This was a particular burden for Latin America's traditional exports of commodities. These exports had reduced in importance, but they were still an important part of the economy of the region. As the period wore on, there was an increasing use of borrowing from foreign financial institutions to cover the imbalance in trade. This buildup of debt is an old story in Latin America that usually does not end well. Unfortunately, the final result of decades of ISI was almost predictable, except for being more severe than would have been expected.

Box 2.9 Latin American debt

Unfortunately, the terms "debt" and "Latin America" are closely connected. As with most such connections, this is not accidental. The history of Latin American debt stretches back to independence. As Latin America freed itself from Spanish colonial rule, the global business and finance communities understood that the region was potentially prosperous. Independence created high hopes of economic success, not only within the region but among foreign investors. The new governments of Latin America needed foreign capital, and at the time the money was readily available. Such borrowing is usually referred to as "sovereign debt", which is a form of debt guaranteed by a government. This form of borrowing was hardly new; it had been routine in Europe for hundreds of years. What followed independence was a wave of borrowing by new and, as it turned out, unstable governments of the region. The result was that much of this new borrowing was not repaid promptly, and the resolution of investor claims took years to sort out. The relative stability of the 1850s ushered in a new wave of lending to the governments of the region. After some of the difficulties experienced by lenders after independence, the lending was more prudent and selective.[33] The success of this lending was given further impetus by the economic success of the region during the Golden Age. Unfortunately, this led to something of a bubble in lending. Sovereign debt is like most things: appropriate in moderation but potentially catastrophic in excess. Lending to the more successful economies, such as Argentina in the late nineteenth century, eventually became excessive. As we will see, like individuals, countries can find themselves in a position where they have taken on more debt than they can comfortably repay. In this as in other cases, default or suspension of debt payments occurs. Debtors and creditors eventually resolve the issue over time. Creditors may not receive all the proceeds that are owed, and defaulting countries lose some or all access to borrowing. The most recent debt crisis in the region, in the 1980s, was no different. Debtors borrowed too much and creditors loaned too much. The borrowing was driven by unsustainable policies, and the lending proceeded on unrealistic assumptions about the ability of the countries of the region to repay debt. The oil shocks of the 1970s exposed both the problems of policy and the excessive optimism of the lenders. However, one should realize that the debt crisis of the 1980s was not something novel for the region; rather, it was an old story being repeated one more time.[34]

The Lost Decade of the 1980s

By the early 1970s, ISI was putting a significant strain on the economies of the region. Most countries were still attempting to maintain fixed exchange rates, as was the norm for the time. Unfortunately, the domestic inflation common in Latin America meant that the prices of imports and exports were becoming increasingly unrealistic. In the face of domestic inflation and a fixed exchange rate, imports were becoming ever cheaper. Countries pursued ever more restrictive policies designed to control the level of imports. Tariffs reached very high levels. Quotas on imports were commonplace. Exchange controls had to be used to ration the increasingly scarce foreign exchange. For many domestic producers, all was well. Imports of crude materials and intermediate products could always access sufficient foreign exchange. Others trying to import less "necessary" products might not be so fortunate. Likewise, exporters in the region were finding life increasingly difficult. With a fixed exchange rate, Latin American exports were becoming increasingly expensive in world markets. The region was still rather dependent on exports of commodities. In commodity markets, price may be the only relevant variable. As a result, Latin American commodity exports suffered. Exporting nontraditional products was difficult at best. Aside from the exchange rate, the industry that had developed in the region was designed to replace imports. It had developed behind a number of different forms of protectionism and thus was not internationally competitive.

The rapid growth of imports, coupled with the difficulty of exporting, resulted in chronic imbalances in international payments. Imports virtually always exceeded exports. In the absence of changes in the exchange rate, these imbalances were frequently resolved by countries borrowing in the international capital markets. As long as the amount of borrowing was relatively small, this solution was not a problem. However, the situation changed dramatically in 1973. The explosion in oil prices hit Latin America hard. While the region is abundant in resources, it is surprisingly poor in oil. Only three countries

(Venezuela, Mexico, and Ecuador) are oil exporters. For the rest of Latin America, this meant a dramatic increase in the value of imports. The response to this increase in imports was ever greater borrowing. The difference was that the volume of borrowing had increased dramatically. Any hope of managing this situation ended with the second oil shock in 1979. As the 1970s ended and the 1980s began, it became increasingly difficult for the countries of the region to borrow more to service previously accumulated debt. In the end, countries were finally forced to devalue their currencies. It had become necessary to finally resolve the macroeconomic imbalances fostered by import substitution. The results were horrendous. As we will see in later chapters, a major change in the exchange rate can mean both higher inflation *and* lower real GDP. In Latin America, these effects were particularly harsh. The region was already suffering from inflation, and this became even worse in many countries. The global recession of the late 1970s and early 1980s would have meant difficulties for the region anyway, as exports of commodities and their prices typically fall. Further, the industrial base of the region had never been internationally competitive. Rising prices for imported inputs, coupled with collapsing demand in domestic markets, doomed many industries in Latin America. Further, governments could no longer afford to subsidize these industries in the face of the need to reinstitute some measure of fiscal responsibility and end the inflationary printing of money. Real GDP growth at first stagnated and then began a slow decline that persisted throughout the decade.

It is difficult to describe the wrenching changes that occurred in the region during the 1980s. The description above is simply an abbreviated introduction to what led to this decade. The causes of this *Lost Decade* are many, and some stretch back decades. In many of the chapters that follow, parts of the explanation of this event are presented. One should be careful not to look for particular villains, plots, or conspiracies. Bad events of any type are usually caused by a multitude of factors that coalesce during a short period of time to produce some particularly bad outcome. The Lost Decade is no different in that regard. We will be able to piece together the explanation as we move through the rest of the book. However, although there is no one cause of the event, it is essential to understand what caused the Lost Decade, as it was primarily the result of a number of poor policy choices that occurred over several decades. One has to understand what went wrong in order for the changes occurring in the region to make sense. The past twenty years have been a positive period for the region as a whole. This is understandable, as better economic policy choices usually led to better economic outcomes.

Key terms and concepts

autarky: a situation in which a country does not engage in economic relations with the rest of the world.

encomienda: the granting of land in the colonies by the government for use by a Spanish citizen during the colonial period in Latin America.

exchange controls: a system in which the government is the only legal buyer and seller of foreign exchange.

human capital: the education, training, and job skills embodied in labor that increase its productivity.

latifundia: large tracts of land held by individuals in Latin America for farming or mining.

Lost Decade: a period of low growth in Latin America during the 1980s.

mercantilism: a restrictive policy imposed on colonies requiring that all international trade be done through the colonial power.

minifundia: small landholdings owned by individuals in Latin America for subsistence farming.

quota: a government policy that limits imports of a product to a certain number of units.

repartida: the portion of the output earned by owners of encomiendas that was owed to the Spanish government in Latin America.

sovereign debt: a debt instrument guaranteed by a government.

state-owned enterprise (SOE): a firm wholly or partially owned and managed by the government.

tariff: a tax on imported goods.

Questions for review and discussion

 1 Describe the link between the discovery of gold and silver in Latin America and the beginning of the encomienda system.
 2 What was the mita system? How is its influence still felt in the twenty-first century?
 3 Describe triangular trade and its relationship to Latin America.
 4 Trace the historical development of latifundia from Spain to Latin America.
 5 Explain the repartida in terms of Latin America and Spain in the colonial era.
 6 Describe the transition of Latin America from the production of gold and silver to the production of agricultural commodities during the colonial period.
 7 Describe how the encomienda system tended to create persistent inequality in the distribution of income in Latin America.
 8 How did mercantilism affect Latin America?
 9 Explain the differences between the colonial experience in Brazil and the rest of Latin America. What accounts for this difference?
10 How did slavery come to Latin America?
11 Why are institutions important for economic development in Latin America?
12 Describe the research by Engerman and Sokoloff (1997) and the extension of their work by Acemoglu and Robinson (2008a).
13 How can the current problems of weak public education and poor infrastructure be traced to developments in colonial Latin America?
14 Describe the effect of the wars of independence and postcolonial turmoil on economic growth in Latin America.
15 Explain what the term "reversal of fortune" means. How does it apply to Latin America?
16 What factors led to the rapid economic growth of the Golden Age?
17 How is Argentina "different" from the other countries of Latin America? Why is this the case?
18 Briefly describe the history of the world economy over the past 150 years. How did this influence Latin America?
19 What changes occurring in the world economy from 1914 to 1945 tended to increase the size of the manufacturing sector in Latin America?
20 How did import substitution affect Latin America?
21 What is meant by the term "Lost Decade"?

Notes

1 For an alternative view of the Spanish government during the colonial period, see Grafe and Irigoin (2012).
2 For more details on this transfer, see Hamilton (1929).
3 For more detail, see Drelichman and Voth (2014).
4 Haciendas were sometimes also engaged in mining or light manufacturing activities.
5 For more on how this affected modern Latin America, see Coatsworth (2008).
6 Although the UK did not formally exist until 1707, we will use the term throughout the book for consistency.
7 All of this was rather imprecise, as the concept of longitude was not well defined until the late eighteenth century.
8 For more on the economic development of Brazil, see Baer (2013).
9 For an excellent history of this topic, see Klein and Vinson (2017).
10 On this point, see Przeworski (2008).
11 An extension of this basic idea, with an emphasis on how climate and geography led to the development of "extractive states," is given in Acemoglu et al. (2001).
12 For more detail, see Vanhanen (1997).
13 For an example of this work and a summary of their previous work, see Acemoglu and Robinson (2008a).
14 An example is detailed in Coatsworth (1974).
15 For more details on the exchange, see Nunn and Qian (2010).
16 The Portuguese royal family fled to Brazil during the Napoleonic wars. After returning to Portugal, the king's son declared the country independent, saving the country the trauma of a civil war.
17 For more on this period, see Bertola and Ocampo (2012). A less pessimistic view of these decades is given in Pados de la Escosura (2017).
18 This period is sometimes referred to as the *belle époque*.
19 See Williamson (1999) for more on the lowering of transportation costs in the late nineteenth century.
20 The current boom in demand for commodities emanating from the growth of China, India, and other large developing countries is a similar story.
21 A more extensive discussion of commodities is included in Chapter 6.
22 Most immigrants from the Middle East came from Lebanon and Syria.
23 The contribution of these groups to the already rich diversity of the region covered in Chapter 1 is a significant positive externality that is difficult to quantify. Imagining modern Latin America without these groups as a part of the economy and culture is difficult.
24 For a review of these issues, see Taylor (2014).
25 For a more complete discussion of this topic, see Reynolds (1983).
26 In a modern Latin American context, the example of Cuba is instructive in this regard.
27 A specific tariff is levied as a certain amount of money per unit imported. An ad-valorem tariff is levied as a certain percentage of the value of imports.
28 For more detail on this, see Fuentes (1998).
29 For more on this period, see Bulmer-Thomas (2014).
30 This is not a universal choice. One could just as easily begin the period in 1930. For an example, see Cardoso and Helwege (1992).
31 A note of caution is in order on this point. There is a counterfactual question: How fast would GDP per capita have grown under another set of policy choices? That is an interesting question for which there is no precise answer.
32 The development and eventual demise of most of these SOEs will be covered in Chapter 7.

33 During the first wave, things got to the point where investors literally loaned to fictitious countries in the region. For more detail on the history of debt in the region, see Reinhart and Rogoff (2009).
34 For a fascinating account of the debt problems of the Spanish monarchy, see Drelichman and Voth (2014).

References

Acemoglu, Daron and James A. Robinson (2008a) "Persistence of Power, Elites, and Institutions," *American Economic Review*, 98 (March): 267–293.

Acemoglu, Daron and James A. Robinson (2008b) "The Persistence and Change of Institutions in the Americas," *Southern Economic Journal*, 75 (October): 282–299.

Acemoglu, Daron, Simon Johnson, and James A. Robinson (2001) "The Colonial Origins of Comparative Development: An Empirical Investigation," *American Economic Review*, 91 (December): 1369–1401.

Baer, Werner (2013) *The Brazilian Economy*, 7th edn, Boulder, CO: Lynne Rienner.

Bertola, Luis and José Antonio Ocampo (2012) *The Economic Development of Latin America since Independence*, Oxford: Oxford University Press.

Bulmer-Thomas, Victor (2014) *The Economic History of Latin America since Independence*, 3rd edn, Cambridge: Cambridge University Press.

Campos, Nauro F., Menelaos G. Karanasos, and Bin Tan (2012) "Two to Tangle: Finance, Instability and Growth in Argentina," *Journal of Banking and Finance*, 36 (January): 290–304.

Cardoso, Eliana and Ann Helwege (1992) *Latin America's Economy*, Cambridge, Mass.: MIT Press.

Coatsworth, John H. (1974) "Railroads, Landholding, and Agrarian Protest in the Early Profiriato," *Hispanic American Historical Review*, 54 (February): 48–71.

Coatsworth, John H. (2008) "Inequality, Institutions and Economic Growth in Latin America," *Journal of Latin American Studies*, 40 (February): 141–169.

Dell, Melissa (2010) "The Persistent Effects of Peru's Mining Mita," *Econometrica*, 76 (November): 1863–1903.

Drelichman, Mauricio and Han-Joachim Voth (2014) *Lending to the Borrower from Hell: Debt, Taxes, and Default in the Age of Phillip II*, Princeton, NJ: Princeton University Press.

Engerman, Stanley L. and Kenneth L. Sokoloff (1997) "Factor Endowments, Institutions, and Differential Paths of Growth among New World Economies: A View from Economic Historians of the United States," in Stephen Haber (ed.), *How Latin America Fell Behind*, Stanford, Calif.: Stanford University Press, pp. 260–304.

Fuentes, Daniel Diaz (1998) "Latin America During the Interwar Period: The Rise and Fall of the Gold Standard in Argentina, Brazil, and Mexico," in John H. Coatsworth and Alan M. Taylor (eds.), *Latin America and the World Economy since 1800*, Cambridge, Mass.: Harvard University Press, pp. 443–469.

Grafe, Regina and M. Alejandra Irigoin (2012) "A Stakeholder Empire: The Political Economy of Spanish Imperial Rule in America," *Economic History Review*, 65 (May): 609–651.

Hamilton, Earl J. (1929) "Imports of American Gold and Silver into Spain," *Quarterly Journal of Economics*, 43 (May): 436–472.

Klein, Herbert S. and Ben Vinson III (2017) "The Establishment of African Slavery in Latin America in the 16th Century," in W. Charles Sawyer (ed.), *Latin American Economics*, vol. I, London and New York: Routledge, pp. 5–37.

Maddison, Angus (2004) *The World Economy: Historical Statistics*, Paris: Organisation for Economic Co-operation and Development.

North, Douglass C. (1995) "The New Institutional Economics and Third World Development," in J. Harriss, J. Hunter, and C. M. Lewis (eds.), *The New Institutional Economics and Third World Development*, London and New York: Routledge, pp. 17–26.

Nunn, Nathan and Nancy Qian (2010) "The Columbian Exchange: A History of Disease, Food, and Ideas," *Journal of Economic Perspectives*, 24 (spring): 163–188.

Prados de la Ecosura, Leandro (2017) "Lost Decades? Economic Performance in Post-Independence Latin America," in W. Charles Sawyer (ed.), *Latin American Economics*, vol. I, London and New York: Routledge, pp. 290–323.

Przeworski, Adam (2008) "Does Politics Explain the Economic Gap between the United States and Latin America?" in Francis Fukuyama (ed.), *Falling Behind: Explaining the Development Gap between Latin America and the United States*, Oxford: Oxford University Press, pp. 99–133.

Reinhart, Carmen M. and Kenneth Rogoff (2009) *This Time Is Different: Eight Centuries of Financial Folly*, Princeton, NJ: Princeton University Press.

Reynolds, Lloyd G. (1983) "The Spread of Economic Growth to the Third World: 1850–1980," *Journal of Economic Literature*, 21 (September): 941–980.

Taylor, Alan M. (1992) "External Dependence, Demographic Burdens, and Argentine Economic Decline after the Belle Époque," *The Journal of Economic History*, 52 (December): 907–936.

Taylor, Alan M. (2014) "The Argentina Paradox: Microexplanations and Macropuzzles," *NBER Working Paper No. 19924*, Cambridge, Mass.: National Bureau of Economic Research.

Vanhanen, Tatu (1997) *Prospects of Democracy: A Study of 172 Countries*, London and New York: Routledge.

Recommended reading

Arroyo Abad, Leticia, Elwyn Davies, and Jan Luiten van Zanden (2012) "Between Conquest and Independence: Real Wages and Demographic Change in Spanish America, 1530–1820," *Explorations in Economic History*, 49 (April): 149–166.

Drake, Paul (1989) *The Money Doctor in the Andes: The Kemmerer Missions, 1923–1933*, Durham, NC: Duke University Press.

Edwards, Sebastian, Gerardo Esquivel, and Graciela Marquez (eds.) (2007) *The Decline of Latin American Economies: Growth, Institutions, and Crises*, Chicago, Ill.: University of Chicago Press.

Engerman, Stanley L. and Kenneth L. Sokoloff (2011) *Economic Development in the Americas since 1500*, Cambridge: Cambridge University Press.

Julif, Dacil-Tania and Joerg Baten (2013) "On the Human Capital of Inca Indios before and after the Spanish Conquest: Was There a 'Pre-Colonial Legacy'?" *Explorations in Economic History*, 50 (April): 227–241.

Mann, Charles C. (2006) *1491: New Revelations of the Americas before Columbus*, New York: Vintage.

Taylor, Alan (2017) "On the Costs of Inward-Looking Development: Price Distortions, Growth, and Divergence in Latin America," in W. Charles Sawyer (ed.), *Latin American Economics*, vol. I, London and New York: Routledge, 207–236.

Taylor, Alan (2003) "Foreign Capital in Latin America in the Nineteenth and Twentieth Centuries," *NBER Working Paper 9580*, Cambridge, Mass.: National Bureau of Economic Research.

Thorp, Rosemary (1998) *Progress, Poverty and Exclusion: An Economic History of Latin America in the 20th Century*, Washington, DC: Inter-American Development Bank.

Williamson, Jeffrey G. (1999) *Globalization and History: The Evolution of a Nineteenth-Century Atlantic Economy*, Cambridge, Mass.: MIT Press.

Williamson, Jeffrey G. (2011) "A Latin American De-industrialization Illustration: Mexican Exceptionalism," in Jeffrey G. Williamson (ed.), *Trade and Poverty: When the Third World Fell Behind*, Cambridge, Mass.: MIT Press, pp. 119–144.

3   Economic growth and Latin America

Introduction

In the previous chapter, we introduced one of the central problems in the economies of Latin America. This problem concerns the rate of growth of GDP in the region. For much of the postwar era, economic growth has been positive. However, the growth of the economies of Latin America has been slow relative to some other regions of the world at a similar stage of economic development. In this chapter, we will begin to address this question in a more systematic way. In order to do this, we must first learn a little about how economists explain economic growth. The study of economic growth is both old and new. It is old in the sense that modern economics traces its roots to the publication in 1776 of Adam Smith's *The Wealth of Nations*. However, the full title of the book is instructive: *An Enquiry into the Nature and Causes of the Wealth of Nations*. In a broad sense, Smith was concerned with economic growth, or what now is referred to as economic development.

Fortunately, the modern study of economic growth has been an active part of the economics literature in the same time frame that we are considering in much of the book: the last half of the twentieth century. During the 1950s, Robert Solow formulated the basic theory of economic growth that is still used to analyze changes in the rate of growth of GDP. This "classic" growth theory explains economic growth in terms of changes in the labor force and the stock of capital. In the first part of the chapter, our task is to explain this basic model and to use it to analyze economic growth in Latin America. As is usually the case, the theory is both instructive and incomplete. The basic factors used in the theory are absolutely essential to understanding the economic growth process for virtually any country. However, it does not consider some important factors involved in the process of economic development. These deficiencies led to the development of "new" growth theory, pioneered by Paul Romer and others. In the second part of the chapter, we will cover the more modern theory of economic growth, which focuses on the accumulation of human capital and the role of technology in economic development. The development of the theory of economic growth will allow us to explain a substantial part of the story of economic growth in Latin America. By the end of the chapter we will be able to better understand why economic growth in Latin America has been relatively low.

Institutional basics

In many areas of economics, there is an implicit assumption concerning some preconditions that need to be in place within a single market (in the case of microeconomics) or the entire economy (in the case of macroeconomics). If these preconditions are not met, the usual theory we use in economics may not work as well. While there are a number of factors that can interfere with the workings of the market, there are two factors that are absolutely critical: property rights and the rule of law. The wretched conditions observed in the poorest countries of the world frequently are the result of the complete lack of either of these preconditions. Indeed, the very definition of a "failed state" is the almost complete lack of either property rights or the rule of law. Fortunately, this extreme lack of either precondition is not the case in modern Latin America. However, neither of these preconditions is a binary variable in the sense that a country either does or does not possess them perfectly. In the world, and in Latin America, there are variations in the degree of respect for property rights and the application of the rule of law. In the following two sections, we will discuss both preconditions in the context of Latin America.

Property rights

Property rights are essential to the workings of a market economy. For markets to work, it must be clear who owns what. If the buyer in a transaction cannot be certain that the seller actually owns the property, the transaction may not occur. Buyers need to be assured that the seller has the right to sell the property. If this is not the case, at some point another party might appear and claim that the seller had no right to sell the property in question. Further, the buyer needs to be confident that once some property is acquired, it cannot be arbitrarily taken away by another individual or the state. The enforcement of property rights has major implications for economic development. The lack of enforcement of property rights makes market participants more reluctant to engage in many economic transactions. The optimum number of economic transactions (all else being equal) would occur in an environment where property rights were perfectly enforced. Any reduction in the enforcement of property rights increases the risk of engaging in transactions. This increase in risk effectively increases the cost of normal economic activity. Of course, these increases in costs reduce the total number of transactions that occur in an economy. Fewer transactions translate into a lower level of overall economic activity and a lower GDP.

The poor enforcement of property rights one observes in a failed state has obvious consequences for economic activity. Transactions grind to a minimum, and output per capita falls to barely subsistence levels. On the other hand, property rights in a high-income country are usually taken completely for granted. As will be the case in many different contexts, Latin America occupies something of a middle ground with respect to property rights. The region did not start out well in this regard, as the modern history of Latin America began with an enormous theft of property by the colonial powers from the indigenous population of the region. In any colonial system, and Latin America was no exception, protection of one's property from a monarchial colonial power was problematic. Protection of property rights was hampered in the postcolonial period by sometimes extreme political instability. In short, the region did not start out in a positive way in this regard. In more recent times, prevention of outright theft of property may be a social problem due to ineffective enforcement of common laws regarding the protection of property. In more complex cases, the settlement of property disputes may be slow and difficult due to the state of the legal system and the courts. Likewise, the existence of corruption makes the rule of law less effective.

Table 3.1 Property rights in Latin America

	Ranking (1–7)
Argentina	3.6
Bolivia	3.4
Brazil	4.3
Chile	5.0
Colombia	3.9
Costa Rica	4.8
Ecuador	3.3
El Salvador	3.4
Guatemala	3.9
Honduras	3.8
Mexico	4.0
Nicaragua	3.4
Panama	4.8
Paraguay	3.6
Peru	3.6
Uruguay	4.8
Venezuela, RB	1.8
Latin America	3.8
Portugal	4.8
Spain	4.6
Canada	6.0
US	5.8

Sorce: World Economic Forum (2019).

Since the subject here is economics, economists like to quantify things. Over the past twenty years, economists have worked to come up with numerical systems that, at least in some sense, quantify factors that may affect the economy, such as the rule of law. The first such set of numbers is shown in Table 3.1. The table contains a measure of property rights obtained from the annual *Global Competitiveness Report* published by the World Economic Forum. This data, derived from surveys of business executives, is on a scale from 1 to 7, where 1 is the poorest protection of property rights and 7 the best. In a number of places throughout the book, we will be presenting measures of this type in an attempt to bring some level of quantification to various economic, legal, and social factors that influence the performance of the economies of Latin America.

The data in Table 3.1 indicates that property rights in Latin America lie somewhere between a total lack of property rights and the observance of property rights indicative of a high-income country. The average of this index for Latin America as a whole is 3.8. However, this masks a substantial amount of variation. The highest scores for Latin America, in Chile, Panama, and Uruguay, are equivalent to scores for Portugal and Spain. While lower than the scores for Canada and the US, they are still quite respectable for middle-income countries. On the other side, scores of 1.8 for Venezuela or 3.3 for Ecuador are somewhat puzzling. Some of the poorer countries of Central America, such as Guatemala and Honduras, have scores above the Latin American average. While research on the effect of property rights on economic growth in Latin America is limited, it is safe to assume that the greater the extent to which property rights are enforced, the more economic growth would be enhanced.

However, on average there is sufficient enforcement of property rights in Latin America to be able to use the model of economic growth discussed later in the chapter with some degree of confidence.

Box 3.1 Squatting in Latin America

In a definitional sense, squatting is the occupation of unoccupied space or buildings without the legal permission to do so. Essentially, squatters are using land that they have no legal right to occupy or use. The phenomenon is so common that it is arguably the largest property-rights problem in the region. Squatting is usually more common in urban areas but is not confined to them. In Latin America, squatting is a very common form of housing for the poor. Virtually any large city in Latin America is ringed by squatter settlements, as the value of land diminishes with the distance from the center of the city. Squatters move onto unoccupied land and proceed to build housing with whatever is at hand. Because they are informal, a major problem with these developments is the lack of the usual infrastructure associated with human habitation. This means no water or sewage service, no electricity, no public education, and few, if any, police services. The phenomenon is so common that squatters and their settlements are part of the common culture in most countries. In Mexico, they are referred to as *paracaidistas* (paratroopers) who literally drop in on unoccupied land. The favelas of Brazil are home to an estimated 25 million people.

This is not just a Latin American problem. The UN estimates that there are nearly a billion squatters in the world. They constitute nearly a third of the world's urban population. The numbers are similar for Latin America, estimated at nearly 130 million squatters. This is nearly a third of the urban population and nearly a quarter of the total population. Laws in the region vary from squatting being a crime in itself to its being a civil matter between the owner of the property and the squatter. The situation is complicated by the fact that many squatters are occupying public land. In some cases, such as in Mexico, squatters can become the de-facto owners of unoccupied land after five years of peaceful occupation. In other cases, the squatters have formed such large communities that evicting such a large number of people is not tenable. An example is the favela of Rocinho outside of Rio de Janeiro, which is home to an estimated 500,000 people. A common public-policy problem in Latin America is the formalization of squatter communities to provide some form of property rights, official recognition, and the provision of public services. Note that the problem originates with a lack of property rights and ends with the recognition of the ultimate necessity of such rights in order for people living in urban areas to have any chance of escaping poverty.[1]

The protection of intellectual-property rights

One of the more widely reported issues in property rights is the protection of intellectual-property rights. Intellectual property can be usefully divided into two main areas. The first is copyrights and rights related to copyright. This applies to the work of authors and musicians. Companies or individuals who helped produce this sort of work may also have rights related to the work. Another sort of intellectual property is industrial property. Again, this type of intellectual property has two components. Companies or individuals with a distinctive product may have a trademark that cannot be used by others. The second type of industrial property is patents for a particular product or process. Intellectual property has been a particular area of interest in international trade negotiations. In general, intellectual property is better protected in developed countries than in developing countries. As the data in Table 3.2 indicates, Latin America clearly falls into this pattern. On the same scale from 1 to 7 that was used in Table 3.1, the Latin American average for the protection of intellectual-property rights is 3.8. It varies from 2.0 in Venezuela to 4.8 in Costa Rica. Almost universally, there is less protection for intellectual property in Latin America than there is for property rights in general. This discrepancy is understandable. The protection of intellectual-property rights involves the collection of royalties and fees for the use of the property and the legal suppression of illegal use. In many cases, the property belongs to individuals and companies outside the region. As a result, the protection of intellectual property is a less important item on the agenda of the governments of developing countries, and Latin America is no exception. Perhaps there is even a hemispheric effect, as the protection of intellectual property in Canada and the US is not exactly perfect. The issue is likely to remain contentious, as the protection of intellectual property is a main goal of the high-income countries in international trade negotiations and for the US when it negotiates trade agreements.

Table 3.2 Intellectual-property protection in Latin America

	Ranking (1–7)
Argentina	3.7
Bolivia	3.2
Brazil	4.2
Chile	4.4
Colombia	4.0
Costa Rica	4.8
Ecuador	3.4
El Salvador	3.2
Guatemala	3.8
Honduras	3.8
Mexico	4.1
Nicaragua	3.2
Panama	4.7
Paraguay	3.4
Peru	3.5
Uruguay	4.7
Venezuela, RB	2.0
Latin America	3.8
Portugal	5.0
Spain	4.5
Canada	5.8
US	5.8

Sorce: World Economic Forum (2019).

The rule of law

> Weapons have given you independence. Laws will give you freedom.
>
> (Francisco Paula de Santander)

The second precondition is the rule of law. Normal economic transactions involve legally binding contracts. Sometimes, contracts lead to disputes among the parties involved. When this occurs, there needs to be a sufficiently developed legal system for the state to determine the appropriate outcome and which parties have what obligations under the contract. If there is no effective referee to enforce business contracts, far fewer business contracts occur. Market participants become reluctant to engage in normal economic activities because they cannot be sure that contracts will be enforced. Once again, the outcome is a lower level of economic activity. As is the case with property rights, the rule of law is never perfectly enforced in any country. Some countries have more rigorous compliance with the law than others. In general terms, enforcement of the rule of law in Latin America is adequate to allow the theory of economic growth that we will describe later in the chapter to be used. However, it is also generally recognized that problems with enforcement of the rule of law are a hindrance to economic growth in the region.

A serious problem in this regard is that the rule of law is difficult to define in a completely precise way. However, there are a number of factors one could consider that would have an impact on the rule of law in any country and are recognizable problems in a Latin American context. All these factors, listed below, have been defined and to some extent measured by researchers at the World Bank.[2] In all cases, the data indicates that the following factors tend to be problems in enforcing the rule of law in Latin America.

Enforcement of contracts

In almost any country, a business contract can be drawn up. The question then becomes one of enforcement. If the process of enforcing a contract involves an inordinate number of procedures or an interminable amount of time, then the existence of a contract may not be of much use. A large number of procedures and slow enforcement may lead to a situation in which the costs of protecting one's rights are prohibitive. The available data on enforcement of contracts in Latin America indicates that the enforcement of contracts in the region can be difficult.

Judicial independence

In order for the rule of law to be observed, it is important for the judicial system to be at least partially insulated from short-run changes in government. In many Latin American countries, this insulation is weak or nonexistent.[3]

Favoritism in decisions of government officials

> To my friends, everything; to my enemies, the law.
>
> (Óscar R. Benavides)

In order for the rule of law to work properly, it is important for the law to be administered impartially. To the extent that the law is not administered in an impartial way, then the overall rule of law in a country is diminished. Notice that this is not the same concept as corruption, it is more a problem of the day-to-day administration of the law. The law may be impartially applied for those who are unknown to the relevant government official. There may be another standard for those who have some connection to the officials. This can lead to a cottage industry of people who are experts in navigating the government bureaucracy and earn a living by expediting any dealings with the government. In any case, favoritism is not conducive to efficient economic outcomes as the administration of the law is uneven.

Efficiency of legal framework

The effectiveness of the rule of law is heavily influenced by the efficiency of the legal framework. In this sense, we mean the ability of the legal system to handle disputes in a reasonable period of time. Further, the system needs to be such that it can be accessed by most, if not all, citizens. Legal systems in Latin America can be extremely slow and difficult for the average person to navigate. In this type of situation, the rule of law is not universally accessible, and its application is diminished.

In all the factors that affect the overall application of the rule of law, the data available indicates that Latin America tends to rank relatively low. This situation is summarized in Table 3.3. Researchers at the World Bank have developed a system of ranking countries from −2.5 to +2.5 on the extent to which the country has an overall tendency to comply with the rule of law. In this case, +2.5 would indicate perfect compliance with the rule of law, and −2.5 would indicate a virtually failed state. The variance in Latin America is large, with the highest score being +0.85 and the lowest score being −1.4.

Table 3.3 The rule of law in Latin America

	Percentile rank (0–100)	*Governance score (−2.5 to +2.5)*
Argentina	46.2	0.16
Bolivia	9.6	−0.39
Brazil	43.8	−0.29
Chile	81.7	0.85
Colombia	40.4	−0.07
Costa Rica	67.8	0.25
Ecuador	25.5	−0.32
El Salvador	20.2	−0.37
Guatemala	13.0	−0.64
Honduras	14.4	−0.51
Mexico	31.7	−0.03
Nicaragua	29.3	−0.64
Panama	54.3	0.01
Paraguay	28.8	−0.81
Peru	33.2	−0.13
Uruguay	72.1	0.42
Venezuela, RB	0.5	−1.4
Latin America	36.0	−0.23
Portugal	84.1	1.33
Spain	81.3	1.03
Canada	95.7	1.85
US	91.8	1.55

Source: World Bank (2017).

The Latin American average is −0.23. To put this into perspective, Portugal and Spain have scores of over 1.0, while Canada and the US have scores between +1.5 and +1.85. The information in the second column expresses the data in terms of a percentile rank for all countries. Viewed this way, the average for Latin America is in the bottom third of the global distribution. The application of the rule of law is not so low that economic growth isn't occurring in Latin America. However, it is a substantial problem, which tends to slow down the rate of growth. This all indicates that Latin America has had a sufficient application of property rights and the rule of law to foster positive economic growth. The basic preconditions are being met, and both are slowly improving. This being the case, we now turn our attention to a more formal model of economic growth. While this model does not provide a complete explanation of economic growth, it does explain a substantial portion of it. Moreover, a more complete model of growth is not entirely novel but builds on this basic model. As for most countries, the basic theory of economic growth will explain much of the growth of the economies of Latin America.

Box 3.2 Judicial independence in Latin America

As indicated above, a critical part of applying the rule of law in any country is the degree of judicial independence. In practice, this means that there needs to be an adequate degree of separation between the executive, legislative, and judicial branches of government. An independent judiciary can play a number of roles in improving the rule of law. First, it can serve as a check on the government by vetoing unconstitutional laws. Similarly, an independent judiciary is essential to act as an impartial referee in the case of legal disputes. Without a referee, the rule of law in a country is about as meaningful as rules in an athletic contest with no officials present. In some countries, the judiciary can play a more active role in the policy process by interpreting the law in a way that amounts to influencing public policy. Finally, the judiciary may play a critical role by acting as a representative for traditionally underrepresented groups in society.

The ability of the judiciary to perform its functions depends critically on several factors. It is essential that the judiciary has sufficient resources to perform its functions and has some budgetary independence from the other two branches of government. Second, the system of appointments is critical. If judges, especially at the supreme court level, can be appointed without sufficient oversight, then the entire legal system may become compromised by short-run political considerations. After the appointment process, judges need a sufficient guarantee of tenure to further insulate their decisions from changes in the government. Finally, the scope of judicial review needs to be broad enough to ensure that all parts of the legal system are subject to judicial review.

There is a general consensus that judicial independence is an impediment to the application of both property rights and the rule of law in Latin America. As described above, judicial independence is a multifaceted phrase that is difficult to condense into simple terms. As in Tables 3.1–3.3, we present data that attempts to do so, albeit in a crude fashion. The World Economic Forum provides survey data on the overall concept of judicial independence for most of the countries of the world. The data for Latin America is shown in Table 3.4. As before, the countries are ranked on a scale from 1 to 7, with the former having the lowest degree

Table 3.4 Judicial independence in Latin America

	Ranking (1–7)
Argentina	3.2
Bolivia	2.6
Brazil	4.1
Chile	4.9
Colombia	3.0
Costa Rica	5.4
Ecuador	1.7
El Salvador	3.2
Guatemala	3.6
Honduras	2.7
Mexico	2.9
Nicaragua	1.6
Panama	2.8
Paraguay	2.1
Peru	3.0
Uruguay	5.6
Venezuela, RB	1.1
Latin America	3.1
Portugal	4.9
Spain	4.2
Canada	6.2
US	5.5

Source: World Economic Forum (2017).

of judicial independence and the latter having the highest. Notice that the range in the region runs from 5.6 to 1.1. Obviously, the region is hardly homogeneous in this regard, but there is a sufficient number of countries with low rankings to indicate that this problem is not insignificant. While such rankings are far from perfect, note that there is a correlation between these rankings and those of Tables 3.1, 3.2, and especially 3.3.

Source: This material in this box is adapted from Inter-American Development Bank (2006).

A basic model of economic growth

In this section, we will build a simple but quite powerful model of economic growth. This model was developed by Robert Solow and refined by many others during the 1950s and 1960s. The model can be variously described, and we still use it today, quite simply because it works. As we will see, economic growth is an extremely complicated process. However, there are some basic factors involved in the process that are common to every country.

Resources

In order for an economy to grow, it needs resources, or what economists call the factors of production. In general terms, these resources are referred to as land, labor, capital, and technology. In the discussion that follows, we assume that land is a constant. The borders of Latin America are now stable, so this particular assumption seems reasonable. More importantly for Latin America, the term "land" in economics refers to not only the land but all resources associated with the land, such as oil, copper, gold, and so on. Latin America is extremely abundant in land in the way it is defined by economists. However, since we are concerned with economic growth, the discussion of natural resources and commodities will be covered in Chapter 6. The following discussion will focus on labor, capital, and technology.

The economic growth of a country can be enhanced by growth in a country's labor force over time. This increase can occur either through an increase in its natural population growth or through immigration. An increase in the labor force will tend to increase GDP. However, there is a potential problem lurking here. In some countries of Latin America, the population is still growing at a fairly fast rate. The ultimate goal is to increase GDP per capita. In the face of positive population growth, GDP must increase more rapidly in order to improve living standards in the region. Data on the population and labor force in Latin America will be shown in more detail in the next section.

Economic growth also requires an increase in the stock of capital. In economic terms, capital is the amount of money invested in business structures and equipment. The latter terms refer not only to the type of equipment that goes into a manufacturing plant but also to the type of business equipment needed to process information, such as computers and software. In the models we use in the next section, economic growth can be enhanced by the ability of an economy to increase the stock of capital as fast as possible. For the developing countries of Latin America, the stock of capital outside the private sector may be critical. In order for capital and labor to produce the maximum output, the economic infrastructure of the country needs to be appropriate to the level of economic development. This sort of infrastructure includes water and sewage systems, paved roads, reliable supplies of electricity, and so on. Since much of this type of capital is developed in the public sector, we will cover this type of investment in the next chapter.

The final factor of production is technology. In economics, technology carries a somewhat different meaning than it does in common usage. Economists define a change in technology as anything that causes resources to be used in a more efficient way. Much of the time, this means a change in technology as we usually understand it, such as an improvement in computer technology. However, for economists, the term is much broader. What we are interested in is the relationship between inputs and outputs. For our purposes, a change in technology means that a country can either produce more output with the same amount of resources or, alternatively, produce the same level of output with fewer resources. This might occur because of better machinery or equipment. However, in this sense, a change in management practices or an improvement in the institutional environment, such as better enforcement of property rights, could have the same effect. In any case, keep in mind that we are discussing technology in a very broad way. One way to express this broadness is to use an alternative phrase to describe this process: *total factor productivity (TFP)*. In much of the discussion of economic growth, the terms "technology" and "TFP" are used interchangeably. Both refer to the ability of an economy to produce gains in output beyond what would be expected from increases in the labor force or the capital stock alone. In the literature on economic growth in Latin America, TFP is the most commonly used term, and we will follow that convention here. As we will see, this term is now also the focus of the literature on this subject. In the next section, we will build a simple model to illustrate the process of economic growth for a typical developing country with adequate preconditions for growth.

The production function

Given the factors of production that we described above, we can now illustrate how these factors interact to produce a higher level of GDP. This relationship is illustrated in Figure 3.1. The vertical axis measures the level of real GDP, and the horizontal axis measures the size of the labor force. To graph the relationship between real GDP and the labor force, we have held the stock of capital and the level of technology or TFP constant. For the moment, we want to look only at the relationship between real GDP and the labor force. This relationship is known as a *production function*. First, note that the relationship between real GDP and the labor force is positive. All else being equal, as the size of the labor force increases, the amount of real GDP that an economy can produce increases. Note that the relationship is not linear. This is because we have assumed that the capital stock and the level of technology are fixed. The changing slope of the production function reflects the phenomenon of diminishing returns. Diminishing returns occur when an increasing amount of a variable factor of production is added to a fixed factor of production. As the amount of the variable factor increases, the resulting increase in output becomes smaller. In this case, the fixed factor of production is the capital stock, and the variable factor of production is labor. When the first few units of labor begin working with a large stock of capital, initially output rises rapidly. This is shown in Figure 3.1. As the amount of labor used increases from L_1 to L_2, real GDP increases sharply from Y_1 to Y_2. However, the slope of the production function is not constant because of diminishing returns. Suppose that the same amount of labor is added, shown by the increase in labor used from L_3 to L_4. In this case, real GDP still increases, but by the smaller amount represented by the movement of real GDP from Y_3 to Y_4. The main concept to keep in mind is that changes in the size of the labor force are represented by a movement *along* the production function.

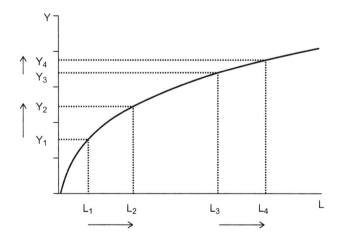

Figure 3.1 The production function and changes in labor.

Box 3.3 Population growth in colonial Latin America

The 500-year history of Latin America is littered with stories of tragedy. However, none is more tragic or important than the story of the change in population that occurred in the region in the sixteenth century. From the start, it must be kept in mind that the historical record is not exact, and there is considerable debate over the actual changes in population that occurred. For example, the population of Latin America in the year 1500 has been estimated to have been as low as 12 million and as high as 40 million. As a sort of average, we'll use the data estimated by the noted economic historian Angus Maddison, as his estimates are somewhere in between these extremes. Maddison estimated that the population of Latin America in 1500 was 17.5 million. By the year 1600, the population was only 8.6 million. The population of the area declined by over 50 percent. Other estimates of the population decline range from a low of 14 percent to a high of 65 percent.[4] This situation is comparable to the Black Death in Europe, which killed 45–50 percent of the population between 1347 and 1351. By any standard, the decline in population was an extreme event in the history of Latin America. Initially, the wars of conquest lowered the population. However, the major source of mortality was simply disease. In this case, the killers were measles and smallpox. The arrival of Europeans led to the introduction of these diseases, against which the population had no natural defenses. The epidemics, combined with the almost total absence of medical care, swiftly decimated the population. According to Maddison, the population recovered in the seventeenth century to slightly over 12 million. By 1820, on the eve of the wars of independence, the population had recovered to 21.2 million.

Such an extreme decline in the population has had permanent effects on the region. Thinking in terms of the production function, one can only imagine the decline in total economic activity engendered by such a severe decline in the population and thus, the labor force. Such a staggering loss of life changed the position of Latin America relative to the rest of the world. In 1500, Latin America accounted for 4 percent of the world's population. It did not regain that relative importance until the dawn of the twentieth century. As one can see from the production function, population matters. A higher population means a higher potential labor force. When we present the statistics on the labor force later in the chapter, this demographic catastrophe should be kept in mind. The current labor force of Latin America is far smaller than it could have been under other circumstances.

Changes in the capital stock and technology

Fortunately, changing the size of the labor force is not the only way to increase real GDP. In the previous section, the stock of capital and the level of technology were held constant. Here, we examine what happens if one or both of these variables changes. First, let us assume that the economy accumulates more capital. In the usual course of economic activity, all current income is not immediately spent. Usually, both consumers and businesses save part of their current income. Even if a country has only a rudimentary financial system, these savings may be loaned to a business. The business may then use the proceeds of the loan to invest in new structures or in plant and equipment.

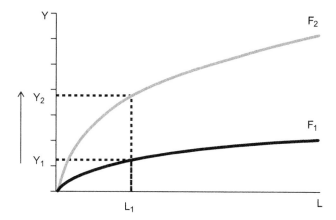

Figure 3.2 The production function and changes in capital or technology.

Note that this new investment is a flow variable that adds to the country's stock of capital. This increase in the capital stock changes the production function, shown in the previous section. Figure 3.2 illustrates this effect. The change in the capital stock shifts the production function upward. If the labor force is at L_1, then the level of real GDP, given the initial production function, is Y_1. An increase in the capital stock shifts the production function from F_1 to F_2. With no change in the labor force, the level of GDP increases from Y_1 to Y_2. The economy can now produce more goods and services for any given size of the labor force. This occurs because the *capital-to-labor (K–L) ratio* has increased. A worker with more capital can produce more goods or services than one with less. As the average K–L ratio rises, real GDP rises. The K–L ratio is one of the most important factors in economics. All else being equal, a worker who has more capital to work with becomes more productive. In other words, the productivity of labor, or output per hour, is positively correlated with the K–L ratio. This is a critical part of the economic development process in Latin America. The more rapidly an economy can accumulate capital, the faster it can grow. Further, increases in the K–L ratio increase the productivity of labor. This is important, as changes in real wages are highly correlated with changes in labor productivity. Logically, this means that the higher the K–L ratio for a country, the higher GDP per capita will be. In a later section of this chapter, data will be presented that illustrates this point.

A similar situation occurs when the level of technology or TFP increases. Remember that technology in this case is the relationship between inputs and output. An improvement in technology should allow the economy to produce more goods and services with the same level of labor *and* capital. In other words, something is happening in the economy that increases the ability to mix labor and capital more efficiently. Graphically, the effect is the same as an increase in the capital stock. An improvement in technology shifts the production function upward from F_1 to F_2. The economy can now increase real GDP from Y_1 to Y_2 in Figure 3.2 with the same amount of labor. However, in this case, the stock of capital has not changed. The increase in real GDP occurs solely as the result of being able to use the same amount of capital and labor to produce more goods and services.

This basic model explains a substantial part of the process of economic growth for virtually any country. Increases in the labor force, the capital stock, and technology will increase real GDP. Moreover, the model is an excellent place to ground one's thinking about economic growth in Latin America. Since it is a developing region of the world, the population and labor force of Latin America is growing faster than most developed countries. However, the theoretical concepts described above need to be given some measure of reality. In the next two sections, we will present the data on the labor force and the capital stock of Latin America.

The Latin American labor market

In this section, we will attempt to explain some of the basic data and characteristics of the labor force in Latin America. To understand the economic growth of the region, it is essential to have some idea of where along the production function Latin America lies and how fast the labor force is growing. However, the labor market in any country or region is nothing like a perfectly free market. While the labor market does have most of the characteristics of any other market, these markets are sufficiently special that there is a whole branch of economics dedicated to their study. For our purposes, they are special in two ways. First, labor markets work, but they work slowly. Changes in labor markets are noticeably slower than in the market for a commodity such as coffee or soybeans. Second, and more importantly, labor markets are among the most heavily regulated markets in any country, and this is particularly true with respect to Latin America. The result of these factors is that one cannot simply infer the supply of labor from data on the population and the available labor force. Imperfections in the labor markets of the region influence the quantity of labor that is being supplied and what form it takes. In this section, we will present the basic data on population and the labor force in Latin America. The more common distortions in the labor market are covered in the next chapter. Finally, the UN estimates that nearly 40 million workers from Latin America are working in the US and other developed countries. This phenomenon is having important impacts on the region and needs to be kept in mind when analyzing the labor market of the region.

The labor force

Table 3.5 shows the basic data on the labor force of Latin America. In 2018, the total number of workers was 314 million. In other words, nearly half of the population of the region is in the workforce. Brazil and Mexico alone account for over 150 million workers. Argentina, Colombia, Peru, and Venezuela have labor forces of over 15 million. In many cases, these statistics fail to capture the millions of workers in the informal sector of the economy. Also missing from the labor force are the substantial number of workers working either legally or illegally in North America or Europe. Another way of putting this is that the labor-force statistics shown in Table 3.5 can be considered very conservative. Compared with the world, Latin America contains 9 percent of the global labor force. Officially, this mirrors Latin America's percentage of the world's population.

The total workforce would allow one to define L in either Figure 3.1 or Figure 3.2. Once one has established the size of the labor force and the production function, real GDP becomes easier to ascertain. As shown in Figure 3.1, the labor force of a country

Table 3.5 The labor force in Latin America (millions of workers)

	1990	2018
Argentina	13.41	20.36
Bolivia	2.76	5.23
Brazil	59.94	106.03
Chile	5.1	9.08
Colombia	14.61	26.64
Costa Rica	1.17	2.34
Ecuador	4.07	8.37
El Salvador	1.92	2.85
Guatemala	3.11	7.04
Honduras	1.77	4.24
Mexico	30.43	58.93
Nicaragua	1.36	2.99
Panama	0.93	2.01
Paraguay	1.71	3.45
Peru	7.85	18.33
Uruguay	1.38	1.77
Venezuela, RB	7.82	14.64
Latin America	172.19	314.13
Low income	143.77	311.67
Middle income	1,684.15	2,523.18
High income	494.17	629.82
World	2,322.09	3,464.67

Source: World Bank (2019).

or a region usually grows over time. This is especially true of Latin America. In 1990, the labor force of the region was 172 million workers. By 2018, it had grown to over 300 million. The region had added over 125 million workers in twenty-three years. In percentage terms, the labor force of the region had grown by over 40 percent. As is usual, this growth contains both benefits and costs. The benefits can be considered using the production function. The rapid growth in the labor force means a rapid movement along a production function. This can potentially lead to faster economic growth. In this circumstance, such growth is essential. With the labor force growing so rapidly, the economy needs to grow at a fast pace in order to absorb the large number of workers entering the labor force. If GDP growth is slow, then problems of unemployment and underemployment become common. If employment is a problem in the face of a rapidly expanding labor force, then the problem may well be that the production function is not shifting upward at a fast enough pace. Inadequate shifts in the production function could be a consequence of either a slow rate of growth of capital investment or slow technological change. As we will see later in the chapter and the next chapter, both factors have been something of a problem.

As important as labor is to economic development, faster economic growth cannot be obtained without the use of capital. In the next section, we will present the basic data on the stock of capital in Latin America. The interaction between labor and capital can produce impressive rates of economic growth. However, if the growth of the capital stock is low, then economic growth may be low as well. In the next section, our task is to combine the information on the labor force with information on the capital stock to give a more complete picture of economic growth in the region.

Capital and Latin America

As we indicated earlier, an important component of the economic growth process is changes in the stock of capital. As the capital stock increases, the production function increases, and GDP rises. As a result, rapid economic growth normally requires rapid increases in the stock of capital. This is especially true when it is combined with labor to form the aforementioned K–L ratio. As this ratio rises, the productivity of the labor force increases. This is critically important. Increases in labor productivity in the long run lead to increases in real wages. This makes sense, as employers can only afford to pay higher wages in real terms if there is a concomitant increase in output per worker. A glimmer of this effect can be seen in Table 3.6. In this table, the K–L ratio is given for each country in Latin America, the high-, middle-, and low-income countries, and the world. GDP per capita is shown in the final column. The K–L ratio for Latin America in 2017 was $3,675. It varies from a high of nearly $13,000 in Panama to a low of $1,332 in Honduras. The K–L ratio in Latin America is higher than for the middle-income countries. However, note that it is substantially below average for the high-income countries. Now compare the K–L ratio with GDP per capita. The correlation between the K–L ratio and GDP per capita is not an illusion. As the K–L ratio rises, GDP per capita tends to rise. Note that this is not only true of Latin America relative to the world; it is also quite striking *within* Latin America. The relatively more prosperous countries have

Table 3.6 The capital–labor ratio and GDP per capita in Latin America

	1990		2017	
	K–L ratio	GDP per capita (constant 2010 US$)	K–L ratio	GDP per capita (constant 2010 US$)
Argentina	1,477	6,224.5	5,882	10,397.1
Bolivia	218	1,358.2	1,634	2,522.8
Brazil	1,555	7,965.1	2,941	10,913.8
Chile	1,685	5,947.8	6,789	15,059.5
Colombia	675	4,310.5	2,649	7,611.7
Costa Rica	1,301	4,921.6	4,491	9,808.8
Ecuador	895	3,720.9	3,343	5,256.0
El Salvador	350	2,158.4	1,496	3,463.5
Guatemala	336	2,146.6	1,342	3,124.2
Honduras	576	1,561.2	1,332	2,210.6
Mexico	2,000	7,661.7	4,592	9,942.9
Nicaragua	139	1,134.2	1,381	2,016.3
Panama	1,511	4,061.5	12,989	11,524.1
Paraguay	609	3,555.7	2,348	5,328.5
Peru	513	2,679.9	2,458	6,172.7
Uruguay	810	6,877.3	4,903	14,362.6
Venezuela, RB	616	11,830.7	8,488	13,709.0
Latin America	1,354	6,513.5	3,675	9,377.6
Low income	117	574.8	–	745.3
Middle income	546	2,102.6	3,789	4,998.6
High income	9,783	28,548.9	17,900	41,655.4
World	2,489	7,188.9	6,081	10,657.8

Source: World Bank (2019) and computation by authors.

Note: GDP per capita for Venezuela, 2014.

substantially higher K–L ratios than the poorer countries of the region. Again, this is not a complete explanation of the differences in GDP per capita, but it is important.

This data highlights the critical role of capital in the process of economic development. All else being equal, the faster the capital stock grows, the faster GDP per capita will grow. The problem for Latin America can be seen from Table 3.6. From 1990 to 2017, the K–L ratio in Latin America increased from $1,354 to $3,675, or over 170 percent. For the middle-income countries, the K–L ratio increased by a substantially larger amount. This difference shows up in GDP per capita. For Latin America, GDP per capita had increased from $6,514 to $9,378. For the middle-income countries, GDP per capita increased by 137 percent. To be fair, Latin America started out at a higher stage of development than many middle-income countries. However, on the other hand, the K–L ratio of the high-income countries increased by over 80 percent over the same time frame. Even accounting for different stages of development, the growth of the K–L ratio in Latin America has been slow. Our next task is to determine why this might be the case.

The data given above is informative, but it is also masking some important issues. If an economy is going to develop rapidly, then either the labor force must grow rapidly, the capital stock must grow rapidly, or the level of technology must improve. More often than not, rapid growth is a function of some combination of the growth of all three. In the next chapter, we will consider why growth in the capital stock has been so low.

New growth theory

The theory of economic growth described above is correct, as far as it goes. However, the theory is an incomplete explanation of the process of economic growth. Part of this incompleteness lies in the basic theory, reinforced by the empirical implementation of the theory. The primary problem is that the model does not explain technology or TFP, which is assumed to be determined by factors outside the model. This is frequently referred to as the condition in which technology is exogenous. As we will see, this is an unsatisfactory state of affairs, especially with regard to Latin America. Empirically, this meant that TFP was being computed as a residual. Once one had accounted for the amount of economic growth caused by changes in labor and the stock of capital, any growth not accounted for was attributed to changes in TFP. Determining something as important as TFP by examining the residual of a regression equation creates more questions than it answers. Just what is determining what this variable is?

New growth theory has evolved since the 1980s in order to address this problem. In these newer models of the growth process, the level of technology is endogenous. That is, it is now explicitly included in the model with other variables determining the level of technology. A key feature of these models is that the level of technology and, by implication, the level of economic growth can be enhanced by the accumulation of knowledge. More knowledge can increase the level of technology and become a driver of economic growth. Knowledge has another important characteristic. It can be accumulated without the constraint of diminishing returns. Indeed, knowledge is usually subject to increasing returns rather than diminishing returns. If the accumulation of knowledge is important to economic growth, then it is obviously of interest to understand what would enhance the accumulation of knowledge. In this regard, two factors are commonly thought to be important. First, the level of education in a society matters. The ability of the population to create and, just as importantly, understand and use new knowledge becomes extremely significant. Another way of expressing this

Table 3.7 Educational attainment in Latin America

	1980s	1990s				2000s			
	Literacy rate (% of people ages 15 and above)	Labor Force with (as % of total)			Literacy rate (% of people ages 15 and above)	Labor Force with (as % of total)			Literacy rate (% of people ages 15 and above)
		Primary Education	Secondary Education	Tertiary Education		Primary Education	Secondary Education	Tertiary Education	
Argentina	93.9				96.1	38.3	32.5	27.8	97.2
Bolivia	74.6	46.4	22.5	15.2	80.0	49.7	24.3	14.2	88.7
Brazil	91.1	15.0	15.8	6.4		42.9	28.9	8.6	88.7
Chile		34.5	49.4	12.6	94.3	24.6	48.8	25.2	95.7
Colombia		25.1	49.9	22.9	86.3				92.7
Costa Rica	92.6	54.0	17.9	12.6		59.0	19.1	16.9	94.9
Ecuador	83.6				88.3	32.4	39.5	25.4	87.6
El Salvador		42.0	15.1	23.8	74.1				82.8
Guatemala					64.2	58.3	12.2	5.4	69.1
Honduras									81.8
Mexico	83.0	43.0	21.0	16.9	87.6	43.9	21.1	21.7	91.3
Nicaragua		58.6	8.8	6.0					77.3
Panama	88.1	44.9	28.5	11.1	88.8	41.3	28.1	22.5	91.9
Paraguay	78.5	63.5	25.3	7.0	90.3	61.5	22.3	13.5	94.6
Peru	81.9	22.4	45.8	25.2	87.2	16.2	49.2	33.1	88.5
Uruguay	95.4				96.8	53.1	22.8	17.3	97.8
Venezuela	84.7				89.8				94.1
Portugal	79.4	68.6	10.9	10.5	87.9	68.0	13.5	11.5	94.6
Spain	92.8	54.3	16.8	22.3	96.5	48.3	21.6	29.6	97.8
Canada		20.6	34.6	44.8		15.8	41.4	42.8	
US		14.3	52.0	33.7		10.9	35.4	53.8	

Source: World Bank (2015).

is that the accumulation of human capital in an economy matters. Human capital is the education, training, and job skills embodied in labor that increases its productivity. Along with human capital, investments in research and development (R&D) can also enhance the level of knowledge. This is by no means an exhaustive list of the factors that can change the level of technology and economic growth. Part of the reason why these are important factors is that they can, to some extent, be quantified. In terms of Latin America, the former is more critical than the latter. Most of the world's R&D occurs in the developed countries, where conditions are most favorable for this kind of activity. To a certain extent this is a positive thing for developing regions such as Latin America. Potentially, it gives them the opportunity to acquire knowledge inexpensively through trade or FDI.

While new growth theory is relatively easy to grasp as a concept, it is not quite so easy to quantify. Although a number of different measures have been proposed, the most usual way to look at the human capital of a country is to examine the educational attainment of the population.[5] The basic data on this is shown in Table 3.7. For a developing country, the first order of business is the reduction of illiteracy to as low a level as possible. One of the greatest success stories in Latin America is the low level of illiteracy. Literacy rates in the region are now approaching the standards prevalent in high-income countries. This is no mean feat, as many developing countries remain mired in poverty as a result of the failure of the government to accomplish this basic function. Past primary education, the data for the region is less promising. For countries for which there is data for both the 1990s and the present decade, there has been some improvement in the number of students finishing secondary education and moving on to tertiary education. However, the situation is worse than the data in Table 3.7 indicates. Even for those students who remain in school, the average quality or actual educational attainment is low by international standards.[6] The problem is not necessarily the percentage of GDP being spent on education relative to other middle-income countries, but the utilization of these resources. Making secondary and higher education more effective in Latin America is one of the most pressing problems in the region.[7]

Box 3.4 Human capital persistence in Brazil

Because economics is a social science, it is difficult to run experiments in the same sense one does experiments in the natural sciences. Frequently, the closest we can get is to find the existence of a natural experiment. A natural experiment is a situation where an abrupt change in an economic variable occurs that allows one to observe the outcome in something like the way you could do so in a controlled experiment. Naturally, economists are always on the lookout for potential natural experiments. In a recent paper, Rocha et al. (2017) were able to perform a natural experiment on the effects of a policy change in Brazil that occurred over 100 years ago. At end of the nineteenth and into the early twentieth centuries, the government established a number of official settlement colonies in the state of São Paulo. The distinctive feature of these settlements was that they were set up to attract immigrants with higher levels of education. The policy forms a natural experiment as these settlements were not different from other parts of the state except for the quality of the immigrants. Further, the settlements were set up before Brazil began to industrialize so virtually the entire state was still agrarian.

The initial effects of the policy were predictable. In 1920, only a few years after the establishment of the last settlements, the literacy rates in the settlements was 27 percent higher than in the rest of the state. What is interesting is the persistence of this policy over time. In 1920, 1940, and 2000, enrollment rates and the number of teachers per student were higher in the settlement areas. In 2000, students in these areas still had more than a half of a year more education than other areas. The effects on income are not surprising. Average income per capita in these areas were 15 percent higher than in other areas. The policy implications of this study are clear. Investments in education pay dividends to current students. That the effects are so far reaching over time show that such investments have a potential rate of return that is far higher than one might think.

For a middle-income country, R&D is a less important factor in economic growth. R&D is a form of investment that societies make. With so many pressing investment needs in Latin America, in both the public and the private sector, it is not surprising that the level of R&D is low. In Latin America, only Brazil and Mexico have R&D spending approaching 1 percent of GDP. For the poorer countries of the region, this percentage is far less. This should not be considered a drag on economic growth. With respect to R&D, the problem has been the historically closed nature of the economies of the region. R&D is normally produced for the most part in high-income countries. The new technology that results from this is then transferred to developing countries directly or indirectly through FDI or international trade. Interfering with the flows of FDI or restricting imports impairs this process. As we will see in later chapters, these impediments to FDI and imports have been substantial in the economic history of Latin America. The result is that technology transfers have not been as high as they could have been, which may have slowed growth somewhat.[8] However, economic situations change over time, and economic growth will make R&D a more important factor. There are already firms in Latin America that produce the sort of high-technology products for which R&D is a critical input. Indeed, you've probably already flown in one: an Embraer jet made in Brazil. At this point, such firms are not the average in the region, but over time their number will grow.

To review, the basic theory of economic growth posits that economic growth is a function of increases in the size of land, the labor force, increases in the stock of capital, and improvements in TFP. The new theory of economic growth adds two factors: increases in the amount of human capital and investment in R&D. While the basic theory and later modifications seem logical, it is always necessary to test theory against the data. This allows one to accomplish two things. First, it can tell you whether the theory is correct or whether it needs to be modified. Second, with respect to economic growth, empirical testing of the theory can be informative in a policy sense. Economic growth in Latin America is no different. In the next chapter, we will consider how the results of tests of economic growth in the region can be used to explain past policy problems and potential modifications in the future.

Key terms and concepts

capital-to-labor (K–L) ratio: the amount of capital per unit of labor used in the production of goods and services.
production function: a graph showing the relationship between real GDP and the factors of production.
total factor productivity (TFP): an increase in GDP not accounted for by changes in the labor force or the stock of capital.

Questions for review and discussion

1   What are the institutional basics necessary for economic growth? Why are they a problem in a Latin American context?
2   Describe the problem of squatting in Latin America.
3   Describe the changes in population in Latin America in the sixteenth century. Using the production function, show how these affected past and current economic growth.
4   List and describe the different aspects of the rule of law.
5   Why is judicial independence critical to the application of the rule of law? Why is this a problem in Latin America?
6   Explain why an increase in the K–L ratio would tend to increase GDP per capita.
7   What happened to the population of colonial Latin America in the sixteenth century?
8   Describe the effects of an increase in K on the production function.
9   Carefully define the term "total factor productivity." Why is it important?
10   What is the size of the labor market in Latin America? How does it relate to the labor market of the world?
11   If Latin America had higher savings and FDI, what would this mean in terms of economic growth?
12   How does new growth theory constitute an extension of the original theory of economic growth?
13   Is the evolution of human capital in Latin America a constraint on economic growth?
14   Why is R&D not a critical factor for economic growth in Latin America?

Notes

1 Field (2007) has made an extremely interesting connection between squatting, the supply of labor, and child labor in Peru. She finds that squatting entails leaving at least one adult home at all times to protect the "property." This leads to a lower labor supply by adults and a higher tendency to put children in the workforce.
2 See World Bank (2018).
3 On this point, see Henisz (2000) or Staats et al. (2005).
4 For more details, see Maddison (2001).
5 For a review of human capital in Latin America, see Gimenez (2005).
6 For more on this point, see Chapter 12.
7 On this point. see Barro and Lee (2001).
8 See Blyde (2004).

References

Barro, Robert J. and Jong-Wha Lee (2001) "International Data on Educational Attainment: Updates and Implications," *Oxford Economic Papers*, 53 (July): 541–563.

Blyde, Juan (2004) "Trade and Technology Diffusion in Latin America," *International Trade Journal*, 18 (fall): 177–197.

Field, Erica (2007) "Entitled to Work: Urban Property Rights and Labor Supply in Peru," *Quarterly Journal of Economics*, 122 (November): 1561–1602.

Gimenez, Gregorio (2005) "The Human Capital Endowment of Latin America and the Caribbean," *CEPAL Review*, 86 (August): 97–116.

Henisz, Witold (2000) "The Institutional Environment for Economic Growth," *Economics and Politics*, 12 (March): 1–31.

Inter-American Development Bank (2006) *The Politics of Policies, Economic and Social Progress in Latin America: 2006 Report*, Washington, DC: Inter-American Development Bank.

Maddison, Angus (2001) *The World Economy: A Millennial Perspective*, Paris: Organisation for Economic Co-operation and Development.

Rocha, Rudi, Claudio Ferraz, and Rodrigo R. Soares (2017) "Human Capital Persistence and Development," *American Economic Journal: Applied Economics*, 9 (October): 105–136.

Staats, Joseph L., Shaun Bowler, and Jonathan T. Hiskey (2005) "Measuring Judicial Performance in Latin America," *Latin American Politics and Society*, 47 (December): 77–106.

World Bank (2018) *Worldwide Governance Indicators, 2018*, Washington, DC: World Bank.

World Economic Forum (2018) *Global Competitiveness Report, 2014–2015*, Davos: World Economic Forum.

Recommended reading

Ferreira, Pedro C., Samuel De Abreu Pessôa, and Fernando A. Veloso (2013) "On the Evolution of Total Factor Productivity in Latin America," *Economic Inquiry*, 51 (January): 16–30.

Loayza, Norman, Ana Maria Oviedo, and Luis Servén (2010) "Regulation and Macroeconomic Performance," in Norman Loayza and Luis Servén (eds.), *Business Regulation and Economic Performance*, Washington, DC: World Bank, pp. 65–117.

Loayza, Norman, Pablo Fajnzylber, and César Calderón (2005) *Economic Growth in Latin America and the Caribbean: Stylized Facts, Explanations, and Forecasts*, Washington, DC: World Bank.

Pagés, Carmen (2010) *The Age of Productivity: Transforming Economies from the Bottom Up*, Basingstoke: Palgrave Macmillan.

Palma, José G. (2011) "Why Has Productivity Growth Stagnated in Most Latin American Countries since the Neo-liberal Reforms?" in José A. Ocampo and Jaime Ros (eds.), *The Oxford Handbook of Latin American Economics*, Oxford: Oxford University Press, pp. 568–607.

Solimano, Andres and Raimundo Soto (2006) "Economic Growth in Latin America in the Late Twentieth Century: Evidence and Interpretation," in Andres Solimano (ed.), *Vanishing Growth in Latin America: The Late Twentieth Century Experience*, Northampton, Mass.: Edward Elgar, pp. 11–45.

Sosa, Sebastian, Evridiki Tsounta, and Hye Sun Kim (2013) "Is the Growth Momentum in Latin America Sustainable?" *IMF Working Paper #WP/13/109*, Washington, DC: International Monetary Fund.

4 Limits to growth in Latin America

Introduction

In the previous chapter, we considered the theory of economic growth and how it applies to Latin America. In considering each factor, we have discussed the data and some of its implications for economic growth in the region. What has been missing is some sense of "putting it all together," so to speak. As we will see, economists have formulated a method of putting most of the factors together in a comprehensible way. In the jargon of the literature, this is referred to as growth accounting. There are obviously a number of factors that influence economic growth. Each of them has a part to play in explaining why the growth of a country or a region has been what it was in the past. By explaining past periods of economic growth, one can perhaps see what went right or wrong over time. In the case of Latin America, such exercises are critical. The growth of the region is generally agreed to have been lower than it should have been. As a result, the results of a growth accounting exercise for Latin America are more than ordinarily important. What we will find is both illuminating and frustrating. Using growth accounting, we'll be able to narrow the scope of the problem of economic growth in Latin America. The bad news is that there is no magic bullet that will suddenly transform Latin America into East Asia. The good news is that the exercises indicate where the bulk of the problems are and that, in theory, these problems can be remedied over time.

In the first part of the chapter, the results of growth-accounting exercises are presented to allow us to get an overview of the problems encountered in Latin America. The second section covers the problem of relatively low capital investment which is familiar from the preceding chapter. The next section covers the central problem of growth in the region: TFP. Unfortunately, the solution to this problem is not entirely clear. The remainder of the chapter deals with what are commonly thought to be the list of suspects contributing to low TFP. The final part of the chapter deals with the structural reforms and institutional issues that are thought to be major contributors to this problem. None of these reforms or issues constitute anything like a complete solution to the problem. However, it would be hard to argue that improving any of them would lower economic growth. In many cases, such as crime, even if improvements did not enhance growth, they would surely enhance the quality of life for the people of the region.

Growth accounting in Latin America

In accounting for growth in a country or region, economists usually put the theory we have described in the previous chapter into a regression equation. With respect to economic growth, the equation usually takes the form

$$Y = F (K, L, H, A) \tag{4.1}$$

where:

> Y = real GDP
> K = the stock of capital
> L = the labor force
> H = human capital
> A = TFP

Equation 4.1 simply expresses the relationship between economic growth and the factors that cause growth. In the equation, the growth of real GDP is expressed as a function of the growth of the labor force, the capital stock, human capital, and TFP.[1] The use of statistics to analyze economic data is known as *econometrics*. The particular statistical tool being employed in this case is regression analysis. The data used in the analysis is available for the countries of Latin America for the past fifty years.[2] The exercise in *growth accounting* is straightforward. Economic growth (Y) becomes the dependent variable in a regression equation. Data on the labor force, the capital stock, and human capital is readily obtainable. One can now "run" the regression through a large variety of statistical software packages.

The results allow one to interpret the effects of changes in the labor force, the capital stock, and human capital on economic growth in a relatively straightforward way. The same cannot be said for TFP. The effect of this factor is not measured directly, but indirectly. In a regression equation, there is a component known as the residual. The residual is where the effects of all factors not explicitly accounted for, such as labor and capital, are lumped together in one place. In growth accounting, the value of the residual is interpreted as a proxy for TFP. This is a convenient convention, but for Latin America, this residual turns out to be critically important.

Despite the explosion of econometric studies on economic growth, the number of specific studies on Latin America is rather small. Since these studies tend to produce rather consistent results, we will focus on a recent study by Cavallo and Powell (2018).[3] The results of this particular study are shown in Table 4.1. The first column shows the average annual growth rate of real GDP per capita in Latin America from 1960 to 2017. While this growth of 2.4 percent is positive, it is a low number by international standards. The next four columns show the breakdown of this growth in terms of growth accounting. As one would expect, the growth of the labor force accounted for 0.66 percent of total growth. Slow population growth is not the source of the problem. The same is true of changes in the capital stock. This factor contributed 1.01 percent of total growth. At this point, note that a very simple model of economic growth accounts for a substantial amount of the total economic growth of the region. However, the importance of adding human capital can be clearly seen. By only a small margin, human capital accumulation is the second most important positive factor in economic growth in

Table 4.1 Average economic growth in Latin America, 1960–2017

	GDP growth (per capita)	TFP	Capital accumulation	Skills	Labor
Advanced Economies	2.71%	0.84%	0.92%	0.76%	0.20%
United States	2.04%	0.79%	0.28%	0.59%	0.38%
Emerging Asia	4.86%	1.72%	1.09%	1.28%	0.77%
Rest of the World	2.60%	0.45%	0.98%	0.98%	0.20%
Latin America and the Caribbean	2.40%	−0.20%	1.01%	0.92%	0.66%

Source: Inter-American Development Bank (2019).

Table 4.2 Growth accounting gaps between Latin America and the world economies

	GDP growth (per capita)	TFP	Capital accumulation	Skills	Labor
Advanced economies	−0.31%	−1.04%	0.09%	0.17%	0.47%
United States	0.35%	−1.00%	0.74%	0.33%	0.28%
Emerging Asia	−2.47%	−1.92%	−0.08%	−0.36%	−0.10%
Rest of the world	−0.21%	−0.65%	0.03%	−0.06%	0.46%

Source: Inter-American Development Bank (2019).

Latin America. While the educational system of the region leaves much to be desired, it is still contributing to economic growth. The contribution of TFP is the puzzling result. The negative sign preceding 0.20 percent is not an error. In this study, TFP growth in Latin America was negative for nearly *six* decades. In terms of economic growth, this is an astonishing result. Unfortunately, for Latin America, this is not uncommon. Virtually all studies of economic growth in the region report that TFP growth is, at best, relatively low. This is not the whole story of the relatively slow growth of the region, but it is a substantial part of it.

To put together the entire picture of Latin American economic growth, comparisons with other parts of the world are shown in Table 4.2. In this table, we compare the growth of the factors of production among Latin America, the advanced economies, the US, emerging Asia, and the rest of the world. Each cell in the table represents the number for Latin America minus the analogous number for another region. Thus, the first column of the table shows that growth in GDP per capita in Latin America has been slower than all other regions with the exception of the US. This is the essence of relatively slow growth in Latin America. GDP per capita growth in Latin America is below the average for the rest of the world, and growth has not even kept up with that in most of the advanced countries. The next four columns indicate why this is so. Obviously, the problem is not the growth of the labor force. Except for emerging Asia, the labor force of Latin America has been growing faster than in the rest of the world. The accumulation of human capital is more of a problem. Relative to emerging Asia and the rest of the world, human-capital growth is lagging behind. Human capital is important for growth but not the most important factor.[4] Clearly, the accumulation of capital also is a problem. Capital growth in the region is only marginally larger than the world average. In particular, the contribution of capital to growth in Latin America is one of the main reasons why it has not grown as fast as emerging Asia.[5] Much of the story is contained in the TFP column. Compared with the rest of the world, the advanced economies, or emerging Asia, TFP growth in Latin America is the largest contributor to the differences in growth. This is precisely what one would expect. Normally, TFP growth is positive in an economy. Putting the usual positive growth for most of the rest of the world together with the negative or slow growth of this factor in Latin America yields this result.

A standard growth-accounting framework has allowed us to do two things in this section. First, we were able to see what has caused economic growth in the region since the 1960s. A standard growth model augmented with some of the newer growth theory explains Latin American growth fairly well. In comparing Latin America with the rest of the world, the picture that emerges is not so encouraging. The accumulation of capital in the region needs to be higher to foster more rapid economic growth. This is a problem that we will cover in the next section. The most serious problem of economic growth in Latin America is the growth of TFP. The final sections of the chapter will try to provide some understanding of why this problem exists.

Capital stock growth

Part of the problem with lagging growth in Latin America has been that increases in the capital stock have not been exceptionally high. This leads to the question of what factors can cause a large increase in the capital stock. In general terms, there are two sources. First, a country could increase its capital stock by increasing the level of domestic savings. Savings generated by the public and the business community could then be funneled through the financial services sector to produce increases in the capital stock. However, in a low- or middle-income country, it may be difficult to raise an optimal level of investment out of the available pool of domestic savings. Since savings is a function of income, lower levels of income tend to generate lower levels of savings. This is especially true in the case of Latin America. Relative to their level of income, Latin American countries do not produce the level of savings that one would predict. While the reasons for this deficiency are not perfectly understood, the general sense is that levels of saving seem to be positively correlated with economic growth. As a result, it is not surprising that the relatively low levels of economic growth in the region have produced relatively low savings rates.[6]

The data on this problem can be seen in Table 4.3. The percentage of GDP that is being saved plus FDI is shown for all the countries of Latin America. In 1990, FDI as a percentage of GDP was less than 1 percent.[7] For any country, this would be a relatively low figure. For most countries, the national savings rates were low by the standards of middle-income countries. The sum of FDI and savings for the region in 1990 was less than 20 percent. Under most circumstances, this percentage is unlikely to lead to a large increase in the production function or rapid economic growth. The data for 2017 is a perfect example of the positive changes that have occurred in the region over the past twenty years. FDI as a percentage of GDP has increased to 3 percent. Savings as a percentage of GDP has fallen. Putting FDI and savings together, the amount of money being invested in the region has not changed substantially as a percentage of GDP. The comparison to the other middle-income countries is painfully obvious. Lower rates of capital investment depress growth rates.

Table 4.3 FDI and savings in Latin America

	1990			2017		
	FDI (% of GDP)	Savings (% of GDP)	Total (% of GDP)	FDI (% of GDP)	Savings (% of GDP)	Total (% of GDP)
Argentina	1.3	16.0	17.3	1.8	13.5	15.3
Bolivia	0.6	9.5	10.1	1.9	15.8	17.7
Brazil	0.2	18.9	19.1	3.4	14.3	17.7
Chile	2.0	23.7	25.7	2.3	20.4	22.7
Colombia	1.0	20.9	21.9	4.5	16.4	20.9
Costa Rica	2.8	19.4	22.2	5.0	14.2	19.2
Ecuador	0.8	17.8	18.6	0.6	25.8	26.4
El Salvador	0.0	11.6	11.6	1.3	14.3	15.6
Guatemala	0.6	10.7	11.3	1.3	14.1	15.4
Honduras	0.9	13.7	14.6	5.5	20.9	26.4
Mexico	1.0	19.8	20.8	2.8	22.9	25.7
Nicaragua	0.1	15.7	15.8	6.5	23.9	30.4
Panama	2.1	16.4	18.5	7.7	29.1	36.8
Paraguay	1.3	19.8	21.1	1.3	24.0	25.3
Peru	0.2	13.1	13.3	3.2	20.2	23.4
Uruguay	0.4	14.1	14.5	−1.6	16.1	14.5
Venezuela, RB	0.9	29.6	30.5	0.2	8.9	9.1
Latin America	0.7	19.5	20.2	3.0	17.3	20.3
Low income	0.2	14.1	14.3	3.3	18.8	22.1
Middle income	0.6	27.6	28.2	1.9	31.3	33.2
High income	1.0	21.5	22.5	2.6	23.0	25.6
World	0.9	23.3	24.2	2.3	25.3	27.6

Source: World Bank (2019) and computation by authors.

Note: Data for Venezuela, 2014; Savings for low income, 2016.

Several factors may be contributing to low savings, low investment, and low FDI in the region. In this case, interest rates may offer a clue. In some countries interest rates are high, which would indicate an inadequate level of savings relative to investment opportunities. However, high interest rates are not universal. Interest rates are relatively low in some countries, which would indicate a lack of profitable investment opportunities. Interest rates are not the only factor. The problem is further exacerbated by somewhat inefficient capital markets. The purpose of capital markets is to efficiently transfer savings into productive investment. To the extent that capital markets are inefficient, the savings being generated in an economy are not being invested as productively as they could be. Obviously, this produces economic growth that is lower than would occur if the savings were being invested in a more productive fashion. The general sense is that capital markets in Latin America are not as well developed as they could be, given the income of the region, and that this is a negative factor in terms of economic growth.[8] TFP is the subject of the next section, but the efficiency, or lack thereof, of the capital markets of the region has a link to TFP. As one might imagine, if capital markets are not allocating capital efficiently, then TFP may be lower. Arizala et al. (2009) have found a strong link between the level of development of capital markets and TFP for Latin America and for other regions. As we develop why TFP growth is so low, it is well to keep in mind that capital market development also may be part of the problem.

TFP growth in Latin America

> The determinants of TFP are quite difficult to grasp.
> (Andrés Solimano and Raimundo Soto)

In the previous section, it was shown that the primary reason for slow economic growth in Latin America was the slow growth of TFP. Research by Duade and Fernández Arias (2010) has provided an answer to an interesting hypothetical question. If labor, capital, and human capital in Latin America were used as productively as they are in the US, what would happen to GDP per capita in the region? Put another way, what would happen to GDP per capita if TFP in Latin America and the US were equal? The startling answer is that it would double. This assumes that changes in TFP would have no effect on the amount of labor, capital, or human capital being used. This is reassuring in the sense that the conclusion concerning GDP per capita is likely to be a conservative estimate of reality. Of course, no one study is definitive, but the literature on growth accounting in Latin America reaches essentially the same conclusion that the most serious growth issue in the region is TFP.

Given the empirical evidence on the importance of TFP for increasing growth in Latin America, one might assume that increasing TFP would be easy to accomplish. A reasonable response would be to design and implement a set of policies designed to increase TFP. In order to do this, one must first understand the determinants of TFP. As the quote at the start of the chapter indicates, the determinants of TFP are uncertain. The overall problem is that TFP can be influenced by a multitude of general factors that are hard to quantify. Research on this subject is ongoing, but there are no precise answers to the problem. In the case of Latin America, the amount of research on TFP is still small. Given these caveats, the literature on the determinants of TFP overall and for Latin America in particular can be used to produce a list of general factors that could be negatively influencing TFP in the region. In the following sections, we will consider infrastructure, the formal sector, the informal sector, structural reforms, and *institutional quality*.

Infrastructure

It is an old truism that much of the problem with Latin America can be boiled down to two things: education and infrastructure. Education has been discussed in the previous chapter and will be discussed further later in the book. In this section, we consider the effects of infrastructure on economic growth. Poor infrastructure makes it difficult both for businesses to operate efficiently and for individuals to obtain maximum utility. In the former case, poor infrastructure reduces TFP and, by extension, economic growth and GDP per capita. In this section, we will consider the dimensions of the problem and the potential for infrastructure investment to increase growth.

The term "infrastructure" does not have an absolutely precise definition. However, some of its more important dimensions are easy to define. The World Economic Forum publishes an annual report that contains the results of an extensive survey of business opinion on a number of factors that affect businesses in countries around the world. Countries are rated on a scale of 1 to 7, where 1 is low and 7 is high. For each factor,

Table 4.4 Infrastructure quality in Latin America (2017–2018)

	Overall quality	*Electricity*	*Roads*	*Railroads*	*Ports*	*Air transport*
Argentina	3.3	3.0	3.3	2.1	3.7	4.2
Bolivia	3.6	2.6	3.3	2.5	2.0	3.2
Brazil	3.1	4.5	3.1	2.0	3.1	3.9
Chile	4.7	6.1	5.2	2.5	4.9	4.5
Colombia	3.1	4.8	3.0	1.5	3.8	4.1
Costa Rica	3.1	5.9	2.6	1.9	3.4	4.5
Ecuador	4.5	4.9	5.1	–	4.6	5.1
El Salvador	–	–	–	–	–	–
Guatemala	3.4	5.7	3.1	–	3.6	3.4
Honduras	3.6	3.5	3.8	–	4.4	4.0
Mexico	4.1	4.9	4.4	2.8	4.3	4.4
Nicaragua	3.5	4.4	4.3	–	3.1	3.8
Panama	4.7	5.2	4.4	4.5	6.2	6.0
Paraguay	2.6	2.6	2.4	–	3.3	2.6
Peru	3.1	5.1	3.0	2.0	3.7	4.1
Uruguay	3.6	6.0	3.3	1.2	4.9	5.3
Venezuela, RB	2.5	2.1	2.8	1.5	2.7	2.7
Latin America	3.5	4.5	3.6	2.2	3.9	4.1
World	4.2	4.5	4.0	3.3	4.1	4.4

Source: World Economic Forum (2019).

there is a global mean against which the performance of a country or a region can be compared. Since infrastructure has a large effect on the ability to do business, the report contains data on the business perception of infrastructure. In Table 4.4, data is presented on overall quality of infrastructure and the quality of electricity, roads, railroads, ports, and air transport. The data in the table is consistent with the widespread perception that the quality of infrastructure in Latin America could be improved. The overall quality is rated at 3.5, with a global mean of 4.2. In every category, the story is the same. The regional average is below the world average. Out of ninety data points, the region is at or above the world average in only twenty-five. The best category is electricity, and by far the worst is railroads. Note also that the world averages are the result of including a number of low-income countries. There are other, more limited, data on infrastructure for the region, but the story remains largely unchanged. The overall state of infrastructure is poor. One can safely say that the conventional wisdom about infrastructure and growth in the region is not unfounded.

As one might expect, the potential to increase growth by increasing investment in infrastructure in Latin America is high. Calderón and Servén (2011) find that infrastructure investment in the region is currently around 2–2.5 percent of GDP. In this study, the authors estimate that if infrastructure investment doubled, GDP growth could increase by as much as 2 percent. If investment at these levels could be maintained for twenty years, infrastructure in the region would catch up with the more successful Asian economies. While this may be true, the necessary money for investment is scarce. As outlined above, private savings in the region are relatively low. Further, public-sector budgets are invariably tight, with a bias toward current spending. A third possibility is FDI in infrastructure, but the available evidence from Barbero (2010) indicates that this type of infrastructure investment is not increasing. Thus, one is left with a frustrating possibility that higher growth as a result of infrastructure investment will be difficult to achieve.

Box 4.1 The human cost of bad roads

In the previous section, we outlined how poor infrastructure can lower TFP and
reduce economic growth. A significant component of the overall infrastructure is
the quantity and quality of roads. The lack of paved roads in the region is a well-
known problem. Just how much of a problem is shown in Table 4.5. Although
the data is not up to date for all countries, the overall picture in the table is not
wildly imprecise. Given available data, only 25 percent of the roads in the region
are paved. This average is biased upward to some extent by the high percentages
observed in Central America. For Mexico and South America, the percentage is
slightly over 20 percent. In some cases, vast distances (Brazil) and mountainous
terrain (Chile, Peru) are deterrents to building roads. Still, the regional average
is less than half the global average. As we showed in Chapter 1, GDP per capita
in the region is close to the world average. In a relative sense, the road network
in the region is poor. This negatively affects TFP, as the cost of movement to
businesses, governments, and people is being hindered by a poor road network.
However, some things go beyond pure economics. In terms of road fatalities per
100,000 inhabitants, Latin America is around the global average. Unfortunately,
the total number of deaths on the roads of the region is nearly 100,000. The
low percentage of paved roads is adversely impacting something arguably more
important than TFP.

Table 4.5 Road quality and road fatalities in Latin America

	Percentage of paved roads	*Road fatalities per 100,000 inhabitants (2015)*	*Total fatalities*
Argentina	32.2 (2011)	14.1	5,619
Bolivia	11.6 (2011)	23.3	2,476
Brazil	13.5 (2011)	22.6	46,935
Chile	23.8 (2011)	11.6	2,179
Colombia	14.4 (2000)	18.9	8,107
Costa Rica	26.0 (2011)	14.9	676
Ecuador	14,8 (2007)	20.7	3,164
El Salvador	53.1 (2011)	19	1,339
Guatemala	44.8 (2011)	19.9	2,939
Honduras	20.0 (2000)	16.5	1,408
Mexico	37.8 (2011)	11.8	15,062
Nicaragua	13.3 (2011)	14.9	931
Panama	41.8 (2011)	10.7	386
Paraguay	15.6 (2011)	23.4	1,408
Peru	13.3 (2011)	13.3	4,234
Uruguay	10.0 (2004)	17.4	567
Venezuela, RB	34.0 (2000)	41.7	–
Latin America	24.7	18.8	97,430
World	64.9 (2011)	18.3	1,240,000

Sources: World Bank (2019) and World Health Organization (2019).

The formal sector

Before beginning the discussion of the informal sector, it needs to be recognized that there are problems in the formal sector of the economy that reduce TFP. Low TFP growth can be somewhat explained by failures of firms to implement new technologies. However, it can also be explained by market failures and policy mistakes that lead to the misallocation of resources. Obviously, an economy with significant resource misallocation will grow more slowly. In the past decade, economists have developed empirical techniques to estimate the losses that economies suffer if resources are misallocated. To think about this, first consider the term *marginal revenue product (MRP)*. MRP is the market value of one additional unit of output. It is calculated by multiplying the marginal physical product by the marginal revenue. In an economy without distortions, all firms should hire labor and capital until the MRP is the same across all firms. In an economy with distortions, MRP differs across firms. Another way of putting this is that there is a substantial amount of heterogeneity among firms in the region. Because overall TFP is low in Latin America, it is a given that there are significant distortions even in the formal study.

Applying this basic idea to Latin America yields startling results. Busso et al. (2012) report that the level of heterogeneity in MRP at the firm level in the region is relatively large. This means that the gaps between the most productive and least productive firms is large. Latin American firms exhibit greater heterogeneity than in the US, and the degree of this is increasing over time. As one would expect, this is leading to losses of total output for the economies. The size of these losses is startling. They can be calculated as the losses that are occurring relative to the situation where the MRP was the same for all firms. Total productivity would rise by at least 41 percent up to 122 percent. For most countries, the gain would be in the 50 to 60 percent range. In Mexico, TFP would almost double. Further, the study considers only gains within industries, there would be further gains by reallocating resources across industries. The study investigates a number of potential causes of these results that we have or will consider in the book. They include: lack of access to capital, restrictive labor regulations, poor functioning of courts, detrimental regulations, institutional instability, and unfair or excessive taxation. It appears that the first two factors are the most important. The problems with the capital markets in the region were discussed earlier, and labor market regulation is covered below. The main point is that the focus of study of TFP problems in Latin America has been on the informal sector that is discussed next. However, one should keep in mind that there are substantial problems in the formal sector that are contributing to the problem as well.

The informal sector

The informal sector of the economy is extremely large in Latin America. This is not surprising. The International Labour Organization (ILO) estimates that nearly 50 percent of workers in low-income countries are in the informal sector. For middle-income countries that are not in Latin America, informal employment is 35 percent. What is different about Latin America is that the region is a collection of middle-income countries, and the percentage of workers in the informal sector is 55 percent.[9] Informality is common in low- and middle-income countries. The distinctiveness of Latin America is that informality is unusually high. Another way of measuring informality is to estimate the percentage of GDP that is in the informal sector. Using such an approach, the smallest estimate of the informal sector for the region is Mexico at 28 percent. The regional average is nearly 43 percent.[10] While these percentages are the result of only two studies, they are representative of almost any study done on the degree of informality in the region. The percentages can never be estimated exactly, but there is little argument over the simple fact that the percentage of economic activity in the informal sector is large on both an absolute and a relative basis.

Informality has been shown to be an important determinant of low TFP in Latin America. Powell (2013) has shown that informality is a significant factor in lowering TFP in the region. Another link between informality and TFP can be found by examining more micro-oriented data. The general sense is that firm size is correlated with informality, and that smaller firms in the informal sector are less productive than larger firms in the formal sector. Busso et al. (2012) have shown this to be the case. Using firm-level data from a large set of countries in the region, they found that productivity in firms with more than 250 workers is more than 150 percent higher than in firms with fewer than twenty workers. Using very detailed data that specifically identifies informal firms, they found that formal firms were 84 percent more productive than informal firms. What the empirical evidence strongly indicates is that a major source of low TFP in Latin America is the high degree of informality in the private sector. The policy conclusion is that reducing the amount of informality would have a positive impact on TFP and GDP per capita.

Structural reforms

Surprisingly, there is little research on the causes of informality in general, or for Latin America in particular. This is peculiar, as the seminal work on informality was done by the Peruvian economist Hernando de Soto (1989). In his work, he identifies the root cause of informality as firms attempting to escape the burden of taxation and regulation. Reducing informality and increasing TFP are intertwined. To reduce the former and increase the latter requires *structural reform*. These are measures that change the institutional and regulatory environment in which firms and individuals operate. In order for an economy to achieve its maximum growth potential, the business environment needs to be conducive to and structured in such a way as to obtain the benefits of regulation without imposing unnecessary costs on firms and workers. As we will see below, Latin America is badly in need of structural reforms.

Reducing complexity

The high informality observed in the region may be related to taxes and complicated business regulation. While it is impossible to quantify these issues precisely, Tables 4.6 and 4.7 present data designed to give an idea of the magnitude of these factors contributing to informality in the region. The essence of informality is that small- and medium-size enterprises (SMEs) in Latin America tend to be informal. An entrepreneur starts a small business and for some reason never registers it with the government. The data shown in Table 4.6 was collected by the World Bank for their annual *Doing Business* report. While this data is far from perfect, it does give a sense of the difficulties of starting a business in the region. The first column shows the number of procedures necessary to start a business. The regional average is over eight, with a range of five to twenty. Of course, complying with these procedures takes time. In this case, the regional average is twenty-eight days. Put another way, it takes nearly a month just to fill out the

Table 4.6 Starting a business in Latin America (2018)

	Procedures (number)	Time (days)	Cost (% of per capita income)	Rank
Argentina	11	11	5.3	119
Bolivia	14	43.5	46	156
Brazil	11	20.5	5	109
Chile	7	6	5.7	56
Colombia	8	11	14	65
Costa Rica	10	23	9.5	67
Ecuador	11	48.5	21.2	123
El Salvador	9	16.5	45.1	85
Guatemala	6	15	18.1	98
Honduras	11	13	40.7	121
Mexico	8	8.4	16.2	54
Nicaragua	7	14	63.6	132
Panama	5	6	5.4	79
Paraguay	7	35	40.3	113
Peru	8	24.5	9.9	68
Uruguay	5	6.5	22.6	95
Venezuela, RB	20	230	391.3	188
Latin America	8.2	27.8	36.8	–

Source: World Bank (2019).

Table 4.7 Business taxes in Latin America (2018)

	Total tax	Time to comply (hours)	Number of payments
Argentina	106	311.5	9
Bolivia	83.7	1,025	42
Brazil	65.1	1,958	9.6
Chile	34	296	7
Colombia	71.9	255.5	11
Costa Rica	58.3	151	10
Ecuador	32.3	664	8
El Salvador	35.6	180	7
Guatemala	35.2	248	8
Honduras	44.4	224	48
Mexico	53	240.5	6
Nicaragua	60.6	201	43
Panama	37.2	408	36
Paraguay	35	378	20
Peru	36.8	260	9
Uruguay	41.8	163	20
Venezuela, RB	64.6	792	70
Latin America	46.3	329	26.4
World	40.4	236.8	23.8

Source: World Bank (2019).

necessary paperwork to start a business. This time has a monetary cost. The regional average cost of starting a business is equal to nearly 37 percent of per-capita income. In addition to the absolute numbers, the World Bank calculates the rank of each country in the world for ease of starting a business. The average rank for a country in Latin America is nearly 102. Even given the limitations of the data, the almost inescapable conclusion is that government policy in the region puts a serious burden on SMEs that contributes to informality.

Taxation

For any business, paying taxes is part of doing business. However, governments need to be careful that the tax burden is reasonable in order to discourage informality. Table 4.7 shows data from the annual *Paying Taxes* report from the World Bank. The regional average tax rate is over 53 percent, which is 10 percent over the global average. Glancing at the data, it is not difficult to see why SMEs would choose to be informal. Part of the burden of paying taxes is the cost to a business of complying with the tax law. The last column shows the number of different tax payments firms have to make. The regional average is nearly twenty-seven, which is not substantially different from the world average. It is the second column, indicating time taken to comply with the law, where Latin America is an outlier in the wrong direction. The world average for compliance is 237 hours. In Latin America, the average is 100 hours over the world average. This is partially driven by the astonishing numbers for Bolivia and Brazil. However, only five countries in the region are below the world average. In most of the countries, high taxes are only a part of the problem. It is difficult to imagine that SMEs in most of the region would have either the time or the resources to comply with the tax laws.

Labor market reform

> The failure to put one key policy in place can be equivalent to multiplying by zero: no matter how much effort a country has put into the other components of reform, the end result will still be zero.
>
> (Sebastian Edwards)

Recent research has indicated that a major contributor to informality and low TFP can be the difficulty of complying with labor laws. Studies by Busso et al. (2013), the Organisation for Economic Co-operation and Development (OECD) (2018), and Ohanian et al. (2018) all lead to the conclusion that labor-market regulation is a serious impediment to growth. As indicated above, the labor markets of Latin America are large, diverse, and subject to substantial distortions. Summarizing this diversity is difficult at best. However, we will attempt to do this using an index developed by Gwartney et al. (2019) that ranks the countries of the world according to a variety of conditions in the labor market. The index is constructed from six different variables measuring conditions in the labor market. These are: (1) hiring regulations and the minimum wage; (2) hiring and firing regulations; (3) centralized collective bargaining; (4) hours regulations; (5) mandated cost of worker dismissal; and (6) conscription. The result allows one to rank the countries of the world based on the relative flexibility of their labor markets. The results are shown in Table 4.8. The data on labor-market flexibility in Latin America summarizes how different the region is in this regard. The average country in Latin America is ranked at 101. However,

Table 4.8 Labor-market flexibility in Latin America

	World rank
Argentina	133
Bolivia	138
Brazil	131
Chile	78
Colombia	85
Costa Rica	54
Ecuador	121
El Salvador	96
Guatemala	124
Honduras	97
Mexico	91
Nicaragua	75
Panama	88
Paraguay	71
Peru	90
Uruguay	112
Venezuela, R B	139
Latin America	101.4
Portugal	38
Spain	67
Canada	9
US	1

Source: Gwartney et al. (2019).

the range runs from 54 to 139. In this regard, Latin America has relatively inflexible labor markets with respect to the world, much less flexible than the two high-income countries in the hemisphere. However, there is a noticeable difference here when comparing Latin America with Portugal and Spain. In terms of labor-market flexibility, Latin America is very close to these countries. Despite being high-income countries, Portugal and Spain have noticeably inflexible labor markets. Whether or not this similarity is spurious is an intriguing question.

The data shown above helps to explain a number of stylized facts about labor markets in Latin America. First, in line with the purpose of this chapter, there is at least a partial explanation of the relatively poor economic growth performance of the region. It is always hard to explain how a region full of hard-working and relatively well-educated workers can produce relatively low economic growth. The mere possession of a quality labor force is not enough. If there are significant barriers to the effective utilization of these workers, the potential productivity of the labor force is diminished. The negative effects on economic growth are obvious. The research on the effects of labor laws in Latin America is not large, but the results are both predictable and consistent. The "classic" reference on this subject is an edited volume of eleven papers by Heckman and Pagés (2004). The first thing to realize is that like any other economic phenomenon is that there are costs and benefits. The benefits are decidedly in favor of workers who have a job in the formal sector. The main problem with Latin American labor law is that workers in the formal sector accrue rights to severance payments that increase with seniority. As a result, it becomes very expensive for employers to terminate workers. The predictable result is that employers are reluctant to hire new workers. In effect, the laws tend to turn labor into something akin to a fixed cost. The laws have been consistently found to have reduced the level of employment as firms are less willing to hire new workers. The flip side of that tendency is that it tends to increase the level of unemployment. The costs are not evenly distributed among the labor force. Workers with the lowest skill levels are bearing the majority of the costs. These are the marginal workers who may well be low-skilled due to a poor education, a not-uncommon problem in the region. Since skills accumulate with age, the burden falls especially hard on younger workers. This effect is not unique to Latin America and can be found virtually anywhere there are rigid labor laws. The link to inequality is not hard to make. Unemployment will be much higher among younger people than among the older segments of the population. Second, the size of the informal labor market becomes more understandable. If employment in the formal labor market involves a large number of relatively inflexible rules, there will be a tendency for employers to evade these regulations in the underground economy.[11] While labor-market regulations cannot form a complete explanation for the existence of the informal labor market, they doubtless contribute to its existence.

Box 4.2 Unions

A discussion of labor-market distortions for any country is incomplete without a discussion of the role of labor unions. Latin America is no different in this regard. The conventional wisdom is that labor unions (*sindicatos*) constitute a significant labor-market distortion in Latin America. As usual, the conventional wisdom isn't wrong, but it needs to be qualified. The whole purpose of a labor union is to obtain wages and benefits for workers that are in excess of what would be provided in a free labor market. As we will see in a later chapter, many of the employers were operating in a domestic market either shielded from foreign competition or subsidized. As a result, there were abnormal profits available, and the development of unions was an understandable response to that. Unions in many countries, such as Argentina and Mexico, were informally allied with the government. In these cases, unions became a potent political force, which perhaps accounts for the impression that their influence in the economy matches their political influence. The rise of military dictatorships in the 1970s and 1980s dealt a heavy blow to unions, as they were outlawed or harassed by governments. Since that period, unions have been forced to refocus their relationships. Instead of being closely allied to the state, they are now more focused on their relationships with firms or industries.

Their actual economic influence is less than usually imagined. In the first place, labor unions include a much smaller percentage of the labor force in the area than was once the case. In every country of Latin America, the percentage of the work force that is unionized has declined over the past several decades. There are currently only two countries where slightly over 30 percent of the labor force is unionized (Brazil and Mexico), and only two other countries over 20 percent (Argentina and Nicaragua). For Latin America as a whole, only 14 percent of the labor force is unionized. While this is not trivial, the picture of the region as one where labor unions dominate the labor markets is not quite correct. The empirical literature on the effects of unions is small, but the results are not surprising. The available evidence indicates that unions cause a small change in the productivity of labor.[12] Coupling that with the percentages above, it is difficult to conclude that a "union-free" Latin America would be substantially more productive.

As indicated at the beginning of the section, informality is a serious problem in Latin America. The research on economic growth shows that the primary problem is low TFP. In turn, low TFP reduces both GDP growth and GDP per capita. As a result, the reduction of informality is an important policy goal. The causes of informality are complex, but part of the problem can be traced to the difficulty of starting a business in the region. This is compounded by tax rates that are higher than the global average and a cost of complying with the tax regulations that is considerably higher than the global average. In a sense, this is encouraging. The social cost of reducing the difficulties involved in starting a business is low. The same is true of reducing the difficulties associated with paying taxes. In both cases, the social benefit of higher economic growth would seem to be well worth this cost. Reducing labor-market inflexibility is a more controversial topic. The current labor laws are there to protect the existing workforce in the formal sector from some of the changes normally associated with the operations of a free market. However, this contributes to the existence of a completely free market in the informal sector, where workers have little or no protection. In addition, overly inflexible labor markets may lower TFP and economic growth and reduce the incomes of workers overall. Finding a balance between these competing social objectives is not going to be an easy task in any country. However, a first step is the recognition that rigid labor laws are not free, and their cost to society and particularly workers in the informal sector should be considered.

Institutional quality

> The best explanation for Latin America's economic trajectory is its institutions.
>
> (James A. Robinson)

In the previous chapter, we considered the usual determinants of economic growth and how they pertained to Latin America. The basic growth theory considering capital, labor, and human capital is a good point to begin a discussion of growth. In this chapter we went on to show that the largest problem with growth in Latin America has been the slow growth of TFP. In the previous section, the effects of poor infrastructure and economic policy on TFP were considered. Improvements in infrastructure and economic policy would no doubt increase TFP in the region to some extent. The reader may have noted previously that the most successful country in the region, Chile, virtually always had high scores with respect to policy. It may also have been noted that this is not invariably the case. Other countries have made significant changes in economic policy with much less success to show for their effort. What this means is that there are other factors affecting TFP, which are harder to address in purely economic terms. In this section, we will discuss these other factors, which are generally referred to as institutional quality.

In a sense, economists have known for a long time that the quality of institutions can affect economic growth. We alluded to this earlier in the previous chapter by pointing out that effective property rights and the rule of law were essential preconditions to economic growth. In this section, we are refining that basic idea. Institutional quality is far more complicated than just these two factors in general. Also, they are not binary variables. A country does not either have or not have the rule of law or property rights. As we saw earlier, there are various degrees to which these factors apply. What follows is a very condensed version of the state of knowledge on institutions and growth and how it may apply to Latin America. The modern study of institutions and growth can be traced back to the work of Ronald Coase, Douglass North, and others. Although this area of study has many variants, it is usually referred to as the "New Institutional Economics."[13] The basic idea of this literature is that economic growth is critically dependent on the quality of institutions in a country. There are startling differences in the level of economic development among countries or even regions that cannot be explained purely on the basis of growth in the labor force, the capital stock, or human capital. Much of the early work in this area was done by economic historians, who focused on identifying institutional factors that tended to encourage economic growth, or the absence of which seemed to retard this process. The problem with studying the role of institutional quality has always been the difficulty of precisely defining what it means. It is understood that institutional quality affects economic growth through TFP. Unfortunately, the link between the two is very difficult to quantify due to the difficulty of precisely defining what institutional quality is.[14] Some of the factors that are important in this context were discussed in the previous chapter: the rule of law, respect for property rights, an independent judiciary, and so on. At this point, we will not attempt to come to any definitive answer to that question. Rather, we will present data for a number of different indexes of institutional quality and look for a common story. That story can be seen from the numbers presented in Table 4.9.

The table contains four different measures of institutional quality that are widely available for most of the countries in the world. Each cell in the table represents a country's global rank on this measure. The first column contains the widely cited measure of corruption in a country, produced by Transparency International. This is

Table 4.9 Measures of institutional quality in Latin America

	Corruption (world rank)	*Government effectiveness (world rank)*	*Doing business (world rank)*	*Competitiveness (world rank)*
Argentina	85	74	119	81
Bolivia	132	120	156	105
Brazil	105		109	72
Chile	27	42	56	33
Colombia	99	91	65	60
Costa Rica	48	68	67	55
Ecuador	114	114	123	86
El Salvador	105	119	85	98
Guatemala	144	140	98	96
Honduras	132	125	121	101
Mexico	138	89	54	46
Nicaragua	152	141	132	104
Panama	93	87	79	64
Paraguay	132	154	113	95
Peru	105	97	68	63
Uruguay	23	59	95	53
Venezuela, RB	168	179	188	127
Latin America	106.0	106.2	101.6	78.8
Portugal	30	26	34	34
Spain	41	34	30	26
Canada	9	7	22	12
US	22	16	8	1

Sources: Transparency International (2019); World Bank (2019); World Economic Forum (2019).

the first measure presented for a reason. Ask virtually anyone in a developed country what the most important problem is in Latin America, and the answer frequently is corruption. Of course, corruption is a problem in the region. However, a glance at the table indicates that this is hardly peculiar to Latin America. Note that the regional average shows Latin America to be rather average by global standards. Further, the region is nothing like uniform with respect to corruption. For some reason, the common perception of corruption in Latin America is not totally consistent with the data. The next column presents the rankings for Latin America reported by the World Bank on the ease of doing business in a country. It is a composite of factors involved in running a business, such as employing workers, paying taxes, enforcing contracts, and so on.

It is here that one can visualize the difficulties of doing business in the region. The regional average is worse than the global average, and there are many countries where doing business is obviously very difficult. This difficulty in doing business is compounded by relatively ineffective governments. Again, the World Bank publishes data on government effectiveness around the world. On this measure, the governments of Latin America are relatively ineffective. Comparing these numbers with those for corruption, the latter is hardly the region's most serious problem. While none of these indexes is definitive, the overall picture is of a region with moderate problems with corruption, a poor business environment, and relatively ineffective governments. Under these circumstances, the econometric evidence presented in the previous section should not be surprising. Increasing TFP in this kind of environment would not be easy.

Despite the bleak data on institutional quality, there must be something about the region beyond these numbers. The final column presents data from executive surveys gathered by the World Economic Forum. This data is a ranking gathered from a composite of indicators on social and economic conditions in a country that make it more or less competitive in the world economy. Rather than being worse than the global average, the index of competitiveness is far better than the other reported measures. These numbers represent something—obviously not honest government officials, a good business environment, or effective government. This data is derived from surveys of business executives. Executives are usually thinking not just about the present but also about the future. Perhaps the data is simply expressing expectations. If so, the economic future of Latin America looks brighter.

Box 4.3 Crime

It is hardly news that crime is the worst social problem in Latin America in the twenty-first century. Latin America is home to 8 percent of the world's population, and a third of the homicides occur in the region. Since 2000, more than 2.5 *million*. The homicide rate is 21.5 per 100,000. This is over three times the global average. On current trends, this rate could reach nearly 40 by 2030. The violence is concentrated in four countries: Brazil, Colombia, Mexico, and Venezuela. The violence is not limited to the large countries. The highest homicide rate in the region is in El Salvador at 60 per 100,000. More than half of these homicides are related to the activities of gangs, organized crime, or robberies. The majority of the focus tends to be on homicides for technical reasons. International crime statistics frequently contain definitional problems. Unlike other crimes, what constitutes a homicide is clear. For Latin America, other data paints a similar picture. Robbery rates are around 400 per 100,000 in the region, which is far higher than global averages. Another measure of the problem is the percentage of the population that reports being the victims of crime. The Latin American average is 36 percent with the rates approaching 50 percent in Mexico and Venezuela. While the causes of this level of crime are beyond the scope of the book, one thing is clear. The level of crime in the region reflects a widespread inability of governments to perform one of its most basic functions: the protection of people's lives and property.

This failure of government policy has serious economic consequences. Jaitman et al. (2017) has estimated that the cost of crime for the region now amounts to 3.5 percent of GDP. The figure for Central America is over 4 percent. It is not hard to see why this is the case. The homicide rate is so high that the size of the labor force is being affected in many countries. Capital investment also is affected. High levels of crime deter both domestic and foreign investment. Blanco et al. (2017) and others have shown the effects of crime on FDI in the region. This is a part of the low investment problem discussed above. Aside from the effects on labor and capital accumulation, there surely are effects on TFP. If the government cannot adequately control crime, then the private sector will need to spend resources to do so. With a lower crime rate, these resources could be used to produce other goods and services. Crime also affects the spatial location of economic activity. High crime is not spread evenly across the region. Higher crime rates in some countries or regions within countries may be causing substantial distortions in the levels of economic activity. Crime may well be driving some activities into places that are not optimal for that activity. The negative TFP growth observed in the region is no doubt being influenced by crime. As indicated above, if nothing is done, crime over the next decade could get worse. If so, then one could safely assume that the current economic losses could rise as well.

Key terms and concepts

econometrics: the use of statistical techniques to analyze economic data.

growth accounting: an examination of the factors that explain economic growth in a country or region.

institutional quality: a broad concept that captures law, individual rights and high quality government services.

marginal revenue product (MRP): the market value of one additional unit of output. It is calculated by multiplying the marginal physical product by the marginal revenue.

structural reform: measures that change the institutional and regulatory environment in which firms and individuals operate.

Questions for review and discussion

1 Using growth accounting, explain why Latin America tends to have relatively slow economic growth.
2 Why is TFP critical for economic growth in Latin America?
3 Is infrastructure an economic growth problem in Latin America? Why is this so?
4 If MRP is different across firms in a country, why is this a problem for economic growth?
5 Describe what would happen if MRP was equal across firms in Latin America.
6 How can one describe informality in terms of employment and percentage of GDP? Why is Latin America abnormal in this regard?
7 What does structural reform mean in a Latin American context?
8 What government policies tend to encourage informality?
9 Describe the difficulties involved in starting a business in Latin America?
10 Suppose that you wanted to open a bodega (a corner store) in Latin America. What would make this difficult?
11 Compare complying with the tax laws in Brazil and Chile.
12 Why is labor market flexibility such a problem in Latin America? Are unions the primary problem?
13 What is the link between institutional quality and economic growth? How has this affected economic growth in Latin America?
14 Corruption is the most pressing economic problem in Latin America. Explain why this statement is true or untrue.
15 How does high levels of crime affect growth in Latin America?

Notes

1 As explained in the previous chapter, R&D should be a negligible factor in Latin American economic growth and is generally excluded from consideration.
2 Economic data for Latin America prior to World War II is still being developed. The causes of economic growth in the region prior to that time is a field of study still in its infancy.
3 Similar results may be found in Cole et al. (2005), Fernández-Arias et al. (2005), or Solimano and Soto (2006).
4 These results are in line with research by Bils and Klenow (2000) on human capital accumulation and growth. Their results include data on a number of countries in Latin America.
5 Restrictions on FDI will be covered in Chapter 9.
6 For a more complete discussion of this point, see Reinhart and Talvi (1998).
7 The data ignores outflows of FDI from the region. With the exception of Chile, these outflows are insignificant.
8 This problem is extensively analyzed in de la Torre et al. (2006) and Blanco (2009).
9 For more details, see ILO (2012).
10 For more details, see Vuletin (2008).
11 For a case study of the Colombian labor market, see Mondragón-Vélez et al. (2010).
12 For more details, see Rios-Avila (2014).
13 An early example of this work is North and Thomas (1973).
14 For an example of the difficulties in selecting institutional quality variables, see Sawyer (2011).

References

Arizala, Francisco, Eduardo A. Cavallo, and Arturo J. Galindo (2009) "Financial Development and TFP Growth: Cross-Country and Industry-Level Evidence," *IDB Working Paper no. 682*, Washington, DC: Inter-American Development Bank.

Barbero, José (2010) *Infrastructure in the Comprehensive Development of Latin America*, Caracas: Development Bank of Latin America.

Blanco, Luisa (2009) "The Finance-Growth Link in Latin America," *Southern Economic Journal*, 76 (July): 224–248.

Blanco, Luisa R., Isabel Ruiz, W. Charles Sawyer, and Rossitza Wooster (2017) "Crime, Institutions and Sector Specific FDI in Latin America," SSRN No. 2607682.

Busso, Matías, Lucia Madrigal, and Carmen Pagés (2012) "Productivity and Resource Misallocation in Latin America," *IDB Working Paper no. 306*, Washington, DC: Inter-American Development Bank.

Calderón, César and Luis Servén (2011) "Infrastructure in Latin America," in José A. Ocampo and Jaime Ros (eds.), *The Oxford Handbook of Latin American Economics*, Oxford: Oxford University Press, pp. 659–687.

Calvallo, Eduardo and Andrew Powell (2018) *A Mandate to Grow: Latin American and Caribbean Macroeconomic Report*, Washington, DC: Inter-American Development Bank.

Cole, Harold L., Lee E. Ohanian, Alvaro Riascos, James A. Schmitz, Jr. (2005) "Latin America in the Rearview Mirror." *Journal of Monetary Economics*, 52 (January): 69–107.

de Gregorio, José and Jong-Wha Lee (2017) "Growth and Adjustment in East Asia and Latin America," in W. Charles Sawyer (ed.), *Latin American Economics*, vol. I, London and New York: Routledge, pp. 89–134.

de la Torre, Augusto, Juan Carlos Gozzi, and Sergio L. Schmukler (2006) "Capital Market Adjustment: Whither Latin America?" *World Bank Policy Research Working Paper 4156*, Washington, DC: World Bank.

de Soto, Hernando (1989) *The Other Path*, New York: Basic Books.

Duade, Christian and Eduardo Fernández-Arias (2010) "On the Role of Productivity and Factor Accumulation in Economic Development in Latin America and the Caribbean," *IDB Working Paper Series #IBB-WP-155*, Washington, DC: Inter-American Development Bank.

Fernández-Arias, Eduardo, Rodolfo Manuelli, and Juan S. Blyde (2005) "Why Latin America Is Falling Behind," in Eduardo Fernández-Arias, Rodolfo Manuelli, and Juan Blyde (eds.), *Sources of Growth in Latin America: What Is Missing?* Washington, DC: Inter-American Development Bank, pp. 3–54.

Gwartney, James, Robert Lawson, and Joshua Hall (2019) *Economic Freedom of the World: 2018 Annual Report*, Vancouver: Fraser Institute.

Heckman, James and Carmen Pagés (2004) *Law and Employment: Lessons from Latin America and the Caribbean*, Chicago, Ill.: University of Chicago Press.

International Labour Organization (2012) *Key Indicators of the Labour Market*, Geneva: International Labour Organization.

Jaitman, Laura, Dino Caprirolo, Rogelio Granguillhome Ochoa, Philip Keefer, Ted Leggett, Jamanes A. Lewis , José A. Mejía-Guerra, Marcela Mello Heather Sutton, and Iván Torre (2017) *The Costs of Crime and Violence: New Evidence and Insights in Latin America and the Caribbean*, Washington, DC: Inter-American Development Bank.

Mondragón-Vélez, Camilo, Ximena Peùa, and Daniel Wills (2010) "Labor Market Rigidities and Informality in Colombia," *Economia*, 11 (fall): 65–95.

North, Douglass C. and Robert P. Thomas (1973) *The Rise of the Western World: A New Economic History*, Cambridge: Cambridge University Press.

Ohanian, Lee E., Paulina Restrepo-Echavarria, and Mark L. J. Wright (2018) "Bad Investments and Missed Opportunities? Postwar Capital Flows to Asia and Latin America," *American Economic Review*, 108 (December): 3541–3582.

Organisation for Economic Co-operation and Development (2018) *The Informal Economy in Latin America and the Caribbean: Implications for Competition Policy*, Paris: Organisation for Economic Co-operation and Development.

Powell, Andrew (2013) *Rethinking Reforms: How Latin America and the Caribbean Can Escape Suppressed World Economic Growth*, Washington, DC: Inter-American Development Bank.

Reinhart, Carmen M. and Ernesto Talvi (1998) "Capital Flows and Saving in Latin America and Asia: A Reinterpretation," *Journal of Development Economics*, 57 (October): 45–66.

Rios-Avila, Fernando (2014) "Unions and Economic Performance in Developing Countries: Case Studies from Latin America," *Levy Economics Institute Working Paper No. 787*, Annadale-on-Hudson, NY: Levy Economics Institute.

Sawyer, W. Charles (2011) "Institutional Quality and Economic Growth in Latin America," *Global Economy Journal*, 10 (January): 1–13.

Solimano, Andres and Raimundo Soto (2006) "Economic Growth in Latin America in the Late Twentieth Century: Evidence and Interpretation," in Andres Solimano (ed.), *Vanishing Growth in Latin America: The Late Twentieth Century Experience*, Northampton, Mass.: Edward Elgar, pp. 11–45.

Transparency International (2018) *Corruption Perceptions Index, 2018*, Berlin: Transparency International.

Vuletin, Guillermo (2008) "Measuring the Informal Economy in Latin America and the Caribbean," *IMF Working Paper WP/08/102*, Washington, DC: International Monetary Fund.

World Bank (2015) *World Development Indicators*, Washington, DC: World Bank.

World Bank (2018) *Worldwide Governance Indicators, 2018*, Washington, DC: World Bank.

World Bank (2019a) *Paying Taxes 2019*, Washington, DC: World Bank.

World Bank (2019b) *Doing Business, 2019*, Washington, DC: World Bank.

World Economic Forum (2018) *Global Competitiveness Report, 2014–2015*, Davos: World Economic Forum.

World Health Organization (2018) *Global Health Observatory Data*, Geneva: World Health Organization.

Recommended reading

Bils, Mark and Peter J. Klenow (2000) "Does Schooling Cause Growth?" *American Economic Review*, 90 (December): 1160–1183.

Chong, Alberto and Luisa Zanforlin (2004) "Inward-looking Policies, Institutions, Autocrats, and Economic Growth in Latin America: An Empirical Exploration," *Public Choice*, 121 (December): 335–361.

Ferraz, João C., Michael Mortimore, and Márcia Tavares (2011) "Foreign Direct Investment in Latin America," in José A. Ocampo and Jaime Ros (eds.), *The Oxford Handbook of Latin American Economics*, Oxford: Oxford University Press, pp. 438–460.

Ferreira, Pedro C., Samuel De Abreu Pessôa, and Fernando A. Veloso (2013) "On the Evolution of Total Factor Productivity in Latin America," *Economic Inquiry*, 51 (January): 16–30.

Hausman, Ricardo (2011) "Structural Transformation and Economic Growth in Latin America," in José A. Ocampo and Jaime Ros (eds.), *The Oxford Handbook of Latin American Economics*, Oxford: Oxford University Press, pp. 519–545.

Lemos, Sara (2007) "The Effects of the Minimum Wage in the Private and Public Sectors in Brazil," *Journal of Development Studies*, 43 (December): 700–720.

Loayza, Norman, Ana Maria Oviedo, and Luis Servén (2010) "Regulation and Macroeconomic Performance," in Norman Loayza and Luis Servén (eds.), *Business Regulation and Economic Performance*, Washington, DC: World Bank, pp. 65–117.

Loayza, Norman, Pablo Fajnzylber, and Calderón, César (2005) *Economic Growth in Latin America and the Caribbean: Stylized Facts, Explanations, and Forecasts*, Washington, DC: World Bank.

Lora, Eduardo (2012) "Structural Reforms in Latin America: What Has Been Reformed and How to Measure It," *IDB Working Paper Series No. IDB-WP-346*, Washington, DC: Inter-American Development Bank.

Meghir, Costas, Renata Narita, and Jean-Marc Robin (2015) "Wages and Informality in Developing Countries," *American Economic Review*, 105 (April): 1509–1546.

Pagés, Carmen (2010) *The Age of Productivity: Transforming Economies from the Bottom Up*, New York: Palgrave Macmillan.

Palma, José G. (2011) "Why Has Productivity Growth Stagnated in Most Latin American Countries since the Neo-Liberal Reforms?" in José A. Ocampo and Jaime Ros (eds.), *The Oxford Handbook of Latin American Economics*, Oxford: Oxford University Press, pp. 568–607.

Sosa, Sebastian, Evridiki Tsounta, and Hye Sun Kim (2013) "Is the Growth Momentum in Latin America Sustainable?" *IMF Working Paper #WP/13/109*, Washington, DC: International Monetary Fund.

Tokman, Victor E. (2011) "Employment: The Dominance of the Informal Economy," in José A. Ocampo and Jaime Ros (eds.), *The Oxford Handbook of Latin American Economics*, Oxford: Oxford University Press, pp. 767–789.

5 Growth and the environment in Latin America

Introduction

In the previous chapter, we focused on the sources of economic growth in Latin America. Until the 1980s, economists were primarily interested in the process of raising GDP per capita. This is understandable, given the pressing economic needs of the majority of humanity residing in low- or middle-income countries. The study of economic growth in Latin America was no different in this regard. However, the rest of the world caught up with economics. The environmental movement, born in the 1960s, filtered into the discussions of economic growth in the 1970s and 1980s. The situation now is such that discussing economic growth without considering the environmental consequences would seem odd. Rapid economic growth in a low- or middle-income country can create extremely high levels of pollution and degradation of the environment. As countries move from low to middle income, levels of pollution can rise dramatically as the country industrializes and energy consumption by both producers and consumers rises rapidly. Globally, the focus of growth and the environment has been China. With less fanfare, Latin America is experiencing many of the same difficulties. In many parts of Latin America, drinking a glass of water or breathing can be hazardous to your health. When traveling in the region, this is just a nuisance. Unfortunately, for hundreds of millions of people living in Latin America, environmental problems are a part of daily existence that is continually shortening lives and diminishing the quality of life. This is occurring even though economic growth in the region has been relatively slow. If the rate of economic growth picks up at some point, the problems could quickly become more acute.

In this chapter, we will attempt to provide an overall picture of growth and environmental problems in Latin America. In order to do this, the beginning of the chapter will explain why pollution is a difficult economic problem to deal with and the interactions between economic growth and environmental quality. Next, we will consider the policy options available to governments in their attempts to deal with the difficult trade-offs between economic growth and environmental quality. Since every region of the world is different, we will then focus on those environmental problems that are most serious in a Latin American context. Since international trade and economic growth are related, we will consider how the two interact to affect the environment. The final section of the chapter deals with how global climate change has the potential to influence the economies of Latin America in the twenty-first century.

Pollution as a negative externality

> Without contradiction, this land is the best of all for the life of man: the air is exceptionally healthful, and the soil extremely fertile, all that is before you is delightful and pleasing to the human eye to a great degree.
>
> (Pero de Magalhaes de Gandavo)

For the average person, pollution is a bad thing and should be got rid of, like the household trash. As we will see, pollution occurs for reasons that are plain to an economist. However, it cannot be completely eliminated. It is more a matter of a society generating the amount of pollution that is consistent with other societal goals. In order to understand the economic problem of pollution, we will first look at the supply and demand for some everyday good. Then we'll examine another good, the production of which creates pollution, and see how they differ. At that point, the problem of pollution and what to do about it will become clearer.

We will start by looking at the demand and supply of a simple product: a book. The price of a book is determined by the supply and demand for books. This can be shown with a simple supply and demand graph, such as Figure 5.1. In the figure, the demand for books is shown, as usual, as sloping downward and to the right. As the price of books changes, the *quantity demanded* of books changes. The relationship is inverse, so if the price of books increases, the amount of books demanded decreases, and vice versa. The usual supply curve is also shown in the figure. It slopes upward and to the right, indicating that as the price of books increases, the *quantity supplied* of books likewise increases. As you will probably have learned in a previous class, the intersection of the demand and supply curves shows the equilibrium in this market. The market price is shown in Figure 5.1 as P_e, and the equilibrium quantity in the market is Q_e. These are an equilibrium price and quantity for the entire economy. All else being equal, this will maximize social welfare. The economy is producing the correct number of books, and the books are being sold at the correct price. What do we mean by the term "correct"? The price and quantity in this case are correct because all of the benefits and costs have been completely accounted for. When you buy a book, all of the benefits of using the book accrue to you. You paid the price, and you receive

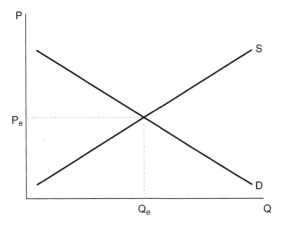

Figure 5.1 Equilibrium price and output with no externalities.

all the benefits. The same is true for the producer. The producer incurred all of the costs of producing the book and is paid the market price for incurring those costs. In other words, all of the benefits and costs have been *internalized* by the market. The buyer receives the benefits, and the producer incurs the costs. No third party has been affected by the production or consumption of the book. Free markets are very efficient at finding the correct equilibrium if all benefits and costs have been internalized or accounted for. If this is not the case, then the equilibrium price and quantity may not be correct. We now consider such a possibility.

In this case, suppose we are analyzing the market for paper. We use this example because of a technical characteristic of the production of paper. A paper mill without pollution-control equipment is capable of emitting an astonishing amount of pollution. The production of paper is very energy-intensive. One way or another, the production of energy causes some pollution. Therefore, industries that are energy-intensive may be more pollution-intensive than they seem at first glance. This is a particular problem in Latin America, as the production of energy may well be more pollution-intensive than energy production in a high-income country. Second, a paper mill produces air pollution. Third, the production of paper produces a substantial amount of by-product waste. The point of using paper as an example is that a simple and ubiquitous product produces a substantial amount of pollution that may not be immediately obvious. What is even less obvious is that not all of the benefits and costs have been internalized in the market. In other words, there are costs to society of the pollution caused by producing paper that are not being paid by the producer. In turn, this causes the supply of paper to be incorrect. If the amount of paper being produced is wrong, then both the quantity demanded of paper and the price are also incorrect. If not all of the benefits and costs of producing paper are internalized in a market, then the resulting equilibrium is not socially optimal. A cost to society that has not been internalized in the market is referred to as a negative externality. This situation is shown in Figure 5.2. The demand curve looks much the same as before. All of the benefits of the consumption of paper have been internalized by the buyers of paper. The problem is not with the demand side of the market. The difficulty is on the supply side. The production of paper is resulting in costs to society that are not included in the costs of production for the paper-producing firm.

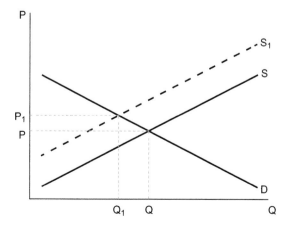

Figure 5.2 Equilibrium price and output in the presence of negative externalities.

There are negative externalities that produce costs being paid by society and not the firm. This means that the cost of production is too low. If the firm had to pay for all of the costs, the supply curve would not be at S. It would be further to the left, at S_1. Note that if the firm paid all of the costs, there would be a decrease in supply. For any given quantity of production (Q), the production costs would be higher along S_1 than along S. This makes sense, because S includes all of the relevant costs of producing paper. Now, combine this new supply curve with the demand curve for paper. If there are negative externalities and these are not being included in the costs of production, then the market price of paper is too low and the production of paper is too high. In this case, the market is not producing the correct amount of paper, and the price is wrong, because the market cannot automatically internalize these negative externalities. Including all costs, the quantity produced should be at Q_1, and the price should be at P_1. To solve the problem, it is necessary to calculate the value of the negative externalities associated with paper production and include them in the costs of production for the producer, and then the correct amount of paper will be produced at the right price.

Everything that has been said about pollution and solving the pollution problem is theoretically correct. The problem of pollution in Latin America should be coming into focus. If an area is heavily polluted, then where are the supply curves for pollution-intensive products? They are closer to S than to S_1. The difference between the two supply curves is some form of pollution control by the government. Market forces alone won't solve the problem. If there are negative externalities involved in the production of a product, some regulation may be needed, or the product will be overproduced, and pollution levels will be too high.[1] This is a classic example of a *market failure*. Actually, the problem is even worse. If paper is too cheap, then, to take our first example, books will be too cheap. A misallocation of resources in one market can lead to misallocations in others. Distortions caused by not regulating important negative externalities in one market can have important secondary effects. Since regulating the negative externalities associated with pollution is important, the next section of the chapter takes up that issue.

Box 5.1 Natural disasters in Latin America

Desolating earthquakes and hurricanes overtake us unawares, and we live in perpetual ambush of inevitable geographic cataclysms.

(Antonio S. Pedreira)

No discussion of the environment in Latin America would be complete without mentioning natural disasters. Unfortunately, hardly a year goes by without some type of natural disaster occurring in some country of the region. Natural disasters are grouped into four broad categories: (1) floods and related disasters—floods, landslides, and mudflows; (2) windstorms—hurricanes, winter storms, tornadoes, and tropical storms; (3) geological disasters—earthquakes, volcanic eruptions, and tidal waves; and (4) droughts and related disasters—droughts, extreme temperatures, and wildfires. Using these definitions, Latin America has suffered 898 natural disasters between 1974 and 2003. Because of the disparity in location and size of the countries of the region, a comparative measure of the extent to which natural disasters are a problem is the number of people killed or affected by natural disasters per 100,000 of population. This data is shown in Table 5.1.

Table 5.1 Natural disasters in Latin America (number of people killed or affected per 100,000 of population)

Argentina	1,456
Bolivia	2,767
Brazil	1,196
Chile	778
Colombia	337
Costa Rica	1,390
Ecuador	638
El Salvador	1,773
Guatemala	2,774
Honduras	2,916
Mexico	173
Nicaragua	2,196
Panama	255
Paraguay	811
Peru	1,313
Uruguay	55
Venezuela	117
Latin America	1,232
World	3,135

Source: Guha-Sapir et al. (2004).

Table 5.2 Major natural disasters in Latin America, 1974–2003

Country	Year	Type of disaster	% of previous year GDP
Guatemala	1976	Earthquake	27
Bolivia	1982	Flood	14
El Salvador	1982	Flood	8
Bolivia	1983	Droughts	31
Chile	1985	Earthquake	8
El Salvador	1986	Earthquake	27
Costa Rica	1991	Earthquake	9
Nicaragua	1991	Wildfires	8
Bolivia	1992	Landslide	7
Ecuador	1993	Landslide	4
Nicaragua	1994	Drought	9
Nicaragua	1991	Hurricane	51
Honduras	1998	Hurricane	42
El Salvador	2001	Earthquakes	21

Source: Guha-Sapir et al. (2004).

Note that by global standards, Latin America as a whole looks rather tranquil. However, there is a significant variation among countries of the region, from a low of 55 to a high of 2,767. Further, note an unfortunate pattern in the data. The countries most likely to be affected by a natural disaster are the poorer countries of Central America and Bolivia, and the effects can sometimes be devastating in purely economic terms. Table 5.2 lists some of the major natural disasters that have occurred in these countries between 1974 and 2003 and the damage in terms of the previous year's GDP. In many countries of Latin America, natural disasters are a significant barrier to economic development.

Pollution and environmental policy

There are no solutions, only trade-offs.

(Thomas Sowell)

In the previous section, we considered the concept of pollution as a negative externality. We went on to show that if the production of a product was associated with a nontrivial amount of pollution, then the supply of the product would be too high. In turn, this would lead to prices for the product that are too low and production of the product that is too high. Conceptually, the solution to this problem was to shift the supply curve far enough to the left to generate a price and output solution that would be more appropriate in the presence of pollution. While this looks easy on a graph, in practice, finding the right price and output combination is hard to accomplish. This section considers the difficulties associated with reducing pollution in a country to a level that more closely approximates a social optimum. From the outset, one needs to understand that these issues rarely have a "perfect" solution. The relatively pristine environment of Latin America that existed in 1491 is not going to return. However, the current state of the environment in the region is clearly not a desirable state. The first part of this section outlines a mental framework for thinking about environmental issues. In the next two sections, two widely used mechanisms for addressing pollution control are covered. Because environmental issues require government intervention, institutions and government effectiveness are critical factors in addressing environmental issues.

Cost–benefit analysis

Like most things in economics, decisions need to be based on the cost of something relative to the benefits. Pollution is no different in this regard. Pollution has obvious costs, such as poor air quality, polluted water, or a scarred landscape. However, one must keep in mind that pollution also has benefits. People engage in activities that generate these costs because they have benefits. Even in the simplest society, a person might tolerate breathing polluted air to obtain the benefit of consuming cooked rather than raw meat. In a modern economy, these problems multiply with the level of economic activity. Life without cars and trucks is hard to imagine, yet the refining of oil can be a very pollution-intensive activity. Modern economies face the task of balancing the costs and benefits of pollution. As shown in the previous section, this is difficult, because pollution is not internalized in the market price. In this case, to achieve a better social price and output, one needs to calculate the costs of pollution that are passed on to society but not included in the market price. In reality, this is not an easy process. This is particularly true for a middle-income country where growth in GDP per capita is still a high priority. However, assuming that some estimate of the social cost can be computed, the total cost of production is higher than just the producer's cost of production. This is important in order to conduct a *cost–benefit analysis*. If this ratio is greater than 1, then the total costs to society are in excess of the benefits, and the activity needs to be curtailed to lower the ratio. This is frequently the case for pollution. Since not all of the costs of production are included in the market price, the market "overproduces." Notice that in a market without negative externalities costs and benefits are likely to match. It is the presence of negative externalities, such as pollution, that can yield a ratio greater than 1. In the case of Latin America, this is obviously occurring. Poor air quality, polluted water, deforestation, and so on, are all manifestations of costs to society that are not being included in the market price.

A further complication is that economic decisions need to be made at the margin. In other words, pollution should be controlled up to the point where the marginal costs of more pollution control are equal to the marginal benefits. The marginal benefits of any activity tend to be highest for low levels of output and decline as more is consumed. The reverse is true of marginal cost. It usually starts out at a low level and rises with the amount produced. This is shown graphically for pollution in Figure 5.3. The marginal benefits to society start out high and gradually fall. This means that the initial benefits of any pollution are quite high but fall as the environment becomes more polluted. The reverse is true for the costs of pollution. They start out quite modest and rise. The optimal amount of pollution would occur where the two curves intersect at Q_0. Figure 5.3 is mostly a useful way to think about the right level of pollution control. Few, if any, countries are precisely at Q_0. However, it does give one a point of reference. How many countries, much less major urban areas, in Latin America are at Q_0? Simple intuition would suggest that many areas of the region are to the right of Q_0. In this case, the marginal cost is far greater than the marginal benefit. Social welfare could clearly be improved by moving in the direction of Q_0. This would mean that the extra costs associated with pollution control are considerably less than the extra benefits. Finally, note that to the right of Q_0, the gap can be quite large. A thought exercise for Latin America might suffice to illustrate this. How far away from Q_0 is Mexico City?

Cost–benefit analysis can theoretically solve environmental problems. It simply requires a calculation of the social costs that are not included in the market price. In many cases, this is not an easy thing to calculate. For example, what is the social cost of air pollution in a large city in Latin America? One would, at a minimum, compare disease and mortality rates in the current situation with rates in a situation with less

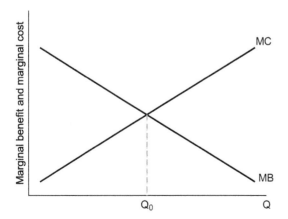

Figure 5.3 The marginal cost and marginal benefit of pollution.

air pollution. Note that the comparison is not with *zero* air pollution. The optimum level of pollution is not zero; recall that economic activities that produce pollution also create benefits. The situation becomes more complicated in that some of the costs are not borne by society immediately but may be passed on to future generations. These costs also need to be included in the calculation of social costs. Even more difficult is the fact that some environmental problems impose costs on neighboring countries or in some cases, the planet. The point is that the calculation of environmental costs is very hard. As a result, a middle-income country is unlikely to achieve a perfect balance of costs and benefits. However, when pollution reaches very high levels, the costs of doing nothing become very high. In the next two sections, two common methods of dealing with pollution are outlined. Neither can be perfectly implemented, but they are indicative of the way governments deal with pollution now or in the future. However, keep in mind that pollution control is a relatively new policy even in high-income countries. A perfect template for pollution control has yet to be designed. As a result, the countries of Latin America are struggling with a social and economic problem that has not been perfectly solved even by two of the world's richest countries north of the region.

Command and control

Refer again to Figure 5.3. The optimal amount of pollution, given the marginal costs and marginal benefits of pollution, is Q_0. Assume for the moment that one knows the level of pollution associated with Q_0. If this is the case, then one solution to the problem is to force firms that pollute to cut their levels of pollution to Q_0. In the jargon of environmental economics, this is known as the *command and control (CAC)* method of lowering the level of pollution. This would force the firm to do one of two things. First, they could cut their level of output to reduce the level of pollution they are discharging. Second, they could install pollution-control equipment to reduce their levels of emissions to allowable levels. In either case, the level of pollution has been reduced. Notice that there is still some pollution. Producing goods and services has benefits, so the optimal solution is not zero pollution. Rather, it is a level of pollution that to some extent is more consistent with a socially optimal level of output for a pollution-intensive good. The great virtue of the CAC method of controlling pollution is its relative simplicity. Government officials determine the level of pollution, and firms must adjust their operations to that level. Since environmental regulations are relatively new in Latin America, CAC is commonly used as a means of pollution control. However, as the next section indicates, CAC is generally considered to be a second-best method of pollution control.

Market-based initiatives

> A strong market-based instrument decentralizes decisionmaking to a degree that the polluter or resource user has a maximum amount of flexibility to select the production or consumption option that minimizes the social cost of achieving a particular level of environmental quality.
>
> (Robert M. Huber, Jack Ruitenbeek, and Ronaldo Seroa da Motta)

While CAC is a frequently implemented means of controlling pollution, it is usually considered inferior to what are known as *market-based initiatives (MBIs)*.[2] Theoretically, it is possible to solve the pollution problem using a CAC policy. However, CAC has one major drawback. Once a producer has met the government-mandated pollution standard, there is no further incentive to reduce pollution. Producers are almost always in the best position to know how to reduce the level of pollution. With the right set of regulations, a government can give producers an incentive to use that knowledge in a way that both lowers pollution and reduces the production cost for the producer. The easiest market-based system is a pollution tax. The government first determines the social cost of pollution that is not included in the private cost of production. The producer is then charged a pollution tax equivalent to this cost. In terms of Figure 5.2, this would shift the supply curve for the pollution-intensive product to the left by the correct amount. In a purely static sense, a pollution tax would yield the same result as a CAC policy. In the long run, there would be a difference. The producer now has a clear incentive to determine how to lower the amount of pollution produced per unit of output. If they could do this, the firm would become more profitable as the tax burden diminished. Also, this could be a source of competitive advantage vis-à-vis other firms in the industry. The use of MBIs seems to be increasing in Latin America. However, they should not be seen as a panacea. They can be difficult to administer, and changing regulations from CAC to MBIs may not always be easy.

While pollution taxes are preferable to CAC, environmental policy can be improved further. Environmental policy should be concerned with the overall level of pollution in the country. A pollution tax sets the price of pollution but does not necessarily control the overall level of pollution in a country. The most commonly used method of controlling the overall level of pollution and providing the incentives of a pollution tax is to issue pollution permits. Permits issued to firms could then be traded to other firms, and the market would set the price of the permits. Permits would then flow to industries where the marginal benefits of pollution are highest. While such a system is theoretically appealing, the actual implementation is difficult. While it is unlikely that such a system will develop within Latin America in the near future, the policy is still of some relevance to the region. Global negotiations on controlling the total amount of greenhouse gases for the planet include an envisioned global system of tradable pollution permits. The implementation of this system on a global basis would no doubt speed up any movement from CAC or pollution taxes to a tradable permit system. In the next section, some of the advantages of tradable permits are more closely examined.

Box 5.2 Exporting environmentalism

In analyzing efforts to control pollution in Latin America, one tends to forget that environmental legislation is relatively new in *developed* countries. Using the US as an example, the Environmental Protection Agency (EPA) was not formed until 1970. Further, the US has been refining its regulations almost continuously since the formation of the EPA. Environmental issues are difficult, and the US experience is not atypical. From the beginning, a focus of US environmental regulation has been the chemical industry. By its very nature, the industry is pollution-intensive. The production of chemicals generates hazardous and nonhazardous waste, consumes energy heavily, relies on nonrenewable resources for its raw materials, and may release substances that enter the food chain or biological systems. Until the 1970s, the attitude of the US industry had been to fight regulation. This effort yielded limited success, as the focus of US environmental policy shifted from pollution control to pollution prevention. The industry gradually came around to the notion that pollution prevention could be a source of competitive advantage and simultaneously put it less at odds with government and environmental groups. This led the US industry to adopt a policy known as Responsible Care. In general, the goal of the policy was to better align industry practices with the social environment it operates in and to stay ahead of the curve in terms of industry environmental policy. The development of Responsible Care coincided with the expansion of the industry into other markets, some of them in the more important developing countries, such as Mexico and Brazil. In these markets, the companies took the concept of Responsible Care with them. In many senses, these countries are now on the same path as the US decades ago, and firms understand that operating in a socially responsible way can be a source of competitive advantage.

Mexico is a good case in point. The country passed its first comprehensive environmental legislation in 1987. The beginning of free trade in the 1990s offered the possibility of exports to the US, but only under the condition that Mexican firms were in full compliance with Mexican law. US firms also started investment in chemical plants in Mexico, as they were now facing a much more open FDI environment. As they increased operations in Mexico, the US firms took the Responsible Care program with them. In the US, the program had become just a normal part of doing business, and it was obvious that it was perhaps even more important in the context of a US firm operating in a foreign country. It is perhaps slightly more surprising that the Mexican chemical industry decided that the same program was a good idea. Mexican firms now routinely work with government, environmental groups, and community groups to try to find environmental solutions to the problems that are inherent in the industry. In a sense, the US chemical industry is "exporting" a form of environmentalism. Limited data on this issue indicates that US firms operating in Mexico are more pressured by corporate headquarters and colleagues than by the Mexican government. The program has been less successful in Brazil in terms of participation by Brazilian firms. However, another study of Brazilian industry indicates that foreign firms or firms with significant foreign ownership spend more resources than local firms on reducing pollution.[3] Obviously, industry groups and FDI are not going to solve the problems of pollution control in Latin America. It remains to be seen whether the nascent government agencies in the region can avoid the "regulatory capture" that can occur with government and industry cooperation. However, it does seem that FDI by firms from developed countries has the potential to create a positive externality for the region in terms of environmental quality.[4]

The role of institutions

Legislation is really not the critical factor in environmental improvements. Legislation cannot guarantee that the intent of the legislator will be implemented in practice. The major problems result from the difficulty of establishing control and enforcement mechanisms to apply the legal provisions.

(UN Environmental Programme)

In the previous sections, the theory of environmental protection has been presented, as well as some of the common means of mitigating environmental problems. Attempts to address environmental problems in Latin America have focused on passing initial legislation to deal with these problems. This is a necessary first step, as these problems will not be adequately dealt with in the absence of some form of government intervention. However, in the context of Latin America, it is unrealistic to expect the level of environmental control that one typically observes in a high-income country. The purpose of this section is to raise some of the more common problems that have to be overcome in the process of making the actual enforcement of environmental regulations more congruent with the regulations themselves.

First, and foremost, is the issue of government funding of pollution-control efforts. The government of any developing country faces an almost impossible task of allocating scarce resources among many pressing and competing needs. Sadly, pollution control is just one of many pressing needs. One is tempted to say that environmental concerns are absolutely fundamental. However, allocating resources among the environment, health care, education, and so on is no easy task. There is little formal study of this allocation, but the general sense is that spending on environmental enforcement in Latin America is low and may be declining.[5] A related problem is that effective pollution control is not inexpensive. To be effective, the government agencies in charge of this must have well-trained personnel and expensive equipment. Both of these resources are obviously less available in Latin America than they are in high-income countries. This problem may be mitigated to some extent by the location of industry in Latin America. Most heavy industry tends to be heavily concentrated in a few areas.[6] Also, industries that are pollution-intensive are now well known. This may greatly reduce monitoring costs and allow the government to reduce pollution significantly at a relatively low cost. This advantage is partially offset by the large informal sector. Producers in the informal sector may be pollution-intensive, and controlling discharges in this environment may be difficult. On the other hand, the informal sector may also be producing a low percentage of output relative to the large firms in the formal sector.

The structure of government finance in Latin America may make MBIs an attractive proposition relative to CAC. CAC is a less flexible form of pollution control. However, the government is shouldering the costs of monitoring pollution and is receiving no revenue in the process. Pollution taxes now become doubly attractive. As mentioned above, they provide incentives for firms to find ways to produce output in a less pollution-intensive manner. They also produce revenue. Tax revenue in a developing country is always difficult to raise. In this case, revenue has been gathered in the process of obtaining another social goal. Offsetting this is the fact that many MBIs may be more difficult and expensive to monitor than CAC. There is some evidence of a movement toward pollution taxes in Latin America as a means of raising revenue.[7] Also, governments in middle-income countries have to be aware that pollution control may constitute a regressive form of taxation. Spending by firms on pollution control may be passed on in the form of higher prices for consumer goods. This implicit pollution tax may be easily borne in a high-income country but may be much more burdensome in a country where GDP per capita is significantly lower. Tradable pollution permits would, in theory, solve many of these problems. First, they allow governments to control the overall level of pollution. Second, they solve the difficult problem involved with pollution taxes concerning what is the correct tax. Auctioned permits that are tradable force firms to reveal in a market what the right to pollute is worth. And they also raise revenue needed by the government. Given these advantages, one may assume that the global move to tradable permits will eventually reach Latin America.

Environmental issues in Latin America

In this section, we move from the general to the specific. In the first part of the chapter, the focus was on developing a framework for analyzing environmental problems in the context of Latin America. In this section, the focus will be on a short list of environmental problems that are especially acute in Latin America. This list is by no means exhaustive. Latin America has many of the same environmental problems as much of the rest of the developing world. However, each region of the world is different. For example, drought is a much less serious problem in Latin America than in Africa. Latin America is far from overpopulated by global standards, so some of the environmental issues in Latin America are different than in parts of Asia. The issues covered in this section are water quality, air pollution, and deforestation.

Water pollution

Water quality has long been a serious environmental problem in Latin America. Polluted water is associated with a host of diseases, such as amoebic dysentery, cholera, trachoma, and others. Such conditions can easily lead to death, especially in small children. Aside from this, frequent illnesses associated with polluted water lower the productivity and earnings of the labor force. Less obviously, if clean water is scarce, people may have to waste resources by transporting water from a clean source or using part of a meager income to purchase clean water. In short, water pollution can carry a heavy economic and social cost. The statistics on access to clean water are shown in Table 5.3. The first four columns indicate the access to improved (clean) water in rural and urban areas of Latin

Table 5.3 Access to clean water and sanitation in Latin America

	Access to improved water source (%)				Access to improved sanitation (%)			
	Rural		Urban		Rural		Urban	
	1990	*2015*	*1990*	*2015*	*1990*	*2015*	*1990*	*2015*
Argentina	69	100	97	99.6	69	93.6	89	95
Bolivia	41	78.9	91	99.3	41	26.8	41	64.5
Brazil	68	86.6	96	99.3	31	58	79	90.9
Chile	48	100	99	100	53	98.9	91	100
Colombia	69	86	98	99.8	41	72	82	88.3
Costa Rica	87	99.5	99	99.7	83	94.3	93	98
Ecuador	61	80.4	84	99.5	37	80.3	74	89.4
El Salvador	59	83.4	91	97.8	30	87	70	93.2
Guatemala	75	89.4	91	97.5	49	53.1	81	80.7
Honduras	60	84.3	92	98.7	33	75.1	70	83.7
Mexico	59	93.7	92	99.5	35	80.7	78	91.4
Nicaragua	54	60.7	92	97.4	26	62.8	59	85.8
Panama	67	87.3	98	98.9	41	59.2	76	85.7
Paraguay	24	98.4	83	99.2	14	80.7	62	98.3
Peru	44	72.4	88	94.6	16	58.2	71	81.9
Uruguay	75	93.7	98	99.5	81	94.9	94	95.7
Venezuela, RB	71	86.4	93	98.8	45	72.3	89	97.7
Latin America	60.6	87.1	94.3	98.8	42.6	73.4	76.4	89.4

Source: World Bank (2019).

America. In 1990, less than two-thirds of the rural population had access to water from an improved source. By 2015, the percentage was over 80 percent. For the urban population, the percentage increased from 94.3 to 98.8. As in so many other areas of life in Latin America, conditions in urban areas are considerably better than in rural areas. The fifth to eighth columns show access to improved sanitation in the two areas. In this case, in 1990, 42.6 percent of the rural population had such access. By 2015, over 70 percent had access to improved sanitation. In the urban areas, the percentages improved from nearly 77 percent to over 85 percent. The two are not unrelated. The lack of improved sanitation also frequently means water quality problems. The cholera epidemics that have affected parts of Latin America can be traced to this link. More recently, water pollution has been caused by runoffs from agricultural land as well as from industry.

Solving the problem of clean water has been a vexing problem in Latin America for a long time. Water pollution from industrial sources can be dealt with using some mix of CAC and MBIs, which have already been discussed. Since polluters in the formal sector are frequently small in number and geographically concentrated, dealing with industrial water pollution should be a problem even a small and underfunded bureaucracy can deal with. Industrial pollution emanating from the informal sector is much more difficult to deal with, but again, while these producers are numerous, the amount of pollution coming from this sector should be small. Again, pollution coming from the informal sector is just another example of problems created by a policy mix that encourages economic activity in this sector rather than in the formal sector of the economy. The largest problem affecting the average person in the region is the poor quality of water produced by the public sector in municipalities. In the first two chapters, the problem of institutional weakness in Latin America was covered at several points; this is just another specific example of this general problem. In this case, a potential solution to this problem is to privatize the public water system. In practice, this frequently means FDI in this critical sector. However, in Latin America, this potential solution is not a panacea. The provision of water and sanitation services is a natural monopoly, and private companies must be efficiently regulated if private provision is to work properly. The record in this regard is mixed. Privatization has led to riots in Cochabamba, Bolivia, and a large-scale privatization in Argentina during the 1990s has been partially rolled back. Once again, government effectiveness is crucial. The private sector can potentially help solve this long-standing problem in the region, but only in conjunction with effective government regulation.

The other element of water pollution in Latin America is emissions by industry into the water supply. Table 5.4 presents data on the extent of the problem in the region. The first two columns show the absolute amount of water pollution by industry in 1990 and 2006.[8] In general, the data is discouraging. The absolute amounts have increased in most countries, substantially in some. The numbers in the first two columns are just part of the environmental costs of economic growth in low- to middle-income countries. Also, note that water pollution per worker is not increasing very much. As is evident from the data for the reference developed countries at the bottom of the table, the relationship between economic growth and pollution is not totally straightforward. With respect to environmental policy, industrial water pollution is one of the least difficult environmental problems to control. The largest sources of this pollution are normally quite visible, and the number of firms engaging in the pollution is small. While industrial water pollution is not a trivial problem in the region, it is easier to make progress in this area than in others.

Table 5.4 Industrial water pollution in Latin America

	Kilograms per day (thousands)		Kilograms per day worker	
	1990	*2006*	*1990*	*2006*
Argentina	186.7	155.54	0.2	0.23
Bolivia	8.4	11.54	0.24	0.25
Brazil	780.4	–	0.19	–
Chile	66.8	92.5	0.22	0.25
Colombia	93.2	86.99	0.19	0.2
Costa Rica	27.3	–	0.2	–
Ecuador	25.6	44.75	0.23	0.28
El Salvador	7.7	–	0.22	–
Guatemala	16.1	–	0.27	–
Honduras	17.8	–	0.23	–
Mexico	174.3	370.81	0.18	0.19
Nicaragua	10.5	–	0.27	–
Panama	9.7	13.72	0.26	0.32
Paraguay	3.3	10.81	0.28	0.28
Peru	56.1	–	0.2	–
Uruguay	38.7	–	0.23	–
Venezuela, RB	96.5	–	0.21	–
Portugal	147.9	105.04	0.15	0.15
Spain	320.3	379.73	0.17	0.15
Canada	321.5	310.28	0.17	0.16
US	2,565.20	1,897.50	0.15	0.14

Source: World Bank (2006).

Air pollution

Much like water pollution, air pollution is a pressing environmental problem in almost any metropolitan area in Latin America. Many cities in the region are set in breathtakingly picturesque environments that can be glimpsed only through a screen of smog. This is annoying, but the effects of air pollution on the health of the inhabitants of these cities is all too real.[9] Part of the problem is the location of industry in major urban areas. Industrialization is usually not a rural phenomenon. The other part of the problem is the increasing affluence of the population of the region, leading to a large increase in vehicle use. In turn, this leads to a greater amount of air pollution generated by these vehicles.

The data can be seen in Table 5.5. For most of the countries, there has been a dramatic increase in the number of vehicles. As the data for the four developed countries at the bottom of the table indicates, Latin America is in the process of "catching up" with the world's high-income countries in terms of the number of vehicles. As a result, CO_2 emissions are also rising. Air quality is a problem in the countries of the region, and it is getting worse. The good news is that it is getting worse at a slower rate. Note that Spain and Portugal are moving in the same direction as Latin America. However, the two developed countries indicate that at some point, air quality will begin to improve. In a later section of the chapter, the economic logic behind this sort of movement will be explained.

Table 5.5 Urban air pollution in Latin America

	CO_2 emissions (metric tons per capita)		Motor vehicles per 1,000 people
	1990	*2014*	*Recent years*
Argentina	3.4	4.7	316 (2015)
Bolivia	0.8	1.9	72 (2015)
Brazil	1.4	2.6	350 (2019)
Chile	2.5	4.7	230 (2015)
Colombia	1.7	1.8	116 (2018)
Costa Rica	1.0	1.6	224 (2015)
Ecuador	1.6	2.8	141 (2015)
El Salvador	0.5	1.0	41 (2015)
Guatemala	0.5	1.2	115 (2015)
Honduras	0.5	1.1	18 (2017)
Mexico	3.7	3.9	297 (2015)
Nicaragua	0.6	0.8	79 (2015)
Panama	1.1	2.3	171 (2015)
Paraguay	0.5	0.9	98 (2015)
Peru	1.0	2.0	78 (2015)
Uruguay	1.3	2.0	280 (2015)
Venezuela, RB	6.2	6.0	145 (2015)
Latin America	1.7	2.4	163
Portugal	4.2	4.3	566 (2015)
Spain	5.6	5.0	591 (2015)
Canada	15.7	15.1	670 (2016)
US	19.3	16.5	837 (2016)

Sources: World Bank (2019); Wikipedia (2019).

Box 5.3 Urbanization and the environment

In the previous two sections, we have covered problems with water and air pollution in Latin America. Part of what was being conveyed in those sections is that the thought of Latin America as an area where most of the population is living in an idyllic rural environment is not quite accurate. Economic development in the region has drawn countless millions of people from rural villages and smaller cities into very large metropolitan areas. In 1975, only slightly more than half the population lived in urban areas. By 1990, this figure was 70 percent, and by 2013, it was nearly 80 percent. Note the variation in the data. Urbanization tends to be lowest in the countries with the lowest GDP per capita. As these countries develop, urbanization rates are likely to rise and bring the regional average even higher. Latin America is already more urbanized than most regions of the world and seems poised to become as urbanized as the countries of North America.

The increasing urbanization of Latin America exacerbates environmental problems. High levels of discharges of pollution into the water supply and air, combined with high population densities, can contribute to the poor quality of life of the increasing number of people crowded into the large cities of Latin America. This makes progress on environmental issues more urgent, since they can be expected to impact ever more people as the countries of the region become even more urbanized.

Deforestation

As we have alluded to earlier and will cover in more detail in Chapter 6, Latin America is a region with a substantial amount of natural resources. One of the richest of these resources comes from the immense amount of natural forest. Forests cover over 40 percent of the land area of Latin America. As a result, forest products have always been a major industry in the region and are currently the major source of income and employment for millions of people. The forest resources of Latin America are also a global resource. Twenty-four percent of the world's forest resources are in Latin America. The basic data on forest resources is shown in Table 5.6. When considering forest resources in Latin America, there is a natural tendency to think almost exclusively in terms of the rain forests of the Amazon basin in Brazil. Given the amount written about this area, this is perfectly understandable. Note from the data that 40 percent of Latin America's forests are outside Brazil. The point is that forest resources are an important environmental issue in virtually every country in the region.

As we saw in an earlier section, pollution is a negative externality. In terms of air pollution, there are growing fears that the emission of carbon from industrial production and transportation equipment has the potential to change the climate of the entire planet. Carbon emissions are now seen as a global, not just a local, environmental issue. Forests play a key role in this. In essence, forests act as a natural way to reduce the amount of carbon in the atmosphere. It is for this reason that losing a significant part of the world's forests is an important environmental problem. Further, preventing

Table 5.6 Urbanization in Latin America

	Percentage of population in urban areas	
	1990	*2017*
Argentina	87	92
Bolivia	56	69
Brazil	74	86
Chile	83	87
Colombia	69	80
Costa Rica	50	79
Ecuador	55	64
El Salvador	49	71
Guatemala	42	51
Honduras	40	56
Mexico	71	80
Nicaragua	53	58
Panama	54	67
Paraguay	49	61
Peru	69	78
Uruguay	89	95
Venezuela, RB	84	88
Latin America	63	74
Portugal	48	65
Spain	75	80
Canada	77	81
US	75	82

Source: World Bank (2019).

deforestation is a far cheaper way to reduce carbon emissions than pursuing alternative strategies to reduce carbon emissions. In more technical terms, forests produce a positive externality. A positive externality exists when a product produces benefits to society that are not included in the market price. Forests obviously produce a *positive externality*. There is a benefit for which the owner of forest products cannot charge the world. In turn, this implies that the indiscriminate cutting of forests yields a *negative externality*. In effect, trees are too cheap, and since the market is not accounting for the externalities associated, the result is deforestation.[10] Basically, we are getting the same results as are shown in Figure 5.2. The supply is too large, prices are too low, and the equilibrium in the market is too high. This leaves owners of forest lands with the incentive to clear-cut forests and then develop the cleared land for other uses such as agriculture or ranching. Unfortunately, high prices for commodities can encourage this trend. Since the owner of the forest is not being compensated for the positive externality, the incentives for deforestation remain in place. In any region, this makes forest resources difficult to develop in an appropriate way. Forest products yield income in the current period, but the resources can take many years to replace. In a sense, trees are a crop, but a crop with a very long growing cycle. In Latin America and the rest of the world, the "farming" of trees is a growing part of the forest products industry. From Table 5.7, one can see that tree plantations are still a small part of the total forest resources of Latin America, but the growth rate of this part of the industry is extremely fast. This cannot offset the deforestation occurring in most countries of the region, also shown in Table 5.7. While the annual rates of deforestation are small, the compound effects over decades lead to striking losses of a critical resource. Deforestation is an old story, and

Table 5.7 Deforestation in Latin America

	Total forest area (thousands of hectares) (2015)	Average annual percentage change (1990–2015)	Plantation forests	Average annual percent change (1990–2015)
Argentina	27,112	−0.88%	1,202	2.28%
Bolivia	54,764	−0.51%	26	1.20%
Brazil	493,538	−0.39%	7,736	2.21%
Chile	17,735	0.65%	3,044	3.13%
Colombia	58,501.74	−0.37%	70.9	5.60%
Costa Rica	2,756	0.30%	17.6	−3.76%
Ecuador	12,547.88	−0.57%	55.24	1.00%
El Salvador	265	−1.19%	16.2	2.10%
Guatemala	3,540	−1.02%	185	6.40%
Honduras	4,592	−1.74%	0	–
Mexico	66,040	−0.21%	87	11.90%
Nicaragua	3,114	−1.24%	48	1.41%
Panama	4,617	−0.34%	80.4	9.70%
Paraguay	15,323	−1.10%	98	3.06%
Peru	73,973	−0.20%	1,157	3.10%
Uruguay	1,845	1.25%	1,062	3.24%
Venezuela, RB	46,683	−0.41%	557	0.00%
Portugal	3,182	−0.29%	891	0.44%
Spain	18,418	1.34%	2,909	1.71%
Canada	347,069	0.01%	15,784	9.79%
US	310,095	0.10%	26,364	1.88%

Source: Food and Agriculture Organization of the United Nations (2018).

many of the high-income countries went through a similar process at an earlier stage of development. For Latin America to break out of this historical pattern is not going to be an easy task, as the incentives to use the resource to produce income and jobs in a middle-income country are high.

The problem is compounded in this case by the frequent absence of property rights. Many of Latin America's forest resources are on public land. In the Amazon basin, less than a quarter of the land is privately held.[11] The rest is owned by the state. If this resource is not carefully policed, the possibility of a *tragedy of the commons* exists. This occurs when there is a resource available and there are no clear property rights. In such a case, the resource may be depleted because of a lack of incentives for anyone to conserve the resource. If forest resources exist on public land, and there is no effective control of the use of that resource, then deforestation can occur on land that is technically owned by the state. If government effectiveness is low, then the control of the destruction of forests on public land is a distinct possibility. This is especially true if the resource is geographically remote. In some countries, the sheer enormity of the resource makes adequate policing of its use virtually impossible. The Amazon basin is one and a half times the size of India.

This shows that one of the most critical environmental problems for Latin America is deforestation. Forests form such a large percentage of land in the region that the effective use of this resource is obviously important. Effective use will not be easy. Forest resources are more likely to be used efficiently on private land, but there is no guarantee of this. There are currently no tax or subsidy schemes in place that would adjust market prices to reflect the loss of a resource that produces a positive externality for the region and the world. A more pressing problem is that, theoretically, much of this resource in the region is on public land, where the use is more easily controlled. Unfortunately, a mix of the vastness of the forest's resources and weak institutions for protecting it means that deforestation is occurring on land that should be protected. Even with more effective institutions, the incentive to develop the resource quickly is strong in middle-income countries. Government policy is caught between protecting a critical resource and economic growth. At a certain level of GDP per capita, stopping and reversing deforestation are possible, as shown by the data for the high-income countries in Table 5.7. Applying this sort of situation to Latin America at this point in time is not realistic. No government in the region is going to stop the development of this resource for purely environmental reasons. In the meantime, the focus of policy in the region is on slowing the rate of deforestation. While this is not a perfect outcome, governments in the region are now influenced by environmental concerns and are trying to balance these with economic growth. The task is not one that anyone would envy.

Biodiversity

An environmental issue frequently related to deforestation is biodiversity. Biodiversity refers to the number of different forms of life that occur in a local ecosystem or on the earth as a whole. Biodiversity provides a number of benefits. First, as noted with forest resources, plant life can be an important component of pollution control. Second, a lack of diversity in agriculture may make the food supply more vulnerable to problems with a single crop. The Irish potato famine of the 1840s is a classic example of this risk. Currently, about 80 percent of human food comes from just twenty types of plants. Biodiversity is a health-industry issue, as a large number of currently used and potential medications are derived from plant and animal life. A reduction in the number of species in the world potentially reduces the supply of medicines. Business and industry rely on a large number of plants and animals for the production of countless goods and services. Finally, a diverse environment provides aesthetic benefits to mankind. In economic terms, biodiversity is potentially very important. It is also a positive externality, potentially a very large one.

This implies that deforestation in Latin America is even more important than indicated above. Deforestation involves a loss of habitat for many species. Even without deforestation, development in forests may reduce the number of species. The issue is especially important for Latin America. Five of the top ten countries of the world in terms of biodiversity are in Latin America: Brazil, Colombia, Ecuador, Mexico, and Peru. Ten percent of the plant and animal species in the *world* are found in Colombia alone. Overall, Latin America (including the Caribbean) is home to 34 percent of the world's plant species and 27 percent of the mammals. Preserving these resources is in some senses an even more formidable task than preventing defor- estation. The benefits of biodiversity are large, but what is the size of the externality? Even if that could be determined, what would be an optimal policy with respect to biodiversity? This area is difficult to deal with even in a high-income country. With respect to environmental policy in Latin America, it will be difficult to implement on a large scale. However, it is almost certainly true that any estimates of the costs of deforestation are low because the positive externality of biodiversity hasn't been included. Because of biodiversity losses, the problem of deforestation is even more pressing than indicated above.

Box 5.4 Paper parks

On the surface, it appears that the governments of the region are doing an admirable job of preserving the important biodiversity of the region. A fifth of the region's land has been set aside for conservation. This is noticeably higher than the world average of 13 percent. Unfortunately, simply designating an area as "protected" is not enough. The region is home to a number of "paper parks." This is a term used to refer to land that has been set aside by the government for conservation but is not being adequately protected. Without proper protection, protected areas can suffer from a number of problems that can dilute the social benefits they can confer. Part of the problem is the extension of agriculture onto protected land or use for grazing. Illegal logging is a problem in many countries, especially Brazil. Recently, illegal mining in protected areas, particularly for gold, is becoming a serious problem. In this case the mining is not only degrading protected areas, it presents serious envir- onmental problems. The urban sprawl mentioned earlier in the chapter also is a problem. One can only sadly wonder what some of the large cities in Latin America once looked like to realize what has been lost. Finally, protected areas that are not really protected can become havens for criminal activity in a region that can ill afford the provision of safe havens for these activities.[12]

Normally, we think of property rights in terms of the private sector. As noted above, 20 percent of land in the region is owned by the government. Paper parks exist due to the inability of the government to exercise its property rights. The enormity of the protected areas has the potential to create large social benefits for Latin America and the world. Unfortunately, these benefits are not free. The problems cited above are directly attributable to a lack of funding to protect areas designated for conservation. The World Bank (2012) estimates that the countries of the region spend less than 1 percent of their total environmental budgets on conservation. This is considered to be roughly half of what would need to be spent to cover basic needs. Flores (2010) estimates that the gap between actual spending and what would be optimal is less than $1 billion with nearly half of the total accounted for by Brazil. While government budgets always are tight, the amount of money necessary in terms of the GDP of the region does not seem large in relation to the benefits of protecting a fifth of the region's land.

The environment and growth

A relationship that was mentioned at several points in the previous section was the trade-off between environmental issues and economic growth. It is frequently the case that protection of the environment will involve either CAC policies or MBIs, which will make economic activity more expensive. In turn, this expense may result in a slower rate of growth of real GDP. In a low- or middle-income country, this is a difficult trade-off. A polluted environment or the overuse of natural resources is not a desirable outcome. On the other hand, increasing GDP per capita is an important consideration. How to think about reconciling the two is the purpose of this final section of the chapter. In a sense, the earlier sections are concerned with the microeconomics of pollution problems in Latin America. This section covers some of the more general issues involved in the process of balancing the environment and growth. The first part concerns obtaining a level of growth that is environmentally sustainable. In the next section, the results of a substantial amount of research about GDP per capita and pollution are summarized and put in a Latin American context. The interactions among FDI, international trade, and pollution are covered, as both FDI and trade are increasingly important contributors to economic growth. A final section considers the implications of climate change in the twenty-first century for the economies of the region.

Sustainable growth

Over the past two decades, the concept of sustainable growth has become a more important part of the literature on economic development. Over the same time frame, sustainable growth has become an increasingly complicated term. At this point, sustainable growth can mean different things to different people. In other words, it is becoming hard to define the term. Sustainable growth originally applied solely to environmental issues. Over time, the concepts of economic and social sustainability came to be associated with the term. In this case, it is small wonder that the term is now difficult to define. For our purposes here, we will confine the discussion to sustainable growth in an environmental sense, for two reasons. First, once one leaves the area of environmental sustainability, there is much less agreement about what sustainable growth means. Second, in this chapter the focus has been on environmental issues. Discussing sustainable growth in terms of the environment is a convenient way to summarize many of the environmental issues that have been covered so far.

Sustainable growth in the context of the environment begins with the concept of natural capital. Natural capital is the endowment of nature's resources possessed by a country or region. These resources, such as fresh air and clean water, can be used at various rates. In addition to natural capital, there is also land, as it was defined in the previous chapter. The question then becomes: at what rate should these resources be consumed? There are three possibilities. If the consumption of natural capital is larger than nature's ability to replenish it, this leads to environmental degradation and is obviously a nonsustainable situation. A second possibility is that the use of natural capital roughly matches nature's ability to replenish the resource. The final situation is where the economy is using natural capital at a lower rate than it is being replenished.

After reading the previous paragraph, it is fairly clear where Latin America is in terms of sustainability overall. The air pollution in the major cities is a classic example of nonsustainable growth. The same situation holds for water pollution. The deforestation that is occurring in much of the region is just another form of nonsustainable development. The vast forest resources of Latin America are being used at a faster rate than they can be replaced. In many cases, in the past and in the present, natural resources such as precious metals or other minerals have been used at nonsustainable rates. Most of the previous parts of this chapter have been specific examples of nonsustainable growth. It is a chronic problem in the economies of Latin America. The problem is even worse than was initially described. Some of the problems outlined are irreversible. The resources extracted in the colonial era, in many cases, cannot be replaced. The loss of biodiversity, in many cases, cannot be reversed. Nonsustainable growth can have long-run consequences that may be extremely serious.

Making growth sustainable requires the use of the policies we described earlier in the chapter, but usually on a larger scale. Market prices cannot be expected to include costs imposed on future generations in the current market price. In calculating the negative externalities associated with certain types of production, it is now necessary to calculate not only the current effects but also effects into an indefinite future. Of course, this makes the negative externalities and the associated reduction in production even larger. The cost–benefit analysis changes considerably when one starts accounting for costs and benefits well into the future as well as in the current situation. Using either CAC or MBIs to control pollution becomes increasingly complicated, as the analysis becomes much more complex.

What the above means is that in an environmental sense, sustainable development is a desirable social goal. However, implementing it in practice is very difficult. Done well, it would involve accounting for all the costs that the production of a good or service is imposing on current and future generations that are not being included in the market price. In practice, even high-income countries would be hard pressed to accomplish this. In an area where governments may not be completely effective and the institutional environment is weak, an aggressive program aimed at sustainable development may not be possible. Even though sustainable growth may not be immediately achievable in Latin America, it is a useful benchmark. Like perfect competition or perfectly rational expectations, one may rarely observe perfect sustainable growth policies. This hardly makes the concept useless. It can serve as a guide for comparing current policy with some optimum. While Latin America is certainly far from perfectly sustainable growth, an important question is whether environmental policy in the region is moving toward that optimum or away from it. In the context of middle-income countries, perhaps movements of policy and reductions in measurable levels of pollution should be seen as the progress they represent and a hope for a greener future. The next section presents a concept, now common in economics, indicating that such hope is not unrealistic.

The environmental Kuznets curve

For nearly twenty years, there has been a lively debate and a large amount of empirical research on the relationship between economic development and levels of pollution.[13] The debate was started by the results of a paper by Grossman and Krueger (1993). The paper introduced the concept of the *environmental Kuznets curve*. The curve is named after the relationship between GDP per capita and the distribution of income discovered by Simon Kuznets in the 1950s. In his research, Kuznets found an inverted U-shaped relationship between income distribution and GDP per capita. As the latter grew, the distribution of income would tend to worsen initially, peak, and then decline as GDP per capita increased. The environmental Kuznets curve is derived from the relationship that is frequently found in studying the interaction of GDP per capita and levels of pollution. A common relationship shows that as a country moves from low to middle income, levels of pollution tend to worsen. However, at some point, the level of pollution peaks and then declines as a middle-income country moves to the high-income level. A typical Kuznets curve is shown in Figure 5.4.

The environmental Kuznets curve is now a common part of the lexicon of economic growth. Used simplistically, it carries a potentially important idea. This is that environmental concerns in developing countries will, in time, fix themselves. Pollution levels naturally rise as consumers in middle-income countries obtain goods such as cars and industry becomes a larger percentage of GDP. The curve indicates that eventually GDP per capita will become high enough that environmental conditions will improve. Among policy-makers, this has become almost an unfortunate article of faith. In a middle-income country, growth in GDP per capita is usually the most important economic policy goal. With this constraint, environmental concerns are seen as *temporarily* being considered of secondary importance. Unfortunately, the empirical research on the environmental Kuznets curve indicates that this view of the relationship between economic growth and the environment is not quite so simple, for a number of reasons. First, the peak of the curve is in an uncertain place. Various estimates have put it from around the middle of the world distribution of income ($3,000–$4,000) to as high as

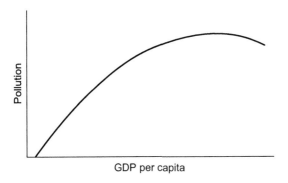

Figure 5.4 The environmental Kuznets curve.

$15,000. The higher estimates would imply that much of Latin America has not reached that turning point, and may not for a nontrivial amount of time. A second problem is that much of the empirical work on this subject uses data from developed countries. Extrapolating these results to the developing countries of Latin America runs the usual risk of transplanting results across countries with widely different institutional settings. What little research has been done using data from developing countries is yielding relationships that are not as neat as Figure 5.4 implies. Another drawback of the literature is that the empirical work to date covers a relatively small number of pollutants for which data is conveniently available. This is not reassuring, given that the potential number of pollutants produced by consumption and production is large. Another difficulty is that environmental damage that occurs early in the process of economic development may in some cases be irreversible. Deforestation of virgin forests is a prime case in point in Latin America, although it may also apply to other forms of environmental degradation. Finally, the literature indicates that assuming that pollution is simply a function of GDP per capita is simplistic at best. In a careful study of pollution in Mexico, Gallagher (2004) found little or no evidence of Mexico having reached the peak of the curve. Even less is known about the rest of the region. It is probably safe to assume that at some point environmental issues will become more important in the region, but few if any countries are now at that point. In the meantime, decades of environmental damage, some of it irreversible, may occur. With poverty and inequality still significant problems in the region, it will be difficult for policy-makers to make environmental policy a higher priority. More study of these issues is badly needed to show that the current costs of pollution are quite high, and the cost to future generations in the region may be extremely high.

Trade, FDI, and the environment

Over the past two decades, there has been an active literature in economics on the effects of international trade on the environment.[14] While there are endless variations of this literature, the basic idea can be expressed in a straightforward way. As an economy develops, three effects occur that can influence the overall level of pollution in an economy. First, there is the scale effect. All else being equal, when real GDP increases, the overall level of pollution will tend to rise. Second, there is the technique effect. A higher real GDP increases incomes. This increase normally generates both the ability and the willingness of a society to reduce the level of pollution. Finally, there is the composition effect. Over time, the industrial structure of any country changes. This is important in terms of the environment. As has been previously discussed, some industries are naturally more pollution-intensive than others. All else being equal, a change in industrial structure in a country can change the overall level of pollution. For example, a decline in the steel industry coupled with an increase in the information-technology industry might lower overall levels of pollution. With these three concepts in mind, we can now more easily think about the interactions among pollution, international trade, and FDI.

As we will see in Chapter 8, barriers to international trade have been falling since the 1950s. As trade barriers fall, the volume of international trade rises. In turn, as the amount of trade increases, the economic output of countries that trade more increases.[15] Thinking about the scale effect leads to the conclusion that international trade increases the overall level of pollution. On the other hand, trade leads to increases in real GDP per capita. In turn, these increases tend to reduce pollution via the technique effect. If nothing else changes, then the latter effect will frequently be larger than the former effect. However, there is still the composition effect to consider. International trade changes the industrial structure of a country. Export-oriented industries tend to become larger, and industries competing with imports become smaller. The increased volume of trade leads to a reorganization of world production whereby some countries produce more goods in a particular industry and some less. This reorganization occurs as a result of differences among nations in the costs of production.[16] With the arrival of environmental regulations in the high-income countries, a new factor determining world production and trade was recognized. Countries have differential costs of production, but they also have differences in the regulation of pollution. In general, low- and middle-income countries have fewer environmental regulations than high-income countries. This implies that countries with low levels of regulation could have lower costs of production in pollution-intensive industries. This could skew the world pattern of production toward these countries and lead to an overall higher level of pollution for the world. This might also lead firms to invest more heavily in pollution-intensive industries in these countries, exacerbating the basic problem. A convenient way to express this idea is to refer to these countries as potential *pollution havens*. The basic idea seems compelling, but the research indicates that this is not happening to any great extent in the world economy. As we will see in later chapters, the FDI investment decision is influenced by a host of factors, of which the level of environmental regulation is just one of many. In most cases, any savings realized by lower levels of environmental regulation pale in comparison to other factors involved in the decision. In other words, in most cases, lax regulation occurs in countries where producing complicated products would at best be difficult. The small amount of research on Latin America is consistent with the overall results mentioned above. There is scant evidence of this phenomenon in the region.[17] A key finding has been that there is little evidence of this occurring in Mexico, which has less strict regulation than the US and is geographically close, with few barriers to trade. As has been shown throughout the chapter, Latin America has significant environmental problems. Fortunately, the research on this subject for the region indicates that becoming a pollution haven in the world economy is not one of them.[18]

Box 5.5   The North American Free Trade Agreement and the environment

In 1994, Mexico joined the *North American Free Trade Agreement (NAFTA)*, which previously included Canada and the US. Critics of NAFTA in the US noisily predicted that a large number of US manufacturing firms would relocate to Mexico in order to obtain lower wages and escape environmental regulations in the US. With respect to the environment, the implication for the region was clear. Firms would close relatively clean plants in the US and open much dirtier plants in Mexico. This would damage the environment both in Mexico and potentially in border areas of the US. With the passage of fifteen years, there is now enough data to analyze the outcome of that forecast of NAFTA as the source of potentially large environmental problems. Fortunately, two careful studies of this issue have concluded that NAFTA has had little impact on the environment in Mexico. At first glance, this may seem puzzling. Pollution is a serious problem in Mexico, and it seems logical to conclude that NAFTA is part of the problem. Perhaps it is a part of the problem, but only a small one. The reason is that the reduction in trade barriers has two effects. First, it might change the composition of industry in Mexico by encouraging pollution-intensive industries. Gallagher (2004) and Gamper-Rabindran (2006) have found that this does not seem to be the case. Factors other than environmental regulation have influenced the composition of industry in the post-NAFTA era. On the contrary, over time, industry in Mexico is shifting to a mix of industries that is less pollution-intensive than in the past. What does influence the level of pollution in Mexico is economic growth. As the economy grows, overall industrial production in Mexico is rising, and this in turn generates more pollution. Again, we are back at the trade-off between growth and the environment. This is where trade and the environment have the potential to cross. It is widely accepted that increasing international trade in a country enhances economic growth. Since the point of reducing trade barriers is to enhance international trade, it is quite possible that these agreements increase growth and, to some extent, the level of pollution. Thus, trade agreements may lead to some increases in the level of pollution, just not in quite the same way many believe they do.

Climate change

One of the most complex challenges facing the world is climate change. In most cases, it is prudent for a country to prepare for the possibility of adverse events even if the probability of such an event is low. For example, both Chile and Mexico must prepare for the possibility of earthquakes. Climate change in the twenty-first century is a similar problem. There is a high probability of adverse changes in the climate of the region. However, the extent of the problem and the timing of the changes are unknown. In such a situation, it would be prudent for any country to prepare for the projected adverse effects of climate change as a form of insurance. With respect to climate change, there are a number of different projected outcomes, and not all are negative for all countries or regions of larger countries. However, the potential for climate change to adversely affect economic growth in the region in a significant way is a very real threat. This is unfortunate, as Latin America is in an asymmetrical position with respect to climate change. The region produces a negligible amount of global pollution, but, as we will see, climate change may have a large effect on the region. The available evidence indicates that the effects of climate change are already observable. Since the mid 1970s, temperatures in the region have risen by about 1 degree Centigrade. Climate projections indicate that temperatures could rise by 1.6 to 4 degrees.[19] Current estimates of the effects of a 1–5 degree Centigrade increase in global temperatures would put 10 million to 180 million people in the region under severe water stress. Many of the glaciers in the Andes would either be reduced or disappear. The threat of drought in some parts of the region could seriously impact the production of electricity. Latin America is unique in that 65 percent of the regions power is hydro. This is in contrast to a global average of 16 percent. Given the already problematic power production in the region, the threat to economic growth is not trivial. At higher temperature levels, 25–40 percent of the tree species in central Brazil and the Amazon basin would die out.[20]

As one can imagine, climate change would have noticeable effects on overall economic activity for a number of sectors and in total. On the assumption of a 2.5 degree increase in temperatures, GDP in the region would fall by 1.5 to 4 percent. The most affected sector would be agriculture. The agriculture sector accounts for about 5 percent of the GDP of the region. Further, it employs 14 percent of the labor force and accounts for 23 percent of exports. Potentially adverse effects in the agricultural sector have the potential to worsen absolute poverty in the region, as incomes in the sector are typically lower than in other parts of the economy. The losses in agriculture are partially driven by higher temperatures reducing water availability. There are potential effects outside agriculture, such as a more limited water supply to urban areas and a reduction in the production of hydroelectric power. As noted above, climate change could produce noticeable reductions in the biodiversity of the region even outside the Amazon basin. Such changes could adversely affect the tourism industry, as rising sea levels would affect not only forests but beaches, reefs, and glaciers that attract both domestic and foreign tourists. While Latin America cannot prevent these changes, it can take steps to mitigate the damage. Estimates by Kober et al. (2016) put the potential costs of these efforts at approximately 0.5 percent of GDP. While this is not an inconsequential sum for a poor region, the benefits to the region of offsetting the costs of lost GDP would seem to indicate that this is an investment in future growth that may be well worth the costs.

Appendix: demand and supply

In this chapter and subsequent chapters we will be using the basic concepts of supply, demand, and elasticity. The purpose of this appendix is to provide a simple a review of these basic concepts. These concepts probably are familiar, but perhaps in need of a review. We start with the concept of a demand curve which is shown in Figure 5.5. The curve slopes downwards and to the right reflecting the inverse relationship between the price and the quantity demanded. If the only thing that changes is the price, then the demand curve does not shift and the price is the only relevant variable. However, the demand curve may shift in response to underlying factors that initially were held constant.

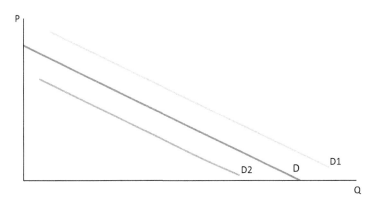

Figure 5.5 Demand curve.

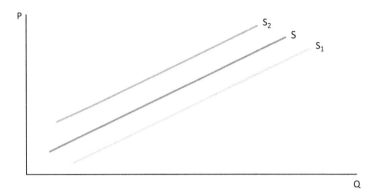

Figure 5.6 Supply curve.

The curve might shift the right or to the left indicating either an increase or decrease in the quantity demanded, respectively. The first factor to be considered that could cause a shift in demand is income. An increase in income could cause a rightward shift of the demand curve. This means that for any given price, the sales of the product would rise. This makes sense as people with more income normally will purchase more. The same would hold true for a decline in income. An example for Latin America would be the export of commodities that are products that the world would like to consume but are not exactly necessities such as wine from Argentina. If the world economy is doing well, this would tend to shift the demand curve for wine to the right. A global recession that occurred in 2007–2008, would have the reverse effect. Both of these shifts are shown in Figure 5.6 as the demand curve increases from D to D_1 or decreases from D to D_2. The second factor that could shift the demand curve is the price of substitutes or complements to the good in question. The price of a substitute for wine, such as beer, can affect the demand for wine. If the price of beer increases relative to the price of wine, then the demand for wine would tend to increase shown by a shift to the left. The logic is symmetric. If the price of beer decreases relative to the price of wine, then the demand for wine would shift to the left as consumers bought more beer and fewer wine. Again these shifts are analogous to the changes in income discussed above. The same sort of logic would apply to goods that are complements for wine, such as cheese. If the price of cheese falls, consumers would purchase more cheese and also more wine. A decrease in the price of cheese would increase the demand for wine. The reverse would be true. If the price of cheese rose then the demand for wine might shift from D to D_2.

A third factor would be changes in consumer tastes and preferences. Wine from Argentina is a good example. Until the late twentieth century, wine from Argentina was not popular outside of Latin America. As consumer awareness of the quality of the product in other parts of the world increased, the demand for wine from Argentina increased substantially. The prices the product now commands in the market reflect this increase in demand. A reverse case is oil exported from Venezuela. Venezuelan oil is considered to be relatively low-quality product because it is more difficult to refine. As a result, the price of Venezuelan oil is typically lower in world markets. Finally, many of the products exported from Latin America are commodities that will be covered in the next chapter. As we will see, commodity prices can be quite volatile. Part of this volatility can be attributed to changes in what buyers expect to happen in the future. The mere expectation that prices will change in the future can influence the demand for the product in the present. One can frequently observe this in practice. The spot price for a commodity is the price one pays today. The future price is what one must pay for delivery of the commodity at some point in the future. It is common for the two prices to differ, sometimes by a substantial amount.

Now that we have reviewed changes in the quantity demanded and changes in demand, we need to move to the supply curve. A supply curve slopes upwards and to the right as shown in Figure 5.6. If the only thing that changes is the price, then this is represented by a movement from one point to another on the supply curve S. Price and the quantity supplied are directly related. At higher prices producers are willing to supply more than at lower prices. To use a personal example, you might be more willing to work more hours for $50 an hour as opposed to $10. However, as was true of the demand curve, the supply curve can shift as well.

The first factor is a change in input prices. Wine is a good example. If the price of grapes fall, then the cost of producing wine would decrease. In Figure 5.7, this would be shown as a rightward shift of the supply curve from S to S_1. At any given price, more wine could be produced with lower-priced grapes. If the price of grapes rises, then the cost of production would rise and the supply curve would shift from S to S_1. Second, the number of producers could change. If the number of producers increases, then so would the supply as exhibited by a shift to the right. Likewise, if the number of producers falls, then the supply curve would shift from S to S_2. The global market for wine over the past several decades is a good example. The number of producers of wine in the world has increased dramatically and the price of inexpensive wine has fallen as a result of the increase in supply. Third, technological change can influence the supply curve. Irrespective of the details of the process, an improvement in technology improves the relationship between inputs and outputs. More output can be produced with the same amount of inputs or the same output can be produced with fewer inputs. Better technology would produce a shift of the supply curve from S to S_1. Because agricultural commodities are important to Latin America, natural events such as changes in the weather or natural disasters such as earthquakes can influence the supply curve. Adverse weather conditions can produce lower crop yields which can decrease the supply just as favorable weather can increase supply. As the prices of commodities are set in world markets, it is not just local conditions that matter. A drought in California could raise the prices of grapes and wine for producers in Latin America. Finally, it is not just the current conditions that matter. Expectations of future conditions can affect the current supply. If producers in Latin America expect adverse supply conditions in other parts of the world, this may induce them to produce more now in expectation of higher prices in the future. Long-run changes may also matter. The anticipated increase in global demand for batteries may well increase the current supply of lithium.

The interaction of demand and supply is shown in Figure 5.7. P_e indicates the equilibrium price that balances the demand and supply of wine. This equilibrium also shows that Q_e balances the quantity demanded with the quantity supplied. Any changes in either curve will change both the equilibrium price and quantity. Rightward or leftward shifts of the demand curve as shown in Figure 5.5 would increase both the equilibrium price and quantity in Figure 5.7. Changes in the supply curve that were shown in Figure 5.6 would likewise change the equilibrium price and quantity. A rightward shift

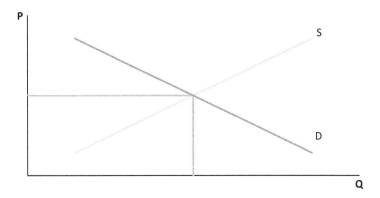

Figure 5.7 Interaction demand and supply.

of the supply curve would lower price and increase quantity. A leftward shift would have opposite effects. Changes in both the supply and demand curves would have a variety of effects. The main point is to shift the curves in the correct direction and determine where the new equilibrium price and quantity would be. Keep in mind that the effects may be uncertain and depend on the magnitude of the shifts. For example, an increase in demand coupled with a decrease in supply would clearly increase the price. However, the effect on quantity is dependent of which of the two shifts is larger. As a result, attempts to memorize outcomes could lead to errors. Carefully drawing a graph for each situation will give one a clearer picture of the particular situation.

For our purposes, the concept of elasticity is important. So far, we have not mentioned that the slopes of the two curves can be distinct. In some cases they can be relatively steep and in others much less so. Economists think about this in terms of the elasticity of the supply and demand curves. More formally, elasticity is the percentage change in the quantity divided by the percentage change in the price. The price elasticity of demand shows how much the quantity demanded changes as a result of a price change. If the number is 2, then quantity demanded is rather sensitive to changes in prices. If the price rose by 10 percent, the quantity demanded would fall by 20 percent. The reverse could be true. If price rose by 10 percent and the quantity demanded fell by 2 percent, then the elasticity of demand is 0.2. In this case the quantity demanded is not very sensitive to changes in price. An elastic of 1 is a cut point. If the value of the elasticity is over one, we refer to this as elastic demand. If the elasticity is less than one it is considered inelastic. The price elasticity of the supply curve is analogous. In this case, changes in the price are inducing a change in the quantity supplied. The quantity supplied could be sensitive to a change in price (elastic) or less sensitive to a change in price (inelastic).

As we will show in Chapter 6, the case of both inelastic demand and inelastic supply are important in the context of Latin America. Such a situation is shown in Figure 5.8. Many of the products exported from Latin America are commodities such as minerals or agricultural products. The demand for commodities tends to be relatively inelastic. For example, if the price of oil changes by 10 percent, the quantity demanded likely will change by less than 10 percent. The same is true for the supply curve. The supply curve for commodities is likely to be inelastic as well. In the short run, it is difficult to change the supply of a mineral product such as oil or an agricultural product such as coffee.

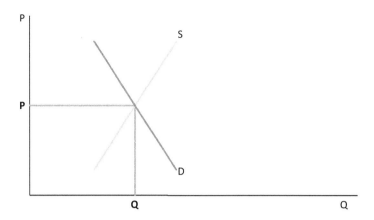

Figure 5.8 Inelastic demand and supply.

A bit of thinking about Figure 5.8 shows a general result. If both the demand curve and the supply curve are steeply sloped (inelastic) then most of the effects of any shifts of the curves are reflected in the price. The effects on quantity are much less pronounced. The result is that the price of commodities tends to be volatile. In some cases the volatility can be extreme. As a thought exercise, consider an increase in demand coupled with a decrease in supply. The main point is that the simple concepts of demand, supply, and elasticity can frequently explain many of the factors that have significant effects on the economies of the region.

Key terms and concepts

command and control (CAC): a policy to control pollution that sets an allowable level of pollution for producers.

cost–benefit analysis: an analysis using all relevant costs and benefits to determine the appropriate level of economic activity.

environmental Kuznets curve: a curve showing the relationship between GDP per capita and the level of pollution.

market failure: a situation where the production or use of a good or service does not occur at the point where the marginal costs equals marginal benefits for society as a whole.

market-based initiatives (MBIs): the use of market signals to influence producer behavior with regard to pollution.

negative externality: a cost to society of producing a product that has not been included in the market price.

North American Free Trade Agreement (NAFTA): an agreement to establish a free-trade area consisting of Canada, Mexico, and the US.

pollution haven: the idea that a country with lower levels of environmental regulations may be able to produce and export pollution-intensive products more cheaply than countries with stricter regulations.

positive externality: a benefit to society of a good or service that is not included in the market price.

tragedy of the commons: a situation in which individuals acting solely in their self-interest may end up depleting a limited natural resource.

Questions for review and discussion

1　What is a negative externality? Describe an obvious example related to the environment in Latin America.
2　Using a supply-and-demand graph, show why gasoline in Latin America might be selling at too low a price if there were no regulations on air pollution by oil refineries.
3　Are natural disasters a significant economic development problem in Latin America?
4　A common policy in Latin America is the sale of diesel fuel at low prices as a subsidy to industry. Discuss the costs and benefits of this policy.
5　Why would a country in Latin America use CAC to control pollution if there are better policies available?
6　Why are MBIs superior to CAC as a means of controlling pollution? Why are pollution permits even better?
7　How could a country in Latin America import pollution control?
8　How are institutions and pollution control related?
9　Describe the problem of water pollution in Latin America.
10　How does urbanization contribute to environmental problems, especially air pollution, in Latin America?
11　Explain the factors that lead to deforestation in Latin America. How does this relate to biodiversity?
12　Is economic growth in Latin America sustainable?
13　Describe the environmental Kuznets curve. How does it potentially apply to Latin America?
14　Because of low levels of environmental regulation, Latin America is likely to become a pollution haven. Is this statement true or false?
15　How could the reduction of trade barriers increase the level of pollution in the world? Has this happened in the case of NAFTA?
16　Describe the potential changes in climate in Latin America in the twenty-first century. How will these affect economic growth?

Notes

1 However, it is not appropriate to try to correct small negative externalities if the cost of dealing with them is larger than the externality.
2 In this section, only the two most common examples of MBIs are presented. However, there is a much larger number of these instruments available. For examples in a Latin American context, see Huber et al. (1998).
3 See Seroa da Matta (2003).
4 This section draws heavily from the outstanding case study by Garcia-Johnson (2000).
5 See Gallagher (2004) for evidence on Mexico.
6 A further mitigation is the privatization of many firms in Latin America over the past three decades. Huber et al. (1998) have found that public-sector firms tend to have less incentive to control pollution than private-sector firms.

7 See Huber et al. (1998).
8 More recent data is unavailable, as it is no longer published by the World Bank.
9 For example, see Foster et al. (2009).
10 The discussion deliberately ignores the negative externality of degradation of the land that may occur because of deforestation. This externality exists, but it is harder to quantify and does not occur in all cases.
11 Even this figure is uncertain, as many private titles to land may not be legally valid.
12 For an interesting case study of Colombia see Canavire-Bacarreza et al. (2018).
13 This section draws heavily on Gallagher (2004).
14 Because the literature on these issues for Latin America is quite limited, the best overall reference in this area is Copeland and Taylor (2003).
15 The correlation between increasing openness (more trade) and economic growth is not something about which there is much doubt. See Edwards (1993) on this point.
16 This highly simplified explanation of trade will be covered in more detail in Chapters 6 and 7.
17 For an early empirical test, see Birdsall and Wheeler (1993). Most subsequent research simply confirms their findings.
18 For a thorough discussion of these issues, see Copeland and Taylor (2003).
19 For more detail, see Economic Commission for Latin America and the Caribbean (2014).
20 For more detail, see World Bank (2010).

References

Birdsall, Nancy and David Wheeler (1993) "Trade Policy and Industrial Pollution in Latin America: Where Are the Pollution Havens?" *Journal of Environment and Development*, 2 (Winter): 137–149.

Canavire-Bacarreza, Gustavo, Julian E. Diaz-Guiterrez, and Mark Hanauer (2018) "Unintended Consequences of Conservation: Estimating the Impact of Protected Areas on Violence in Colombia," *Journal of Environmental Economics and Management*, 89 (January): 46–70.

Copeland, Brian R. and M. Scott Taylor (2003) *Trade and the Environment: Theory and Empirical Evidence*, Princeton, NJ: Princeton University Press.

Economic Commission for Latin America and the Caribbean (2014) *The Economics of Climate Change in Latin America and the Caribbean: Paradoxes and Challenges*, Santiago: Economic Commission for Latin America and the Caribbean.

Edwards, Sebastian (1993) "Openness, Trade Liberalization, and Growth," *Journal of Economic Literature*, 31 (September): 1358–1393.

Flores, Marlon (2010) "Protected Areas," in A. Bovarnick, F. Alpizarw, and C. Schnell (eds.), *The Importance of Biodiversity Ecosystems in Economic Growth and Equity in Latin America and the Caribbean: An Economic Evaluation of Ecosystem*, New York: United Nations Development Program, pp. 203–237.

Food and Agriculture Organization of the United Nations (2018) *The State of the World's Forests 2018*, Rome: Food and Agriculture Organization of the United Nations.

Foster, Andrew, Emilio Gutierrez, and Naresh Kumar (2009) "Voluntary Compliance, Pollution Levels, and Infant Mortality in Mexico," *American Economic Review*, 99 (May): 191–197.

Gallagher, Kevin (2004) *Free Trade and the Environment: Mexico, NAFTA, and Beyond*, Palo Alto, CA: Stanford University Press.

Garcia-Johnson, Ronie (2000) *Exporting Environmentalism: US Multinational Chemical Corporations in Brazil and Mexico*, Cambridge, Mass.: MIT Press.

Grossman, Gene M. and Alan B. Krueger (1993) "Environmental Impacts of a North American Free Trade Agreement," in Peter M. Garber (ed.), *The Mexico–US Free Trade Agreement*, Cambridge, Mass.: MIT Press, pp. 13–56.

Guha-Sapir, D., D. Hargitt, and P. Hoyois (2004) *Thirty Years of Natural Disasters 1974–2003: The Numbers*, Louvain: Presses Universitaires de Louvain.

Huber, Richard M., Jack Ruitenbeek, and Ronaldo Seroa da Motta (1998) *Market-Based Instruments for Environmental Policymaking in Latin America and the Caribbean: Lessons from Eleven Countries*, World Bank Discussion Paper No. 381, Washington, DC: World Bank.

Jenkins, Rhys (2003) "Has Trade Liberalization Created Pollution Havens in Latin America?" *CEPAL Review*, 80 (August): 81–95.

Kober, Tom, Philip Summerton, Hector Pollitt, Unnnada Chewpreecha, Xiaolin Ren, William Wills, Claudia Octaviano, James McFarland, Robert Beach, Yongxia Cai, Silvia Calderón, Karen Fisher-Vanden, and Ana Maria Loboguerrero Rodriguez (2016) "Macroeconomic Impacts of Climate Change Mitigation in Latin America: A Cross-Model Comparison." *Energy Economics*, 56 (May): 625–636.

Seroa da Matta, Ronaldo (2003) *Determinants of Environmental Performance in the Brazilian Industrial Sector*, Rio de Janeiro: Research Institute of Applied Economics.

Wikipedia (2019) List of countries by vehicles per capita. http://en.wikipedia.org/wiki/List_of_countries_by_vehicles_per_capita.

World Bank (2006) *World Development Indicators*, Washington, DC: World Bank.

World Bank (2010) *The Costs to Developing Countries of Adapting to Climate Change: New Methods and Estimates*, Washington, DC: World Bank.

World Bank (2011) *World Development Report*, Washington, DC: World Bank.

World Bank (2012) *Biodiversity: Finding the Funds to Keep Latin America Green*, Washington, DC: World Bank.

World Resources Institute (2008) *World Resources Report, 2008: Roots of Resilience—Growing the Wealth of the Poor*, Washington, DC: World Resources Institute.

Recommended reading

Blanco, Luisa, Fidel Gonzalez, and Isabel Ruiz (2013) "The Impact of Sector Specific FDI on CO_2 Emissions in Latin America," *Oxford Development Studies*, 41 (1): 104–121.

De Miguel, Carlos J. and Osvaldo Sunkel (2011) "Environmental Sustainability," in José A. Ocampo and Jaime Ros (eds.), *The Oxford Handbook of Latin American Economics*, Oxford: Oxford University Press, pp. 130–158.

de la Torre, Augusto, Pablo Fajnzylber, and John Nash (2009) *Low Carbon, High Growth: Latin American Responses to Climate Change*, Washington, DC: World Bank.

The Economist (2009) "The Future of the Forest," June 13. Available at http://www.economist.com/node/13824446 (accessed August 23, 2019).

The Economist (2011) "Black Sand in the Desert," September 3. Available at http://www.economist.com/node/21528288 (accessed August 23, 2019).

Gamper-Rabindran, Shanti (2006) "NAFTA and the Environment: What Can the Data Tell Us?" *Economic Development and Cultural Change*, 54 (April): 605–633.

Lora, Eduardo, Andrew Powell, Bernard M. S. van Praag, and Pablo Sanguinetti (eds.) (2010) *The Quality of Life in Latin American Cities: Markets and Perception*, Washington, DC: Inter-American Development Bank and World Bank.

Miller, Shawn William (2007) *An Environmental History of Latin America*, Cambridge: Cambridge University Press.

Munasinghe, Mohan, Raúl O'Ryan, Ronaldo Seroa da Motta, Carlos de Miguel, Carlos Young, Sebastian Miller, and Claudio Ferraz (2006) *Macroeconomic Policies for Sustainable Growth: Analytical Framework and Policy Studies of Brazil and Chile*, Northampton, Mass.: Edward Elgar.

Romero, Aldemaro and Sarah E. West (eds.) (2005) *Environmental Issues in Latin America and the Caribbean*, Dordrecht: Springer.

6 Latin America and primary commodities

Introduction

In the previous chapters, we touched on the importance of the production and export of commodities in Latin America. The first purpose of this chapter is to explain in more detail why commodities have been an important factor in the economic development of the region. Second, commodities are going to be an important part of the future of the region, so an understanding of this part of the economy is important for an overall understanding of the history of the region and its future. In some regards, commodities are just another product to be analyzed using the familiar tools of supply and demand. However, commodities have their own peculiarities. Supply and demand still works, just somewhat differently in commodities markets. Third, if commodities are a significant percentage of total exports and GDP, then changes in commodities markets can have ramifications for the entire economy. Since this is true for many of the economies of the region, we will introduce some of these issues.[1] Further, countries have policy choices concerning economic development. For a country that possesses commodities, there may be noticeable differences in economic development policy. Finally, commodities potentially can distort the entire structure of an economy. This can happen even in a high-income country. For the middle-income countries of Latin America, commodities can be like dynamite: useful if handled with care but potentially dangerous. The brief history of commodities in Latin America in the next section begins to illustrate both the costs and the benefits of commodities for a country or region.

Commodities in Latin America: a brief history

> We are poor, living in the midst of our riches.
>
> (Juan Miguel Castro)

In previous chapters, we have touched on the importance of commodities in Latin American economic history. Commodities have not only been important in the past, they continue to be an important part of the economic landscape of the region. The purpose of this section is to briefly review this importance and finish with the current data on commodities in the region. To begin with, it is necessary to recognize two important characteristics of commodities. First, the production of commodities has a tendency to follow a boom-and-bust cycle. Commodity booms tend to have two sources. On the one hand, it is sometimes the case that a boom in a commodity follows its discovery and subsequent widespread use. Latin American examples of this would be coffee and tobacco. In another case, the boom may be caused by the discovery not of the product itself but of a new source of supply. Newly discovered supplies of gold and silver in Latin America would be examples. As we will see in the next section, these booms usually contain the seeds of their own destruction. If commodities are important in a country or a region, this can make either economic development or economic management in the shorter run more difficult. This has been a significant economic problem in the region from the beginning. A somewhat less problematic, but still important, problem with commodities is price volatility. Everyone is familiar with the gyrations in price in the world oil market over the past few decades. Oil is not a special case. In commodity markets, this price volatility is *normal*. If this seems a bit puzzling, the reasons behind this volatility are covered in the next section. At this point, one needs to understand that volatile commodity prices should be considered an economic fact of life. It's been this way for hundreds of years. Like commodity booms and busts, commodity price volatility makes economic management in many countries more difficult. Not only is the price of oil volatile, but prices of other commodities produced and exported in the region are also volatile. Other than oil, some other important commodities are copper, soybeans, bananas, wheat, meat, hides, mutton, wool, coffee, sugar, and tobacco.

The history of commodity booms and busts is shown in Table 6.1. As everyone knows, the early booms in the region were fueled by gold and silver. The data presents a story that is somewhat less obvious. The major supplies of gold were quickly exhausted. Silver soon replaced gold as the primary source of commodity income for the region and had a considerably longer production run. Two other booms started in the mid sixteenth century. Cochineal was a red dye, superior to what was available in Europe, and was wildly popular. Indigo had been used since antiquity, but Latin America provided a larger and cheaper source of supply.

Tobacco, coffee, and sugar were soon in great demand in Europe. The first two were "new" products that were soon very popular consumer items. Of course, sugar was an old product. However, increasing supplies from the Western Hemisphere drove

Table 6.1 Commodity booms in Latin America

Commodity	Years	Countries
Gold	1492–1550	Mexico, Peru
Silver	1550–1650	Mexico, Peru
Cochineal	1550–1850	Mexico, Guatemala
Indigo	1560–1880	Brazil, Guatemala, Honduras
Tobacco	1600–1700	Cuba, Brazil
Sugar	1625–1750	Brazil
Gold	1700–1760	Brazil
Coffee	1720–1850	Brazil, Colombia
Diamonds	1725–1860	Brazil[a]
Guano	1840–1880	Bolivia, Chile, Peru
Henequen	1860–1910	Mexico
Rubber	1879–1912	Brazil
Oil	1910–1920	Mexico
Oil	1973–1982	Ecuador, Mexico, Venezuela

Note: (a) A smaller boom occurred in the late nineteenth century with the discovery of secondary deposits in Venezuela.

down the price. This decrease in price now allowed average consumers in Europe to purchase increasing amounts of sugar. The sugar-laden products that are now commonplace were new products in the eighteenth century, made possible by cheap imported sugar. Note from Table 6.1 that Brazil was a relatively late participant in the commodity booms. Large-scale production of sugar did not begin until the seventeenth century, and the gold and diamond booms occurred about 100 years later. The nineteenth century saw smaller booms in guano, henequen, and rubber. All of these booms succumbed to the exhaustion of the resource (guano) or changes in technology (henequen and rubber). Like the global oil industry, the industry in Latin America was fueled by high prices for oil caused by World War I.[2] The end of this boom was followed by relatively low oil prices that persisted for over half a century. Historically, high oil prices are a relatively recent phenomenon. Since commodity booms have been a staple of the economy of Latin America for hundreds of years, it is unlikely that the phenomenon will ever completely disappear. Busts are sometimes caused by falling global demand for a product that reemerges at a later date. The possibility of new booms cannot be discounted. An increase in the global demand for batteries is starting yet another commodity boom in western South America. Guano is economic history, but lithium is beginning a boom. An old story is repeating itself in the same part of the region.

Along with the booms and busts in commodity markets, there is the more usual issue of price volatility. Commodity prices are naturally more unstable than most prices because of the demand and supply conditions in these markets. For example, consider a product such as coffee. Coffee is a popular product, but it is in fact just another mundane agricultural crop. However, the price of coffee is subject to large fluctuations. If the problem were just coffee, then it would be a problem for Brazil and Colombia, but not for the rest of the region. The difficulty is that this sort of thing affects *all* commodities. Commodity prices as a whole are subject to large fluctuations. Since Latin America exports many commodities, price volatility influences the regional economy. Table 6.2 shows the movements of an index of many commodity prices from 2006 to 2013. For commodities overall, the price fluctuations can be extreme. This is particularly true for oil, as shown in the last row. Most of us know about oil price fluctuations, but these are not an isolated case. Many other commodities exhibit price fluctuations that are just as extreme. The overall message being conveyed from the data is that the prices of individual commodities can fluctuate substantially. As we will see in more detail,

Table 6.2 World commodity prices, 2006–2013 (percentage change over previous year)

	2006	2007	2008	2009	2006	2007	2008	2009	2010	2011	2012	2013
All commodities	31.5	37.0	-2.0	-23.5	31.5	37.0	-2.0	-23.5	36.2	25.5	-13.9	-5.1
Food and tropical beverages	22.8	27.8	17.2	-5.9	22.8	27.8	17.2	-5.9	21.7	30.4	-1.9	-1.3
Vegetable oilseeds and oils	-2.7	50.0	41.4	-39.1	-2.7	50.0	41.4	-39.1	31.6	35.5	-11.2	-16.7
Agricultural raw materials	9.6	22.2	4.5	-17.6	9.6	22.2	4.5	-17.6	20.3	37.3	-10.7	-7.1
Minerals, ores, and metals	49.7	43.4	-10.2	-26.3	49.7	43.4	-10.2	-26.3	46.8	19.1	-17.7	-3.4
Crude petroleum	21.7	11.1	35.9	-35.7	21.7	11.1	35.9	-35.7	27.7	35.5	1.6	-2.3

Source: United Nations Conference on Trade and Development (2015).

the possession of commodities is a mixed blessing. The products contribute to the real GDP and exports of a country. However, they can be risky in terms of their contribution to the economy.

The microeconomics of commodities

In the previous section, it was shown that the production of commodities is subject to booms and busts. Even in the absence of these extremes, commodity prices are normally quite volatile. In this section, we will review the simple microeconomics of commodity markets. While the gyrations of these markets are a puzzle to most people, the reasons behind this volatility are not difficult to explain. As with most products, the prices of commodities and the amounts produced and consumed are determined by supply and demand. A simple supply-and-demand model of a representative commodity is shown in Figure 6.1. To start with, note that the demand curve has a negative slope. This indicates the usual inverse relationship between the price and the quantity demanded. If the only thing that changes is the price of the product, then there is a movement from one point to another along the same demand curve. If anything changes other than the price, then there is a shift of the entire demand curve. Such a shift is referred to as a change in demand. An increase in demand is shown by a rightward shift in the demand curve, and a decrease in demand is shown by a leftward shift. Such changes could be caused by a change in the population or a change in income. Notice that in Figure 6.1, the demand curve has been drawn with a very steep slope. This was not accidental. It shows that the demand for this product is *inelastic*. In the context of a demand curve, this means that changes in price do not have a very large impact on the quantity demanded. Oil is a classic example of this effect. An increase in the price of oil reduces the quantity demanded, just not by a large amount. Inelastic demand curves are common for commodities. They will also help to explain why commodity prices are so volatile.

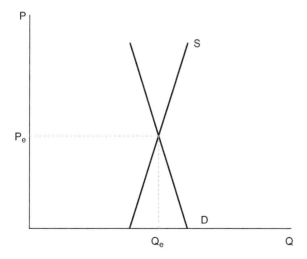

Figure 6.1 Equilibrium price and output for a commodity.

Box 6.1 Cochineal

In Table 6.1, one can be excused for wondering what cochineal is. It is now an uncommon word, but it was once an important commodity in the world economy. Cochineal or carmine dye produces a red color. It was first cultivated by the Mayas, and later the Aztecs, in Mexico and Central America. Upon their arrival, the Spanish were immediately struck by the richness of the red color the dye produces, which was far superior to anything available in Europe. The dye is derived from an insect that is a parasite of the cactus plant. A chemical produced by the insect to protect it from predators is the source of the dye. As one can imagine, the production of the dye is very labor-intensive. The dye was so popular that production in the Oaxaca province of Mexico grew rapidly. After silver, cochineal was Mexico's second largest export in the colonial period. Prices of cochineal were regularly quoted on the Amsterdam and London commodity exchanges.

Mexico's war of independence in the early nineteenth century disrupted the production of the product. Commercial production of cochineal then began in Guatemala. Unfortunately, in the mid nineteenth century, artificial red dyes were developed in Europe. By the end of the century, cheaper dyes spelled the end of the industry in Latin America. Production of cochineal survived only as a small cottage industry. The story does not end there. In the late twentieth century, it was determined that artificial red dyes may be carcinogenic. As with many other products, the "natural" alternative is regaining popularity. The production of cochineal is now commercially viable again.

The supply curve for a commodity is also shown in Figure 6.1. Analogous to the demand curve, a change in the price is represented by a movement along the supply curve. This is referred to as a change in the quantity supplied. If the only change that occurs is a change in price, then there is a movement from one point to another along the same supply curve. A change in supply occurs when something other than the price changes. An increase in supply would be shown by a shift of the supply curve to the right, and a decrease in supply by a shift of the curve to the left. Changes in supply can occur for reasons such as a change in the number of producers or a change in the costs of inputs into the production process. As with the demand curve, the supply curves for many commodities are relatively inelastic. Changes in price do not have a very large impact on the quantity supplied. For agricultural commodities, there may be only one growing season per year. A change in price after the crop has been planted may have only a minimal impact on the quantity supplied. For minerals such as oil or gold, it may be possible to increase the quantity supplied in the short run by a small amount. Larger increases in supply may take years, as new supplies have to be developed, with heavy capital investment.[3] The intersection of the demand and supply curves in Figure 6.1 determines the equilibrium price and quantity in this market. If there are no changes in either curve, then the price will be P_e and the equilibrium quantity Q_e.

Commodity booms and busts

In commodity markets, both P_e and Q_e are subject to large fluctuations. We are now in a position to show in more detail why this is true. The demand for commodities can shift

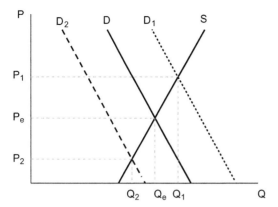

Figure 6.2 Equilibrium price and output with changes in demand.

substantially to the left or the right. This is shown in Figure 6.2. The discovery of new products in Latin America in the sixteenth century, such as coffee, tobacco, or cochineal, can lead to an enormous increase in demand. In the figure, this is shown as a shift of the demand curve from D to D_1. Because the supply curve is inelastic, any increase in demand translates primarily into an increase in price. The price moves from P_e to P_1. The increase in the quantity supplied is much smaller. This movement is only from Q_e to Q_1. Thus, it is rather easy to set off a commodity boom. Given market conditions, increases in the demand for a commodity can cause large changes in the price. A commodity bust is also easy to imagine. Cochineal is a good example. The appearance of a good substitute for the product caused a large decrease in the demand. In the figure, this is shown as a movement of the demand curve from D to D_2. A large drop in the demand causes the equilibrium price and quantity to fall to P_2 and Q_2, respectively. In this case, a large drop in the demand can cause a collapse in the price of the commodity. Cochineal is not an isolated example. Many of the booms presented in Table 6.1 ended in the same way. Particular cases include indigo, henequen, and rubber. The effects on countries or regions of countries can be devastating. Latin America is dotted with once prosperous areas that subsequently fell back into relative poverty after the end of a commodity boom.[4]

Like the demand curve, changes in the supply curve can cause a commodity boom. The demand for some commodities, such as gold, silver, or diamonds, is so high that even a relatively large increase in supply may not lower prices by a substantial amount. This situation is shown in Figure 6.3. In this figure, the initial demand and supply curves are D and S, respectively. The original equilibrium yields a price P_e and a quantity Q_e. Notice that the initial price of gold is rather high, because the demand is very large relative to the supply. The discovery of gold and silver in Latin America in the sixteenth century can be shown as an increase in the supply curve. This is represented by a shift of the supply curve from S to S_1. The new equilibrium price is lower at P_1. However, the lower price is not all that much lower. The world demand for gold is so great that the decrease in price is not that large.[5] An increase in the supply of a valuable commodity has caused a boom. However, if the resource is exhaustible, the boom can quickly turn into a bust. This has happened in Latin America. The large supply of gold

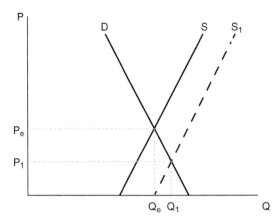

Figure 6.3 Equilibrium price and output with changes in supply.

was exhausted by the mid sixteenth century. The production of silver began declining 100 years later. The story for diamonds in Brazil and Venezuela and guano in Bolivia, Chile, and Peru was essentially the same. In this case, the supply curve might shift back to S. In such a case, a "new" equilibrium might occur at P_e and Q_e.

A commodity bust can happen even if the resource is not exhaustible like guano. The sugar boom in the seventeenth and eighteenth centuries is a good historical example. Increasing supplies of sugar, coupled with rising incomes in Europe, created a combination of both rising prices and output of sugar. However, unlike gold, the production of sugar could be expanded to new regions, such as the Caribbean. Eventually, the demand for sugar ceased to rise as rapidly as the supply of sugar was increasing. This creates a situation much like that shown in Figure 6.3. Increases in the supply of the commodity begin to drive down prices. If this persists for some time, the once expensive commodity can become quite cheap. With the use of supply-and-demand graphs, commodity booms and busts become more understandable. Changes in demand can cause both a commodity boom and also a subsequent bust if demand falls or simply does not grow at such a fast rate. Likewise, the exhaustion of a natural resource can cause a commodity bust as production falls. The reverse case can occur if production of a high-priced commodity can be extended to new areas, and supply increases. One can take almost any of the cases in Table 6.1 and graph the trajectory of the boom and bust based on supply and demand conditions.

Box 6.2 The commodity supercycle

The term "commodity supercycle" refers to the tendency for the prices of commodities in general to increase for a period of years followed by a decrease. The basic idea has a long history in economics but has only recently been quantified. Erten and Ocampo (2017) have studied commodity prices in general for the period 1865–2009. During this long period, they have identified several periods when nonoil commodity prices tended to have a distinct trend. Prices rose strongly from the 1890s and peaked during World War I. Prices then fell and bottomed in the Great Depression. Prices began to increase again in the 1930s, peaked in the 1950s, and faded away during the 1960s. Prices rose sharply in the 1970s and then began falling until the early 1990s. Since 2000, prices have risen strongly. The evidence is one of periods that last thirty to forty years. In each period, prices are 20 to 40 percent higher or lower than normal. Except for oil, these price cycles seem to be related to global economic growth. This means that commodity prices appear to be most heavily influenced by demand factors. The recent surge in commodity prices is usually related to increases in demand from large countries such as China or India. The point is that the concept of a commodity supercycle is not just a concept but a real phenomenon that can be seen in a long time series. Unfortunately, being able to identify turning points when they actually occur is much more difficult.

The application of this concept to Latin America is apparent. Part of the Golden Age in the region was also a period of high commodity prices. The distress of the Great Depression was transmitted to the region partially through low commodity prices. The past two decades have seen relatively strong growth in Latin America, partially due to high global commodity prices. The more recent concern is whether or not the period of high prices is coming to an end. Forecasts of commodity prices over the next five years are for prices that will be stable to somewhat lower. Recent research has yielded models of economic growth that allow one to translate changes in commodity prices into potential changes in economic growth. Using such models, Gruss (2014) finds that stable commodity prices over the remainder of this decade would mean that growth in the region would fall by at least 1 percent. If prices were to trend lower, the effects would be more negative. While this is just a forecasting exercise, it still shows how dependent economic growth in the region is on global commodity prices. These prices are an exogenous factor that has a troubling impact on growth. As a result, the possibility of a turn in the commodity price cycle becomes a major factor in determining the growth of the region in the short to medium run.

Price volatility

For many commodities, there may not be spectacular booms and busts. In some cases, an initial boom followed by a bust is then followed by market conditions that are typical for commodities: price volatility. This is exactly what is illustrated in Table 6.2. Commodity prices in the world economy are naturally volatile. Fortunately, we can adapt Figure 6.1 to show why this is true. We start with the effects of fluctuations in demand. These are shown in Figure 6.2. Because the supply of commodities is typically inelastic, small changes in demand can have noticeable impacts on prices. An increase or decrease in demand from D to D_1 or from D to D_2 can have a large impact on the price. A difference between P_e and P_1 or P_2 could easily be 10 percent. This means that the difference between the highest and lowest prices for this commodity could be 20 percent in total. All the determinants of the demand for a product could easily produce these sorts of fluctuations in price. In world commodity markets, an important determinant of world prices is the growth of the world economy. Commodity prices tend to be high when the world economy is growing rapidly, and the demand for commodities is like D_1. A global slowdown tends to produce a demand for commodities more like D_2. Countries that produce and export commodities may well benefit greatly from a global boom but suffer disproportionately from a global downturn. Recall the Golden Age in Latin American economic history. It is not accidental that this period coincided with a global boom. Less favorably, the recent global economic downturn has seriously depressed the prices of some Latin American commodities, such as copper. Notice also that changes in demand for commodities are normally exogenous. This means that demand is primarily determined outside the country or the region. Thus, the prices Latin America receives for its commodities are determined by global supply and demand. The prices the region receives then become something like the weather: sometimes good and sometimes bad. As we will see, this compounds the problem of economic management for a country or a region. Fluctuations in world demand are particularly noticeable for commodities used in manufacturing. For Latin America, the most important of these products are oil, copper, and nickel.[6]

The supply of commodities can also shift, as shown in Figure 6.3. An increase in supply is shown by a rightward shift of the supply curve from S to S_1. This has a large effect on the equilibrium price, lowering it from P_e to P_1. The opposite effect occurs if the supply curve decreases from S_1 to S. Prices rise substantially from P_1 to P_e. In both cases, the movements in price are large because the demand curve is inelastic. In commodity markets, changes in supply are easy to imagine. For agricultural products, there are years of reduced production or crop failures due to weather. In other years, more favorable conditions produce a larger supply than is normal. Latin America is no different in this regard. Weather reports from Brazil are closely watched by soybean traders. Coffee traders watch crop conditions in Brazil, Colombia, and Central America. Chilean weather affects what Americans pay for certain fruits and vegetables. Inelastic demand for soybeans, coffee, and vegetables leads to the sometimes large fluctuations in the prices of these products. The supply curve for nonagricultural commodities can also change. The rate at which minerals can be extracted in the world economy can fluctuate. The rate at which new supplies of commodities are depleted in one area is not always perfectly matched by new finds elsewhere. This can lead to temporary reductions in supply and higher prices. At other points in time, the reverse can occur.

New supplies may come on to the market at a faster rate. The fluctuations in supply may not be as large from year to year as is sometimes true in agricultural markets, but they are still there. Extremely large fluctuations in prices occur under the right set of circumstances. Figure 6.4 is a simple illustration of what can occur in commodity markets. In this figure, there are two demand curves: D_l and D_h. They represent relatively low demand for a commodity and a correspondingly high demand, respectively. There are two analogous supply curves, labeled S_l and S_h. For convenience, the two most extreme price solutions are labeled P_l and P_h. A combination of relatively high demand and a low supply leads to a relatively high price, P_h. On the other hand, low demand coupled with high supply leads to a relatively low price, P_l. Notice that the difference between P_h and P_l is extremely large. These effects are what led to the large values observed in Table 6.1. It is also not difficult to see the cause of more minor volatility. As noted above, the demand for commodities in general is related to the state of the world economy. Global growth changes from year to year. As a result, the demand for commodities fluctuates somewhat each year. Also, the supply of agricultural commodities

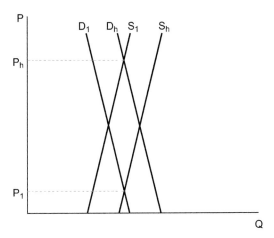

Figure 6.4 Changes in supply and demand in commodity markets.

can literally fluctuate with the weather. The supply of nonagricultural commodities can also fluctuate from year to year, as new discoveries of supplies often don't perfectly match use of the resources. As we will see in the next section, this price instability of commodities has macroeconomic implications for many of the countries of the region.

Box 6.3 Quinoa: a boom and bust example

A fascinating commodity story, by the standards of economists, in the twenty-first century is quinoa. Quinoa is a food product that has long been a staple of life in the Andes. While food fads come and go, quinoa is arguably one of the most complete foods produced anywhere in the world. In the local environment of Bolivia and Peru, it was usually thought of as a food consumed primarily by poor people. Early in this century, quinoa was "discovered" by health-conscious consumers in North America, Europe, and Asia. The result was literally an explosion in the demand for quinoa. A quick look at Figure 5.2 shows this situation. However, the graph does not do justice to what happened. Between 2005 and 2013, the price of quinoa increased by *600 percent*. The price of a pound of quinoa increased from 25 cents to $4. The next part of the story is predictable. Traditionally, the production of quinoa was concentrated in the Andean highlands on marginal land where crop yields were low. The higher prices induced production in areas of Peru where yields were far higher. In addition, the new producers had access to more capital and better agricultural technology. In just two years, 2013 and 2014, Peruvian production more than doubled. Commercial production also began in a number of other countries as diverse as China, India, and Italy. Quinoa may well end up following the trajectory of potatoes. Potatoes were once a purely Andean crop that become a global staple food.

Associated with the boom and bust of quinoa, was the effect on the original farmers of the crop. As the price increased rapidly, income for these farmers increased as well. The hope was that quinoa might lead to a sustainable increase in income in some of the poorest areas of Latin America. Unfortunately, the rapid increases in supply and the subsequent crash in prices cut off that path to development. One has to be careful in concluding that the boom and bust left farmers permanently worse off. Fortunately, quinoa was never a food staple in the sense of a commodity like rice in Asia. It has always been a supplemental food and the rise in price had a minimal impact on food budgets in the region. Second, the current price of quinoa is about $1 per pound. While the income from the production of quinoa is down dramatically from the peak, it is still much higher than before the boom began.

The macroeconomics of commodities

The periodic booms and busts in commodities and the perpetual price instability are more than a nuisance to producers and consumers. In the case of Latin America, commodities are sufficiently important that changes in commodity prices can affect the entire economy. To see why this is true, we need to review the concept of real GDP that we introduced in Chapter 1. Specifically, we need to consider the components of GDP. These are given in Equation 6.1.

$$Y = C + I + G + (X - M) \qquad (6.1)$$

where:

Y = real GDP
C = consumption by the public
I = residential and nonresidential investment
G = government spending on goods and services
X = exports of goods and services
M = imports of goods and services

From Equation 6.1, the effect of exporting a new commodity or changes in the price of exported commodities becomes clear. If commodity exports are a high percentage of total exports, then changes in commodity prices can significantly affect the total value of exports. In turn, this would change the trade balance $(X - M)$. Now, if exports are a high percentage of GDP, logic would lead one to the conclusion that changes in commodity prices can affect the entire economy. A boom in commodity prices could either lead to a trade surplus or reduce the size of the trade deficit. Everything else being equal, this would tend to increase real GDP. The reverse would also be true. A large decline in commodity prices would either reduce the trade surplus or make it negative. This could have the effect of reducing real GDP. The link from commodity prices to the entire economy is relatively simple. A boom in commodity prices can cause rapid growth in GDP, and falling commodity prices may constitute a drag on the entire economy.[7]

The critical part of the analysis is the percentage of exports that are commodities and the ratio of exports to GDP. In the case of Latin America, these numbers are rather high. The data is given in Table 6.3. Commodity exports make up 61.3 percent of total exports. In virtually any year, commodity exports comprise the majority of the total

Table 6.3 Commodities' share of exports and GDP in Latin America (2017) (millions of current dollars)

	Commodity exports	*Exports (merchandise)*	*Commodity/ exports*	*Commodity exports/ GDP*
Argentina	39,072	58,622	66.7	6.1
Bolivia	6,423	7,846	81.9	17.1
Brazil	134,706	217,826	61.8	6.6
Chile	59,621	69,230	86.1	21.5
Colombia	28,168	37,881	74.3	9.0
Costa Rica	4,298	9,556	45.0	7.5
Ecuador	17,772	19,122	92.9	17.0
El Salvador	1,374	5,760	23.9	5.5
Guatemala	6,358	11,001	57.8	8.4
Honduras	3,351	8,675	38.6	14.6
Mexico	67,085	409,401	16.4	5.8
Nicaragua	2,493	5,170	48.2	18.0
Panama	1,050	11,093	9.5	1.7
Paraguay	7,702	8,680	88.7	19.4
Peru	33,007	45,275	72.9	15.6
Uruguay	6,305	7,888	79.9	11.2
Venezuela, RB	72,277	74,714	96.7	15.0
Latin America			61.3	11.8

Source: World Trade Organization (2019).

Notes: Venezuela data 2014.

exports of the region. Now we can take the logic one step further. The final column in the table shows commodity exports as a percentage of GDP. For the countries of Latin America, this averages 12 percent. In other words, over 10 percent of the overall GDP of the region is accounted for by commodity exports. This information can be related to the data in Table 6.2. Commodity prices are very volatile. This price volatility naturally translates into volatility in overall exports. Since these exports represent a relatively high percentage of GDP, the rate of growth of real GDP in many of the countries of the region can be substantially impacted by changes in commodity prices. This is an important point that we will return to again in Chapter 12. For now, one can see that commodity price volatility makes the management of GDP in Latin America more difficult than it would be if commodities were not such an important part of total exports and GDP.

Commodities and economic development

> The gratification of wealth is not found in mere possession or in lavish expenditure, but in its wise application.
>
> (Miguel de Cervantes)

The endowment of commodities is not evenly distributed around the world. Some countries have mineral resources, and others do not. Some countries are able to produce certain agricultural commodities, and others cannot. Latin America is a perfect case in point. Few of the world's regions are so richly endowed with *both* types of commodities.

Commodities can be used as the basis for a more comprehensive development strategy. If managed wisely, commodities can be used to enhance the economic development of a country. If not, then the possession of commodities can be detrimental to economic development.

First, the production and export of commodities can be quite profitable. If the product is cheap to extract or easy to cultivate, production costs may be lower than the world market price. As a result, commodities can be a major source of tax revenue. In these cases, the government may be able to use this tax revenue to enhance economic development. Countries tend to move in stages from a dependence on agricultural production to a stage where manufacturing becomes more important. However, the development of manufacturing may require a substantial investment in the country's infrastructure. Revenues from the production of commodities may allow the country to finance this more easily than a country without such resources. The result is that the country may be able to grow faster. Second, the development of infrastructure may require imports, such as capital equipment, from developed countries. In turn, these imports will require foreign exchange. The export of a commodity can allow the country to more easily afford these types of imports. This should be a familiar story from the Golden Age of Latin American economic history. Third, a country with commodities may find it easier to transition into manufacturing than a country without such resources. Many commodities are the start of the process of producing a final good. For example, sugar can be refined into a product that is sold to consumers essentially as is. It can also be used to produce more sophisticated products such as candy or rum. The obvious first step in this process for a country with commodities is to add value to the primary product. As a result, countries with commodities may be able to make the transition to manufacturing more easily than countries without commodities.

In practice, the scenario outlined above has been fraught with difficulties. In fact, these difficulties are so common in Latin America and elsewhere that they are sometimes referred to as the *resource curse*. Since Latin America is a large and heterogeneous region, not all of these problems apply to all countries. However, elements of the resource curse are, to a greater or lesser extent, part of the economic story of Latin America.[8] For example, the initial colonization of the region shows the resource curse in an extreme form. The initial motivating factor for Spanish settlement of the region was the extraction of gold and silver for shipment back to Spain. Very little of this wealth was used for economic development. The indigenous population was decimated by European diseases, and much of the labor force worked in mining and other activities in less than free-market labor conditions. It is difficult to imagine that the possession of gold and silver was producing positive economic results for the region.

In the post-independence era, the possession of commodities has still been problematical for the region. Since the production of commodities can be quite profitable, the division of these profits between the private and public sectors can be troublesome. Understandably, private-sector producers of commodities wish to hold on to their earnings. Governments, on the other hand, may see taxing commodities as a relatively easy way to raise revenue in a poor country. Under ideal circumstances, the government would find an optimal tax rate that maximizes revenue without discouraging production. This revenue would then be funneled into spending on infrastructure, education, and so on, which would promote faster economic growth. However, even under the best of circumstances, using commodities to finance development can create tension between producers and the government.[9] Sadly, the production of commodities can also lead to corruption. Producers of commodities are vulnerable to the ability of the government to take part of the profits earned. Once the money has left the private sector, there is no guarantee that it will be wisely used. Aside from outright corruption, the problems may be more subtle. Revenues from commodities may be used to purchase support from the population that otherwise might not exist. Government employment may rise faster than would be the case if such revenues were not available. In short, the production and export of commodities may not lead to faster economic growth. Indeed, it is not difficult to imagine commodity earnings leading to relatively slow growth. At least some of these tendencies are evident in Latin America. Despite being rich in commodities, the region is poor in infrastructure. Education and health care also suffer funding problems. This is always hard to reconcile. As we saw in Chapter 4, corruption is a problem in the region. One has to be careful not to blame this problem totally on commodities. However, a simple thought question might be helpful. Would there be less corruption in many Latin American countries if they had no significant commodities? The same sort of question applies to government employment and imports. Has income from commodities been used in some cases to finance a larger civil service and to support higher levels of imports of consumer goods? The direction of these effects is probably clear. The magnitudes vary from country to country depending on the amount of money generated by commodities and the quality of government. Overall, it is difficult to say that the possession of commodities has been an unalloyed benefit to the region since independence.

Things become even more complicated with the involvement of foreign firms in the production of commodities. The extraction of mineral wealth or certain agricultural commodities may require capital and technical expertise that the country may not possess. The production of commodities in a low- or middle-income country may require FDI. Negotiations between *multinational corporations (MNCs)* and the host country may be difficult in many circumstances. It is especially difficult if the commodity is an exhaustible resource. Conditions of entry, tax rates, and other variables can all influence the final outcome.[10] During the Golden Age, the conditions were usually national treatment. Foreign firms faced similar taxes and regulations to domestic firms. However, with relatively weak governments in the region, coupled with low taxes and light regulation, *national treatment* became an increasingly unacceptable form of regulation of MNCs, especially for exhaustible natural resources. In other cases, export enclaves developed where MNCs were receiving preferential treatment rather than national treatment. In the twentieth century, the balance of power slowly shifted from the MNCs to the governments of the region. Taxes and regulations became stiffer. In some cases, the local assets of the MNCs were expropriated, with varying degrees of compensation.[11] In any event, the relationship between the governments of the region and MNCs involved in extracting natural resources has been difficult. In these cases, many countries have opted to produce their own resources using SOEs. As we will see in the next chapter, SOEs have a checkered history. In theory, SOEs allow the country to extract all of the value from its commodities, but in practice this has proven to be difficult. The oil industry in Mexico and the copper industry in Chile are well-known examples that have produced somewhat different results.

Box 6.4 Pemex and Petrobras

Not surprisingly, the two largest companies in Latin America are based on commodities. In this case, the commodity is oil. Ever since independence, the countries of the region have struggled to strike a balance between the development of natural resources and dealing with MNCs that have the money and technology to exploit these resources. In different ways, both Pemex and Petrobras illustrate the difficult trade-offs that exist even in the twenty-first century. For a long time, it has been recognized that the Mexican oil industry is dysfunctional. The hope was that a public–private partnership in the oil industry in Brazil would prove to be a new model. Unfortunately, the search for a model relationship between public and private interests in commodities in the region continues.

Pemex (Petróleos Mexicanos) was created by the famous nationalization of foreign oil interests under the presidency of Lázaro Cárdenas in 1938. From this expropriation, Pemex evolved into one of the world's largest oil companies. Along the way, the fortunes of Pemex became inextricably linked to the Mexican government. As a monopolist in the Mexican oil market from production to retailing, Pemex was spectacularly profitable. However, these profits were transferred to the government in the form of high taxes. These tax revenues account for a third of government revenues. The result has been that Pemex now routinely loses money and has a total debt of $60 billion, not counting $100 billion in unfunded pension liabilities. One of the results has been that the company has not been able to invest enough to replace lost output in old fields. With declining production and the loss of tax revenue, the Mexican government is now doing what was once unthinkable: allowing foreign participation in the Mexican oil industry. As is frequently the case, a state-owned monopoly has not worked well in the long run.

Until recently, the model firm in this regard has been Petrobras (Petróleo Brasileiro). Like Pemex, it was formed as a national oil monopoly, in 1953. This monopoly was broken by the government in 1997, allowing private companies to compete in the Brazilian market. From this point, Petrobras began working with foreign oil companies to further develop oil production in the country, especially production in deep offshore fields. Discoveries in these new fields were partially financed by a spectacular stock offering of $72.8 billion. By 2010, the company was hailed as a successful example of a public–private partnership. More recently, enthusiasm has waned. With rising profitability, the company was able to accumulate over $170 billion in debt. Political interference in the company's operations has taken a toll. The accumulation of debt, the imposition of price controls, and lower oil prices have left the company struggling. A more recent problem is an old story: corruption. It appears that the wall between the political system and the company was somewhat porous.

Finally, it has been difficult for Latin America and other regions to leverage their commodities into manufacturing based on these resources. The reasons for this are many, but a primary problem has been the level of tariffs, and in some cases quotas, in the developed countries. The *structure of protection* in developed countries is set up to encourage the processing of commodities there. This is done by escalating the tariffs according to stage of processing. For example, raw commodities frequently have a low or zero tariff. If the product is processed into an intermediate commodity, the tariff rate rises. If the commodity is further processed into a finished good, the tariff is still higher. The point of this policy is to import commodities as cheaply as possible. The tariff then encourages the processing of the commodity in the developed country rather than the developing country. This makes it very difficult for the developing countries of Latin America to establish manufacturing industries based on their plentiful commodities. This is not the only factor inhibiting industrial development in the region, but it has not helped. As we have seen in this section, the possession of commodities can theoretically aid economic development. For Latin America, the possession of commodities has no doubt made the region better off. It is hard to imagine Latin America without commodities. It is also difficult to say that the potential benefits of these commodities have been used to their fullest to enhance economic development. The resource curse has not afflicted the region as badly as has been the case in other parts of the world. On the other hand, traces of this effect are not difficult to find in the region.

Box 6.5 Latin America and China

Over the past thirty-five years, China has grown from an economically irrelevant backwater to the world's second largest economy. The effects on the world economy have been profound. Likewise, the effects of the rise of China have been important for Latin America. In this case, the rise of China has been a mixed blessing. Rapid economic growth in China has created a voracious demand for the commodities that Latin America exports. These commodities include oil, iron ore, soybeans, copper, meat, and pulp and paper. Until recently, China's demand for raw materials has been growing at double-digit rates. The effect on commodity prices has been predictable. These rising commodity prices, in turn, have had a favorable effect on the terms of trade for the region. With stable prices for imports and rising prices for exports, the terms of trade over the past decade were strongly positive. As shown in the previous section, this has had a positive effect on economic growth in Latin America. In this sense, the rise of China has been a positive development.

In another respect, the rise of China has created an uneasy feeling in the region. China's growth has been fueled by booming exports of labor-intensive manufactured goods. The early exports of simple goods such as toys has been followed by an increasing amount of exports of more sophisticated goods. An obvious example is cell phones, but there are other products, such as automobile transmissions, that are less visible but no less important. While exports of manufactured goods from Latin America have grown significantly over the past several decades, this growth pales in comparison to the rate of growth from China. The situation is not precisely a zero-sum game, but there is the sense that the relative success of China has come partially at the expense of growth in exports from Latin America. The reasons for this disparity are not clear. They may be related to the usual list of suspects, such as relatively poor infrastructure, low human capital related to education, and rigid labor laws. Whatever the causes, the rise of China has tended to benefit Latin America in a way that is an old story: booming commodity prices. The cost may be another lost opportunity for the region to diversify out of its traditional pattern of development.[12]

Commodities and Dutch disease

In economics, *industrial structure* refers to the percentage of output that is accounted for by each industry within a country. If a country has significant production of commodities, this can affect its industrial structure. Since Latin America definitely falls into this category, the effects of commodities on the industrial structure of the region are worth considering. In a sense, these effects are obvious. A country with commodities will naturally commit resources to their production. In the short run, more resources, in the form of capital and labor, in commodities means fewer resources elsewhere in the economy. The commodities, and industries tied to them, will be larger, and other parts of the economy will be smaller. In the short run, this has to be true. However, there are other, less obvious effects at work when a country possesses commodities.

First, consider a commodity boom. Profits are extremely high in this sector of the economy. These high profits act as a magnet for resources in the other parts of the economy. Capital will naturally be invested, as the rate of return will be relatively high. This is important in a low- or middle-income country, because capital is a scarce resource. Other sectors of the economy may not be able to grow as fast as they are growing now if they have to compete for capital in a market where it was not plentiful to begin with. Marginal borrowers of capital get "crowded out" as the price of capital rises. The same thing happens with labor. Part of the high returns in the booming sector of the economy accrues to labor in the form of wages. In turn, wages may rise in other parts of the economy. This may make the production of goods outside the booming sector less competitive. The effect on the labor market does not just involve wages. The booming sector may also attract workers with the most human capital. In a country where human capital is a scarce resource, this may make growth more difficult in other parts of the economy. In sum, an economy with a commodity boom may start becoming distorted, and not only in terms of industrial structure. Scarce resources such as capital and human capital are being diverted to one part of the economy. Wages may rise in the entire economy. While things are going well in the booming commodity sector, other parts of the economy are having a more difficult time growing.

As shown in Figure 6.2, commodity booms frequently end in a sometimes spectacular bust. In a frictionless model of economic activity, resources would be briskly transferred to other sectors of the economy with few transaction costs. Another way of putting this is that a bust would lead to a costless change in industrial structure as the commodity-producing sector of the economy shrinks and the other parts of the economy now grow faster. In reality, the transitions are not always that smooth. The result of the bust is that resources are released from the production of commodities. In the short run, which might take many years, the other parts of the economy cannot grow fast enough to absorb these resources. Even if they can, many of the physical and human resources may have become sector-specific. Mining machinery may not be easy to adapt to other uses. Workers have built up useful skills in the commodity sector, but these skills may not be easily transferrable to another sector. The inability of an economy to easily transfer resources from the former booming sector may lead to a prolonged slump in overall economic activity. A commodity boom may create an industrial structure in a country that is not easy to change once the boom ends. Similar, but smaller, effects of this type occur due to commodity price volatility. As the prices of a commodity rise, more resources may be temporarily pulled into the sector. Again, there are adverse effects for other parts of the economy. A dramatic fall in prices sets up a less serious version of the situation described above. How much these effects matter is related to how important a commodity is to the economy. A good example for Latin America would be the oil industry in Mexico and Venezuela. Oil is important to the Mexican economy. However, the Mexican economy is highly diversified, and oil is just one important industry among many. Mexican goods and services are sold all over the world, and oil is just one more important export. High oil prices are good for the Mexican economy, but not critical. Venezuela is a different story. The oil industry dominates the economy of the country. The production of nonoil goods languishes for the reasons given above. High oil prices mean relative prosperity, and low oil prices invariably mean lower growth for the economy. The effects described in this section exist in both countries, but to different degrees.

On top of the description given above, in a floating-exchange-rate world, a commodity boom can affect the exchange rate. Foreign buyers of the commodity must first purchase the domestic currency of the commodity-producing country in order to purchase the commodity. This increase in demand for the commodity translates into an increase in demand for the local currency. In turn, this can cause the exchange rate to appreciate. This appreciation has several effects. First, it makes imports cheaper.[13] This increases the relative price of domestically produced goods that compete with imports. Such industries are not only paying more for capital and labor; they may also face downward pressure on prices. Second, exports of goods and services other than commodities become more expensive for foreign buyers. These price increases tend to lower the demand for a country's exports. In total, a commodity boom means a more difficult environment for the tradable goods sectors of the economy. The booming commodity sector leads to more imports and lower domestic production. It also can mean fewer exports and lower production in that part of the economy. This effect can be exacerbated if the booming sector is also pulling FDI into the country for its development. The effects on industrial structure caused by the exchange-rate appreciation are in addition to what would be occurring even if exchange rates were unaffected.

The effects of commodities on industrial structure are referred to in general as *Dutch disease*. The term refers to the effects on the economy of the Netherlands that were noticed after the country began to export natural gas. It is now used to refer to a set of conditions that typically accompany a commodity boom. A boom in the commodity-producing parts of the economy tends to cause hardship in other parts of the economy. In a small country with a large commodity boom, the ultimate effects can be a badly distorted domestic economy that is very vulnerable to a fall in commodity prices. The description of Dutch disease given above is a minimal outline of the effects. To a greater or lesser extent, the effects of Dutch disease are easy to find in Latin America. Commodity booms have attracted more resources into those parts of many economies, with lasting effects on industrial structure. Adjusted for productivity, wages in Latin America tend to be high. This has worked to retard the development of other economic activities not related to commodities. Scarce investment capital has been attracted to commodities, as they frequently offer higher returns. As we will see in Chapter 9, Latin America has a history of overvalued exchange rates. This has encouraged imports and discouraged exports of products other than commodities. These effects have been felt most strongly in the manufacturing sector of the region. As we will see in the next chapter, Dutch disease cannot account for all of the problems of industry in Latin America. However, it is an important component of the overall picture.

Box 6.6 The lithium triangle

Commodities are important to Latin America partially because the arrival of new commodities that the world wants and the region has an abundance of. In the twenty-first century, lithium is exhibit A. Currently, all of our electronic devices are powered by lithium ion batteries. If that was not enough demand, then the movement toward battery-powered cars and the need to store electricity using these batteries almost guarantees rapid growth the demand for lithium for the forseeable future. The supply of lithium is rather concentrated in three countries in Latin America. Argentina, Bolivia, and Chile together account for over half of the world's lithium resources. The scramble to extract this resource is reminiscent of the silver boom centered around Potosí in the sixteenth century.

   The order of countries given above matches the relative size of lithium deposits in the three countries. The actual production figures are almost reversed. Chile is producing nearly twice as much as Argentina, and Bolivia literally has barely begun production. The reasons for this mismatch are a classic case study. Chile is the most developed country in the region and has by far the best overall institutional quality. Lithium is produced by extracting brine from wells, evaporating the water to form a concentrate, and then processing the concentrate into lithium carbonate. The product then must be transported to a port for shipment of importing countries. Chile's lead in production would be even larger but for controls on production due to lithium being designated as a strategic product. Also, the government is moving cautiously as the ecosystem of the high Andean desert is fragile. Although Chile has the lowest production costs, Australia is rapidly catching up even with higher costs. It is still much easier to do business in a developed country than any country in Latin America. Production in Argentina is another matter. Exchange controls prevent companies from repatriating profits. Export taxes have made lithium production less profitable, and controls on imports makes investment in machinery more difficult. Further complications involve the fact that provincial governments, not the national government, actually own the minerals. In the midst of these complications, the mere existence of production and exports is remarkable. The case of Bolivia is almost like a Latin American time warp. The right to extract lithium is a state monopoly. The Uyuni salt flat near Potosí is the largest deposit of lithium in the world. The SOE set up for extraction way behind schedule, well over budget, and lacks the technology and human capital for large-scale production. Putting an important commodity together with three national strategies for production and export is a good lesson on the more general theme of economic development in Latin America.

Key terms and concepts

Dutch disease: a term used to describe the effects of commodity exports on other parts of the economy.

industrial structure: the percentage of output that is accounted for by each industry within a country.

inelastic: the property of a demand or supply curve that changes in price have only a small impact on the quantity demanded or supplied.

multinational corporation (MNC): a corporation with operations in more than one country.

national treatment: the situation in which a country's laws are blind with respect to nationality.

resource curse: the empirical regularity that countries rich in commodities frequently experience low economic growth.

structure of protection: an analysis of the variation in tariffs in a country.

Questions for review and discussion

1 Explain the two major problems that a country that produces primary commodities may face.
2 List the major commodity booms that have occurred in Latin America since 1500. Other than lithium, try to construct a scenario for another new commodity boom in the region.
3 Describe the volatility in world commodity markets since 2006.
4 Describe the rise, fall, and rise of the cochineal market in the world economy.
5 Graph a commodity boom for an exhaustible resource and the subsequent bust. How does the boom-and-bust cycle differ for a commodity of which the supply can be increased?
6 What is the commodity supercycle? How did it affect Latin America in the past and, potentially, how will it affect it in the future?
7 Explain how changes in commodity prices affect real GDP.
8 How can the possession of commodities in a country enhance economic development?
9 Explain the resource curse. How has it affected Latin America?
10 How has the structure of protection in developed countries hindered the development of industry in Latin America?
11 How has the relationship between the governments of Latin America and commodity-oriented MNCs changed over time?
12 Describe Pemex and Petrobras. Why has one been more successful than the other? What is the common problem in both cases?
13 What is Dutch disease? How does it apply to Latin America?

Notes

1 Some of these issues will be covered in more detail in Chapters 9 and 12.
2 The term "black gold" was coined in this period.
3 In many cases, the production of nonagricultural commodities is capital-intensive.
4 Many of these areas left a legacy of spectacular architecture that allows one a glimpse of the wealth commodity booms can confer.
5 This should be easy to imagine. Suppose that in the twenty-first century a new, large supply of gold was discovered. This extra supply might depress the price of gold for a time, but the effects are not likely to last long, as world demand is continually increasing.
6 More technically, the income elasticity of demand for nonagricultural commodities is usually higher than for agricultural commodities.
7 A more detailed explanation of macroeconomic management with commodity exports will be given in Chapter 12.
8 For an alternative view of the resource curse, see Lederman and Maloney (2008).

9 This issue is a problem that rarely vanishes completely. The recent tension between exporters of agricultural commodities in Argentina and the government is just the most recent example of a long-standing problem.
10 The outcome is not always final. See Manzano and Monaldi (2008) for examples from the oil industry in Latin America.
11 Perhaps the most famous of these nationalizations was the takeover of American oil interests in Mexico in 1938.
12 For more detail on these issues, see Gallagher and Porzecanski (2010).
13 These effects will be covered in more detail in Chapter 9.

References

Erten, Bilge and José Antonio Ocampo (2017) "Super Cycles of Commodity Prices since the Mid-Nineteenth Century," in W. Charles Sawyer (ed.), *Latin American Economics*, vol. I, London and New York: Routledge, pp. 131–165.
Gallagher, Kevin P. and Roberto Porzecanski (2010) *The Dragon in the Room: China and the Future of Latin American Industrialization*, Palo Alto, Calif.: Stanford University Press.
Gruss, Bertrand (2014) "After the Boom: Commodity Prices and Economic Growth in Latin America and the Caribbean," *IMF Working Paper 14/154*, Washington, DC: International Monetary Fund.
Lederman, Daniel and William F. Maloney (2008) "In Search of the Missing Resource Curse," *Economia*, 9 (fall): 1–39.
Manzano, Osmel and Francisco Monaldi (2008) "The Political Economy of Oil Production in Latin America," *Economia*, 9 (fall): 59–98.
Smith, Geri (2007) "Beating the Oil Curse," *Business Week*, June 4, pp. 48–49.
United Nations Conference on Trade and Development (2015) *Trade and Development Report*, Geneva: United Nations Conference on Trade and Development.
World Trade Organization (2015) *Trade Profiles*, Geneva: World Trade Organization.

Recommended reading

Bacha, Edmar L. and Albert Fishlow (2011) "The Recent Commodity Boom and Latin American Growth: More than New Bottles for an Old Wine?" in José A. Ocampo and Jaime Ros (eds.), *The Oxford Handbook of Latin American Economics*, Oxford: Oxford University Press, pp. 394–410.
Gibbon, Peter (2001) "Upgrading Primary Production: A Global Commodity Chain Approach," *World Development*, 29 (February): 345–363.
Haber, Stephen, Noel Maurer, and Armando Razo (2003) "When the Law Does Not Matter: The Rise and Decline of the Mexican Oil Industry," *Journal of Economic History*, 63 (March): 1–31.
Mandel, Benjamin (2011) "The Dynamics and Differentiation of Latin American Metal Exports," *Federal Reserve Bank of New York Staff Report No. 508*, New York: Federal Reserve District Bank of New York.
Pineda, José G. and Francisco Rodríguez (2011) "Curse or Blessing? Natural Resources and Human Development," in José A. Ocampo and Jaime Ros (eds.), *The Oxford Handbook of Latin American Economics*, Oxford: Oxford University Press, pp. 411–437.
Sinnott, Emily, John Nash, and Augusto de la Torre (2010) *Natural Resources in Latin America and the Caribbean: Beyond Booms and Busts?* Washington, DC: World Bank.
Talbot, John (1997) "The Struggle for Control of a Commodity Chain: Instant Coffee from Latin America," *Latin American Research Review*, 32 (2): 117–135.

Topik, Steven and Allen Wells (eds.) (1998) *The Second Conquest of Latin America: Coffee, Henequen, and Oil during the Export Boom, 1850–1930*, Austin, Tex.: University of Texas Press.

Topik, Steven, Carlos Marichal, and Zephyr Frank (eds.) (2006) *From Silver to Cocaine: Latin American Commodity Chains and the Building of the World Economy, 1500–2000*, Durham, NC: Duke University Press.

7   Import substitution in Latin America

Introduction

As we saw in Chapter 2, the Great Depression marked a turning point in the economic history of Latin America. The relative openness of the Golden Age ended in the protectionism of the 1930s. The ending of World War II also marked another turning point for Latin America. In the postwar era, much of the world began to slowly remove the protectionism developed during the 1930s. Latin America did not.[1] Moreover, Latin America went further than simply not reducing the level of protectionism. A large number of different policies were constructed to build up industry in the region. Not only trade policy, but industrial policy, exchange-rate policy, and policies for the financial markets were harnessed together in support of the development of industry. As we will see in the last section of the chapter, this headlong rush to industrialize the region ended badly. That is why it is important to outline in more detail in the next section of the chapter the original thought behind this movement.

Structuralism, dependency theory, and ISI

Latin American structuralism

To understand the origins of ISI in Latin America, one needs to briefly return to the Golden Age. Latin America prospered during this period by exporting commodities and importing products that it could not produce or that could be produced more cheaply in other parts of the world. In more formal terms, the region exported products in which it had a comparative advantage and imported comparative-disadvantage products. This sort of trade worked well for Latin America in the late nineteenth and early twentieth centuries. On average, commodity prices were high, and export earnings were substantial. This allowed the region to easily import the manufactured goods that were needed for consumption and economic development. The onset of the Great Depression seriously dented faith in this sort of trade, not only in Latin America but in much of the world. The export earnings of the region were falling, but the prices of the manufactured goods being imported were not falling nearly as fast. This was creating serious strains in the *balance of payments*. As a result of this, a group of economists at the Central Bank of Argentina began researching this problem. By the late 1930s, Raúl Prebisch and his colleagues had started to develop some economic reasoning on this issue. Part of the problem was introduced in the previous chapter. The supply of most commodities is inelastic. Thus, when the Great Depression hit, the prices of most commodities fell dramatically. On the other hand, it was posited that the supply of manufactured goods was much more *elastic*. This implies that if the demand for these goods falls, the price will not fall by a substantial amount. This is a reasonable explanation for some of the balance of payments problems Latin America experienced during the Great Depression. The prices of commodities fell much faster than the price of manufactured goods.

Following World War II, the UN set up the Economic Commission for Latin America (ECLA). As director of ECLA, Prebisch published an enormously influential book *The Economic Development of Latin America and Its Principal Problems* (1950). This book was partially based on an earlier UN report, but the basic argument was expanded into a much more sweeping thesis. The start of the argument concerns the declining *terms of trade* that may face developing countries such as those in Latin America. Rather than being a short-run problem caused by a global downturn, it was asserted that the prices of commodities were falling relative to the price of manufactures over the long run. The declining terms of trade for developing countries would mean that over time, more and more commodities would have to be exported to obtain any given amount of manufactured goods. Taken to another level, this argument contains an unusual conclusion: trade is making the developing countries of Latin America worse off. The reverse would be logically true. This trading relationship should be making the developed countries better off. For Latin American countries, a major problem was the structure of the economy, which was geared toward exporting commodities and importing manufactured goods. In order to break out of this, it would be necessary to change the structure of their economies. This came to be known as *structuralist economics*, or the basic idea that the structure of an economy can have important effects on economic outcomes.[2] In the case of developing countries, an economic structure composed primarily of commodities was condemning these countries to poverty.

From structuralism to dependency theory

Prebisch's argument contained another idea that became enormously influential in the 1950s and 1960s. He argued that the world economy was divided into the developed countries, which are the center of the world economy, and the periphery countries, which comprise the developing countries. The center countries produce technologically advanced manufactured goods, which are sold in both the center and the periphery countries. However, the periphery countries, being unable to produce these goods, must purchase them from the center at ever higher prices in terms of the commodities they produce. Under these circumstances, the countries of the center are gaining vastly more in terms of international trade than the countries of the periphery. With its overwhelming amount of commodity exports and relatively little industry, the idea that Latin America was not benefiting from trade with the rest of the world was a compelling idea. It was so compelling that it was later extended to a whole school of thought in economic development, known as "dependency theory." In this view, the countries of the center were viewed as the *cause* of the relative poverty of the developing countries. The world economy was viewed as a system in which the developing countries produced raw materials that the center countries needed for their prosperity. In return, the developing countries received as little as necessary from the center. The periphery was seen mainly as a hapless victim of the economic activities of the center. Further, the institutions of the world economy were arranged in a way that made progress in the periphery countries difficult at best. An important component of dependency theory was the thought that underdevelopment was something that was external to the developing countries. Dependency theory was extremely popular in much of the developing world, including Latin America. The idea that the world economy was a rigged game and that the destiny of the region was being set outside the region has some obvious appeal.[3]

Both structuralism and dependency theory contain ideas that are superficially plausible. Economic structure matters, as can be seen in any industrial organization textbook. Bolivia is not Belgium, and differences in the economic structures of the two countries influence economic outcomes. *Dependency theory* springs from the obvious fact that the developed countries have more wealth and power than the developing countries. However, both types of analysis lead to a radical conclusion. This conclusion would not matter much if the theories were just the normal intellectual parlor games of academics. However, as Keynes pointed out long ago, the ideas of academics and scholars are sometimes extremely important. In the case of Latin America, these ideas turned out to have very serious consequences.

The argument for ISI

The basic ideas of Prebisch and others can be summarized in this way. The structure of developing countries led them to export commodities and import manufactures from the developed countries. Because of the declining terms of trade, in the long run, this pattern of trade would not be beneficial for the developing countries. The implication of this is that the traditional theory of *comparative advantage* doesn't work for developing countries. This conclusion flies in the face of 200 years of economic theory. In retrospect, the acceptance of this thesis seems incredible. However, one should keep in mind that in the early 1950s, there was virtually no *empirical* evidence on the benefits of trade based on comparative advantage. The declining terms of trade argument was at that point buttressed by data.[4] For the time, this was unusual. In any case, the argument that the traditional trade of the developed countries with the developing countries was injurious to the latter became something like a conventional wisdom. The solution implied that developing countries could only break out of this pattern of trade by developing domestic manufacturing industries. There were two possible options. The first option would involve developing low-wage manufacturing based on an abundance of cheap labor. This is in line with the traditional theory of comparative advantage, whereby a country exports products it can produce cheaply and imports products in which it has a *comparative disadvantage*. However, if one believes that trade based on comparative advantage is not a welfare-maximizing policy for developing countries, this may not seem to be an optimal policy. The second option was to partially close off the economy to trade and develop industries not for export but to replace imports from the developed countries. In this manner, it was hoped to both change the structure of the domestic economy and reduce the imports of manufactures that were partially the source of the declining terms of trade.

In the early 1950s, this argument neatly fit much of the thinking on economic development. In a sense, economic development as a field of study was being born at this time. A large number of former colonies were going through the transformation from colony to nation that Latin America had accomplished over 100 years earlier. The new countries were obviously poor relatives to the developed countries. The common perception was that these countries were poor because the agricultural or commodity sectors of their economies were large. The perception was that the developed countries had become that way by a process of moving out of agriculture into industry. The influence of structuralist economics can be related to this perception. It was widely perceived that the developing countries would not be able to industrialize in a world economy where the developed countries already had a large amount of productive industry. The inevitable conclusion of this logic was that in order to industrialize the developing countries would need to heavily protect their domestic markets. In particular, they would need to pursue policies that substituted domestic production for imports. An adjunct to industrialization was increasing the rate of investment. At the time, the process of development was viewed as being closely related to increasing the amount of investment in industry and raising the K–L ratio. As we saw in Chapter 3, this would tend to increase GDP per capita. This was being confirmed by the theoretical work done on growth theory at the time. With optimism that in retrospect seems unwarranted, the process of economic development seemed simple enough. Use protectionism to develop domestic industry, increase the rate of capital investment, and the developing countries would soon catch up with the developed countries.

This approach to economic development found widespread acceptance in Latin America. Latin American proponents of this approach also went somewhat further down this road. Embodied in much of the thinking of the period was a general feeling that market forces were a poor guide for the development process. This led to two other aspects of ISI in Latin America. First, the thinking was that wage rates were not very important and that wages could be raised to address poverty with no loss of employment.[5] In a similar fashion, the exchange rate was controlled at a low rate. This made the importation of capital goods cheaper to aid in the process of industrialization. It was assumed that this did not matter very much in terms of exporting commodities. Further, a low exchange rate could help dampen inflation.

As will be shown in this and later chapters, the policy did not work as planned. It was slowly abandoned in the 1980s, and some of the policies put in place in the 1950s and 1960s are still in place. The above is not a justification for ISI. It is, rather, an attempt to explain why it was put in place. Sixty years ago, the process of economic development seemed simple. The developed countries were rich because they had industry that the developing countries of Latin America lacked. It seemed totally obvious that the path to becoming a developed country involved moving from agriculture to industry. To accomplish this, it was necessary to engage in a program that involved developing domestic industry using a variety of government interventions. Heavy capital investment was assumed to be an important part of the process, and once again, government intervention of various types would be needed to do this. Given standard growth theory, this heavy capital investment would quickly raise GDP growth and GDP per capita. Government intervention in investment was necessary as it was felt that market forces would not produce the intended results. The acceptance of ISI in Latin America was further enhanced by the fact that one of its most articulate proponents was the most famous economist in the region. Ultimately, these policies failed to accomplish their purpose. In retrospect, they were the cause of many difficulties that the region is still coping with in the twenty-first century. However, the policies were born out of a misplaced sense of optimism and a poorly developed understanding of the process of economic development. As with virtually any failed economic policy, ISI was implemented in the 1950s, with the best of intentions, as a simple solution to a complex problem. The initial implementation of these policies should perhaps be viewed as an honest mistake. However, they continued long after the policy failures were becoming apparent. The reasons for that problem can be related to the details of how ISI was implemented, given in the next section.

Box 7.1 Raúl Prebisch (1901–1986)

The name of Raúl Prebisch is inextricably linked to ISI in Latin America and to dependency theory. In some quarters, his work is still considered seminal and important, while in others it is considered in a somewhat less favorable light. In a common Latin American story, Prebisch was born in Argentina, but his parents were German immigrants. He showed early promise, publishing six articles before finishing an MA in economics at the University of Buenos Aires. His early work mirrored the times, as the Argentina of the 1920s was an example of a country prospering on the basis of the standard theory of comparative advantage. As for many others, the Great Depression changed his thinking. Working at the Central Bank of Argentina, he and his colleagues began research on why the country's terms of trade were deteriorating. This was the beginning of both the declining terms of trade argument and the concept of the world economy divided into a center and periphery. His move to the ECLA in the later 1940s was a natural extension of his earlier thinking on Latin America and the world economy. The ECLA quickly became a center for heterodox economic thought in both Latin America and the world. His ideas proved influential in a policy sense, as ISI became the dominant development policy of the region and, to a lesser extent, for many other countries outside Latin America. His early work on the composition of the world economy became the basis for the later work on dependency theory. In the 1960s, Prebisch helped start the United Nations Conference on Trade and Development (UNCTAD). In broad terms, UNCTAD's agenda was to promote a "new world economic order" in which the countries of the periphery would receive more equitable treatment in the world economy. While his term at UNCTAD and the organization itself were less than successful, his views on economic development had obviously changed. He had publicly given up on ISI as a development strategy. Instead, he was an early proponent of the sort of internal reforms discussed in Chapter 4. He also worked for trade preferences for developing-country exports and regional integration among developing countries.

   The legacy of Raúl Prebisch is hardly that of a radical. As director-general of the Central Bank of Argentina, he was an inflation hawk and an advocate of fiscal responsibility. Revealingly, he was forced out of the central bank by Juan Perón. He was far ahead of his time in advocating the importance of central-bank independence. In the 1930s, he worked on a multilateral plan to stabilize world commodity prices, which have always been a problem for both producers and consumers. The plan failed, but it reflected both his overriding interest in practical problems and his ability to recognize what works and what doesn't. For example, by the late 1950s, he was already becoming skeptical of ISI and worried about the neglect of exports from Latin America. His later work at UNCTAD reinforced this. ISI had failed, and he had recognized the importance of outward-oriented trade strategies for developing countries. After leaving UNCTAD in the late 1960s, he sounded the alarm about the growing debt burden of the region and the possible consequences. In hindsight, it is easy to criticize his work on ISI. While responsible for its creation, he cannot be held responsible for the subsequent thirty years of its heavy-handed application in Latin America. Aside from ISI, his other work during his career was surprisingly mainstream. The constant of his career was concern about economic development and policies to enhance growth in developing countries.[6]

How ISI worked

In the previous section, we outlined the theoretical justification for ISI. It may have been a flawed justification, but the policies were implemented nonetheless.[7] The basic idea was to develop domestic industry that would not otherwise have developed. In general terms, this was accomplished by protecting new industries from foreign competition through trade policy and enacting a wide-ranging set of programs to make industry more profitable than would otherwise have been the case. In a developed country, this collection of policies to guide the development of industrial structure would be known as industrial policy. Among economists, industrial policy can create an uneasy feeling. On the one hand, all countries have an *industrial policy* of some sort. Changes in the regulation of business that are not universal inevitably favor one industry over another. Pollution-intensive industries are regulated more heavily than other industries. This is appropriate if there is some positive or negative externality associated with the industry. On the other hand, unease over industrial policy occurs when the government chooses to favor an industry because it will enhance economic growth. For this to work, it must be the case that the government can pick which industries will grow faster than average in the future.[8] In a developed country, the industry is usually favored with a mix of tax breaks, government subsidies, and protectionism. In theory, the money spent is an investment, as faster growth in this industry will yield faster overall growth in the future. In a rich country, the social cost of a failed industrial policy would usually be some waste of resources and somewhat slower growth.

Industrial policy in a developed country is usually applied at the industry level. ISI in Latin America was industrial policy writ large. Subsidies were not the odd tax break or higher tariff for a particular industry. Rather, there was an overall development strategy composed of a number of policies directed at industry *in general*. These policies were so important that they affected not only industry but the economy as a whole. This was intentional. Recall that the basic idea was to change the structure of the economy from agriculture and commodities to industry. The forecasted outcome was an acceleration of the rate of economic growth and an increase in GDP per capita. Unfortunately, policies can have unintended outcomes, and this was the case for ISI. ISI worked in the sense that Latin America shifted more toward industry than might otherwise have been the case. In order to understand ISI and its effects, this section presents the highlights of its major components.

Trade policy

Invariably, encouraging the development of industry in Latin America meant wholly or partially excluding imports from competing with domestic firms. Almost always, this will mean higher tariffs. Recall that tariffs in Latin America were raised during the Great Depression. However, after World War II, the paths of Latin America and the rest of the world diverged. By the mid 1930s, it was recognized in the developed countries that the global trade war ignited by the US in 1930 had been a costly disaster for the world economy. After World War II, these countries quickly started trying to dismantle the protectionism of the 1930s. In particular, trade negotiations were started under the *General Agreement on Tariffs and Trade (GATT)* in 1947. To put it mildly, the countries of Latin America were not enthusiastic participants in GATT. Few countries joined at the beginning, and many countries did not join until decades later.[9] However, this fits with the development of ISI. Under ISI, imports from the developed countries needed to be reduced. The whole point of GATT was to reduce protectionism. Given this incompatibility, many of the countries in Latin America did not bother to join GATT. As we will see in the next chapter, tariffs were not reduced from the levels of the 1930s. Instead, the level of protectionism increased after World War II. In many cases, tariffs were not sufficient to reduce the level of imports to desired levels. Frequently, tariff protection was supplemented by quotas. The combination of high tariffs and quotas led to astonishingly high levels of protection of industry in the region. In summary, trade policy was the most fundamental tool of ISI. Most of the other components of ISI would not have been very effective in promoting industry if similar goods could have been imported.

Exchange-rate policy

As was mentioned earlier, a key component of ISI was an artificially low exchange rate. In terms of industrialization, this had the advantage of making the importation of capital goods more inexpensive. The industries developed under ISI in Latin America tended to be oriented toward the production of consumer goods to replace imports. While these industries were able to produce goods for the domestic market, they were not capable of producing the capital equipment necessary for their production. These capital goods had to be imported from the developed countries. Since these goods are expensive, a low exchange rate could substantially reduce the initial cost of setting up an "industry" in a Latin American country. A hypothetical transaction may be useful to illustrate this point. Assume that a firm in a country needed machinery to produce car batteries that cost $1 million. Further, assume that the exchange rate is fixed at 10 pesos to the dollar. To the domestic producer, the cost of the machinery would be 10 million pesos. As will be shown in Chapter 9, this fixed exchange rate was commonly far below the equilibrium. For example, it is not difficult to imagine that the equilibrium exchange rate may well have been 20 pesos to the dollar. At this exchange rate, the identical piece of machinery would have cost 20 million pesos. In these situations, the lower exchange rate would constitute a very large subsidy to this industrial firm. This implicit subsidy did not end there. The imported capital equipment, of course, needed parts and sometimes foreign services. The same subsidy would apply to any subsequent imports associated with keeping the equipment running. In the three decades of ISI in Latin America, such transactions were commonplace. Whole industries were being developed from scratch in much of the region. Exchange rates were fixed at rates usually below market rates. Industrial activities were much cheaper to start up and keep running than would otherwise have been the case. This was intentional. Governments needed means to increase the profitability of new industries, and exchange-rate policy was one of them. Further, initially, the policy was inexpensive.

However, as will be seen in later chapters, maintaining a low exchange rate eventually became extremely expensive.

Targeted lending and financial repression

Usually, industries being developed under ISI were capital-intensive. Remember that this capital intensity was to some extent intentional. The larger the increase in the capital stock, the larger the increase in the production function for the country. This capital intensity also served to increase the country's K–L ratio. The hoped-for effect would be to increase wages in the capital-intensive industry and in an indirect way raise wages in the economy overall. The problem then became how to provide an adequate amount of capital for the initial investments required. Neither trade policy nor exchange-rate policy would provide the start-up funds needed. Private-sector banks might be understandably reluctant to loan large sums of money to finance the creation of new firms in industries with no historical track record in these countries. The problem was exacerbated by the small amount of capital available. Middle-income countries are usually abundant in labor, but capital is scarce. The operation of an ISI development strategy required large amounts of capital in capital-scarce countries. The solution in many cases was the development of state-owned or state-subsidized development banks. Such financial institutions were set up all over the region to loan to industry in general or a particular industry. Capital could then be raised by the state, allocated to development banks, and then loaned out to firms at relatively low interest rates. Thus, the desired subsidy for investment in industry had been supplied by the state.

Financial subsidies sometimes came in a different form. Financial systems in some Latin American countries were subject to varying degrees of *financial repression*. Financial repression refers to government policies that influence the savings and investment decisions of individuals and financial institutions. These sorts of controls can consist of limits on interest charged or paid or government control over the flow of financial resources. For example, laws could limit the amount of interest paid to savers in order to provide less expensive financing for industry. Financial repression can have several effects. First, it can reduce the amount of savings, as individuals may either choose to save less or keep their savings in other less liquid forms, such as land.[10] This can be a particularly serious problem if the interest rate paid to savers is low relative to the rate of inflation. As we will see in Chapter 10, inflation has been a persistent problem in the region. The amount of savings is partially dependent on the real interest rate. The *real interest rate* is the nominal interest rate minus the expected rate of inflation. This relationship raises the possibility that a seemingly reasonable nominal interest rate could leave savers losing money. For example, suppose that the rate paid by financial institutions to savers is fixed at 5 percent. This leaves savers with a positive rate of return only if the rate of inflation is less than 5 percent. Couple this interest rate with a 20 percent rate of inflation, and the financial system is inflicting horrific losses on anyone trying to save for the future.[11] Second, financial repression can also result in the misallocation of capital. To start with, it should be recognized that capital markets free of government intervention have been known to misallocate capital. The question becomes whether or not government allocation decisions are better. Among economists, the general thinking is that markets make fewer mistakes than governments. Prior to the 1980s, it was not uncommon for governments in Latin America to be involved in the allocation of over 50 percent of a country's investment funds.[12] This large-scale intervention by governments in the region in the allocation of capital led to widespread misallocations. This statement is not a value judgment. A country that is naturally capital-scarce can ill afford to waste a scarce resource. Much of the capital directed by government intervention went into capital-intensive industries. The result was that much of the region's capital was being allocated to industries that were very unlikely ever to be internationally competitive due to the mismatch between the resources of Latin America and the type of industries being developed. This was based on a superficially plausible idea: invest heavily, and growth will follow. Unfortunately, investing heavily in the wrong industries may lead to results that are less than expected.

Box 7.2 Capital flight and currency substitution

There are two phenomena potentially related to financial repression that anyone familiar with Latin America will recognize, even if they don't know the exact economic terminology. The first is capital flight. *Capital flight* is the term used to describe the movement of money out of a country in response to adverse political or economic events. Usually the term is used in the context of a massive amount of capital moving in a short period of time. We will see this sort of capital flight again in Chapter 9. However, the movements are often more subtle, as money may be moving more slowly over a longer period of time for exactly the same reasons. Financial repression can cause this sort of capital flight. With low interest rates and high inflation, the real rate of interest can easily be negative. With few alternative assets available in the capital markets of a middle-income country, the temptation to move money to another country where financial assets offer a positive real rate of return can be substantial. For example, a bank account in Miami or Panama is not exactly an uncommon thing in Latin America. This kind of capital flight does not make the headlines precisely because it is so "normal." This very normality is telling an economist that something is wrong.

  For the less well-off, a bank account in a foreign country may be an impossible dream. Even an account with a domestic bank may not be easy to obtain. However, a point that many may miss is that the poor may lack education, but this hardly means that they are not financially astute. Making ends meet in a middle-income country frequently requires financial agility worthy of a modern financier. For this group, holding savings in a form that is not depreciating means holding on to any stable foreign currency that becomes available. In Latin America, this is usually US dollars. Hoarding savings in the form of dollars has been a common practice in the region. This holding of financial assets in foreign currency as a protection against losses is known as *currency substitution*. This phenomenon is not restricted to the poor. Wealthier investors may also engage in currency substitution. Note that the definitions of capital flight and currency substitution are somewhat similar. In both cases, people are trying to protect themselves from financial loss. This hoarding behavior adversely affects long-run growth. A bank account in Miami or $100 hidden at home have the same effects. There is less money to be invested in the domestic economy.

SOEs

The drive to industrialize the countries of Latin America under ISI sometimes led to the development of SOEs. The protection of domestic industry through trade policy, the implicit subsidy of a low exchange rate, and the availability of cheap credit were sometimes not enough to create the sort of new industries governments were interested in. These sorts of industries usually fell into one of three categories. First, governments frequently desired the establishment of "heavy," that is, capital-intensive, industries present in high-income countries. Frequently, these industries were producing intermediate goods that were felt to be essential to the ultimate development of other upstream industries. In the mid twentieth century, a prime example of this was the steel industry. The thinking was along the lines of "How can a country industrialize without steel?" Even under the conditions described above, there were no private investors available to start a steel company in a country without iron ore and coal. The solution in some cases was to set up an SOE to provide the desired industry. A later tendency was to develop "new" or "modern" industries that were human-capital-intensive. Since Latin America was not well endowed with human capital in the 1960s and 1970s, enticing private-sector firms into these industries was difficult. Brazil attempted to set up computer and aerospace industries using SOEs in the absence of any private-sector participation.[13] A final type of investment in SOEs occurred for a different reason. Natural resources in many parts of the world are considered a national patrimony, which makes exploitation of these resources even by domestic private-sector firms difficult. This is the case in Latin America as well. Following the model of the oil industry in Mexico, many countries chose to develop their natural resources using SOEs. In some cases, such as the copper industry in Chile and the oil industry in Brazil, SOEs have been successful. In other cases, the results have been disappointing.

Box 7.3 Brazilian SOEs

As a general rule, the operation of SOEs in Latin America was not very successful. This is not a purely Latin American phenomenon. This organizational form has a poor track record in virtually every country of the world. In running an SOE, bureaucracy and inefficiency tend to be the norm. The usual profit motive is diluted by the state as whole or partial owner. If the entity runs a loss, the usual associated penalties may not exist. Losses are the taxpayers' problem. Just breaking even is a success for an SOE. As a result of the financial crisis of the 1980s, many of the SOEs in Latin America were closed or privatized. The governments of the region entered the decade with government finances in poor condition. The crisis widened budget deficits, and the losses being made by most SOEs became too large to continue to support. There were some exceptions, such as Pemex in Mexico and Codelco in Chile, but these two have control of important natural resources. In Latin America, SOEs not engaged in other areas are now a part of economic history.

In general, the same is true for Brazil. However, the country has produced two SOEs that have become internationally competitive companies. The more famous of the two is Petrobras, which is engaged in the exploration and production of oil. The company began as a result of the controversial nationalization of all private oil reserves in the country. Unlike Pemex, Petrobras restricted its activities to the exploration and production of oil and left the wholesale and retail sides of the industry to the private sector. Brazil has historically been an oil importer, so the company has had a high incentive to find and produce oil. In this process, the company has been successful both in finding oil and in developing the technology to produce oil offshore in deep water. Its recent discoveries of two new fields in the Atlantic could turn Brazil into a major oil exporter. However, as we saw in the previous chapter, interference by the government in the company's operations has severely diminished its standing in the world oil markets.

An even more interesting company is Embraer (Brazilian Aeronautics Company). The idea of a Brazilian aircraft industry was conceived by the government in the 1940s. This led to the creation of aerospace research institutes in the country, which helped to create the industry-specific human capital that was a prerequisite for any high-technology industry. In the 1960s, the infant industry was able to design, successfully test, and build military transport planes. These planes were adapted for civilian use, and Embraer was born in response to a project that was becoming a successful company. Like Petrobras, the company was started as a joint venture between the government and private investors. Other types of planes were designed and produced in the 1970s and 1980s. The company was completely privatized in 1988, as the government was withdrawing from SOEs in general. The lack of new products in the late 1980s and 1990s led to the near death of the company. However, in the 1990s Embraer developed the regional jet, which has become an enormously successful product. In 2008, the company delivered 204 planes and is now the third-largest aircraft manufacturer in the world. Note that the common thread here is the public–private character of both companies. These are not the only examples of Latin American companies that are successful in the world economy. They are unusual only in the sense that they began life as creations of the state and have been successful. As in most parts of the world, this is unusual.

ISI and multinational corporations

In the drive to industrialize the region, MNCs became part of the process. As we have seen, in some industries the subsidies being offered to the private sector were inadequate to produce the desired result: an industry. In other cases, even SOEs were not feasible due to the lack of industry-specific human capital necessary to begin production. In these cases, the participation of MNCs in the development of the local industry became essential. For an MNC, there is frequently a choice to be made between exporting to a country and producing the product locally. This export versus FDI decision is dependent on a large number of variables. In the case of Latin America, the choice to engage in FDI frequently was not difficult. The high tariffs in the region, coupled with the existence of quotas, often made exporting to these markets unprofitable. If the domestic market was large enough, FDI became an attractive option. In general, the three largest markets in the region were the ABM (Argentina, Brazil, and Mexico) countries. These countries had large and growing populations that were profitable markets for firms selling consumer goods such as automobiles. Once established in these markets, MNCs had access to some of the same benefits as domestic firms. They were shielded from foreign competition and might have access to inexpensive foreign exchange. The plants set up needed inputs and parts produced outside the region. To keep these plants running, governments had to provide access to foreign exchange for inputs and parts. MNCs could further enhance the profitability of these operations by using plant and equipment that was old or obsolete by developed-country standards. New cars in Argentina were frequently models that had been out of production for years in the MNC's home markets. Although the production volumes of these plants were relatively low, profits could still be reasonable due to high prices being charged for outdated products. While the country could obtain an "industry" in this manner, the consumers of a middle-income country were paying an implicit tax for this form of industrialization.

The relationship between the MNCs and the governments of the regions in this situation was complicated. The countries desired industry and reluctantly allowed FDI as a less than preferred means of accomplishing that end. FDI was virtually never on a national treatment basis but was usually negotiated on a case-by-case basis. During this period, the activities of MNCs were viewed with some suspicion, and governments strove to maximize the benefits of FDI and limit the perceived costs. This was not unreasonable, as the source of profits in many cases was some sort of government policy that resulted in a relatively noncompetitive domestic market. For the MNCs, these investments were seen as the only feasible way to obtain access to growing markets. However, the production volumes were frequently small, and the countries of the region are not easy places to do business. This was especially true for MNCs, which sometimes faced restrictions that the typical domestic firm did not. While there was a nexus of interests between governments of the region and MNCs, the relationship was uneasy. Governments obtained industry from the MNCs, but often one that was a pale shadow of the industry in the source country. MNCs gained access to desirable markets, but this access came in a form that was profitable only under a certain set of government policies. ISI created a certain type of FDI designed to "jump" over trade barriers and obtain certain kinds of subsidies. Not surprisingly, neither side of the bargain was ever entirely happy with the result.

The results of ISI

In theory, ISI was supposed to transform Latin America from a relatively poor region in the world economy to relative prosperity. The goal seemed achievable, as parts of the region had been prosperous at various times in history. In the 1940s, it seemed obvious how to do this. The high-income countries had moved out of agriculture and into industry and got rich in the process. It seemed obvious that if Latin America could move out of commodities and agriculture and industrialize, the same result would follow. Further, the new development theory indicated that economic development was a relatively simple process. If a country could increase its capital stock and the K–L ratio, then GDP per capita would surely rise. In the previous section, we indicated that things did not work out as planned. GDP per capita in the region increased from 1950 to 1980, but at a relatively slow rate. This was disappointing, but the collection of policies created numerous unintended consequences. In this section, we review a partial list of these problems.

Industrialization

The main purpose of ISI was to produce industry in a country as rapidly as possible. In the case of Latin America, the policies produced a dramatic increase in the ratio of manufacturing to GDP. If it were true that rapid industrialization automatically meant rising GDP per capita, all would have gone to plan. However, one needs to go back and think about the phrase "import substitution" for a moment. Simple trade theory indicates what should be occurring in foreign trade and by extension, what domestic production should look like. A country should be exporting products that it can produce more inexpensively than other countries. The earnings from these exports can then be used to buy imported products. The products that a country imports should be products that can be made in other countries more inexpensively than domestic producers can make them. This is how a country maximizes its welfare by trading. One of the main benefits of trade is that a country can improve its welfare by buying goods cheaply from foreigners as opposed to producing them domestically at a high cost. In the jargon of economics, a country exports goods in which it has a comparative advantage. It imports goods in which it has a comparative disadvantage. Now consider the likely results of ISI. By definition, a country imports products for which it has a comparative disadvantage in production. By pursuing ISI, a country is deliberately building up industries in which it has already demonstrated that it has a comparative disadvantage in production. Imports will be replaced, but at a cost that is guaranteed to be higher than the cost of imported goods. Industry will be developed, but it will be industry in which the country has a comparative disadvantage in production. Industry has been developed, but it is an artificial and fragile sort of industry. It is a bit like growing a pine tree in a desert. It may be possible to do this, but only with a lot of care and feeding.

One of the main problems with ISI was the mismatch between the labor abundance of Latin America and the capital intensity of the industries being developed. A labor-abundant region should have a comparative disadvantage in the production of capital-intensive industries.

In a region that is relatively capital-scarce, what capital was available was being poured into *capital-intensive industries*. Capital acquired through FDI was also funneled into these industries as a result of trade policy. By the 1960s, industry in Latin America had developed along the following lines:

- The typical industry that had developed was very capital-intensive. Although capital was scarce in the country as a whole, targeted lending meant an adequate supply of cheap capital.
- If imported inputs were necessary for production, these could be imported inexpensively, as the exchange rate was being held below equilibrium.
- Troublesome foreign competitors could not profitably sell in markets with very high tariffs and quota protection.
- The local firm may not have faced much domestic competition either. In a small market, there may have been room for only one firm.
- Even an inefficient firm could be quite profitable in these circumstances.
- These profits made generous labor laws possible. High wages and higher administrative costs could be passed on in the form of higher prices. This was easier to accomplish considering the chronic inflation problems of the region.

By the 1970s, many countries of the region had developed a sort of ISI enclave within the economy. The industrial sector was highly profitable, and workers fortunate enough to have jobs in this part of the economy were relatively well-off by local standards.

However, virtually the whole industrial sector was built not on the foundation of comparative advantage but on the existence of a certain set of government policies. Any combination of increases in interest rates, a depreciation of the currency, and changes in trade policy could severely damage industry. Since everyone was aware of this, the policy was difficult to change. Firms and workers (unions) both shared an interest in the continuation of ISI. Governments everywhere are not likely to change a policy supported by *both* business and labor. Government-supported SOEs were going to be difficult to close. Too much capital had been invested, and such firms had an especially close relationship with government. Many MNCs had invested heavily – not just in the region but also in ISI. Their plants could not withstand a major change in policy. As we will see, it took a major *external* shock to cause a change in policy.[14]

ISI and the informal sector

Industrialization brought prosperity but not to the average citizen of the region. For firms and individuals outside the ISI industries, things did not go as well. For consumers, goods were frequently expensive, and quality was not up to world standards. An understandable reaction in many countries was smuggling to evade tariffs and quotas or small-scale production in the informal sector. For SMEs and consumers, credit was difficult to obtain. Credit was first allocated to ISI industries, and everyone else bid for what was left. Informal moneylenders could fill the gap for some loans, but many sectors of the economy found credit difficult to obtain. A similar situation applied to foreign exchange. Exchange controls favored industry both in terms of access and frequently with respect to price.[15] The usual black markets in foreign exchange were common. Government regulations could be dealt with by large firms with the resources to deal with the bureaucracy. Labor regulations that raised the price of labor above equilibrium meant that official unemployment and underemployment became high. Higher taxes that could be paid by firms in the ISI sector could not be paid by smaller firms. Tax evasion became normal in many countries. Under these circumstances, the development of a large informal sector of the economy was hardly surprising. To be sure, the last three policies were not directly attributable to ISI. However, the presence of large profitable firms made implementation of some regulations and taxes more reasonable. Many economies of the region became an odd mixture of the seemingly modern industrial sector and a large informal sector producing goods and services outside the official regulations of the state. Every economy in the world has an informal sector; the only question is how large it is. The informal sector in Latin America has long historical roots tracing back to excessive regulation in the colonial era. At least part of the abnormally large size of the informal sector in the region can be reasonably attributed to the unintended consequences of ISI.

ISI and agriculture

ISI inherently favored the industrial sector of the economy. As seen in the previous section, it implicitly made doing business in other sectors of the economy more difficult. Many of these effects were unintended consequences. The effects on the agricultural sector of the region were more ominous. The whole development policy was built on the idea of reducing the importance of agriculture relative to industry. The policy worked as intended in this regard. ISI produced a brutally difficult climate for the agricultural sector. Targeted lending was designed to provide the bulk of the available investment funds to industry. As for other sectors of the economy, credit in the agricultural sector became more difficult to obtain. The exchange-rate policy was a particular problem. Agricultural commodities sell in world markets and are usually priced in a major currency. The overvaluation of Latin American currencies was a severe handicap to exports of agricultural commodities from the region. The taxes, labor laws, and business regulations that firms in the ISI sector could withstand made business in agriculture extremely difficult. A farm is not a factory, and government regulations that seem reasonable in the environment of the capital city can make farming in compliance with the law nearly impossible. A further problem was infrastructure. The drive to industrialize meant that public-sector investment in infrastructure tended to be in the large cities where much of the heavy industry was located. Infrastructure investment in rural areas languished. This was especially true of transportation systems. Roads are a crucial part of an efficient agricultural sector. With a poor network of roads, agricultural producers faced a cost disadvantage in exports on top of the frequent exchange-rate problem. In summary, the policies necessary for ISI discriminated against the agricultural sector. As governments sometimes do, the policy favored comparative-disadvantage industries and discriminated against a comparative-advantage industry. Resources were being channeled to industries that might never grow rapidly and moved away from potentially faster-growing industries. As we will see in the next section, this neglect had other consequences.

Urbanization and pollution

For a moment, consider the situation of a young person in a rural area of a Latin American country. The primary source of employment in the area is agriculture. However, production has not increased significantly in decades, and wages are low. Education has been a difficult process. Primary schools are widely available, and illiteracy is now rare. Secondary education is more difficult. Secondary schools don't exist in small villages, and transportation on rural (dirt) roads makes obtaining further education difficult. The young person is facing a future of poorly paid agricultural labor with no real prospect of anything better in the future. Now let's assume that the annual wage for this young person is $500 per year. We will also assume that they can potentially earn $1,500 per year if employed full time in the *informal* sector in a large city. The migration of this young person from a rural village to a large city is hardly surprising. The income gap is easy to explain. Wages are higher in the large city partially because of the existence of high-paying jobs in ISI industries. These high wages tend to increase wages for all workers in the urban area, and the policies of ISI make these wages possible. However, there is a complication. A large number of young people see this gap and decide to migrate. Not all the new workers can find jobs in the formal sector. This drives up the official unemployment rate. There are still jobs available in the informal sector at high wages relative to the rural area. The work available may be sporadic and include periods of unemployment. However, the wage gap is so large that this young person could afford to be unemployed half the time and still be better off than by remaining in the village.

The above is a simplified description of the *Harris–Todaro model* of rural to urban migration. Workers migrate in response to differences in income between rural and urban areas. If the income gap is large, workers may continue to migrate even in the face of high unemployment in the urban areas. Notice that the young person described above could be unemployed half the time and still have a higher income in the urban area. As long as these gaps exist, workers will continue to migrate. In much of Latin America, this gap can be traced to the existence of ISI. Even without this policy, an income gap would have existed that would have induced migration. The major cities of the region were going to become larger under any set of policies. However, policies that depress the agricultural sector and encourage industrialization are going to widen this gap. This encourages more migration than would otherwise have been the case. These major cities are full of workers who migrated from the countryside and who work and often live in the informal sector. A job in the informal sector and living as a squatter is a way of life for many of the poor in Latin America. These migrants may be poor and lack some formal education. Their continuing migration suggests that they are good at basic math, calculating probabilities, and forecasting. They migrate and stay in what appear to be difficult circumstances. Those circumstances can be seen and deplored. One needs to keep in mind that what they left was *worse*. To a certain extent, their situation is part of the collateral damage of ISI. Again, ISI did not *create* this situation, but it no doubt exacerbated it.

Finally, consider the effects of all of this on the environment. Infrastructure in the country is scarce, so heavy industries are locating in major cities, where access to electricity and modern transportation systems is easiest. Also, these cities already have the largest pools of human capital necessary for modern industry. ISI industries are heavily tied to government policy, so locating in the capital city of the country is an advantage. Mexico City would be a textbook case of these effects. The development of industry in the city begins attracting migrants from the rural areas. The initial migrants do very well, and this encourages further migration. As long as the income gap persists, the population of the city continues to grow. An expanding ISI sector and a booming population in the city are not unrelated. The result can also be an environmental nightmare. As described in Chapter 5, many of these industries are inherently pollution-intensive. Environmental regulations are weak, and enforcement may be lax. The booming population generates a larger demand for all forms of power, from electricity to automobiles. Also, pollution standards in this sector are low. The large informal sector and the large squatter population further aggravate the problem. As ISI encourages rapid urbanization, it likewise contributes to environmental problems. The major cities of Latin America would not be pristine without the sort of industries that flourished under ISI, but they would be cleaner and less crowded.[16]

Fiscal and monetary policy

In much of Latin America, ISI put a persistent strain on government finances. In terms of *fiscal policy*, this usually meant a government budget deficit. In many countries, SOEs were a constant source of government spending. The correlation between SOEs and profits is not high in any part of the world. Latin American SOEs are no different. These entities tended to run persistent losses, which had to be covered by the government. Their existence was making government spending higher than would otherwise have been the case. Domestic private-sector firms and MNCs were usually profitable and able to pay taxes. However, the rates they could afford to pay might not have been appropriate for other parts of the economy. This was leading to widespread tax evasion and the growth of the informal sector. The growth of the informal sector creates serious problems on the revenue side of the government budget. The net effect was that government budget deficits were virtually the norm in the region for decades in the mid to late twentieth century. A commodity boom might produce a temporary surplus on occasion, but a balanced budget or surplus was unusual.

In a developed country, fiscal policy can be separated from *monetary policy*. If the government runs a budget deficit, the difference can be borrowed from either domestic or foreign lenders in the form of the sale of government bonds. Such a deficit may or may not be prudent, but it can be financed without affecting the money supply of the country. In a middle-income country, fiscal policy effectively becomes monetary policy. To understand this, consider the options of the government in the face of a fiscal deficit. The government cannot borrow by issuing bonds as in a developed country. No one would buy them. The ability to borrow by issuing bonds requires credibility that most governments of the region did not possess. The alternative became the printing of money and the expansion of the money supply. In this environment, a government budget deficit translates into a loose monetary policy. As we will see in Chapter 11, this usually leads to inflation. In many Latin American countries, the inflation was catastrophic. By the 1980s, "inflation" and "Latin America" were two terms that were uncomfortably related to one another. As before, ISI was not the absolute cause of inflation in the region. However, it contributed to fiscal deficits that, in the institutional environment of the times, contributed to excessive rates of growth of the money supply.

The trade balance

Eventually, the worst effect of ISI was the pressure it put on the trade balance. The ISI industries had a voracious appetite for foreign exchange. Equipment and intermediate goods had to be imported to keep the industries running. These imports were not inexpensive, and as the industrial sector grew so did imports. The low exchange rate necessary to subsidize these imports encouraged other types of imports. Anyone who could get access to foreign exchange at the reduced price probably could make a profit. There was constant pressure on the demand for foreign exchange. In terms of exports, Latin America was still locked in the past. The region had been an exporter of commodities for centuries and remained so. The world economy was changing, but the composition of exports had not. Aside from the occasional commodity boom, prices during this period of time were not high. Agricultural exports languished, as government policy was not focused on growth in this sector. Exports of manufactured goods were limited. Manufacturers in the region were focused on serving the domestic market. Labor costs, taxes, and the burden of regulation made it difficult for firms in the region to successfully export manufactured goods. Difficulties in exporting translate into low foreign-exchange earnings or, more precisely, a limited supply of foreign exchange. Deficits in the trade balance likewise became normal in Latin America. Government rationing of foreign exchange became a common means of dealing with the outcome of a low exchange rate.

This situation was manageable until the 1970s. Two events occurred outside the region that eventually made continuing ISI untenable. First, the global system of fixed exchange rates collapsed in 1971. The developed countries simply converted to floating exchange rates and carried on. The countries of Latin America were reluctant to do this, as the ISI industries were dependent on cheap imports. To a lesser extent, other sectors of the economies of the region were operating under the assumption of a low and fixed exchange rate. The second event was the oil shock of 1973. Most of the countries of the region are oil importers. The increase in the price of oil caused large increases in trade deficits. Imports increased dramatically for most of Latin America, and exports of commodities fell in tandem with the global recession. Trade deficits increased dramatically along with the need for foreign exchange. For some countries, the solution was to borrow foreign exchange from commercial banks. This borrowing grew large as the decade progressed. Depreciations of the exchange also accompanied these problems.

The second oil shock in 1979 was the beginning of the end of ISI. Governments in the region rapidly increased their borrowing. However, by 1982, this borrowing was dramatically reduced, as lenders became increasingly concerned about the ability of countries in the region to repay their debt. The inability to borrow, coupled with depreciations of the exchange rate, came to threaten the entire industrial sector of the region and had a profound impact on consumption by the public.

The Lost Decade

It is easy to turn an aquarium into fish soup. Reversing the process is much harder.

(Lech Walesa)

As we will see in Chapter 12, an *exchange-rate shock* is a traumatic event for any economy. The currency depreciates by a large amount in a very short period of time. In turn, this causes several other effects. First, the cost of all imports rises substantially. The ISI industries of the region, which had been dependent on cheap imports for decades, were unable to continue business as usual. The firms were frequently inefficient and simply could not cope with the increase in costs. The price of imports purchased by consumers also rose dramatically. In effect, there was an economy-wide cost of living increase. In a high-income country, this would be annoying but manageable. In a middle-income country, consumers at the low end of the income distribution suffer real hardship.[17] For this part of the population of Latin America, it was difficult to obtain enough food to stave off malnutrition. There is also an effect on the output of the economy. Real GDP falls, and, as a result, unemployment rises. Again, this is more of a problem in a middle-income country. Social safety nets are weaker, and government assistance to adversely affected workers is not as effective. The exchange-rate shock has caused a very unpleasant combination of higher inflation and higher unemployment. While this situation is not unusual for a single country, it is somewhat more unusual for an entire region to be affected. However, this is precisely what occurred in Latin America. The region as a whole adopted ISI in the 1940s and 1950s. As the policy developed problems in the 1970s, most of the region gradually abandoned fixed exchange rates in the face of two oil shocks. This was accompanied by a large amount of borrowing in foreign currency. Finally, the inability of countries of the region to continue this borrowing brought about a *regional* exchange-rate shock.

Another way of viewing the problem is to consider what a trade deficit really is. Going back to our analysis in Chapter 6, consider the components of GDP.

$$Y = C + I + G + (X \ M) \tag{7.1}$$

To review, Equation 6.1 shows that GDP (Y) is simply the summation of consumption by the public (C); nonresidential and residential investment (I); government spending on goods and services (G); and exports (X) minus imports (M). The final term is roughly equivalent to the trade balance.[18] Since this is an identity, we can rearrange the terms as follows:

$$Y - C - I - G = (X - M) \tag{7.2}$$

Equation 7.2 allows us to consider what the trade balance is. Y represents the total production of the economy, and C, I, and G represent the various forms of consumption of this output.

Now, if the sum of C + I + G is larger than Y, this means that the economy is consuming more than it is producing. If this is the case, then (X − M) *must* be a negative number, that is, a trade deficit. Fundamentally, a trade deficit is a statement that a country is consuming more than it is producing. This also means that the country is borrowing from the rest of the world. The imports must be paid for with foreign exchange. If the country does not have previously accumulated sources of foreign exchange, then it will need to borrow it. This is exactly what Latin America as a region did in the 1970s. Rising oil prices dramatically increased the cost of imports. The export of commodities could not rise fast enough to cover this increase. The governments of the region borrowed to cover the trade deficits. In essence, the region was living beyond its means. Domestic consumption was higher than production, and the difference showed up as trade deficits covered with borrowed money. As with an individual, the day of reckoning came when the countries of the region were unable to make agreed-upon payments on the debt. When this borrowing was no longer possible, the wrenching adjustments associated with an exchange-rate shock hit virtually the entire region. The result was nearly a decade of inflation coupled with declines in real GDP and abnormally high unemployment.

In most cases, an exchange shock is the sort of unpleasant macroeconomic experience described above. The higher inflation and lower real GDP occur quickly after the depreciation and dissipate over one to three years. In the case of Latin America, there were economic aftershocks that took nearly a decade to work through. In addition to the macroeconomic consequences, the economies of Latin America had to be fundamentally restructured. The decades of ISI had left the region with a large industrial sector that was uncompetitive in the world economy. ISI firms began to fail, and the drain of SOEs on the public finances became unsustainable. Resources needed to flow out of the old ISI industries and into other parts of the economy that were more productive. Such a process is never easy. The labor and capital tied up in the ISI industries could not be costlessly transferred into other parts of the economy. To regain some degree of balance in international trade, the components of GDP shown in Equation 6.1 had to change. Both consumption and government spending had to be reduced. At the same time, investment had to increase to allow the transition to a different kind of industrial structure. In the short run, these adjustments usually mean that the resources coming out of the declining sectors of the economy may be unemployed. In the jargon of economics, this causes a substantial amount of *structural unemployment*. This unemployment occurred on top of the unemployment that follows an exchange-rate shock alone. In summary, the region was dealing with two problems at the same time: short-run macroeconomic difficulties and a fundamental restructuring of the economies of the region. In addition, the region was searching for a model of economic development with a sounder base than ISI.

The above is the briefest possible description of the Lost Decade. Completely understanding the economic upheaval in the region requires more economic analysis than can possibly be covered in one chapter. Further, the region responded to this shock by making substantial changes in economic policy in a number of areas. In the next six chapters, a better understanding is precisely what we will try to accomplish. Much of the first six chapters concerned the economic history of the region and its effects on the current structure of the economies of Latin America. Going forward, more detailed chapters on trade policy, exchange-rate policy, and macroeconomics will be necessary to obtain a more complete understanding both of what happened and of the policy options facing governments of the region going forward.

Box 7.4 ISI and the American automobile industry

One of the more difficult things to understand is changes in industrial structure. Such changes occur continuously in a healthy economy. Consumer demand and costs of production are constantly changing. When we say GDP is growing at 3 percent, this does not mean that all sectors of the economy are growing at that rate. Some are growing faster and are comprising a relatively larger percentage of total economic activity. Some are growing more slowly and are in relative decline. Finally, some sectors may even be shrinking in absolute terms. Declining industries are just as important as expanding ones. For the expanding industries to grow to their potential, resources must be released from the declining industries. The economist Joseph Schumpeter referred to this process as "creative destruction." It is a normal part of economic growth. However, it is not unusual for a government to attempt to interfere with this process and direct resources into declining industries. These attempts can end badly if there is not a sufficient positive externality occurring. The result can be resources being tied up in industries that are no longer competitive and that are dependent on the government for support. Further, this support can serve to make the industries even less competitive over time. The government can find itself in a vicious circle whereby the initial support leads to less efficiency and the need for more support later. By the 1970s, much of the industry of Latin America had fallen into this pattern. The presumed externality of ISI was faster growth. In reality, this externality didn't exist, and the industry and workers had become dependent on the government.

The same sort of thing can happen elsewhere. The US automobile industry was becoming less competitive in the 1970s. Years of dominance of the industry by three firms had led to companies that were more like bureaucracies than private-sector firms. As competition from Japan intensified, the firms and labor unions sought protection in the early 1980s, and one of the three firms was rescued by the government. This protection allowed the industry to avoid the uncomfortable adjustments necessary to compete successfully. The recent economic crisis led to the failure of two of the three firms.

Again, the government rescued both firms. Even with the protection and bailouts, the adjustments have been difficult. The owners of the firms have lost billions, and tens of thousands of workers have lost their jobs with little hope of employment in the short run. In the case of the US, this is a problem for a small portion of the population and the government finances. This is not a short-run problem, and it will take years for the industry to return to normal. Now imagine this sort of problem occurring in a large number of industries at the same time in the same country. If you can imagine this situation, you now have an inkling of the trauma of the Lost Decade for the people and governments of Latin America.

Key terms and concepts

balance of payments: a summary of all the international transactions of a country's residents with the rest of the world during a year.

capital flight: the movement of money out of a country in response to adverse political or economic events.

comparative advantage: the ability of a country to produce a good at a lower opportunity cost than another country.

comparative disadvantage: the situation where a country can produce a good only at a relatively high opportunity cost.

currency substitution: the holding of financial assets in foreign currency as a protection against losses.

dependency theory: the idea that the world economy is a system controlled by the developed countries (the center) to the detriment of the developing countries (the periphery).

elastic: the property of a demand or supply curve that changes in price have a large impact on the quantity demanded or supplied.

exchange-rate shock: a large depreciation of a country's currency that occurs in a short period of time.

financial repression: government policies that influence the savings and investment decisions of individuals and financial institutions.

fiscal policy: a macroeconomic policy that uses government spending and/or taxation to affect a country's GDP.

General Agreement on Tariffs and Trade (GATT): a trade agreement reached after World War II, designed to reduce the level of protectionism in the world economy.

Harris–Todaro model: the theory that rural to urban migration is caused by differences in the relative incomes obtainable in the two areas.

industrial policy: a policy or set of policies designed to stimulate the growth of an industry or affect the industrial structure of a country.

monetary policy: the policy of the central bank with respect to the growth rate of the money supply and interest rates.

real interest rate: the nominal interest rate minus the expected rate of inflation.

structural unemployment: unemployment that occurs as labor moves from one part of the economy to another.

structuralist economics: the idea that the structure of an economy can have important effects on economic outcomes.

terms of trade: the price of exports divided by the price of imports.

Questions for review and discussion

1 Explain how a global downturn could cause balance-of-payments problems in a country that exports commodities.
2 What is structuralist economics? How did it apply to Latin America?
3 Describe the link between structuralist economics and dependency theory.
4 Describe the process that led many countries in Latin America to adopt ISI development policy in the 1950s.
5 Who was Raúl Prebisch? Why was he important?
6 What is industrial policy? How is it related to ISI?
7 How was trade policy used to implement ISI?
8 Explain the role of exchange-rate policy in ISI.
9 What is financial repression? How did it relate to ISI?
10 How were capital flight and currency substitution related to ISI?
11 How were ISI and SOEs related?
12 Describe the relationship among ISI, FDI, and MNCs.
13 List and describe the characteristics of industrialization under ISI.
14 How was ISI related to the rise of the informal sector?
15 How did ISI damage the development of the agricultural sector?
16 How did ISI contribute to the urbanization and pollution problems of the region?
17 Describe the Harris–Todaro model, and think of a Latin American example.
18 Describe the link between ISI and inflation in Latin America.
19 What was the link between ISI and the trade balance?
20 How did ISI lead to the Lost Decade of the 1980s?

Notes

1 A more detailed description of Latin American trade policy is given in the next chapter.
2 We will encounter structuralist economics again in a discussion of inflation in Latin America. It has reappeared more recently in the more rigorous work of Lance Taylor.
3 In a Latin American context, the Brazilian economist Celso Furtado was the best-known proponent of this approach. For details see Furtado (1963).
4 See United Nations Department of Economic and Social Affairs (1949).
5 That may have turned out to be the case. Higher wages in the formal sector simply meant more jobs in the informal sector.
6 For anyone with an interest in either the man or the times, the biography by Dosman (2008) is required reading.
7 The flaws will become more obvious as we move through the material.
8 An old joke among economists is that if government officials could actually do this, they would be much better off working for an investment company.
9 More information on Latin America and GATT will be presented in the next chapter.
10 This is part of the problem of the generally low rate of savings in the region, which hinders economic growth.
11 This situation would be unlikely to occur if the rate paid on savings were not being controlled. In defense of the countries of Latin America, such controls were not unknown in the *developed* countries before the 1980s.
12 For more details on this, see Edwards (1995).
13 In defense of Brazil, some high-income countries in Europe attempted the same approach with similar results. Even the World Bank partially funded the efforts of the Brazilian government.

14 For an early, but very accurate, analysis of ISI and industrialization, see Baer (1972).
15 Many countries used multiple exchange rates in which the price of foreign exchange depended on the proposed use.
16 For an excellent description of this process in Mexico City, see Ross (2009).
17 This point will be clearer in Chapter 12 on poverty and income distribution.
18 At this point, we are omitting some details, which will be covered in Chapter 9. These details do not alter what follows in any important way.

References

Arezki, Raban, Kaddour Hadri, Prakeash Loungani, and Yao Rao (2013) "Testing the Prebisch–Singer Hypothesis since 1650: Evidence from Panel Techniques that Allow for Multiple Breaks," *IMF Working Paper No. 13/180*, Washington, DC: International Monetary Fund.

Baer, Werner (1972) "Import Substitution and Industrialization in Latin America: Experiences and Interpretations," *Latin American Research Review*, 7 (spring): 95–122.

Dosman, Edgar J. (2008) *The Life and Times of Raúl Prebisch*, Montreal: McGill-Queen's University Press.

Edwards, Sebastian (1995) *Crisis and Reform in Latin America: From Despair to Hope*, Washington, DC: World Bank.

Furtado, Celso (1963) *The Economic Growth of Brazil: A Survey from Colonial to Modern Times*, Los Angeles, Calif.: University of California Press.

Mendoza, Plinio A., Carlos A. Montaner, and Alvaro V. Llosa (2000) *Guide to the Perfect Latin American Idiot*, Lanham, Md.: Madison Books.

Ross, John (2009) *El Monstruo: Dread and Redemption in Mexico City*, New York: Nation Books.

United Nations Department of Economic and Social Affairs (1949) *Relative Prices of Exports and Imports of Underdeveloped Countries: A Study of Post-war Terms of Trade between Underdeveloped and Industrialized Countries*, New York: United Nations.

Recommended reading

Aizenman, Joshua (2005) "Financial Liberalisations in Latin America in the 1990s: A Reassessment," *World Economy*, 28 (July): 959–983.

Bruton, Henry J. (1998) "A Reconsideration of Import Substitution," *Journal of Economic Literature*, 36 (June): 903–936.

Cypher, James M. and James L. Dietz (2014) *The Process of Economic Development*, 4th edn, London and New York: Routledge.

Edwards, Sebastian (2003) "Financial Instability in Latin America," *Journal of International Money and Finance*, 22 (December): 1095–1106.

Kaminsky, Graciela L. and Carmen M. Reinhart (1998) "Financial Crisis in Asia and Latin America: Then and Now," *American Economic Review*, 88 (May): 444–448.

Prebisch, Raúl (1950) *The Economic Development of Latin America and Its Principal Problems*, New York: United Nations.

8   Latin American trade policy

Introduction

As we saw in the last chapter, one of the key features of ISI was the deliberate reduction of imports in the region. In parts of the discussion, one probably picked up the impression that substituting domestic production for imports may not have improved the economic situation of Latin America. The purpose of this chapter is to show why the trade-policy part of ISI led to such poor results. In order to do this, it will be necessary to show why unrestricted international trade is normally an optimal trade policy. Sadly, this is rarely the policy that governments in Latin America or anywhere else pursue. Although there a number of government policies that interfere with trade, the most important for our purposes are tariffs and quotas. The second section of the chapter shows how these policies affect the domestic economy. The subsequent sections of the chapter cover the history of trade policy in Latin America before, during, and after the implementation of ISI. This history is critical in understanding Latin America's relative isolation from the world economy, the Lost Decade, and the lingering effects of ISI in the region.

Comparative advantage

It is a truism in economics that trade enhances the welfare of a country. Countries prosper by selling to the rest of the world goods that can be produced cheaply and buying goods that are expensive to produce domestically from other countries. As a result, ISI was always viewed with some suspicion, as one of its foundations was that trade was not enhancing the welfare of Latin America. In this section, we will gradually cover the standard theory of international trade that has been developed over the past 200 years. In the previous chapter, we mentioned the concept of *comparative advantage*. Our purpose here is to explain comparative advantage in more depth. This explanation will more clearly show that a substantial part of ISI had questionable foundations. The next part of this section will cover what determines comparative advantage. The concepts of comparative advantage and disadvantage will allow us to more clearly understand how ISI distorted the economies of the region. These distortions impeded the economic integration of Latin America and have made the integration of the region into the world economy more difficult.

Trade based on absolute advantage

To start with, we need to return to the previously introduced concept of *mercantilism*. As we explained in Chapter 2, mercantilism was the idea that countries could maximize their welfare by adding to their stocks of gold and silver. To accomplish this, countries tended to pursue policies designed to suppress imports and promote exports. While deeply flawed, the concept was the conventional wisdom concerning international trade for hundreds of years. The mercantilist policies imposed on the region during the colonial period were standard for the time. Writing in the late eighteenth century, Adam Smith was the first economist to question the validity of mercantilism. The device he used to do so employed the concept of *absolute advantage*. Absolute advantage is the ability of a country to produce a good using fewer resources than another country. A simple numerical illustration can be used to illustrate the concept. Table 8.1 shows the production of two sorts of goods: machines and commodities. Machines are simply shorthand for the sort of complex manufactured goods that Latin America has imported from more developed countries for the last 500 years. Analogously, commodities are shorthand for the minerals and agricultural products that have comprised the bulk of Latin America's exports to the rest of the world over the same time frame. For convenience, we are analyzing Latin America's trade with the rest of the world. The table shows that a worker in Latin America could produce either two machines per day or fifteen units of a commodity.[1] A worker in the rest of the world could produce five machines per day or ten units of a commodity. If we compare workers in the two regions, Latin American workers are more productive at producing commodities. Workers in the rest of the world are more productive at producing machines. All else being equal, machines will be cheaper in the rest of the world, and commodities will be cheaper in Latin America. Note that both regions gain from trade. Latin America can purchase machines much more cheaply than they can produce them domestically. The rest of the world get to purchase commodities at a lower price than they could produce them domestically. Smith was just showing that countries gain by selling products to the rest of the world and importing products that would be more expensive to produce domestically. The table also indicates that the *world* is better off by trading. Note that if Latin America specializes in the production of commodities, it will start moving labor out of machines and into the production of commodities. As one worker is shifted, the production of commodities rises by fifteen units and the production of machines falls by two. In the rest of the world, the production of machines rises by five and the production of commodities falls by ten units. As a result of shifting labor in both regions, world output of both machines and commodities rises by three and five units, respectively. Countries engage in trade to increase their welfare. However, in doing so, the economic output of the world rises. This is a kind of positive externality for the world that frequently isn't mentioned. Trade is not an n-sum game in which one country's gain is another country's loss. It is a positive sum game in which all countries, and thus the world, benefit.

Trade based on comparative advantage

Given the hundreds of years that mercantilist policy had been in place, proponents of the doctrine were not going to accept a different theory of trade based solely on Smith's

Table 8.1 Trade based on absolute advantage

	Machines	Commodity
Latin America	2	15
Rest of the world	5	10

Table 8.2 Trade based on comparative advantage

	Machines	Commodity	Relative prices
Latin America	1	5	1/5 machine = 1 commodity
Rest of the world	5	15	1/3 machine = 1 commodity

work. This was aided by the fact that there was a potential flaw in his argument. To illustrate the problem, consider the data in Table 8.2. In this table, the numbers of machines and commodities produced for each region have been changed slightly. In this example, a worker in Latin America can produce one machine per day or five units of commodities. A worker in the rest of the world can produce five machines per day or fifteen units of commodities. The difference here is that the rest of the world has an absolute advantage in the production of both products. Using absolute advantage as a basis for trade, there is no reason for the rest of the world to trade with Latin America. The rest of the world has an absolute advantage in the production of both products.

The proponents of free trade initially had no answer for this criticism. In the eighteenth century, the UK could produce most goods under conditions of absolute advantage. It wasn't obvious that free trade would enhance a country's welfare. From the publication of the *Wealth of Nations* until 1817, there was no explanation for the superiority of free trade over mercantilism. It was left to David Ricardo to show the gains from trade based on comparative advantage. In order to understand this, one needs to look at the fourth column of Table 8.2. This shows the relative price of the two goods in the two regions. In Latin America, the relative price of machines is five units of commodities. This represents the *opportunity cost* of producing an extra machine. To produce an extra machine, the region must sacrifice the production of five units of commodities. Another way of looking at the relative price is that a unit of commodities costs one-fifth of a machine. In the rest of the world, a worker can produce either five machines or 15 yards of cloth. This means that the relative price of one machine is three units of commodities. In the rest of the world, the production of an extra machine means an opportunity cost of three units of commodities. As before, another way of expressing the relative price is that one unit of commodities costs one-third of a machine. This particular bit of arithmetic is important. Looking only at absolute advantage, the rest of the world can produce both goods more cheaply than Latin America. However, the prices of the two goods in the two regions are different. Commodities are cheaper in Latin America. They cost only one-fifth of a machine, while in the rest of the world they cost one-third of a machine. This is because the opportunity cost of producing commodities is Latin America is lower. The reverse is true for the rest of the world. A machine costs only three units of commodities, while in Latin America a machine costs five units of commodities. Latin America has a low opportunity cost of producing commodities, and the rest of the world has a low opportunity cost of producing machines. This gives Latin America a comparative advantage in commodities and the rest of the world a comparative advantage in machines. Both countries can now benefit from trade even if the rest of the world has an absolute advantage in both products.

We can now consider trade in a way that is very relevant to Latin America. In autarky, in order to produce a machine, Latin America would have to sacrifice five units of commodities. The rest of the world only has to sacrifice three units of commodities to produce a machine. By purchasing machines from the rest of the world with commodities, Latin America can obtain a machine for three units of commodities rather than five. By trading, the region can either obtain the same number of machines for fewer commodities or buy more machines. The problem with ISI should now be clear. In attempting to industrialize, Latin America substituted domestic production for imports. In the process, all of these domestically produced goods were more expensive than imports. Resources were being diverted from industries in which the region had a comparative advantage to comparative *disadvantage* industries. While this is technically feasible, the economic argument for doing so isn't clear. Notice that the example applies to a single industry. Now consider the opportunity cost to a country of diverting pro-duction in this way across a large number of industries. If the policy is pursued vigor-ously enough, the losses to the economy can become quite large.

Comparative advantage and ISI

At this point, we can now form a tentative link between the discussions of compara-tive advantage in this chapter and ISI in Chapter 7. One of the underpinnings involved in the adoption of ISI was the idea that trade was harming the economic interests of Latin America. As we have shown above, to an economist, this is a puzzling assertion. Raúl Prebisch and others argued that because the region was experiencing a decline in the terms of trade, trade with the developed countries was not enhancing the economic development of the region. This view may be related to a common problem associated with analyzing the gains from trade. To understand the problem, it will be necessary to refer back to Table 8.2. In Latin America, the relative price of a machine is 1M = 3C. In the rest of the world, the price is 1M = 5C. These domestic prices determine the limits to trade. No one in Latin America would pay more than 5C for a machine. Likewise, no one in the rest of the world would take less than 3C for a machine. The domestic prices have set the limits to mutually beneficial trade. No rational seller in either market would sell at a price lower than what could be charged in the domestic market. In this situation, both countries can benefit from trade at any price between 1M = 3C and 1M = 5C. One of the limitations of our example is that the *exact* price that would pre-vail under free trade cannot be determined from the data. However, it is certain that no one in Latin America would pay more than 1M = 5C. The only feasible price for traders in the region is some price less than this.

However, there is a general principle that can be shown. For Latin America, the closer the price is to the price in the rest of the world (1M = 3C), the better off the region will be. This is because the region would be giving up fewer commodities to obtain a machine. The reverse is true. The closer the price is to 1M = 5C, the worse off Latin America will be relative to the rest of the world. While both regions gain from trade, free trade does not ensure that both regions will gain equally. As the price approaches the domestic price of your trading partner, your welfare will improve. As it approaches your own domestic price, your welfare diminishes.

It is here that perhaps the proponents of ISI came to an unfortunate conclusion. Unless traders in Latin America were irrational, it was virtually impossible for trade to be making the region worse off. No rational trader would have paid more for foreign goods than for domestic goods. If domestic manufactured goods were not available, there was a reason for this. The opportunity cost of producing them was too high. It was cheaper for the region to trade commodities for goods that would have been too costly to produce. However, it may well have been true that the relative price of commodities was declining in relation to that of machines.[2] This would mean that Latin America was receiving fewer of the gains from trade. In our example, this would mean that the relative price was moving toward 1M = 5C over time. While such a movement would reduce the benefits of trade to the region, it is *not* true that trade was making the region worse off. A decline in the terms of trade reduces the benefits of trade, but it is not an argument for replacing imports with domestically produced goods that are more expensive than imported goods. That policy will make the region worse off. Spending 10 pesos to produce a good domestically that can be purchased in the world market for 5 pesos is equivalent to buying machines at a price of 1M = 10C. Sadly, this situation, which would virtually never occur in a free market, became a normal state of affairs for many of the countries of the region.

Box 8.1 The terms of trade in Latin America

In the previous chapter, we covered the role of the terms of trade in the formation of ISI in Latin America. The argument was that the terms of trade were declining for Latin America, and this implied that reducing international trade would improve economic performance in the region. While that argument was unfortunately not the case, this does not imply that the terms of trade are unimportant. Under normal circumstances, trade will always benefit a country. However, as we saw in the preceding section, the distribution of the gains from trade are not necessarily evenly distributed. In a crude way, economists measure the distribution of the gains from trade by looking at the ratio of export prices (Px) to import prices (Pm). Px and Pm are measured as export and import price indexes, respectively. While the calculation of price indexes is always fraught with difficulties, they do convey some useful information about the gains from trade. If the terms of trade are trending upward for a long period of time, this would indicate that a country or region is obtaining more of the gains from trade and is experiencing an improvement in economic welfare. Less pleasantly, the reverse would be true. From independence to the late nineteenth century, the terms of trade for the region were, on average, rising. This is part of the story of the Golden Age of Latin American economic history. From that peak, the terms of trade declined almost continuously until the late 1940s.[3] The architects of ISI were right in one regard. During the period for which they had data, the terms of trade for Latin America were, in fact, declining. Also, this relates to the problems discussed in Chapter 6. If a region is a heavy exporter of commodities, the terms of trade will quite likely be subject to large swings. As a result, the economic fortunes of the region may be strongly influenced by changes in the terms of trade. Unfortunately, this is not the end of the terms-of-trade story. Such changes still influence overall economic conditions in the region in the twenty-first century. One should keep this in mind for reference during some of our later discussion on macroeconomics, the exchange rate, and the balance of payments.

Comparative advantage, factor prices, and the distribution of income

While the analysis of the gains from trade given above is useful, it is also incomplete. The basic theory of comparative advantage does not really explain what *causes* comparative advantage. In this context, comparative advantage is a result of differences among countries in the opportunity cost of producing goods. That begs the question of what causes differences in opportunity costs. In the next section, we will present a basic theory concerning this issue and apply it to Latin America. Also, this theory is very useful in examining the influence of trade on the prices of the factors of production. Since trade influences factor prices, it has a discernible effect on the distribution of income.

The Heckscher–Ohlin model

In the early twentieth century, Eli Hecksher and Bertil Ohlin produced a more complete theory of the causes of international trade. In the *Heckscher–Ohlin model*, the costs of production are determined by the relative abundance of the factors of production. In its most simple form, the model uses two factors of production: capital and labor. To start with, we will assume that Latin America is relatively labor-abundant. On the other hand, we will consider the rest of the world to be relatively capital-abundant. Using a term we developed in Chapter 3, Latin America and the rest of the world would have a low and a high K–L ratio, respectively. This difference in the K–L ratio affects factor prices. In Latin America, labor would be relatively cheap, and capital would be relatively expensive. In the rest of the world, the reverse would be true. Labor would be relatively expensive, and capital would be cheap. The model assumes that countries will naturally have different K–L ratios. These differences can be seen in Table 8.3, which shows the K–L ratios for the countries of Latin America and some high-income countries. Note that relative to these countries, the K–L ratios for Latin America are low. In general, the region is abundant in labor.

To complete the model, we will make an assumption about the production process for machines and commodities. The production of machines is always *capital-intensive*. This means that the production process always uses a lot of capital relative to labor. The production of commodities is always *labor-intensive*. It naturally uses a lot of labor relative to capital. From these assumptions, we can now determine the cause of comparative advantage. If the production of machines is capital-intensive everywhere, then it will be cheaper to produce machines in a capital-abundant country. In other words, the rest of the world will have a comparative advantage in the production of machines because capital is cheap. Latin America would have a comparative advantage in commodities because commodities are labor-intensive and the region possesses cheap labor. Using a mix of factor abundance and factor intensities explains comparative advantage. The principle can be summarized thus: A country will have a comparative advantage in goods whose production intensively uses its relatively abundant factor of production. This is one of the most powerful statements in economics. It goes a long way toward explaining the pattern of trade for any country. In the context of Latin America, it is also important to keep in mind the other side of the coin: comparative disadvantage. A country will tend to have a comparative disadvantage in products that intensively use its scarce factor of production. For Latin America, capital would tend to be scarce and expensive.

Table 8.3 Capital-to-labor ratio in Latin America

	1990	2017
	Capital/labor	*Capital/labor*
Argentina	1,477	5,882
Bolivia	218	1,634
Brazil	1,555	2,941
Chile	1,685	6,789
Colombia	675	2,649
Costa Rica	1,301	4,491
Ecuador	895	3,343
El Salvador	350	1,496
Guatemala	336	1,342
Honduras	576	1,332
Mexico	2,000	4,592
Nicaragua	139	1,381
Panama	1,511	12,989
Paraguay	609	2,348
Peru	513	2,458
Uruguay	810	4,903
Venezuela, RB	616	8,488
Latin America	1,354	3,675
Low income	117	–
Middle income	546	3,789
High income	9,783	17,900
World	2,489	6,081

Source: World Bank (2019) and computation by authors.

Note: Data for Venezuela is from 2014.

As a result, the region would have a comparative disadvantage in the production of capital-intensive products.

Other factors influencing comparative advantage

In its simplest form, using two countries, two products, and two factors of production, the Heckscher–Ohlin model can logically explain comparative advantage. The results of the model can be generalized to many countries, many goods, and more factors of production. Fifty years of empirical research on the determinants of international trade have shown that there are factors other than just labor and capital that are important in explaining trade flows. First, the assumption that labor is homogeneous can be an empirical problem. When we use the term *labor-abundant*, we usually need to refine what we mean by the term *labor*. Aside from just the number of workers, there is the human capital embodied in the labor force. For some products, the key to comparative advantage is the abundance of human capital. As was shown in Chapter 3, the accumulation of human capital is currently a problem in Latin America. What this means is that Latin America on average would have a comparative disadvantage in human capital-intensive products. To an even larger extent, the same holds true for R&D. Some products are R&D-intensive. Their production relies on an abundance of R&D expenditures. Like most middle-income countries, the countries of Latin America spend a small percentage of GDP on R&D. As a result, the region tends to have a comparative disadvantage in R&D-intensive goods.

Trade, factor prices, and the distribution of income

One of the important insights that followed the development of the Heckscher–Ohlin model of trade was that international trade can affect the distribution of income in a country. To see this, consider what happens to industrial structure following a movement from autarky to trade. In our example, there are two industries in Latin America: commodities and machines. The former is the comparative advantage industry, and the latter is the comparative disadvantage industry. As trade opens up, the commodities industry will start to expand to satisfy both domestic consumption and the export market. On the other hand, the machine industry will begin to contract, as some domestic production will be replaced by imports. However, these changes will influence the prices of labor and capital. Commodities are labor-intensive. As the industry expands, the demand for labor will increase substantially. There will be an increase in the demand for capital as well, but it will be relatively small, given production conditions for commodities. Where will the labor and capital for this expansion come from? The answer lies in the decline of the machine industry. As imports of machines increase, domestic production of machines will fall. This reduction will release labor and capital that are no longer needed in that industry. There is a mismatch at work here. The machine industry is capital-intensive. As it shrinks, it is releasing a lot of capital and much less labor. The needs of the expanding commodity industry are the reverse. The industry needs a lot more labor and not much capital. This will affect the price of labor and capital. The demand for labor is rising faster than the increase in the supply of labor. As a result, the price of labor rises. The reverse is true for the price of capital. The large increase in the supply of capital is occurring with only a small increase in the demand for capital. The result is that the price of capital falls. These effects are known as *factor-price equalization*. Trade has a tendency to diminish the differences in factor prices between countries that trade. While trade does not usually lead to perfect factor-price equalization, it will influence wages and the return to capital in a systematic way. We can now take this logic one step further. Specifically, trade increases the price of the *abundant* factor of production. It also decreases the price of the scarce factor of production. What this implies is that labor is now getting a larger share of national income. On the other hand, trade is diminishing the welfare of the owners of the scarce factor of production, capital. With trade, capital is receiving a lower percentage of national income. As one might expect, trade not only influences factor prices, it also influences the distribution of income between labor and capital. The abundant factor tends to get a larger share of national income, and the scarce factor loses. These effects of trade on the distribution of income are known as the *Stopler–Samuelson theorem*.

Now consider what this means in terms of Latin America. The region is clearly labor-abundant. A movement from autarky to free trade would tend to change the industrial structure of the region. Labor-intensive industries would tend to become larger. In turn, this would increase the number of jobs in these industries. Because of factor-price equalization, wages would tend to increase. This increase in wages would increase the percentage of national income received by labor. Since Latin America is labor-abundant, trade would tend to increase the welfare of workers in the region. The same is not true for the owners of capital. Trade would tend to reduce the return to capital and lower the percentage of national income going to the owners of capital. In developing countries, trade has the potential to improve the distribution of income. Laborers are generally poor, and trade tends to improve their welfare by raising wages. On the other hand, trade tends to reduce the welfare of the owners of capital. In autarky, they benefit from the ownership of a scarce factor of production. With trade, the return to the scarce factor falls. Since the owners of capital are usually well-off, their loss of income improves the distribution of income. As we will see, this has an unfortunate implication. To the extent that the owners of capital understand that trade is not in their best interest, they will have a tendency to resist it. This helps to make the high trade barriers in Latin America somewhat more understandable. To the extent that the owners of capital have any influence on government policy, they are unlikely to be enthusiastic about international trade. This is an unfortunate result, given the chronic income-distribution problems of the region. As we will see, policies that reduce the amount of trade in Latin America tend to harm the interests of labor and improve the welfare of the owners of capital. Unfortunately, the story does not end there. Most countries do not allow free trade in goods and services. The world economy, and Latin America is no exception, is riddled with various barriers to trade. Although free trade maximizes the welfare of society as a whole, the benefits are not evenly distributed. Free trade produces losses for some industries and workers. To the extent that these groups can avoid these losses, they will attempt to do so. In the next section, we consider how barriers to trade tend to protect these groups and how the economy loses in the process.

Box 8.2 Trade, factor endowments, and inequality in the nineteenth century

In Chapter 2, emphasis was placed on the role of institutions in the economic development of Latin America over the centuries. To briefly review, the argument is that the initial endowments of Latin America produced a certain set of institutional arrangements in the region. In turn, these institutions tended to shape economic outcomes of the region, such as a high level of income inequality, which still persists. While this train of thought is important, income inequality is a complex phenomenon, which may well be influenced by other factors. Along with the impact of institutions, factor endowments and international trade may well have played a role. Another contribution to explaining income inequality stresses the movement of the region into and out of the world economy at different points in time. However, in both cases, there is not nearly as much empirical research on these issues as one might want.

In a recent article, Arroyo Abad (2013) has been able to show the effects of changes in factor endowments and trade on income inequality in the nineteenth century for four countries: Argentina, Mexico, Uruguay, and Venezuela. Specifically, the study investigates the influence of changes in the terms of trade and the relative abundance of land and labor. The early decades of the nineteenth century saw the dismantling of the Spanish colonial empire. This transformation included the ending of mercantilism, covered in Chapter 2. The result was that the countries of the region were now free to trade with the rest of the world and fully participate in the global economy. Since most of the exports of the region were commodities, their prices were volatile. This volatility affected the distribution of income. To the extent that the commodities were based on land, high prices tended to increase inequality. This was also a period of mass migration into the region. This migration affected the relationship between the returns to land and the returns to labor. The result of migration tended to increase inequality, as it reduced the return to labor. With migration, new areas of land could now be developed, which had the effect of reducing inequality. The result was that then, as now, international trade and globalization can have important effects on the distribution of income. While the idea that institutions had an important effect on the economies of the region is correct, one should be careful not to assume that this is the *only* factor at work.

The economic effects of tariffs and quotas

However protection may affect special forms of industry it must necessarily diminish the total return to industry-first by the waste inseparable from encouragement by tariff, and second by the losses due to transfer of capital and labor from occupations which they would choose for themselves to less profitable occupations which they must be bribed to engage in. If we do not see this without reflection, it is because our attention is engaged with but a part of the effects of protection. We see the large smelting-works and the massive mill without realizing that the same taxes which we are told have built them up have made more costly every nail driven and every needle full of thread used throughout the whole country.

(Henry George)

In the preceding chapters, we have implied that free trade will tend to maximize the welfare of society. In this section, we will show this in a more formal way. Once we have established the benefits of free trade, we will be in a better position to understand how trade barriers reduce welfare. This is a particularly important point in the context of Latin America. The region has a long history of high barriers to trade. This historical protectionism has lingered into the twenty-first century. In order to assess the damage this has done to the region, it is necessary to examine the effects of tariffs and quotas in more detail.

The effects of free trade

To analyze the effects of free trade, consider the supply and demand curves shown in Figure 8.1. Following our earlier example, we will look at these effects for the machine industry. Latin America has historically had a comparative disadvantage in the production of certain types of products. Again, we can think of machines as a generic example of the sort of products the region is likely to import. As is usually the case, the demand for machines slopes downward and to the right, and the supply curve slopes upward and to the left. In a state of autarky, the price of machines would be P_d, and the equilibrium quantity would be Q_d. We can now examine the welfare effects in this market. For consumers, the *consumer surplus* would be equal to the triangle A. This is the area below the demand curve and above the market price. It represents the improvement in welfare that is obtained by consumers because of the difference between what they would have been willing to pay and the market price of P_d. Analogously, area B represents *producer*

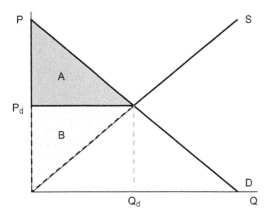

Figure 8.1 Equilibrium price and output in autarky.

surplus. This is extra welfare that the producers receive as a result of being able to obtain a market price that is above their cost of production.[4]

Now suppose that there are other producers in the world economy that can produce machines at a price lower than P_d.[5] In this case, Latin America would start importing machines. Graphically, importing machines would be equivalent to adding domestic suppliers in the region. Imports would show up as an increase in supply. Foreign machine producers would keep shipping machines to Latin America as long as the price they could obtain there was higher than the price they could get elsewhere. In other words, they would increase exports to Latin America until the price in the region matched the world market price. In the end, this process would yield a new equilibrium in the region of P_w and Q_2, shown in Figure 8.2. Domestic sales have increased because prices have fallen. However, domestic production has fallen from Q_d to Q_1. Domestic consumers are clearly better off, and domestic producers of machines are worse off. Society is better off because the gains to consumers are larger than the losses to producers. To show why this is true, we need to examine the changes in consumer and producer surplus that are shown in Figure 8.2. As the price drops from P_d to P_w, consumer surplus grows from area A to area A + B + C + D. The domestic producers are not so fortunate. Producer surplus falls from area B + E to area E. The overall effects are clear. Consumer surplus increases by B + C + D. Producer surplus falls by B. The gains to consumers are far larger than the losses to producers. Society as a whole is far better off than was the case with autarky. Unfortunately, this optimal state is not the norm in Latin America. Governments in the region have historically used barriers to trade to offset the effects on producers. The effects of these barriers are shown in the next section.

The effects of tariffs

We can now use the concepts of consumer and producer surplus to analyze the effects of restricting trade. Our analysis begins with the case of a country whose imports constitute a very small portion of world imports. The importing country is referred to as a price-taker because it is so small that it cannot influence world market conditions. For Latin America, this is not an unreasonable assumption.[6] In Figure 8.3, the domestic

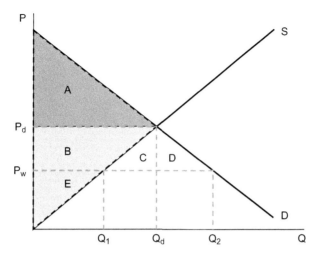

Figure 8.2 Changes in welfare resulting from trade.

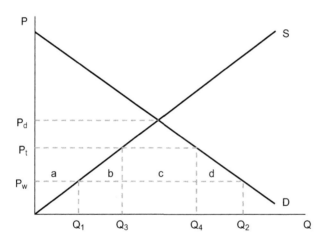

Figure 8.3 The effects of a tariff.

demand and supply of machines are illustrated. Before international trade, equilibrium price and output in the domestic market occur at P and Q, respectively. Now, assume that the small country has a comparative disadvantage in the production of machines and decides to engage in international trade. In this case, the country will be able to import at the world price (P_w), which is below the domestic price P. As we indicated earlier, this new equilibrium is clearly beneficial for the consumers of machines. It is as though a market-wide sale of cloth were occurring, as the price of cloth declines from P without imports to P_w with imports. In addition, the quantity of cloth that consumers are willing and able to buy increases from Q to Q_2. However, with free trade, the amount supplied by the domestic cloth industry contracts from Q to Q_1 as the price of cloth declines and imports increase.

Unfortunately, in Latin America, this has been a historically unusual result. Either to raise revenue or to protect domestic industry, governments in the region have typically imposed tariffs on imports. Given this, let's assume that the domestic government imposes a tariff on machines of the amount T to restrict imports. Because we have assumed that the importing country is small, it cannot influence world market conditions. In this case, the world price of cloth will remain constant at P_w. The imposition of a tariff raises the price of cloth in the importing country by the full amount of the tariff, T. The result is that the price of cloth in the importing country rises from P_w to P_t.

The higher price of imported machines has two effects. First, the quantity imported falls from the horizontal difference Q_1 to Q_2 to the smaller amount Q_3 to Q_4. The decline in imports is a result of lower domestic consumption of cloth—Q_2 to Q_4—and greater domestic production—Q_1 to Q_3. Second, consumers of cloth are clearly worse off. The price of cloth has increased, and the quantity of cloth consumers buy has declined. As a result, consumer surplus in the country has declined. Specifically, the loss in consumer surplus is represented by the area (a + b + c + d). As a result of the government imposing a tariff, consumers in the country lose. The remaining question is: Who gains? The gainers in the case of a tariff are the domestic government and domestic producers.

The rectangular area c represents the tariff revenue that the domestic government collects. The quantity imported after the tariff is imposed is the horizontal difference between Q_3 and Q_4. The tariff (T) is the difference between the world price, P_w, and the price paid by domestic consumers, P_t. Multiplying the quantity imported by the amount of the tariff gives us the total tariff revenue collected by the government: area c. As a result, the government gains this area, and the consumers lose it. If one assumes that the utility derived from government spending is the same as that derived from private consumption, there is no net loss to society as a whole from the consumer losing area c and the government gaining it. Area a represents a transfer of consumer surplus to producer surplus. This transfer of welfare from consumers to domestic producers represents the domestic producers' gains from a tariff.

From the standpoint of the domestic cloth producer, a tariff is not as good as autarky, but it is preferable to free trade. The small triangle b represents the cost of resources transferred from their best use to the production of more machines—Q_1 to Q_3. This represents a loss to society because in a free market these resources would have been used to produce a product in which the importing country has a comparative advantage.[7] Transferring resources to the tariff-ridden industry necessarily entails a loss of resources to some other more productive industry. Finally, area d represents a consumption effect caused by a tariff as consumers purchase less cloth—Q_2 to Q_4.

Areas a and c are redistributed from consumers to the producers and government, respectively. The net loss to society and the loss of consumer welfare are composed of area (b + d).

Box 8.3 Uniform tariffs in Chile

Although there are no efficiency reasons for uniform import tariffs, there are practical political economy considerations for advocating a flat import structure.

(Sebastian Edwards)

Most countries have a rather complicated tariff schedule with a different tariff for literally thousands of different product categories. An alternative to this is to have a *uniform* tariff or a single tariff for *all* imports. This neatly solves a number of problems with a complicated tariff structure. First, the tariff becomes easy to administer, because customs officials do not have to worry about classifying a product into whatever category it might best fit. Second, a uniform tariff makes lobbying for protectionism much harder. If an import-competing industry wants an increase in the tariff, the tariff would have to increase on all imports. This is likely to create some resistance, for several reasons:

- A general increase in the tariff is unlikely to pass by consumers completely unnoticed.
- Other industries capable of lobbying the government would likely do so.
- Firms purchasing imported intermediate products would see the increase in the tariff as a direct increase in their costs and would complain to the government. Under most supply and demand conditions, the firms would not be able to pass all of this cost increase on to consumers, and profits would fall.
- The same would be true of firms that are purchasing imports for final sale to the consumer.
- Firms that export may find tariff increases especially harmful, as these may dilute their ability to compete in international markets. The net result is that more firms may lose from the tariff than the number of firms that might gain from it.
- Given the above, the optimal public choice strategy for a politician may well be *lower* tariffs.

What we have just described is much like what happened in Chile during the past thirty years. In the early 1970s, Chile had tariffs that were high and very complex. These tariffs were replaced by a 10 percent uniform tariff in 1979. In response to an economic crisis in the 1980s, the uniform tariff was raised to 35 percent. Since the mid 1980s, the tariff has fallen to 7 percent.

This loss to society is referred to as the *deadweight loss* of a tariff. The deadweight loss represents a real loss to the country, since it is not transferred to another sector of the economy, and it represents a waste of resources in economic terms.

Trade and transportation costs

The analysis we used to analyze tariffs can also be used to consider the effects of transportation costs. Positive transportation costs increase the cost of supplying foreign markets and shift the supply curve back to the left. The result is that transportation costs both reduce the amount of trade and raise the price of imports. In effect, they act as a natural barrier to trade. The reverse holds true if transportation costs fall. A reduction in transportation costs would move the supply curve to the right. International trade would increase, and prices of products in world markets would fall. These transportation costs affected the economic development of Latin America. In the sixteenth century, transportation costs in international trade were extremely high. The sailing ships of the time were enormously expensive to operate, as they were very labor-intensive. In addition, unfavorable weather conditions and difficult maintenance could drastically increase the cost of a voyage from Europe to Latin America. The hurricane season in the Caribbean and the difficulties of navigating around the tip of South America made voyages at certain times of the year risky. All of these factors served to make a now routine voyage expensive. Under these circumstances, it was only profitable to carry products that had a high value to weight ratio. The ships were incapable of carrying large volumes of cargo, so international trade was mostly confined to very valuable goods. A look back at Table 5.1 confirms this. Prior to the mid nineteenth century, only expensive luxury goods were exported from Latin America. Note that after 1850, more prosaic commodities began to be exported. This was not an accident. The global boom in commodities trade that occurred in the second half of the nineteenth century was related to technological change. The widespread use of metal ships, coupled with steam power, dramatically changed international trade. These ships were capable of carrying large amounts of commodities at a very low price. Suddenly, commodities such as guano, henequen, rubber, or oil could be profitably transported over long distances. The subsequent boom in exports contributed to the Golden Age of Latin American economic history. Further changes in technology made it possible to export commodities such as beef from Argentina to European markets. Finally, the widespread use of railroads made it possible to transport commodities from the more remote parts of the region to the ports for transportation to foreign markets. This revolution in transportation costs fundamentally changed the nature of international trade. Traded items increased from almost purely luxury goods to a much wider group of products. These changes fundamentally changed the nature of the world economy. The changes were even more pronounced for Latin America. The ability to sell a wider range of products to the world was the source of the globalization of Latin America in the late nineteenth century. The region we observe today is still to a large extent the product of technological change and the resultant drop in transportation costs.

Transportation costs still affect Latin American trade. Recent research indicates that transportation costs for Latin American imports are nearly twice as high as those for the US. Even worse, transportation costs for *intra*-Latin American trade are just as high as for trade with the rest of the world. Examples of this can be seen in Table 8.4. For a sample of seven countries in the region, transportation costs amount to an ad-valorem tariff equivalent of 7.2 percent. The percentage for the US is almost half of this. The average tariff for these countries on a trade-weighted basis is 7.6 percent. Putting the two together yields a tariff that is effectively nearly 15 percent. The lesson is that reducing transportation costs is going to be an essential part of lowering overall

Table 8.4 Trade and transportation costs in Latin America

Country	Tariff equivalent transportation costs	Tariff	Total
Argentina	5.1	12.1	17.2
Brazil	5.5	10.0	15.5
Chile	7.5	6.0	13.5
Colombia	6.7	9.2	15.9
Peru	8.5	1.5	10.0
Paraguay	15.0	6.2	21.2
Uruguay	5.7	8.3	14.0
Average	7.2	7.6	14.8
US	3.7	2.1	5.8

Sources: Mesquita Moreira et al. (2008) and WTO (2014).

trade barriers in Latin America. These higher transportation costs impose tariff-like losses on the region. Also, they may partly explain the low openness to trade of the region. These high transportation costs are primarily related to two factors. First, it is true that products with a low value-to-weight ratio have higher transportation costs. For example, it costs more to transport cement than diamonds. As Latin America both exports and imports a substantial amount of commodities, this adversely affects transport costs. This is yet another example of the burden imposed on the region by dependence on commodities. In the short run, there is little government policy in the region can do to change this. The other factor is the efficiency of the ports. Port efficiency, like other forms of infrastructure, is positively related to GDP per capita. However, Mesquita Moreira et al. (2008) have shown that most of the countries of Latin America have ports that are of poorer quality than one would predict given their GDP per capita. This is one area of government policy in which the cost benefit of infrastructure investment is exceptionally clear.

Box 8.4 Brazilian soybean exports

One of the best-known examples of how transportation costs affect trade in Latin America is the difficulties associated with exporting soybeans from Brazil. Brazil is the second largest exporter of soybeans (the first is the US). In the competition for exports in the world market, Brazil and the US are direct competitors, and the differences in transportation costs are crucial. Soybeans are produced in several regions of Brazil. The highest-cost regions have production costs equal to those in the US. However, soybeans from the low-cost regions can be produced at a significantly lower cost than the most efficient US producers can achieve. In the low-cost regions of Brazil, over 50 percent of the crop is exported. These low production costs are slowly eroded by high transportation costs. The distance from the fields to the ports can be as much as 2,000 kilometers. Virtually all of the crop has to be transported by truck over roads that are often "unimproved." As of 2011, fewer than 14 percent of the roads in Brazil were paved. Railroads are almost nonexistent in the areas of the country that produce soybeans. The crop has to be transported a considerable distance to reach any mode of transportation other than trucks. Once differences in transportation costs to the ports are accounted for, the cost advantage of Brazilian soybeans has been seriously reduced. Once the crop has reached the port, it sits for an average of seven days before it is loaded onto a ship. In 2007, a ton of soybeans from an efficient Brazilian producer was sold for $206. By the time it left the port in Brazil, the cost had risen to $315. This is an exceptionally clear example of the problems that poor infrastructure in the region are causing. A lack of paved roads and inefficient ports put very efficient producers at a serious competitive disadvantage in world markets.[8]

The effects of quotas

As was shown above, tariffs are a very effective means of lowering the economic welfare of a country in any region of the world. Unfortunately, quotas are even more effective. In a later section of this chapter, we will discuss why quotas were extensively used as a

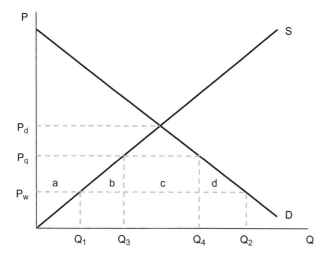

Figure 8.4 The effects of a quota.

trade-policy instrument in Latin America. In a previous chapter, we defined a quota as a quantitative restriction on the amount imported into a country. In this section, we will cover the economic effects of a quota and show that they are even more damaging to national welfare than tariffs.

Fortunately, the effects of a quota are very similar to the effects of a tariff. These effects are shown in Figure 8.4. In the graph, the domestic demand and supply of machines are shown. Again, we will assume that imports of machines lower the price in the domestic market from P_d to P_w. As before, the amount imported in this situation is the difference between the amount consumed (Q_2) and domestic production (Q_1). In this case, instead of using a tariff to raise the price of machines, a quota is imposed on the amount imported. In Figure 8.4, the maximum amount that can be imported is reduced, which effectively reduces the supply of imports. This reduction in supply reduces the quantity imported to the difference between Q_4 and Q_3. As before, the loss of consumer surplus is represented by the area a + b + c + d. The gain to domestic producers is area a. The deadweight loss due to the quota is b + d. The difference with a quota is area c. With a tariff, this area represents government revenue. However, with a quota, this revenue is lost. In this case, area c is transferred to the foreign exporters. They can charge a higher price for their product and legally avoid paying a tariff. As a result, under almost any conceivable set of circumstances, a quota is worse for the country than a tariff. Things can get even worse in the long run. If machines are at least a normal good, the demand for machines will tend to shift to the right as incomes increase. If the quota does not increase, then any change in demand is captured completely by the domestic producers. From their narrow point of view, a quota is better than a tariff. They only have to deal with a limited amount of foreign competition, and if demand increases, they capture all of this increase in demand. For domestic consumers and the government, the situation is not as satisfactory. Any increase in demand leads to further losses in consumer surplus and lost revenue for the government.

Note that Figure 8.4 is suspiciously similar to Figure 8.3. The effects of a quota and a tariff are indeed similar. Under most circumstances, they are equivalent. In this case, the quota causes a gap between the world price (P_w) and the quota-constrained price (P_q). If one expresses this difference as a percentage of the latter price, one arrives at the *ad-valorem equivalent* (AVE). AVE simply converts the degree of protectionism embodied in a quota and makes it comparable to an *ad-valorem tariff*. In many cases in Latin America, imports faced both a tariff *and* a quota. Under these circumstances, the losses to consumers and the economy as a whole become even larger than would be the case if either instrument of trade policy were used in isolation. The AVE equivalent will become important in a later context. International trade rules prohibit the use of quotas as an instrument of trade policy. However, countries that begin the process of complying with these rules are not asked to simply eliminate quotas. They are allowed to convert quota protection into tariff protection. Under these circumstances, the resulting tariff would be the AVE.

Latin American trade policy

In economics, trade policy refers to government actions that influence the flow of goods and services to and from a country. In this section, we will briefly review the history of trade policy in Latin America. As is frequently the case in Latin America, there have been relatively distinct historical periods in which there were relatively uniform policy changes. In the next section, we will cover trade policy in the region from independence to the Great Depression. As we saw in the previous chapter, the 1930s were characterized by a substantial shift in overall economic policy in the region. These changes included changes in international trade that will be covered in the section on trade policy and ISI. The next two sections consider how ISI influenced the participation of countries in the region in international trade negotiations and movements toward other forms of economic integration.

Pre-import-substitution-industrialization trade policy

From the start, there is a need to acknowledge an uncomfortable historical fact. For virtually all of its history, Latin America has had the world's most protectionist trade policy. As shown in the previous section, protectionism distorts domestic economic activity and lowers growth. Typically, it favors certain industries and workers at the expense of the welfare of society at large. Precisely why Latin America has been more prone to protectionism is not entirely clear.[9] The material that follows will focus on the known history of trade policy in Latin America rather than on why this was the case.

In a sense, Latin America since 1492 has always been protectionist. As you will recall from Chapter 2, the new rulers of the region enforced the policy of mercantilism. Colonies were not free to sell to other markets, and imports from anywhere other than Portugal or Spain were severely restricted. What is easy to forget is that this high level of protectionism lasted for over *300* years. Given the historical precedent, it would have been very unusual for the region to have swiftly moved from mercantilism to a trade policy with low levels of protectionism. Given the historical legacy of mercantilism, what occurred was perhaps what one would have expected: high levels of protectionism. As we will see, there were other factors involved in the determination of trade policy. However, the initial conditions were not conducive to free trade.

The end of Spanish colonial rule created another unfortunate effect. During the colonial era, there was at least free trade among the various parts of the region. With the exception of trade between the Spanish colonies and Brazil, goods could move freely around Latin America. In modern terms, the region was a de-facto customs union. Independence ended this situation. The wars of independence of the 1820s left Latin America balkanized into a large number of separate countries. Each country eventually erected its own barriers to trade and created its own currency. Both trade barriers and the lack of a common currency hinder growth. Many countries were too small to develop significant industry as there was no possibility of achieving economies of scale in many industries. The damage to growth in the region that this initial condition caused cannot be calculated. However, one way to think about the problem is to think in terms of the development of North America. Suppose that instead of two countries developing in the region, the region had fragmented into nearly sixty separate countries. Each of these "countries" would have its own barriers to trade and a separate currency. Intuitively, one can comprehend that this would have damaged the historical growth of the region. Just how serious this damage would have been is not certain, but the direction of the effect is clear. Unfortunately, this is precisely where Latin America started. Part, though by no means all, of the difference in the economic histories of North and South America can be traced to the unfortunate start of the latter region. This balkanization was exacerbated by small populations and low GDP per capita.[10]

Again returning to Chapter 2, the early decades after independence in the 1820s were marked by political instability and the violence that frequently goes with it. In this environment, during this period of history, this frequently meant high tariffs. The discussion above was focused on *protective tariffs*. The purpose of a protective tariff is to protect a domestic industry from foreign competition. Prior to the twentieth century, tariffs were often levied primarily as a means of raising revenue. A *revenue tariff* is a tariff whose primary purpose is raising revenue for the government as opposed to protecting specific domestic industries. In the circumstances, it was essential for governments to raise as much revenue as possible. The boundary disputes and internal violence created a large need for revenue by governments of the region. New countries frequently have limited options in terms of raising revenue. This was especially true for Latin America, because independence destroyed the old colonial systems of raising revenue. The new countries of Latin America were left with a low ability to tax and few bureaucratic resources. In these circumstances, tariffs become an attractive means of generating revenue for the government that is both feasible and low cost. With violence and instability lasting for decades, tariffs were raised to extremely high levels to finance military expenditures. Finally, tariffs in this period were normally *specific tariffs*. A specific tariff is expressed as a certain amount of money per unit, such as pesos per liter. In more modern times, tariffs are usually expressed as ad-valorem tariffs. An ad-valorem tariff is expressed as a percentage of the value of the imported good.[11] In the situation faced by Latin American countries in the nineteenth century, specific tariffs had two advantages. First, they were easier to administer and were attractive in an environment where bureaucratic resources were scarce. Second, specific tariffs made it more difficult for dishonest customs officials to appropriate part of the tariff revenue. Aside from the details, tariffs before the Golden Age were quite high.

During the Golden Age of Latin American history, the region became much more integrated into the world economy. The end of Latin America's relative isolation was primarily on the export side of trade. As discussed in Chapter 2, lower transportation costs for commodities, coupled with a boom in the world economy, produced large gains in trade for much of the region. However, there was far less of an opening on the import side. Recent research on tariff rates in the region indicate that tariffs did not fall during the Golden Age but instead rose and peaked in the late nineteenth century.[12] Tariffs fell sharply after World War I but began a long climb in the 1920s. As a result of the global trade war sparked by the passage of the Smoot–Hawley tariff in the US in 1930, tariffs in Latin America rose dramatically along with the general worldwide increase in protectionism.

The history of trade policy in Latin America before ISI can be summarized in this way. The mercantilist policies of Portugal and Spain left the region with a historical legacy of protectionism. The conditions surrounding independence exacerbated a preexisting condition. Tariffs remained high, as the governments of the region needed revenues for national defense and to maintain internal stability. While the region became more open to international trade during the Golden Age, the opening was more pronounced on the export side. Tariffs were high during this period. After a brief fall associated with World War I, tariffs in the region climbed during the 1920s and rose sharply during the global trade war of the 1930s. As we will see in the next section, ISI was less of a sharp break with the past than a continuation of a long historical record of protectionism. Latin America has virtually *always* had one of the highest levels of protectionism in the world. The degree to which this reduced growth in the nineteenth and early twentieth centuries is unknown. However, the direction of the effect is clear.

Box 8.5 The optimum tariff in Latin America

As we have seen on p. 180, tariffs can be used to raise revenue and to protect domestic industry. If one observes high tariffs, a reasonable question to ask is: What are the forces driving this? In the case of Latin America in the nineteenth century, the reasons for high tariffs seem reasonably clear. New and weak governments had few ways to collect revenue. Taxes on foreign trade were far easier to collect than other taxes, so tariffs were a convenient solution to government revenue problems. However, governments setting tariffs to maximize revenue have to be cautious about imposing the ad-valorem tariff that will maximize revenue. If the tariff is too low, then the government is not maximizing its revenues. On the other hand, if the tariff is too high, revenues likewise will not be maximized, and smuggling will be encouraged. Although it was not known in the nineteenth century, there is a convenient formula for calculating the optimum tariff or the tariff that will maximize government revenue from the tariff. The formula is:

$t^* = 1/(1 + e)$ where:
t^* is the optimum tariff.
e is the price elasticity of the demand for imports.

The critical variable is e. As the price elasticity varies, the optimum tariff will vary. In the nineteenth century, there is no way that governments in the region could have had explicit knowledge of these details. However, Coatsworth and Williamson (2002) have concluded that the observed tariffs in the region are consistent with available estimates of the price elasticity of import demand for the period. As in many other cases, economic agents, in this case governments, may act as if they have more formal economic knowledge than one might guess.

Trade policy under ISI

As we learned in the previous chapter, the argument for protectionism as an economic development strategy gained ground in Latin America during the 1940s. This occurred as a result of the confluence of one old and one new factor in the region. First, encouraged by the work of Raúl Prebisch and others, protectionism as a means of industrialization and economic development seemed plausible. Second, the region has always been one of the most protectionist regions in the world.[13] Prior to and during the Great Depression, tariffs in Latin America were high. The difficulty was that after World War II they were not reduced. As we will see in the next section, much of the rest of the world learned a hard lesson from the trade war of the 1930s. This lesson was that trying to increase domestic production through protectionism doesn't work well. Unfortunately, thinking on this issue in the region did not follow these global trends. ISI provided a veneer of respectability for the idea that a country or a region might be better off trying to industrialize and more generally develop by reducing imports and thus stimulating domestic production. In the postwar era, tariffs in Latin America began a slow climb during the 1950s and 1960s. Tariffs peaked during the 1970s and have declined significantly since then. While most of the rest of the world was reducing tariffs, in Latin America they were *increasing*.[14]

Unfortunately, tariffs understate the actual amount of protectionism in the region. The high tariffs were frequently supplemented with protection by quotas, which were covered earlier in this chapter. In this period, many countries in Latin America were still able to implement quotas with impunity. There were also other instruments of trade policy used for protectionism that are less well known but extremely protectionist in nature. An import license is a permission to import, issued by the government. Under import licensing, a potential importer must not only be willing to pay the world market price plus the tariff but also obtain explicit permission from the government to engage in this transaction. At a minimum, the time involved in obtaining permission constitutes an additional implicit tariff. In addition, governments in the region sometimes required an import deposit before the product could be imported. Effectively, this would require the importer to prepay for the goods in order to begin the transaction. Because exchange rates were fixed during this period, governments in the region were free to set different exchange rates for different sorts of transactions. These multiple exchange-rate systems frequently became an implicit means of protection, as different classes of importers had access to foreign exchange at different exchange rates. Moreover, the system was frequently ad-hoc in nature. Governments in the region during this period were often under extreme balance of payments pressure. Some of the measures described above were implemented more to conserve scarce foreign exchange than to provide explicit protection. However, the effects usually resulted in higher levels of protection, intended or not.

Box 8.6 Rent-seeking

From the discussion of tariffs and quotas above, it would seem logical that most countries would pursue a policy of free trade. Trade barriers impose significant economic losses on a country. However, public policy in a democratic society is often more complicated than merely finding the optimal economic policy and implementing it. Trade policy is a good case in point. As we saw above, free trade maximizes the welfare of society. However, the gains from trade are not evenly distributed. The government loses tax revenue, and producers lose some of their producers' surplus. In addition, workers in sectors of the economy that compete with imports have the same incentives as the firms they work for. A reduction in domestic production caused by imports may threaten jobs. As a result, both firms and workers have an incentive to lobby the government for restrictions on trade. While such restrictions may not benefit society as a whole, they do benefit certain groups. This lobbying for government policy that will aid particular groups but may harm society as a whole is known as *rent-seeking*. Economic rents can occur when an individual or a group can earn money by manipulating policy as opposed to earning profits from production. In this case, the firms and workers are attempting to increase their income by obtaining economic rents rather than producing more goods and services. In their desire to maximize votes, government officials may conclude that the granting of rents may in some cases produce more votes.[15] This can occur because trade has the peculiar asymmetric quality that the gains from trade are widely diffused while the losses are very concentrated.

Rent-seeking can be particularly damaging in the context of developing countries. In a small market, there may be only one or at most just a few firms in the industry. In this case, the costs of organizing the firms in the industry to lobby the government for protection can be relatively low. Such a situation is frequently the case in Latin America. In addition, manufacturing firms in the region are frequently unionized. Further, in many Latin American countries, unions are a powerful political force. Adding to the pressure is that manufacturing centers in much of Latin America are either in or close to the capital city. Throw even a modest amount of corruption into the mix, and rent-seeking can yield a rather high rate of protection for many of a country's industries. Unfortunately, rent-seeking is not confined to trade policy. Any form of government policy that can affect the economic interest of any group in society is susceptible to rent-seeking behavior. If one is ever prone to wonder why a country in Latin America is having a difficult time implementing a policy that would clearly improve the welfare of society, rent-seeking behavior may well be the answer.

The effective rate of protection

While the tariffs in Latin America were high, the situation during the ISI period was actually considerably worse than indicated. To understand why, we need to explain the concept of the *effective rate of protection*. The actual purpose of a tariff is to encourage domestic value added in an industry. If a product produced in a country incorporates any foreign components, then the structure of protection can affect the amount of protection afforded to a domestic industry. A simple example will suffice to illustrate the point. Suppose a producer of a consumer good in Latin America is importing 50 percent of the value of the product, and the product sells for 100 pesos. The value added domestically is 50 pesos. If the tariff on the product is 20 percent, then the tariff-inclusive price is 120 pesos. Because of the tariff, the domestic value added is now 70 pesos. The effective rate of protection is the percentage increase in the domestic value added. In this case, it has risen by 40 percent. Thus, the degree of protection afforded to the domestic producer is not 20 percent but 40 percent. The general formula for determining the effective rate of protection (ERP) is

ERP = (Tf aTc)/(1 a) where:

Tf is the tariff on the final product.

Tc is the tariff on imported components a is the percentage of imported components.

Although the number of outcomes of this calculation is infinite, it is very common for the ERP to be higher than the nominal tariff. This is because it is common for countries to have lower tariffs on inputs into domestic production than on final goods. Latin America was no different in this regard, but ISI aggravated this situation. Many ISI industries were operating with a substantial amount of imported intermediate goods, with final production occurring in the region. Under these circumstances, a nominal tariff of 35 percent could yield truly astonishing effective rates of protection. Effective rates of protection above 100 percent were not uncommon.[16] The important point is that any nominal tariff rate has to be considered in light of the ERP. In many cases, the actual level of protection is considerably higher than the posted tariff indicates.

The extremely high levels of protection profoundly distorted the economies of the region. On the one hand, as one can imagine, the losses for the consumers and the economies of Latin America were immense. On the other hand, domestic production rose, and manufacturing for these protected domestic markets was strongly encouraged. Moreover, these policies had two other effects. As the markets in Latin America closed to imports, firms wishing to sell in these markets began pursuing FDI. With the level of protection so high, FDI became a way to "jump over" the tariff wall and more profitably serve a protected domestic market. It also stimulated the use of SOEs when even high levels of protection could not entice the private sector into domestic production. Unfortunately, both domestic and foreign firms were almost completely focused on producing in the most profitable way for a highly protected domestic market. Implicitly, the protection was encouraging the development of industries in which Latin America did not have a comparative advantage. In many cases, the reverse was occurring. Firms were prospering in areas in which the region had a comparative disadvantage. By the end of the ISI period in the 1980s, the industrial base of the region could not compete domestically without protection and was incapable of competing in international markets. As we will see in later chapters, ISI induced chronic balance-of-payments problems. The protected firms required imported inputs to continue to produce. This was coupled with an inability to obtain foreign exchange via exports. For a while, the way out of this dilemma was an increasing amount of debt. Once the amount of debt became unsustainable, then fundamental policy changes became unavoidable. An interesting question at this point is how Latin America was able to pursue protectionism for so long when the rest of the world was liberalizing trade. The answer is that much of the region simply avoided participating in the institutions that were fostering that process. In the next section, we detail the history of that nonparticipation.

Box 8.7 Why your coffee is not processed in Colombia (or Brazil)

The ERP explained above has had an effect on exports from the developing countries due to tariffs in the developed countries. In countries such as the US, it is all too common for tariffs to increase with the level of processing (tariff escalation). In other words, tariffs are low on primary commodities, higher on intermediate products, and still higher on finished goods. For example, consider coffee beans, roasted and ground coffee, and instant coffee. In such circumstances, the ERP is escalating with the level of processing. This structure of protection becomes an effective barrier for developing countries that could develop simple industries based on the processing of raw materials into semifinished or finished goods. Given the preponderance of commodities in the region's exports, this is not a small matter. Further, this can be a more general problem of industrialization. The processing of commodities is frequently the first step in industrialization. The lessons learned in doing simple manufacturing form the basis for more complicated processes later. If learning the basics of manufacturing doesn't occur, then industrialization becomes somewhat harder.

Table 8.5 shows the structure of protection for coffee in the European Union (EU), Japan, and the US. This is just an example, but the principle is quite general. Given Latin America's comparative advantage in commodities, the loss of value added in processing those commodities is not trivial.[17]

Table 8.5 Average ad-valorem tariffs on coffee

	EU	*Japan*	*US*
Coffee: not roasted	4	0	0
Coffee: roasted	8	12	0
Coffee: mixtures and extracts	12	39	12

Source: Cheng (2007).

Latin America and the General Agreement on Tariffs and Trade/World Trade Organization

The trade war of the 1930s marked a new era for both the world economy and Latin America. Most of the world outside Latin America quickly reached the conclusion that the trade war had been a catastrophic mistake. As early as 1934, the US had begun passing legislation that would eventually lay the groundwork for reducing the level of protectionism.[18] The latter half of the Great Depression and World War II prevented a major liberalization of world trade in the 1930s and 1940s. However, toward the end of the war, the US and the UK had begun negotiations on the establishment of institutions that would turn out to be of critical importance for Latin America.

In 1944, the Allied countries met at a conference in Bretton Woods, New Hampshire, to consider building institutions that would help to avoid a return of poor economic conditions after the end of the war. In Chapter 1, we mentioned the World Bank, or more technically the International Bank for Reconstruction and Development. The initial purpose of the World Bank was to assist countries in rebuilding from the devastation of World War II. With that task largely accomplished, the institution began loaning money in Latin America and other developing countries for specific economic-development projects. The second institution proposed at the conference was the *International Monetary Fund (IMF)*. Prior to the Great Depression, most of the countries of the world maintained a system of fixed exchange rates tied to gold (a gold standard). The economic stresses of the Great Depression led most countries to abandon the gold standard. In doing so, they effectively allowed their exchange rates to float. In the aftermath of these problems, there was a general realization that a return to a classical gold standard was not possible. However, there was consensus for a return to fixed exchange rates. Fixed exchange rates without a gold standard required an international body to oversee such a system. The IMF was the institution set up to oversee this new system of fixed exchange rates based on the US dollar rather than gold.

For our current purposes, the importance of the Bretton Woods conference was with respect to international trade. There was general agreement among countries that the trade war of the 1930s had contributed to the global economic contraction. As a result, there was a general desire to find a mechanism to reduce tariffs to something like their prewar levels and construct a mechanism for preventing a reoccurrence of global protectionism. The result was a proposal to establish the International Trade Organization (ITO). The actual negotiations to create the ITO were conducted from 1945 to 1948 and were concluded in Havana, Cuba. The refusal of the US Congress to ratify membership in the ITO meant that the organization never came into being. However, the backup position was not an organization but a treaty: the General Agreement on Tariffs and Trade (GATT). Under the auspices of GATT, the developed countries, increasingly joined by the developing countries, conducted international trade negotiations designed to gradually reduce the excessively high tariffs caused by the trade war of the 1930s. The focus of GATT was twofold. First, it required contracting parties to agree to two basic principles.[19] One was that tariffs were required to be on a most-favored-nation (MFN) basis. MFN embodies the principle of nondiscrimination. The lowest tariff for a product charged to any contracting party must be used for all contracting parties. More important for Latin America was the prohibition of the use of quotas as a means of protection. The mechanism for the liberalization was a series of *multilateral trade negotiations (MTNs)*. These MTNs were usually referred to as "rounds" of trade negotiations. The first four smaller rounds were followed by larger MTNs known as the Dillon Round (1960–1961), the Kennedy Round (1962–1967), the Tokyo Round (1973–1979), and the Uruguay Round (1986–1994). The current Doha Round began in 2001, and the negotiations are still ongoing. Through the Kennedy Round, MTNs were completely focused on reducing tariffs. Beginning with the Tokyo Round, the subsequent MTNs have been broadened to cover issues such as international trade in services, trade-related intellectual property, and nontariff barriers to international trade. Among the countries that have been participating, trade barriers have fallen substantially over the past fifty years.[20]

Until recently, the participation of the countries of Latin America in this process has been minimal. There are several reasons for this. From the start of the process, the prevailing view in the region was that free trade was unlikely to enhance the economic development of the region. In the twenty-first century, this view seems almost bizarre, but, as discussed earlier, it was the prevailing view of the times. A more important consideration was the issue of trade in agricultural products. Liberalizing trade in agricultural products was the most difficult problem facing the negotiations over GATT and the ITO. The failure of the ITO left the world with GATT. Unfortunately, in order to achieve an agreement, trade in agricultural products was not covered. International trade in agricultural products thus became a free-fire zone in which countries could introduce forms of protectionism that were completely illegal for trade in other types of products. These products were precisely the sort of products in which Latin America has a comparative advantage. As a result, the countries of the region perceived that GATT was almost irrelevant to their interests. This is illustrated in Table 8.6, which shows the dates on which the countries of the region joined either GATT or its successor, the *World Trade Organization (WTO)*. Note that the average date of accession for countries of the region was 1978. There were a few countries that joined early but were never really serious participants in MTNs. The majority of countries in the region did not join until the 1980s, and a number waited until the 1990s. Given the information above, this means that Latin America missed the Kennedy Round, the Tokyo Round, and the majority of the Uruguay Round. It was not until the 1980s that Latin America became active in MTNs. To be fair, this lack of interest in GATT was not confined to Latin America. In general, the developing countries were late to begin participating in the process. As exports of manufactured goods became more important, the developing countries and Latin America all became more active participants in the process. In the current Doha Round, Brazil has become an important voice for the interests of Latin America and the developing countries in general. However, the Doha Round is foundering on the rock of liberalizing trade in agricultural products and limiting the subsidies to farmers in developed countries with little comparative advantage in these products. These efforts have met with limited success. As we will see in the next section, the liberalization of trade in Latin America has followed a different path.

The most important factor illustrated by Table 8.6 is that being outside the official world trading system allowed Latin America to engage in trade practices that would have been illegal under GATT. As already mentioned, the situation left Latin America free to impose quotas on any product. For the contracting parties to GATT, quotas could only be used to protect agricultural products. Second, under GATT, tariffs were bound. This meant that tariffs for contracting parties could only be raised temporarily under certain circumstances.[21] For countries outside GATT, there was nothing to prevent a country from raising tariffs on any product at any time. Through the mid 1970s, the countries of the region tended to increase tariffs because there was no restriction on this behavior. Thus, while the rest of the world was reducing tariffs, the reverse was occurring in Latin America. The region was able to develop industries designed to replace imports by increasing tariffs and using quotas when that level of protection was not adequate. However, by definition, industries designed to replace imports are industries in which the country or region has a comparative disadvantage. This was not an accident but a deliberate policy choice. By the 1980s, the damage had been done. The region was left with industries that could not compete in domestic markets, let alone the world market. During this decade, Latin America began the long, painful switch to industries in which the region has a comparative advantage. Note that the decline in tariffs that began in the 1970s coincides with the more active participation of the countries of the region in international trade negotiations. This participation is in the best interests of the region, but the decades of nonparticipation carried a heavy price. There was less pressure in the large MTNs for liberalizing trade in agricultural products, which would have greatly benefited the region. More importantly, one can only imagine what might have been if Latin American trade policy had been in alignment with the rules of GATT.

Table 8.6 Dates of accession of Latin American
countries to GATT/WTO

Country	Date
Argentina	1967
Bolivia	1990
Brazil	1948
Chile	1949
Colombia	1981
Costa Rica	1990
Ecuador	1996
El Salvador	1991
Guatemala	1991
Honduras	1994
Mexico	1986
Nicaragua	1950
Panama	1997
Paraguay	1994
Peru	1951
Uruguay	1953
Venezuela	1990
Latin America	1978
Portugal	1962
Spain	1963
Canada	1948
US	1948

Source: WTO (2015a).

Regional trade agreements in Latin America

In the post-World War II era, Latin America was becoming more protectionist.
However, in both the world economy and Latin America, a new form of trade liberalization was being born. GATT obliged members to adhere to the principle of MFN
or nondiscrimination in tariffs. However, the original agreement contained an exception. Article XXIV of GATT provided an exception to MFN for free-trade areas and
customs unions. The former is an agreement between countries to eliminate tariffs on
"substantially all" trade within a "reasonable period of time." In practice, substantially
all trade meant virtually all trade in nonagricultural products. Likewise, a reasonable
period of time came to mean fifteen years. A customs union goes one step further. This
sort of agreement also requires the elimination of the various national tariff schedules
and their harmonization into a single tariff schedule for all countries. From the beginning of GATT until the late 1950s, Article XXIV was not particularly important. What
is now the EU was created by the Treaty of Rome in 1957, but the number of other
agreements was limited.

Article XXIV and the creation of the EU did have an impact on Latin America. The
protectionist policies fostered by ISI had the effect of isolating the countries of the
region from one another. Since many of these economies are small, the ability of industries to grow to an optimal size was severely limited by small domestic markets. The
creation of the EU spurred a burst of interest in *regional trade agreements (RTAs)* in
Latin America. Theoretically, such agreements would allow countries of the region to
obtain some of the gains from trade and protect their industries from competition from

countries outside of the region. These thoughts led to the formation in 1960 of the Latin American Free Trade Agreement (LAFTA), which was composed of ten countries in South America plus Mexico. Twenty years of attempted trade liberalization came to an end with the collapse of LAFTA in 1980. Another RTA among the countries of the Andean Region was attempted. The Andean Pact was formed in 1969 as an ambitious project to form a customs union in that part of South America. As in many cases of economic integration, the project proved too ambitious and foundered on the problem of forming a common external tariff (CXT) coupled with political instability in the region. Similar problems plagued the Central American Common Market (CACM). Launched in 1960, the CACM was initially more successful than other integration schemes in the region. However, war and political instability led to the eventual demise of the agreement. While the various economic integration schemes of the 1960s failed, they did set the stage for a renewal of RTAs in Latin America.

From the information given in the previous section, Latin America missed much of the liberalization of trade that occurred in the world economy, fostered by GATT and later the WTO. However, tariffs in Latin America have been falling for over twenty years as a result of increased participation in MTNs and the spread of RTAs. If this seems to be a puzzle, then RTAs are the solution to the seeming contradiction. In this case, Latin America has not been an outlier in the world economy, but is now following a general trend. When GATT was written, Article XXIV was conceived of as an exception to MFN that would probably apply primarily to what is now the EU. In the world economy, this seemed to be the case during the 1960s and 1970s. RTAs were formed in Latin America and elsewhere, but they were more exceptions to the rule, and their fate in other parts of the developing world was not dissimilar to the Latin American experience. Beginning in the 1980s, there was a noticeable increase in the number of RTAs in the world economy. By the 1990s and moving into the twenty-first century, RTAs are now appearing to be the future of trade liberalization. The difficulty of negotiations during the Uruguay Round and the inability to conclude the Doha Round seem to be contributing to this trend. While liberalization under MTNs and RTAs are not mutually exclusive, countries that wish to move to freer trade can now do so more quickly by signing RTAs. This trend is evident in Table 8.7. The initial impetus seems to have been the creation of the Mercado Comun del Sur (MERCOSUR) in 1991. MERCOSUR was formed as a customs union among Argentina, Brazil, Paraguay, and Uruguay. Tariffs among the countries were cut to zero by 2000, and a CXT was completed by 2006. Negotiations are now under way to produce a single market in the same sense in which the phrase is used in the EU.[22] Less noticed, but not unimportant, is the Andean Community (CAN), composed of Bolivia, Colombia, Ecuador, and Peru. As is apparent from Table 8.7, there is an enormous amount of trade liberalization occurring in the region. CAN and MERCOSUR have freed up trade among eight countries in the region. Both Chile and Mexico have been actively signing trade agreements with a number of other countries in the region. Note that every country in the region, with the exception of Venezuela, has signed at least one RTA. In addition, many of the listed RTAs involve free trade with countries outside the region. NAFTA has effectively spread to include Central America and Chile. Finally, there are a number of ongoing negotiations to create further RTAs both within the region and with countries outside the region.

As is always the case in economics, there are benefits and costs associated with the formation of RTAs. As shown earlier in the chapter, movements to freer trade

Table 8.7 RTAs in Latin America

Country	RTAs with
Argentina	CAN, Chile, India, MERCOSUR
Bolivia	CAN, Chile, MERCOSUR
Brazil	CAN, Chile, India, MERCOSUR
Chile	Australia, Brunei, CAN, Canada, China, Colombia, Costa Rica, EFTA, El Salvador, EU, Guatemala, Honduras, Hong Kong, India, Japan, Korea, Malaysia, Mexico, New Zealand, Nicaragua, Panama, Peru, Singapore, Turkey, US
Colombia	CAN, Canada, Chile, EFTA, EU, El Salvador, Guatemala, Honduras, Mexico, US
Costa Rica	Canada, Chile, China, El Salvador, Guatemala, Honduras, Nicaragua, Peru, Singapore, Dominican Republic, EFTA, EU, Mexico, Panama, US
Ecuador	CAN
El Salvador	Chile, Columbia, Costa Rica, Dominican Republic, Guatemala, Honduras, Nicaragua, Taiwan, EU, Mexico, Panama, US
Guatemala	Chile, China, Columbia, Costa Rica, Dominican Republic, El Salvador, EU, Honduras, Mexico, Nicaragua, Panama, Taiwan, US
Honduras	Canada, Chile, Columbia, Costa Rica, Dominican Republic, El Salvador, EU, Guatemala, Honduras, Mexico, Nicaragua, Panama, Taiwan, US
Mexico	Canada, Chile, Columbia, Costa Rica, EFTA, El Salvador, EU, Guatemala, Honduras, Israel, Japan, Nicaragua, Peru, Uruguay, US
Nicaragua	Chile, Costa Rica, Dominican Republic, El Salvador, EU, Guatemala, Honduras, Mexico, Nicaragua, Panama, Taiwan, US
Panama	Canada, Chile, Costa Rica, EFTA, El Salvador, EU, Guatemala, Honduras, Nicaragua, Peru, Singapore, Taiwan, US
Paraguay	India, MERCOSUR
Peru	CAN, Canada, Chile, China, Costa Rica, EFTA, EU, Japan, Korea, Mexico, Panama, Singapore, US
Uruguay	India, Mexico, MERCOSUR

Source: WTO (2015b).

Definitions: CAN: Bolivia, Colombia, Ecuador, Peru, Venezuela; EFTA: Iceland, Lichtenstein, Norway, Switzerland; MERCOSUR: Argentina, Brazil, Paraguay, Uruguay.

are beneficial for the economy as a whole. On the other hand, firms and workers in comparative disadvantage industries normally experience a reduction in output and number of jobs available, respectively. The years of ISI meant the large-scale development of just these types of industries. Freer trade, through either MTNs or RTAs, has led to a substantial amount of change in the industrial structure of the region.[23] The increase in trade caused by reducing trade barriers is technically known as *trade creation*. As tariffs and other trade barriers fall, prices fall and imports increase. If this is done on a multilateral basis, then the increase in imports will come from the most efficient suppliers in the world economy. Unfortunately, the tariff cuts that occur under RTAs are not multilateral. Tariffs are cut for some countries but not for others. RTAs involve explicit discrimination among exporters to a country. This can potentially cause a loss in welfare. To illustrate this, we will use a NAFTA example. Suppose that prior to NAFTA Mexico was importing cars from both Japan and the US and imposing a 20 percent tariff. Further assume that cars from Japan and the US cost $18,000 and $20,000 before imposing the tariff and $24,000 and $21,600 with the tariff, respectively. Prior to NAFTA, Mexican importers would have a tendency to buy more cars from the more efficient Japanese producers. With the introduction of NAFTA, the arithmetic changes. Post-NAFTA, American cars are now cheaper in the Mexican market than Japanese cars, and Mexican imports would tend to shift from a more efficient to a less efficient producer. While both Mexico and the US gain from NAFTA, the Japanese may lose. These losses to the Japanese are known as *trade diversion*. World welfare improves because of an RTA if the agreement causes more trade creation than trade diversion.[24] Economists generally have a dim view of trade diversion, as it entails a loss of overall world welfare. For this reason, there is a strong preference for liberalization through MTNs. If tariffs are reduced for all countries, then there is no trade diversion. One has to keep in mind that world welfare usually improves even with the existence of trade diversion as long as trade creation is larger.

Further, trade diversion is important in the context of Latin America. As countries lower tariffs, trade creation obviously occurs. However, who benefits from trade diversion? Recall that tariffs in Latin America have traditionally been high. Now consider the formation of MERCOSUR. Trade among the member countries will increase as tariff barriers fall. In addition, trade diversion may increase trade further for the member countries. While trade diversion detracts from world welfare, it may improve the export prospects of the members of the RTA. The discriminatory reduction of tariffs may increase the ability of Brazil to compete with the developed countries in the markets of the other three members. Further trade diversion may have something to do with the spread of trade agreements in the region. Because of CAN and MERCOSUR, Chilean exporters may be losing exports to a very large combined market due to trade diversion. The optimum response for Chile is clear. By liberalizing trade with both RTAs, they avoid the losses from trade diversion and gain economic welfare for themselves through trade creation. This logic is general. Any country in the region that is outside any RTA in the region stands to lose exports. Under these circumstances, there will be pressure on countries in the region to effectively join RTAs to avoid losses of exports. This solution is not as elegant as the old LAFTA or the Free Trade Agreement of the Americas proposed by the US in the early 1990s. However, these RTAs appear to be both more durable and more politically acceptable than some grand overall plan for the region. Countries can move in the direction of liberalization at whatever speed they deem to be either economically or politically acceptable to all parties. From Table 8.7, it is obvious that there are large regional differences in these preferences. This is exactly one of the main attractions of RTAs. Liberalization through MTNs can mean large reductions in overall trade barriers for every other member of the WTO. For the historically protectionist countries of the region, multilateral reductions in trade barriers with the rest of the world may be too much liberalization at too fast a rate. RTAs allow smaller liberalizations among countries with similar preferences. In some senses, the development of RTAs is reminiscent of the enlargement of the EU. It has taken forty years for the EU to expand from the original six to twenty-seven countries. Four of the countries of Europe have still not joined. Further, the enlargement was hardly smooth or continuous. It has occurred at a pace that both existing and new members find mutually agreeable. While far less formal, the expansion of trade agreements within Latin America is a work in progress that has been going on for only twenty years. Given the trade barriers that prevailed in the region as late as the 1970s, an amazing amount of liberalization in trade has already occurred.

Box 8.8 Trade diversion in action: the EU–Mexico free trade agreement

Any type of preferential trade agreement creates the potential for trade diversion. Lowering tariffs to zero for one or more of a country's trading partners creates potential losses for other countries that are not party to the agreement. Countries that are outside any preferential trade agreement are placed in an interesting position. If they do nothing, they stand to lose exports to the countries within the agreement. Or they can mitigate or eliminate these losses by joining the party, so to speak. The RTA between the EU and Mexico offers a textbook example of the latter reaction.

On November 24, 1999, the EU and Mexico concluded an RTA. The agreement allows for the bilateral phasing out of tariffs by 2010. The agreement also liberalizes trade in services and covers other issues such as public procurement, investment, competition and intellectual-property rights, and a dispute settlement procedure. While this agreement is interesting, it is, at least superficially, a bit puzzling. When the agreement was signed, EU exports to Mexico were slightly less than $10 billion, and imports from Mexico were slightly more than $4 billion. In percentage terms, each of these numbers was less than 1 percent of EU trade. However, the share of EU imports had been on a downward trend since the mid 1990s. The EU had concluded that the most likely suspect was NAFTA. As tariffs fell for the US and Canada, exporters from the EU were losing business in Mexico due to trade diversion. Since Mexican tariffs are still high, the amount of trade diversion inflicted on outsiders such as the EU could be quite high. In order to prevent this trade diversion, the EU evidently decided that signing an RTA with Mexico was its best option. EU exports to Mexico are over twice the size of EU imports from Mexico. On the Mexican side, the motivation for the agreement is less clear. They may feel that the agreement consists largely of replacing some imports from the US and Canada with competitive imports from the EU. In technical terms, the agreement produces little trade creation. This means little lost production in Mexico. The effects will mostly be felt by producers in Canada, the US, and the EU. This is not quite the end of the story. An RTA between Japan and Mexico came into force in 2005.

Key terms and concepts

ad-valorem equivalent: the level of protection provided by a quota expressed as the percentage difference between the world market price and the domestic quota-constrained price.

ad-valorem tariff: a tariff that is measured as a percentage of the value of the imported good.

capital-intensive: the condition that the production of a good requires a high K–L ratio.

effective rate of protection (ERP): a measure of the amount of protection provided to an industry by a country's tariff schedule.

factor-price equalization: the premise that international trade will reduce or equalize factor prices between countries.

Heckscher–Ohlin model: the theory that a country's comparative advantage is based on its endowment of the factors of production.

International Monetary Fund (IMF): a multilateral agency created in 1946 to promote international monetary stability and cooperation.

labor-intensive: the condition that the production of a good requires a low K–L ratio.

multilateral trade negotiations (MTNs): a process of reducing tariff and nontariff barriers to trade among member countries of GATT or the WTO.

opportunity cost: the cost of a good is the amount of another good that must be given up to release enough resources to produce the first good.

protective tariff: a tariff designed to protect domestic industry from foreign competition.

regional trade agreement (RTA): a trade agreement between two or more countries that provides tariff reductions for only those countries that are members of the agreement.

revenue tariff: a tariff imposed by government whose primary purpose is raising revenue for the government.

specific tariff: a tariff that is measured as a fixed amount of money per unit imported.

Stopler–Samuelson theorem: the premise that international trade will reduce the income of the scarce factor of production and increase the income of the abundant factor of production in a country.

trade creation: the efficiency gain that results from an RTA because more efficient member countries displace less efficient member countries.

trade diversion: an efficiency loss that results from an RTA because less efficient member countries displace more efficient nonmember countries.

World Trade Organization (WTO): the organization created in 1995 to replace GATT. The WTO administers multilateral trade agreements and settles trade disputes.

Questions for review and discussion

1 Briefly explain how trade based on comparative advantage improves the welfare of a country and the world.

2 Describe the changes in the terms of trade for Latin America from the middle of the nineteenth century. How did these changes lead to the conclusion that trade was making Latin America worse off? What is the flaw in that argument?

3 Describe how factor abundance leads to comparative advantage or disadvantage. What does this imply for Latin America's imports and exports?

4 How could trade based on comparative advantage improve the distribution of income in Latin America?

5 Relate the quote at the start of the chapter to the cost of living in Latin America.

6 How do the terms of trade affect Latin America, considering that the majority of exports are commodities?

7 Why is the K–L ratio important for Latin America?

8 Show how tariffs and quotas affect the production and import of a product.

9 How would trade barriers affect the distribution of income in Latin America if the goods being protected were capital-intensive?

10 Describe how poor transportation infrastructure affects trade within Latin America.

11 Explain the concept of rent-seeking. How could this apply to trade policy in Latin America?

12 Describe trade policy before ISI in Latin America.

13 Explain how trade policy was a critical component of ISI.

14 How did ISI produce very high effective rates of protection?
15 Why don't Brazil and Colombia export processed coffee?
16 What was the relationship between Latin America and the GATT/WTO?
17 Describe the evolution of RTAs in Latin America.
18 How could trade diversion be leading to the proliferation of RTAs in Latin America?

Notes

1 All of our examples are based on the labor theory of value. In this context, this assumption makes the analysis easier but no less valid. In a subsequent section, we will consider trade with many factors of production.
2 For an excellent discussion of this issue, see Cypher and Dietz (2009).
3 The discussion is based on data given in Clemons and Williamson (2002).
4 Recall that the supply curve contains a normal profit as a cost of production. A normal profit is defined as the opportunity cost for the producer.
5 At this point, we will consider transportation costs to be zero. At a later point in the chapter, we will show the effects of these costs.
6 There is the somewhat more complicated case of the large country whose imports can affect the world market. As shown in Chapter 1, Latin America as a region would not qualify as a large country, much less any of its constituent countries.
7 What we have shown graphically is the basis for the quote at the beginning of the chapter.
8 For more detail, see Mesquita Moreira et al. (2008).
9 For a more complete discussion of this problem, see Coatsworth and Williamson (2002).
10 For a more thorough discussion of these problems, see Williamson (2003).
11 There is also the possibility of a compound tariff, which is where imports are subject to both a specific tariff and an ad-valorem tariff.
12 For more on the tariff history of Latin America, see Coatsworth and Williamson (2002, 2004).
13 See Clemens and Williamson (2002) for more information on this.
14 For another set of estimates of tariffs in the region, see Franko (2007).
15 Vote-maximizing behavior is a standard feature of the branch of economics known as public choice. The insight is that politicians attempt to maximize votes much as consumers and producers attempt to maximize welfare and profits, respectively.
16 For specific examples, see Cardoso and Helwege (1992).
17 Reducing tariff escalation is a major policy goal for the developing countries in the current round of WTO trade negotiations.
18 Specifically, this was the Reciprocal Trade Agreements Act, which moved the overall conduct of US trade policy from the legislative to the executive branch of government.
19 Because GATT was not technically an organization, it did not have members but contracting parties.
20 Nenci and Pietrobelli (2012) have shown that Latin American participation in this process has had a very positive effect on trade flows in the region.
21 This includes antidumping duties, countervailing duties, and escape-clause cases. For more details, see Sawyer and Sprinkle (2020).
22 A single market entails the harmonization of regulations and taxes that tend to distort trade. Progress within MERCOSUR on this front has been limited. However, as the EU has discovered, this process is exceedingly difficult.
23 Trade liberalization has also been shown to lead to upgrades in technology in Latin America. For an example, see Bustos (2011).
24 Empirically, this is almost always the case.

References

Arroyo Abad, Leticia (2013) "Persistent Inequality? Trade, Factor Endowments, and Inequality in Republican Latin America," *Journal of Economic History*, 73 (March): 38–67.

Bustos, Paula (2011) "Trade Liberalization, Exports, and Technology Upgrading: Evidence on the Impact of MERCOSUR on Argentinian Firms," *American Economic Review*, 101 (January): 304–340.

Cardoso, Eliana and Ann Helwege (1992) *Latin America's Economy: Diversity, Trends, and Conflicts*, Cambridge, Mass.: MIT Press.

Cheng, Fuzhi (2007) "Tariff Escalation in World Agricultural Trade," *Case Study No. 10–11 of the Program: Food Policy for Developing Countries*, Ithaca, NY: Cornell University Press.

Clemens, Michael A. and Jeffrey G. Williamson (2002) *Closed Jaguar, Open Dragon: Comparing Tariffs in Latin America and Asia before World War II*, NBER Working Paper No. 9401, Cambridge, Mass.: National Bureau of Economic Research.

Coatsworth, John H. and Jeffrey G. Williamson (2002) *The Roots of Latin American Protectionism: Looking before the Great Depression*, NBER Working Paper No. 8999, Cambridge, Mass.: National Bureau of Economic Research.

Coatsworth, John H. and Jeffrey G. Williamson (2004) "Always Protectionist? Latin American Tariffs from Independence to Great Depression," *Journal of Latin American Studies*, 36 (May): 201–232.

Cypher, James M. and James L. Dietz (2009) *The Process of Economic Development*, 3rd edn, London and New York: Routledge.

Franko, Patrice (2007) *The Puzzle of Latin American Development*, 3rd edn, New York: Rowman & Littlefield.

Mesquita Moreira, Mauricio, Christian Volpe, and Juan S. Blyde (2008) *Unclogging the Arteries: The Impact of Transport Costs on Latin American and Caribbean Trade*, Washington, DC: Inter-American Development Bank.

Nenci, Silvia and Carlo Pietrobelli (2012) "Does Tariff Liberalization Promote Trade? Latin American Countries in the Long Run (1900–2000)," *Global Economy Journal*, 8 (February): Article 2.

Sawyer, W. Charles and Richard L. Sprinkle (2020) *Applied International Economics*, 5th edn, London and New York: Routledge.

Williamson, Jeffrey G. (2003) *Was It Stopler–Samuelson, Infant Industry or Something Else? World Tariffs 1789–1938*, NBER Working Paper No. 9656, Cambridge, Mass.: National Bureau of Economic Research.

World Trade Organization (2014) *World Tariff Profiles, 2014*, Geneva: World Trade Organization.

World Trade Organization (2015a) *Accessions*, Geneva: World Trade Organization.

World Trade Organization (2015b) *Regional Trade Agreements*, Geneva: World Trade Organization.

Recommended reading

Basnet, Hem C. and Subhash C. Sharma (2013) "Economic Integration in Latin America," *Journal of Economic Integration*, 28 (December): 551–579.

Bertola, Luis and Jeffrey G. Williamson (2003) *Globalization in Latin America before 1940*, NBER Working Paper No. 9687, Cambridge, Mass.: National Bureau of Economic Research.

Blustein, Paul (2009) *Misadventures of the Most Favored Nations: Clashing Egos, Inflated Ambitions, and the Great Shambles of the World Trade System*, New York: Public Affairs.

Blyde, Juan S. (2004) "Trade and Technology Diffusion in Latin America," *International Trade Journal*, 18 (fall): 177–197.

Eichengreen, Barry and Douglas A. Irwin (2009) *The Slide to Protectionism in the Great Depression: Who Succumbed and Why? NBER Working Paper No. 15142*, Cambridge, Mass.: National Bureau of Economic Research.

Giordano, Pablo and Robert Devlin (2011) "Regional Integration," in José A. Ocampo and Jaime Ros (eds.), *The Oxford Handbook of Latin American Economics*, Oxford: Oxford University Press, pp. 341–367.

Haltiwanger, John, Adriana Kugler, Maurice Kugler, Alejandro Micco, and Carmen Pagés (2004) "Effects of Tariffs and Real Exchange Rates on Job Reallocation: Evidence from Latin America," *Policy Reform*, 7 (December): 191–208.

Krueger, Anne O. (1974) "The Political Economy of the Rent Seeking Society," *American Economic Review*, 64 (June): 291–303.

Lora, Eduardo (2011) "The Effects of Trade Liberalization on Growth, Employment, and Wages," in José A. Ocampo and Jaime Ros (eds.), *The Oxford Handbook of Latin American Economics*, Oxford: Oxford University Press, pp. 368–393.

Marquez, Graciela (1998) "Tariff Protection in Mexico, 1892–1909: Ad Valorem Tariff Rates and Sources of Variation," in John H. Coatsworth and Alan M. Taylor (eds.), *Latin America and the World Economy since 1800*, Cambridge, Mass.: Harvard University Press, pp. 407–442.

McKinney, Joseph A. and H. Stephen Gardner (eds.) (2008) *Economic Integration in the Americas*, London and New York: Routledge.

Tussie, Diana (2011) "Latin America in the World Trade System," in José A. Ocampo and Jaime Ros (eds.), *The Oxford Handbook of Latin American Economics*, Oxford: Oxford University Press, pp. 317–340.

9 Exchange-rate policy

Introduction

In this chapter, our focus changes essentially from microeconomics to macroeconomics. In most of the previous chapters, we have discussed industries, exports, imports, industrial policy, and other government policies that affected the economic development of Latin America. GDP was mentioned in Chapters 2 and 4, but the coverage concerned economic growth and identifiable periods of economic history for the region. This is different from macroeconomics. Macroeconomics is focused on the movements of GDP, the level of unemployment, and the rate of inflation over shorter periods of time. Typically, the focus of macroeconomics is one to three years. The focus of the material in the rest of the book inevitably changes in another way. In every country, one is exposed to a steady stream of macroeconomic data concerning the output of the economy, measures of conditions in the labor markets, and various measures of inflation. Even if no domestic data comes out on a particular day, there is always information on other parts of the regional or world economy. What one needs to understand is that prior to World War II, for the most part this data did not exist. Over the past fifty years, economic historians have been painstakingly reconstructing *annual* data for the years prior to 1945. This is still a work in progress. As a result, short-run macroeconomic data on a monthly or quarterly basis before this time hardly exists for the high-income countries of the world. For the economies of Latin America, such data is virtually nonexistent. The result is that our focus for much of the rest of the book will be on the postwar era in the region. A substantial part of this choice is related to the unavailability of data. The other reason for this choice is that macroeconomic policy as we now use the phrase was not really a part of the economic history of the region prior to 1945. Why this is true will become clearer in the first section of this chapter.

The purpose of this chapter is to expand on our previous coverage of international trade. Our emphasis in earlier chapters was more on the microeconomics of international trade, in the sense of how trade affects the industrial structure of a country. At several points, the overall balance of trade was touched on but not covered in depth. The first part of this chapter is a more complete description of a country's economic interactions with the rest of the world. For Latin America, this has always been important, as the region began modern history as a supplier of important commodities to the rest of the world. As we will see, this trade creates inflows and outflows of money. In turn, these flows affect the price of the domestic currency relative to foreign currencies, that is, the exchange rate. Each country in the world has to make a choice about how these flows are allowed to affect the domestic economy and the exchange rate. The countries of Latin

America are no different in this regard. To understand both the history and the present situation of the economies of the region, it is crucial to gain a basic understanding of these choices and what each implies.

The balance of payments

> The produce of a country exchanges for the produce of other countries, at such values as are required in order that the whole of her exports may exactly pay for the whole of her imports.
>
> (John Stuart Mill)

Each country of the world maintains detailed data on imports and exports of goods. What is less commonly known is that each country, to the greatest extent possible, records all inflows and outflows of money. Collectively, this data is referred to as the balance of payments. Within the balance of payments, there are two major subcategories. The first is the current account. The current account is an accounting of international transactions that includes goods, services, investment income, and unilateral transfers. Note that international trade in goods is included in the current account, as well as other types of transactions. However, the current account does not catch all of the flows of money into and out of a country. For example, note that FDI is not included in the current account. FDI and financial transactions are part of the financial account. The financial account is a record of the difference between the holding of foreign assets by domestic residents and of domestic assets by foreign residents. In this section, we will explain in some detail the different sorts of flows embodied in these two accounts. These details and the interactions of the current and capital accounts are essential to understanding the interaction of the countries of Latin America with the rest of the world.

The current account

To begin with, we will present a set of data for a representative country in Latin America (RCILA). Each of the countries in the region is somewhat distinctive with regard to the balance of payments, but also there are some common themes for the region. As a result, we do not present data for a particular country but a set of data designed to illustrate these common themes. This data is presented in Table 9.1. The data in the second column is designed to show a "normal" year for a country in the region that exports commodities and also other goods. Note that there are both positive and negative numbers in the column. Inflows of money are shown as positive, and outflows are shown as negative. The negative signs on outflows should not be interpreted as anything *wrong*. A country with no outflows would be far worse off, as imports of goods, services, and capital are an essential part of a healthy economy. The negative signs are simply an accounting necessity in this case. The first two rows of the table contain data for exports and imports of goods. The difference between the two is the balance on trade. This is the most familiar representation of the interaction of a country with the rest of the world. It can also depict a very distorted picture of these interactions. Countries also export and import services. These can be personal services, such as tourism, or business services, such as financial services. The sum of all service flows forms the balance on services. Added to trade in goods, this is the balance on goods and services. The next

Table 9.1 The balance of payments for a RCILA (millions of pesos)

Current account transactions	
Exports of goods	200
Imports of goods	−180
Balance on trade	20
Exports of services	5
Imports of services	−20
Balance on services	−15
Balance on goods and services	5
Income receipts from RCILA assets abroad	5
Income payments of foreign assets in RCILA	−25
Balance on investment income	−20
Balance on goods, services, and income	−15
Unilateral transfers, net	5
Balance on current account	−10
Financial account transactions	
Change in RCILA assets abroad	−1
Official reserve assets	
Private assets	−2
Change in foreign-owned assets in RCILA	3
Official reserve assets	
Foreign private assets	10
Balance on financial account	10

two items are a little more complicated. Over time, the citizens of countries may invest money in other countries. Eventually, some of the return on these investments (profits, interest, dividends, capital gains) may be repatriated to the home country. This appears as income receipts from abroad. The reverse is also true. Money invested in RCILA would probably create an outflow of money over time. In any given year, the difference between income from and payments to the rest of the world constitutes the balance on investment income. Adding this balance to overall trade in goods and services creates the balance on goods, services, and income. The next item is *unilateral transfers*. In general, a transfer payment is a payment made when there are no services rendered. The textbook case of a transfer payment is official development assistance. However, there are private unilateral transfers that are now equally or more important. Remittances are transfers of money from foreign workers to their home country. These are included in unilateral transfers along with the more familiar official development assistance. The addition of unilateral transfers leads to the balance on *current account*.

With this short description of the current account, we can now proceed to analyze the data in the table. This data is representative of inflows and outflows for RCILA in an average year. If the prices of commodities are favorable, then the country will export 200 million pesos a year. Imports are 180 million pesos, so the trade balance is a positive 20 million pesos. Exports of services are 5 million pesos, earned primarily from tourism and a small amount of business services provided to smaller countries in the region. Imports of services are larger, reflecting domestic citizens traveling to foreign countries and the purchase of business services from high-income countries that have a comparative advantage in such services.[1] Given that capital is relatively scarce in Latin America, the outflows of capital from the region have been historically small. This is reflected in the current account as small earnings from investment income flowing into RCILA. On the other hand, there has been a substantial amount of foreign capital invested in the region. This difference shows up as a deficit in the balance on investment income. Again, this deficit should be viewed as perfectly normal for a middle-income country such as RCILA. In turn, this deficit makes the balance on goods, services, and income smaller than the previous balance on goods and services. For a country like RCILA, unilateral transfers are positive. There may be more or less official development assistance for any given year. Recently, an increasingly important factor in Latin America has been remittances. The addition of unilateral transfers yields the balance on current account. Notice that for RCILA, this balance is a negative 10 million pesos.

Box 9.1 The current account in Latin America

One of the important facts that you should take away from the previous section is the importance of the current account. Despite its importance, data on the current account is not easily available. Unfortunately, the same is not true of the balance on trade. This statistic is put out monthly with a time lag by most of the countries of the world. This is also the case for Latin America. On the other hand, the current account is usually published quarterly, so the data is not as "fresh." Further, data for the current account is frequently released with the data on the rate of growth of GDP. Understandably, the information on the current account gets far less attention. As a result, there tends to be more focus on the balance of trade than on the current account. The problem is that the former can be a very misleading number. To illustrate some of these points, Table 9.2 presents data on the balance on trade and the current account for the larger economies of Latin America. This data is published every week in *The Economist*. Second, notice that four out of the six countries are running a trade deficit. However, in every case, the surplus or deficit is small. Second, notice that only one country is reporting a surplus on the current account. For three out of the six countries, the difference is now more substantial. The lesson here is that the balance on trade is more readily available but should be used with care.

Table 9.2 The balance on trade and current account in Latin America

Country	Balance on trade (billions of $)	Current account balance (billions of $)
Argentina	−8.5	−31.3
Brazil	67.0	−9.8
Chile	4.2	−4.1
Colombia	−8.3	−10.6
Mexico	−10.9	−19.1
Venezuela	43.0	−3.9

Source: World Integrated Trade Solution and ECLAC-cepalstat.

Notes: Data for Venezuela is from 2013 BT and 2016 CAB.

The financial account

While the current account gives a more extensive accounting of inflows and outflows for a country, it is not complete. Other transactions not included in the current account are included in the financial account. The *financial account* records the difference between the holdings of foreign assets by domestic residents and of domestic assets by foreign residents. As shown above, these transactions are done in either the public or the private sector. Changes in official reserve assets are given for both RCILA and the rest of the world. Every government of the world holds foreign exchange for a variety of purposes. Over a year, this stock of foreign exchange will become larger or smaller. If a government acquires foreign exchange, this will be recorded as an outflow of money, as a foreign asset has been acquired. A more important factor is the purchase of foreign assets by domestic residents. These purchases take two forms. First, domestic residents may engage in FDI in foreign countries. Second, they may also purchase financial assets in other countries, which are known as changes in portfolio capital. Both of these items represent outflows of money in the financial account. For Latin America, these flows tend to be small, as the economies of the region are capital-scarce. The other side of the financial account is made up of changes in reserve assets by the rest of the world, inflows of FDI, and portfolio capital flows.

Governments in the rest of the world may acquire the currencies of countries in the region. These purchases show up as inflows of money into the domestic economies of the region. As before, these flows are typically small. The larger inflows come through the private sector in the rest of the world. In a well-managed middle-income country, there should be a substantial amount of incoming FDI and inflows of portfolio capital. The rate of return to capital will frequently be higher in Latin America than it would be in a high-income country. This makes sense, as capital is scarcer in the former than it is in the latter. Similarly, the rate of return on financial assets such as stocks and bonds is usually higher in Latin America than it would be in the high-income countries. The result is that in most years the balance on the financial account would be positive: More capital is flowing into Latin America than is flowing out.[2]

Putting the current account together with the financial account yields an important relationship. The market is continually trying to balance the inflows and outflows of foreign exchange. Over a period of time, such as a year, this means that the sum of the current account and the financial account must equal zero.[3] This means that if the current account is negative then the financial account is positive. The reverse would also be true. If the current account is positive, then the financial account is negative. Another way of putting this is that if one account is in deficit, then the other account is in surplus. The typical situation for a country in Latin America can be described in this way. It is common for the balance on trade to be positive. The country is exporting more goods than it is importing. It is also common for the balance on current account to be negative as a result of trade in services and net investment income. Unilateral transfers would normally be positive. There is nothing untoward about a deficit in the balance on current account. It will be offset by a surplus in the financial account. Money should be flowing into the country in the form of FDI and purchases of financial assets.

This discussion can leave one with the impression that this balancing of inflows and outflows is always a smooth and continuous process. Unfortunately, this is not the case. Both inflows and outflows can fluctuate substantially from one year to the next. A task for any country is to decide how to manage these flows. This decision is partly an internal choice by the government. However, the choices made by other countries also matter. No country in Latin America, or anywhere else, is an island. This management of inflows and outflows involves the choice of an exchange-rate system. Over the next several sections, we will describe the two major types of exchange-rate systems that were common in Latin America and the world during the twentieth century. The choices made by the majority of countries in the region turned out to be an important part of the story of the economic performance of Latin America.

Flexible exchange rates

We start our discussion of exchange-rate systems in reverse chronological order, for two reasons. First, most readers of this book have only lived in a world where exchange rates are allowed to fluctuate just like any other price. If trying to fix an exchange rate sounds a bit strange, don't feel alone. The idea is somewhat alien to an economist as well. Second, it is easier to explain exchange rates by first examining the normal situation in which the exchange rate can move about in response to changes in market conditions. With these basics in mind, it becomes somewhat easier to show the effects of fixing the exchange rate. In this section, the basic analysis of exchange rates is explained. After developing the supply-and-demand model, the basic determinants of the exchange rate are presented and put into a Latin American context.

One of the first places where inflows and outflows show up is in the foreign-exchange market. To understand this, let's consider some common transactions. Suppose that a food company in RCILA wants to purchase wheat produced in the US. In order to accomplish this, the company must first exchange pesos for US dollars. This makes sense, as it would be awkward to try to spend pesos in Kansas. This ordinary transaction illustrates the demand for foreign exchange, in this case dollars. It represents a typical transaction that ends up being an outflow of money from the country. Now, consider an example of inflows. Suppose that a supplier to the building industry in the US needs to purchase water heaters. Considering all costs, it is determined that water heaters produced in RCILA are the best value available. In order to complete this transaction, the firm will need to purchase pesos. This is accomplished by buying pesos and selling dollars in the foreign-exchange market. This selling of dollars creates a supply in the foreign-exchange market. Since these sorts of transactions are so commonplace, there is a lot of trading of pesos for US dollars in the foreign-exchange market. Firms and individuals in RCILA are constantly buying dollars to purchase US goods and services. American firms and individuals are likewise selling dollars in order to obtain pesos. Just like any other market, this constant buying and selling creates the usual set of demand and supply curves. The natural result is a market price: the exchange rate.

Now let's put this information into a more formal framework. The demand for foreign exchange looks like any other demand curve: It slopes downward and to the right. The only real difference is how we express the price. In this case, the price is the exchange rate. In addition, we will look at the foreign-exchange market from RCILA's point of view. This means looking at the peso–dollar exchange rate, or the number of pesos it takes to buy a US dollar. This demand for foreign exchange is shown in Figure 9.1. On the vertical axis is the exchange rate. The horizontal axis is the quantity of dollars, which for RCILA is foreign exchange. To keep things simple, consider an exchange rate of 2P/$. This exchange rate falls roughly in the middle of the demand for foreign exchange. Now consider an exchange rate of 3P/$. In this case, it now takes more pesos

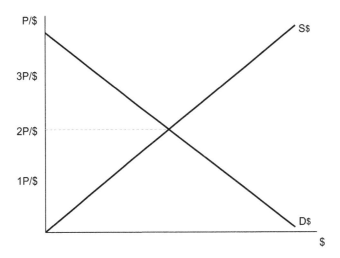

Figure 9.1 The demand and supply of foreign exchange.

to buy a dollar. The peso has *depreciated* relative to the dollar. The reverse is true of an exchange rate of 1P/$. It now takes fewer pesos to buy a dollar, so the peso has appreciated relative to the dollar. In our prosaic example, at 1P/$, US wheat is a bargain. However, at 3P/$, US wheat has become very expensive. Again, if the only thing that happens is a movement in the exchange rate, then one is sliding up or down the existing demand curve for foreign exchange.

As is usually the case, the demand curve can also shift to the left or right. An increase (decrease) in the demand for foreign exchange is represented by a shift of the curve to the right (left). In general, two factors could cause such a shift. An important factor is a change in income in RCILA. If the economy is growing, then the demand for imports will grow and along with it the demand for dollars. This would show up as a shift of the demand for dollars to the right. On the other hand, a recession in RCILA would decrease the demand for imports and shift the demand for dollars to the left. The growth rate of the economy of RCILA will change over time, and the demand for dollars will shift along with these changes. A second factor that will shift the demand for dollars is a change in relative prices. Assume that the rate of inflation in RCILA is 10 percent and that it is 5 percent in the US. If the exchange rate doesn't change, then, over time, goods from the US would become relatively cheaper. In turn, this would increase the demand for dollars and shift the curve to the right. The reverse would also be true. If inflation in RCILA were less than inflation in the US, then over time imports would become more expensive. This would tend to shift the demand curve to the left. These factors set up a couple of important tendencies. First, a booming economy tends to lead to a depreciation of the currency. If everyone is trying to buy dollars, then the number of pesos traders are willing to offer for dollars is going to rise. A booming economy may also mean a rising rate of inflation. Relatively high inflation would also tend to increase the demand for dollars and tend to lead to depreciation of the peso. By the same logic, a recession or low inflation would tend to lead to a depreciation of the currency.

In order to complete the analysis, a supply curve is necessary. In Figure 9.1, the supply of dollars in the foreign-exchange market is shown sloping upward and to the right. The logic behind this slope is straightforward. Suppose that the exchange rate is 1P/$. At this exchange rate, the US demand for imports from RCILA would be low, as a dollar would only buy 1P worth of goods. Following our example, water heaters from RCILA would be expensive. Traders would not be exchanging many dollars for pesos at this exchange rate. Now assume that the exchange rate is 3P/$. From the US point of view, water heaters from RCILA are a bargain. As a result, traders would be exchanging a lot of dollars to obtain pesos. In this case, the supply of dollars is directly related to the exchange rate. As the peso depreciates from 1P/$ to 3P/$, the quantity supplied of foreign exchange increases. The supply curve slopes upward and to the right. This supply curve can also shift for similar reasons to the shifts in the demand curve. In this case, changes in income in the US can shift the demand for goods such as water heaters from RCILA. An increase in income in the US would shift the supply of dollars to the right as traders would need more pesos to buy goods in RCILA. A decrease in income in the US would shift the curve to the left. Relative prices also matter. If inflation in the US is higher than inflation in RCILA, then exports to the US will increase. This will shift the supply curve to the right. The reverse would occur if inflation in the US were lower than inflation in RCILA. US goods would become relatively less expensive, and the supply of foreign exchange would fall as exports reduced. Any shifts in the supply curve would affect the exchange rate. In Figure 9.1, the intersection of the demand and supply of dollars leads to an equilibrium exchange rate of 2P/$. Of course, a change in either the demand or the supply of foreign exchange will change the exchange rate. This potential volatility has been an important factor in the economic development of Latin America.

Fixed exchange rates

Through much of its history, the countries of Latin America maintained fixed exchange rates. In the twenty-first century, the idea of a fixed exchange rate seems peculiar. However, until 1971 it was the norm in the world economy. Prior to the Great Depression, many of the countries of the region were trying to fix their exchange rates under the gold standard or through other means. However, the onset of World War I weakened the system. The arrival of the Great Depression shattered it. Along with the rest of the world, the countries of Latin America slowly left the system.[4] The end of World War II ushered in a new period of fixed exchange rates. Virtually all of the governments of the world wanted to return to fixed exchange rates after the chaotic period of the 1930s. However, it was also realized that a return to the gold standard was not possible. At a conference in Bretton Woods, New Hampshire, in the US in 1944, an alternative system was formulated. The *Bretton Woods system* marked a return to fixed exchange rates. The link to the gold standard was retained, with the US government committing itself to redeem dollars for gold at a fixed price of $35. All other currencies were then fixed to the dollar. The IMF was created to oversee the operation of the system. It maintained a pool of reserves of foreign exchange for countries to borrow to cover current-account deficits. The system eventually broke down in 1971 as the US announced the suspension of the convertibility of the dollar for gold at the official price. As we will see, the countries of Latin America were reluctant to abandon fixed exchange rates and slowly changed to flexible exchange rates in the late 1970s and early 1980s.

Intervention in the foreign-exchange market

Since we covered the basics of exchange rates in the previous section, we now turn our attention to the mechanics of a fixed exchange rate. Our discussion begins with Figure 9.2. As before, the equilibrium exchange rate is 2P/$. However, in this case, the government has committed itself to fixing the exchange rate at this price. Unfortunately, this commitment does not reduce the propensity of the supply and demand curves to fluctuate. To start with, we will consider how the system was supposed to work for a country like RCILA that exports a substantial amount of commodities. Assume that a commodity boom occurs and that the world price of this country's commodity is increasing. As the US has to pay more for the commodity, it will have to trade more dollars in the foreign-exchange market to buy the requisite number of pesos. In turn, this would cause an increase in the supply of foreign exchange. If the exchange rate was not fixed, it would just appreciate, that is, a flexible price would take care of the situation. However, the government is committed to the fixed rate. In this case, it would be necessary to purchase the excess supply of dollars to maintain the fixed exchange rate. The country's *official reserve assets* would rise as it acquired foreign exchange. In a well-managed country, the government would effectively "hoard" foreign exchange as a by-product of fixing the exchange rate. As we saw in Chapter 6, commodity prices can also fall. A fall in commodity prices would lead to a decrease in the supply of foreign exchange. The US would need to exchange fewer dollars to obtain the same amount of commodities. In Figure 9.2, this is shown as a leftward shift in the supply of foreign exchange. With flexible exchange rates, the exchange rate would simply depreciate. In order to maintain the fixed exchange rate, the government will need to sell foreign exchange. This would shift the supply curve to the right and maintain the exchange rate at 2P/$.

Maintaining a fixed exchange rate is difficult for a country that is an exporter of commodities. When commodity prices are high, the government will need to buy up

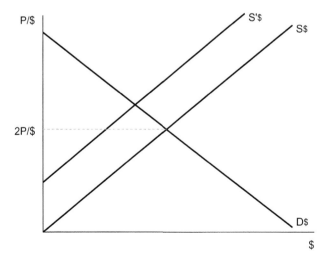

Figure 9.2 Intervention in the foreign-exchange market.

the excess foreign exchange to keep the currency from appreciating. When commodity prices are low, foreign exchange will have to be supplied to the foreign-exchange market to maintain the fixed exchange rate. This is just another example of the old principle that fixed prices create either shortages or surpluses. Since the exchange rate is not being allowed to change, the government at times must accumulate a surplus of foreign exchange. This accumulation will be necessary in order to supply foreign exchange whenever there is a shortage. This buying and selling of foreign exchange is known as *intervention* in the foreign-exchange market. A country that is a commodity exporter has to be careful in managing its stock of official reserve assets. It would need to intervene in the foreign-exchange markets both when there is a commodity bust and, especially, during a commodity boom.

Exchange controls

The previous section presented the management of a fixed exchange rate by efficiently managing the level of reserves of foreign exchange. To review, a country would accumulate reserves when the current account was in surplus. In turn, these reserves would be used during periods when a country is running a deficit. Over time, the country could maintain a fixed exchange rate by wisely managing its reserves. For most of the countries of Latin America, this was not the norm under the Bretton Woods system. During commodity booms or other favorable periods, sufficient reserves were not accumulated to cover the periodic deficits. To be fair, this was hardly a problem peculiar to Latin America. Many countries of the world were unable to do this. As we will see in the next chapter, there are a number of mechanisms that can be used for a country to cover a current-account deficit. The efficient management of reserves is just a preferred option. In this section, we consider another means of managing deficits, which was quite common in Latin America and other parts of the world.

To illustrate the problem, return to Figure 9.2. If the supply of foreign exchange has shifted to the left, the country has a current-account deficit: the demand for foreign exchange is greater than the supply at 2P/$. With intervention, this gap is filled by the government selling foreign exchange. Now, assume that the government does not have sufficient foreign exchange to shift the supply curve far enough to the right. Also, a depreciation of the currency is not an option, as the country is participating in a global system of fixed exchange rates. An answer to this question is a variant of what happens when any price is being forced below equilibrium. A shortage has developed, in this case a shortage of foreign exchange. Without an increase in the price, the government may resort to rationing the available foreign exchange. The usual term for this rationing is exchange controls. Exchange controls necessarily imply discrimination in the market for foreign exchange. With floating exchange rates, the available foreign exchange goes to anyone who is willing to pay the current exchange rate. If a fixed exchange rate creates a shortage of foreign exchange, then the government is going to have to administer the shortage with exchange controls. Since this is not going to be a straightforward process, exchange controls come in a bewildering number of forms. As a result, the discussion that follows refers only to the more common forms they may take.

The most rigorous form of exchange controls gives the government a monopoly on dealing in foreign exchange. In this case, any holder of foreign exchange is obliged to sell it to the government at the official exchange rate. This gives the government an effective monopoly of the supply of foreign exchange. On the other side of the market, there will be more firms and individuals demanding foreign exchange than the supply owned by the government. This is not an agreeable situation. Suppose that the official exchange rate is 2P/$, and the equilibrium rate in a free market is 3P/$. If a firm in Latin America is exporting goods at the official exchange rate, it is well aware of the loss of $1. On the other hand, firms and individuals that can obtain foreign exchange at the official exchange rate are well aware that this is a low price. With an excess demand for foreign exchange, the central question for the government is deciding which demands are more important than others. Some of the rationing is easy, as in the case of oil, food, medicines, or imported inputs to keep the ISI industries functioning. Beyond these relatively easy decisions, one can imagine that the rationing process can become more difficult. One possible response to this is the existence of a system of multiple exchange rates. In this case, the official exchange rate would not be uniform but would vary depending on which the government felt were essential imports and which were less important. For example, the government could set a rate of 1P/$ for essential imports and 3P/$ for imports deemed to be less important. Such systems can lead to an extreme amount of complexity on top of the simple mechanics of managing a bureaucratic system in lieu of private-sector transactions. They also form a sort of de-facto industrial policy. In the context of Latin America, a multiple exchange-rate system could be used to support ISI. Favored industries could obtain foreign exchange at much more favorable rates than other industries. This amounted to a subsidy to ISI industries via exchange-rate policy. Part of the unraveling of ISI that led to the Lost Decade can be traced to the rapid depreciations of exchange rates that were common during this period.

Box 9.2 Black markets in foreign exchange

If there are exchange controls in a country and the currency has become overvalued, the question becomes what the nominal exchange rate "should" be. Recall that domestic residents who possess foreign exchange are legally obliged to surrender it to the government. To a greater or lesser extent, there would be legal sanctions for failing to do this. Suppose that the penalties for illegally possessing foreign exchange are fairly minor—say, a small monetary fine. If the currency becomes sufficiently overvalued, it may become logical (although illegal) not to surrender the foreign exchange to the government at the fixed price. Given that there is excess demand for foreign exchange, it is quite possible that you could find a buyer who would be willing to pay more than the fixed government rate. When the government attempts to fix any price, a *black market* will develop. If one observes that there is a black market for foreign exchange in a country, it is not even necessary to ask whether there are exchange controls. The very existence of a black market means that the government's fixed price for foreign exchange is too low.

In this case, there are only two remaining questions. First, how overvalued is the official exchange rate? The black-market rate is a reliable guide to this. Empirical estimates have shown time and again that the black-market rate will closely approximate purchasing power parity (PPP). This knowledge is both a blessing and a curse. It is good in the sense that one usually does not have to conduct tedious calculations of just how overvalued the exchange rate is. One can simply go out into the street and find out. However, the answer in some cases may be disheartening. If the black market rate is 50 percent above the official rate, there is likely to be a nasty combination of an austerity program and a large devaluation to bring the economy back into balance. Economists will likely be able to identify countries where there is a high probability of a major devaluation. When such a currency crisis will occur is another matter.

The information above refers to exchange controls on the current account. Fortunately, such controls are a part of economic history. In most of the countries of Latin America, such controls on current-account transactions no longer exist. However, there are still exchange controls on financial-account transactions. Recall the data included in Table 9.1 under the financial account. To review, the private-sector component of these flows is composed of FDI and movements of portfolio capital. The outflows from Latin America are not an issue, as they are rather small. As we will see in the next chapter, the inflows can be substantial. Further, the inflows of FDI are not a problem. FDI inflows may be large, but they are not very volatile. Once foreign investors have made an investment in plant and equipment or purchased all or part of a domestic firm, the investment is not likely to flow out quickly. The rate of change of FDI may be volatile. A country might attract a large amount of FDI in one year and somewhat less the next. The point is that once the money has been invested it is not likely to leave quickly. The same is not true of flows of portfolio capital. Portfolio capital is money that is being invested in financial assets such as stocks or bonds. This money can flow easily into a country but can just as easily leave. As portfolio capital flows in, the supply of foreign exchange can shift to the right and the exchange rate can appreciate. The reverse is also true. If foreign investors remove too much portfolio capital in too short a period of time, the supply of foreign exchange can shift to the left, leading to a rapid depreciation of the currency.[5] As we will see in Chapter 11, this capital flight can have disastrous macroeconomic consequences. To summarize the future discussion, capital flight can lead to a mixture of higher inflation and negative economic growth.

Capital flight is an all-too-real risk for developing countries, and especially Latin America. As we saw in Chapter 2, it is just another part of the economic instability embedded in the history of the region. Since independence, foreign investors have been periodically enamored of the economic potential of the region. The ensuing disappointment with these investments led to a number of cases of capital flight from the region. In the wake of the Asian economic crisis of the late 1990s, the term *contagion* has been a popular research topic among economists. Contagion refers to the tendency of investors to withdraw portfolio capital from an entire region in response to perceived economic difficulties in a single country or a subset of countries. While it may be a new topic of interest to economists, it is an old subject in Latin America. As a result, the region may be particularly susceptible to the phenomenon because of the economic history of the region. A recent example may illustrate the point. A series of macroeconomic policy mistakes in late 1994 led to a rapid depreciation of the Mexican peso, known as the Tequila crisis. The crisis was country-specific and not an indication of generalized economic problems in the region. At this point, Latin America as a whole was beginning the process of recovery from the Lost Decade. Nonetheless, the crisis in Mexico led to a large withdrawal of portfolio capital and had adverse economic impacts on the region as a whole.[6]

These risks have led a number of countries to adopt some form of controls on movements of portfolio capital. Such restrictions can serve to limit the inflows and outflows of foreign exchange and thus help to stabilize the exchange rate. As is always the case with any policy, there are costs and benefits. The benefit is that such controls can limit the appreciation of the currency when inflows of portfolio capital are rather high. In turn, this reduces the adverse effects on the country's exports and reduces the tendency for imports to rise. In addition, such controls offer some protection against exchange-rate shocks. Portfolio capital may be unable to leave the country *en masse* and can reduce the severity of the depreciation of the currency. In a sense, controls on the flow of portfolio capital constitute a form of insurance against large changes in the exchange rate in either direction. This form of insurance is not free. The countries of Latin America tend to be capital-scarce. As shown in Chapter 3, capital is a critical input into the process of economic development. Limiting flows of capital may have the consequence of reducing the rate of economic growth. This could also diminish the growth of the K–L ratio, which is an important determinant of real wages. More importantly, it is not completely clear whether or not such controls have the expected effect on the exchange rate. Different studies find varying effects depending on the country or time period studied.[7] At a minimum, assuming that capital controls work perfectly to limit movements in the exchange rate may not be a safe assumption. As a general rule, these restrictions on the free flow of capital are controversial. The traditional view of capital controls is that the growth-limiting aspects of this policy are greater than the benefits of some protection against exchange-rate shocks. More recent research indicates that the cost–benefit analysis may be more complex.[8] This is reflected in the implementation of such controls in Latin America. Controls on movements of portfolio capital in Chile have been extensively studied, and no firm conclusions have been reached on their effectiveness. In response to an appreciation of the exchange rate, Brazil recently began taxing inflows of portfolio capital. While such policies are unlikely to become widespread, they do not appear to be quite ready for the dustbin of economic history in the region.

Box 9.3 Capital controls in Chile

As you have no doubt noticed, in a number of places in the book Chilean economic performance and policy have been presented in a favorable light. This is not an unjustifiable bias by the authors. Chile has been something of a model of good economic policy, not just for Latin America but in some cases for the world.[9] As a result, Chile would seem to be an improbable country to adopt capital controls. However, this is not quite as odd as it may seem at first glance. For more successful developing countries, rapid economic growth carries the risk of large inflows of portfolio capital. Such inflows can cause the exchange rate to appreciate to levels that may cause some of the difficulties described above. In the case of Chile, there is a further problem: copper. Chile produces a third of the world's copper, and it routinely accounts for 40 percent of the country's exports. Unfortunately, copper prices are extremely volatile. The result of this price volatility can be instability in the exchange rate.

From 1991 to 1998, the government of Chile imposed restrictions on capital flows as a means of limiting exchange-rate volatility. These took two main forms.

First, inflows of FDI were subjected to a minimum stay of one year. Controls on flows of portfolio capital were more complex. Chilean firms were limited in their ability to issue stock in foreign markets. More importantly, inflows of portfolio capital were subject to a 30 percent reserve requirement. This amounted to a tax on inflows of portfolio capital. The effects were as one would expect. Inflows of short-term portfolio capital were reduced, and the maturity of capital inflows increased. The effects on the exchange rate are usually estimated to be small. Also, these controls seem to have made it marginally easier for the central bank to conduct monetary policy. The overall evaluation seems to be that in the case of Chile the controls generated small benefits and relatively small costs. However, some of the costs may be less obvious. A recent paper indicates that these controls have an interesting impact. Limiting the flows of short-run capital in a capital-scarce country should have an impact *somewhere*. One of the effects is, in retrospect, obvious. Larger firms were able to avoid the effects of these controls by borrowing in foreign markets. Further, since the regulations were complex, they represented an extra but fixed cost of borrowing. This fixed cost naturally decreased with the size of the firm. However, it was very difficult for banks to avoid the controls. The banking system in Chile, as in other countries, was a major source of capital for SMEs. Edwards (1998) mentions these effects, but in a more focused study Forbes (2007) carefully shows the difference in borrowing costs. During this period, large Chilean firms could borrow in international markets at 7–8 percent. The cost of capital for smaller firms was over 20 percent. The controls had the effect of making capital over twice as expensive for firms that naturally tend to grow faster. While the overall costs to the Chilean economy may have been small, the costs to an important part of the economy seem to have been much larger. Capital controls in Chile were dropped in 1998 as overall capital flows to emerging markets dwindled. They have never reemerged in Chile as a response to inflows of portfolio capital. Perhaps this is just another example of revealed preference.

The real exchange rate

So far in this chapter, all our analysis has focused on the exchange rate that one observes in the market. As is usual in economics, we refer to this as the *nominal exchange rate*. The nominal exchange rate has not been adjusted for changes in inflation. From your previous economics courses, you are probably familiar with the concept of real prices. Real prices are prices that have been adjusted for the effects of inflation. For example, one cannot determine whether or not a price has increased or decreased in real terms by observing the change in the nominal price. It is also necessary to know what the overall rate of inflation is. The same is true for an exchange rate. However, in this case, the analysis is slightly more complicated. One has to consider not only the domestic inflation rate but also the inflation rate in a foreign country. In this section, we explain the concept of the real exchange rate. The real exchange rate is the nominal exchange rate adjusted for changes in both domestic and foreign prices. As we will see, the real exchange rate is important in the context of Latin America. At times in the region, the nominal exchange rate can be quite deceptive. An understanding of the real exchange rate is crucial in understanding the economic changes that have occurred in the region over the past several decades. To borrow a thought from Paul Samuelson, the real exchange rate is an important concept, but it is not obvious. To illustrate this, let's consider a normal economic transaction. Suppose that last year you exchanged a dollar for 1,000 pesos and crossed the border and purchased a bottle of soda. Now, assume that prices in the US are constant and that the rate of inflation in RCILA is 100 percent. A year later, the same transaction might look something like this. You now exchange a dollar for the 2,000 pesos and cross the border and buy a bottle of soda. Notice what has occurred. The nominal exchange rate has changed dramatically. However, a dollar still bought you a bottle of soda. Adjusted for inflation, the real exchange rate has not changed. Just a bit of consideration of this example illustrates how deceptive the nominal exchange rate can be. The example may seem extreme, but, as we will see in Chapter 11, situations such as this were all too real in Latin America in the late twentieth century.

To understand the real exchange rate requires some logic and arithmetic. The starting point is the *law of one price*. The law of one price is the simple statement that identical goods sold in competitive markets should cost the same everywhere when prices are expressed in terms of the same currency. The example above was an illustration. If a bottle of soda cost a dollar in the US, then it should also cost a dollar across the border. One's first reaction may be that this is ridiculous. For any number of reasons, identical goods rarely cost *exactly* the same in two countries. That is also beside the point. The law of one price and other concepts that follow should be viewed as tendencies. If the gap between the prices of goods in different countries becomes too large, then traders will start moving goods from the low-price country to the high-price country to make a profit, that is, arbitrage. When that profit reaches zero, trading stops. Because of trade restrictions, transportation costs, and other barriers to trade, arbitrage may stop before prices are equalized. The point is that prices will tend to move in the direction of equality, not away from it.

Following our earlier examples, we consider the prices in RCILA (Pr) and the US (Pus) and the peso–dollar exchange rate (P/$). The relationship can be expressed as

$$Pr = (P/\$) \times Pus$$

or

$$P/\$ = Pr/Pus$$

Now let's analyze the price of soda example. In this case:

$$1,000P = 1,000P/\$ \times \$1$$

or

$$1,000P/\$ = 1,000P/\$1$$

Now put in the new price of soda in RCILA of 2,000P per dollar. The law of one price would indicate that the price of soda hasn't changed.

Another way of stating the law of one price is *absolute PPP*. Absolute PPP is the theory that exchange rates are related to differences in the level of prices between countries. The key difference here is the term "prices." In our example of the law of one price, we were considering the price of a single good. In analyzing PPP, the focus shifts to the overall price level. This makes sense, as the exchange rate applies to all transactions in the balance of payments not the price of a single good. More specifically, we are referring to a representative market basket of goods and services that is conceptually similar to the sort of market basket used to calculate a price index such as the consumer price index.[10] To illustrate the concept, assume that a market basket of goods in RCILA costs 2P and an identical basket costs $1 in the US. Clearly, this would indicate that the absolute PPP exchange rate should be 2P/$. From the relationship, it becomes relatively easy to calculate changes in the exchange rate that would be necessary to satisfy the condition of absolute PPP.

The concept of absolute PPP can be carried a step further. Changes in the overall level of prices are usually presented in terms of percentage changes. Rather than stating that the market basket for a country has increased from 100 to 105, this change would usually be expressed as inflation being 5 percent. This is the same change as occurs when we move from absolute PPP to *relative PPP*. Relative PPP is the theory that a percentage change in the exchange rate is equal to the difference in the percentage change in price levels. This can be shown in more formal terms as

$$\% \, \Delta \, XR = \% \, \Delta \, Pr \, \% \, \Delta \, Pus$$

where XR is the exchange rate. Notice how easy this makes it to analyze our earlier example. If the inflation rate is 100 percent in RCILA and zero in the US, then the P/$ exchange rate will depreciate by 100 percent.

Box 9.4 Restaurant prices and the Mexican peso

An endless source of fascination for economists has been empirically documenting the concept of PPP. Not surprisingly, the usual finding is that PPP does not hold for every short-run period of time. However, exchange rates tend to move in the predicted direction over sufficiently long periods of time. At a more microeconomic level, if PPP seems to work in the long run, then the law of one price should also be working. Studies on the workings of the law of one price are much rarer than studies of PPP. Finding identical goods for which transportation costs, trade barriers, and other distortions to trade are negligible isn't easy. One famous example is the exchange-rate index published by *The Economist* that is based on the price of Big Macs in different countries. In the context of Latin America, one particularly clever study examines the law of one price between Mexico and the US. Fullerton and Coronado (2001) collected data on the prices of identical items in identical restaurant chains in El Paso, Texas, and Ciudad Juarez, Mexico. The two cities form a large "borderplex" where for restaurants there are few barriers to trade. Citizens of either country are free to eat out wherever they can find the best value. The price ratio in this case is the price of individual menu items in Mexico and the US. Since prices change frequently, one can check to see how price changes relate to the peso–dollar exchange rate. Much like other studies of PPP, changes in the price ratio are an unreliable guide to changes in the exchange rate. One wouldn't want to speculate in foreign exchange by eating out and checking prices on both sides of the border. A further complication is that restaurant food is hard to arbitrage. However, this study found limited evidence that in the long run the price ratio and the exchange rate converge. Subsequent studies using longer time series tend to lend more support to this conclusion. The main point is that the different versions of PPP tend to contain a common theme. Looking for a perfect correlation between the price ratios and the exchange rate is almost accidental. However, in the long run, the ratio and the exchange rate move much as theory predicts.

The discussion of PPP leads directly to the concept of the *real exchange rate*. The real exchange rate can be expressed as a relationship between the nominal exchange rate and prices in the two countries. The real exchange rate between the peso and the dollar can be seen as

$$RXR = P/\$ \ (Pr/Pus)$$

where RXR is the real exchange rate. Now consider the possibilities. Suppose the nominal exchange rate is 2P/$. If prices in both RCILA and the US are equal to 100, then the real exchange rate is also 2P/$. However, what would happen if prices doubled in RCILA and the nominal exchange rate did not change? The real exchange rate is now 4, and the nominal exchange rate is still 2. Consider what this means. Goods in the US have become very cheap relative to goods in RCILA. If one could obtain dollars for 2 pesos, then effectively one could purchase 4 pesos' worth of goods. In the usual jargon, the peso is now *overvalued*. Anyone who can obtain pesos at 2P/$ should clearly do so. The reader is left to imagine the effect on imports into RCILA from the US. The effect on exports is grim. A dollar will only purchase 2 pesos' worth of goods from RCILA. In effect, these goods have become much more expensive. The increase in prices in RCILA will not be accounted for if the exchange rate does not change.

Overvalued exchange rates have been a problem for the economies of Latin America since at least the 1950s. Until the early 1980s, the culprit was the fixed exchange-rate system mandated under Bretton Woods. As this system collapsed in the early 1970s, the governments of Latin America were reluctant to allow their exchange rates to float. The example above gives a glimpse as to why. With generally overvalued exchange rates, ISI industries could purchase needed imports at artificially low prices. Others who had borrowed in dollars could likewise service debts at a reduced cost. On the other hand, exporting anything other than commodities was difficult. Exporting labor-intensive manufactured goods in a competitive world market is very difficult in the face of an overvalued exchange rate.

More recently, the problem can be either high commodity prices or large inflows of portfolio capital. Another numerical example illustrates the point. Assume that prices in RCILA and the US are 100, and there is no inflation in either country. If the nominal exchange rate is 2P/$, then the real exchange rate is also 2P/$. If either high commodity prices or inflows of portfolio capital increase, the nominal exchange rate will appreciate. In this case, we'll assume it moves to 1P/$. This nominal appreciation of the currency now translates into a real appreciation. Imports now become cheap, and exports become expensive. Note that there is a difference. In the case of a fixed exchange rate and high inflation, the real appreciation of the currency occurred as a result of government policy. Low inflation coupled with a floating exchange rate would have prevented an appreciation of the real exchange rate. In this case, the real appreciation has been caused by changes in the world market for commodities or changes in the demand for local financial assets by foreign investors. Note, also, that these same factors could easily cause a real depreciation of the exchange rate. Low commodity prices or capital flight could just as easily cause a real depreciation of the currency. It is precisely these sources of macroeconomic instability that will be addressed in Chapter 12.

Box 9.5 The real exchange rate in Venezuela

It is not exactly a secret that the economy of Venezuela is performing poorly. Large fiscal deficits have been financed by printing money. As we will see in a later chapter, this policy almost invariably leads to high inflation. Compounding this problem is the data we saw in Table 5.3. Oil comprises a staggering 98.3 percent of exports and accounts for 20 percent of GDP. There is literally no other country in the region whose economic fate is so heavily tied to one commodity. With the rate of GDP growth falling, tax revenues tend to fall, creating a larger fiscal deficit and still more difficulties with monetary policy and inflation.

From our discussion on p. 219, it would seem clear what should be happening to the exchange rate. There should be a rapid depreciation associated with falling oil prices and rising inflation. However, the country has chosen not to let this happen. Instead, there is a complicated system of fixed exchange rates, with the central bank rationing the scarce foreign exchange to different sectors of the economy at rates far below the equilibrium exchange rate, while the nominal exchange rate is quietly equilibrating. Over the past ten years, the real exchange rate has appreciated in terms of an index number from around 80 to 320. The rate of appreciation is now almost vertical. Given that the inflation rate in the country is now close to 70 percent and expected to rise further, the appreciation of the real exchange rate is perfectly understandable. This is just an extreme example of the usefulness of the concept of the real exchange rate. With high inflation and a fixed exchange rate, only the real exchange rate can provide information on what the currency is worth.

Managed exchange rates

At the beginning of this chapter, we covered the total inflows and outflows of money into a country by studying the components of the current account. As we saw, these flows have an effect on the exchange rate. As a consequence, countries have to make decisions about how to manage the exchange rate. However, one has to be careful in defining the term "exchange rate." Most of the time, we are referring to the nominal exchange rate posted in the market. However, the related concept of the real exchange rate is important. As shown on p. 220, the real exchange rate can change even if the nominal exchange rate does not. The real exchange rate can have an important impact on the volume of trade and on the economy overall. This makes the choice of an exchange-rate regime important. The *exchange-rate regime* is the system a country uses to manage the exchange rate and the foreign-exchange market. So far in this chapter, we have considered two possibilities: a flexible and a fixed exchange rate. The former is relatively rare, except for a few high-income countries. The latter was formerly common in the world economy, including Latin America prior to the early 1970s. However, since the breakup of the Bretton Woods system, it has become rare even in Latin America. However, a perfectly flexible exchange rate or a fixed exchange rate is an important reference point, in much the same way as perfect competition and monopoly. Most exchange-rate regimes, just like most market structures, are somewhere in between these two extremes. Table 9.3 shows the exchange-rate system used by the countries of the region. At one extreme, Venezuela still has a conventional fixed exchange-rate regime. This is still a workable regime in a country with extremely good economic management. If this is not the case, the effects can be unfortunate. On the other side, Chile and Mexico have freely floating exchange rates, which are the norm in high-income countries. However, since Chile has capital controls, the use of the term "freely floating" is not quite accurate. Four countries have a form of floating that is influenced by monetary policy. Many central banks operate with an inflation target. Given the history of inflation in the region, it is not surprising that the central banks of Brazil, Colombia, Paraguay, and Peru have official inflation targets. This influences the exchange rate, as low inflation should serve to limit the volatility of the exchange rate. Uruguay goes one step further. As we will see in Chapter 10, the money supply can have an effect on the rate of inflation. Uruguay targets a monetary aggregate or the money supply as a further insulation against high rates of inflation, as the rate of inflation is linked to the rate of growth of the money supply. Nicaragua uses what is known as a *crawling peg*. With a crawling peg, the nominal exchange rate is changed by a determined amount at preannounced points in time. The main point of a crawling peg is to limit fluctuations in the real exchange.[11] Three other countries, Argentina, Guatemala, and Honduras, use a crawl-like arrangement, where the goal is to limit fluctuations in the real exchange rate. Bolivia and Costa Rica are doing something similar, without officially stating exactly what factors are guiding exchange-rate policy. In all these cases, the result is that countries use a combination of capital controls, intervention in the foreign-exchange market, and interest-rate changes to influence the value of the exchange rate in order to reduce volatility.[12] Ecuador, El Salvador, and Panama do not have a domestic currency but use the US dollar. Each country is in a currency union with the US. This regime has both costs and benefits. The primary cost is that the country does not have a domestic monetary policy. As a result, macroeconomic stabilization can be accomplished only through the use of fiscal policy. For any country, this constitutes a substantial cost. The benefits of such a policy are twofold. First, the policy limits the possibility of serious inflation in the countries. Given the inflation history of the region, this is not a small consideration. It also limits exchange-rate volatility. In a small country, either capital flows or large changes in commodity prices could have very large effects on the exchange rate. By using a stable currency such as the dollar, the potentially adverse consequences of a domestic currency are avoided.[13] While this choice may seem odd at first glance, it is a perfectly reasonable choice for a small and open economy.

In practice, few if any countries in the region are unconcerned about the exchange rate. As we saw on p. 219, large changes in the nominal exchange rate or inflation can have a substantial impact on the real exchange rate. The countries of the region have learned from bitter experience that large changes in the real exchange rate can have very adverse macroeconomic consequences. Historically, many of these changes were the result of a pegged nominal exchange rate.[14] This experience has led to a reasonable compromise for managing the exchange rates of the region. The nominal exchange rate for most countries is now flexible. This frees the governments of the region from the need to constantly intervene in the foreign-exchange market to peg the exchange rate. On the other hand, the real exchange rate needs to be reasonably close to PPP to avoid inappropriate changes in trade flows. The fact that large, unexpected changes in exchange rates are much less common in the region than they were in the past indicates that the lessons of past policy mistakes have been learned and that current policies are an improvement.[15] This is important, as mismanagement of the exchange rate can have unfortunate consequences for the capital account, which is the focus of the next chapter.

Box 9.6 Fear of floating

In a classic article, Calvo and Reinert (2002) discuss the concept of "fear of floating." This fear of floating exchange rates in emerging markets such as Latin America may be a rational response of central bankers to the situation they are in. In such markets, it is essential for the central bank to have credibility. This is particularly important in Latin America, as central-bank independence is relatively new in the region. In these cases, the central bank may find that it can stabilize either the exchange rate or the interest rate. In order to gain credibility, it is important to stabilize one or the other. Since it may be easier to stabilize the exchange rate, that may be a rational choice. This could lead to perverse pro-cyclical policies. For instance, a commodity boom might cause an unwelcome appreciation of the exchange rate. In response, the central bank might lower interest rates to reduce capital inflows and reduce the appreciation. In their paper, Calvo and Reinert found that countries use a combination of intervention, interest-rate policy, and exchange controls to limit changes in the exchange rate. Specifically, many countries that are commodity exporters have much lower exchange-rate volatility than one would expect. Instead of being freely floating, the exchange rate is being actively managed.

The data in Table 9.3 is a perfect example of the concept as it is evident in Latin America. Only two countries in the region, Chile and Mexico, have freely floating

Table 9.3 Exchange-rate regimes in Latin America (2017)

	Exchange-rate regime
Argentina	Floating, inflation-targeting framework
Bolivia	Stabilized arrangement, monetary aggregate target
Brazil	Floating, inflation-targeting framework
Chile	Free floating
Colombia	Floating, inflation-targeting framework
Costa Rica	Crawl-like arrangement
Ecuador	No separate legal tender, i.e. $
El Salvador	No separate legal tender, i.e. $
Guatemala	Floating, inflation-targeting framework
Honduras	Crawling peg
Mexico	Free floating
Nicaragua	Crawling peg
Panama	No separate legal tender, i.e. $
Paraguay	Floating, inflation-targeting framework
Peru	Floating, inflation-targeting framework
Uruguay	Floating, inflation-targeting framework
Venezuela	Other managed arrangement (03/16)

Source: IMF (2019).

exchange rates. As noted on p. 224, the case of Chile has to be qualified due to the existence of capital controls. In other countries, there is really only a vague commitment to exchange-rate stability. The result is that only one country in the region could be said to have a floating exchange rate in the sense that it applies to high-income countries. To be fair, the countries that are floating with some form of monetary policy target are a long way from a conventional peg. "Fear of floating" seems to be present in the data, but the movement toward truly floating exchange rates is evident.

Key terms and concepts

absolute purchasing power parity: the theory that exchange rates are related to differences in the level of prices between countries.

Bretton Woods system: the global system of fixed exchange rates that functioned between 1946 and 1971.

contagion: the tendency of investors to withdraw portfolio capital from an entire region in response to perceived economic difficulties in a single country or a subset of countries.

crawling peg: an exchange-rate regime in which the nominal exchange rate is changed at regular intervals to stabilize the real exchange rate.

current account: an accounting of international transactions that includes goods, services, investment income, and unilateral transfers.

exchange-rate regime: the system a country uses to manage the exchange rate and the foreign-exchange market.

financial account: a record of the difference between the holding of foreign assets by domestic residents and of domestic assets by foreign residents.

intervention: the buying and selling of foreign exchange in order to maintain a fixed exchange rate.

law of one price: the proposition that identical goods sold in competitive markets should cost the same everywhere when prices are expressed in terms of the same currency.

nominal exchange rate: the exchange rate observed in the market.

official reserve assets: government holdings of gold or foreign exchange used to acquire foreign assets.

real exchange rate: the nominal exchange rate adjusted for changes in both domestic and foreign prices.

relative purchasing power parity: the theory that a percentage change in the exchange rate is equal to the difference in the percentage change in price levels.

unilateral transfers: grants or gifts extended to or received from other countries.

Questions for review and discussion

1   The balance on trade can give one a misleading impression of inflows and outflows into the countries of Latin America. Explain how this can happen.
2   For the countries shown in Table 9.2, explain what must be happening to the financial account.

3   Show what would happen to the exchange rate if there was an increase (decrease) in the demand or supply of foreign exchange.

4   Suppose there is high inflation in an RCILA. What would happen to the exchange rate?

5   If the exchange rate is fixed, then a commodity exporter would need to accumulate foreign exchange when commodity prices are high. Show why this is true.

6   If a country has a fixed exchange rate and a current-account deficit, how can intervention be used to maintain the fixed rate?

7   Explain how exchange controls can be used to maintain a fixed exchange rate. What country in the region is currently using exchange controls?

8   Why would a black market for foreign exchange exist? Which countries in the region now have black markets for foreign exchange?

9   Show how capital flight could lead to a rapid depreciation of the exchange rate.

10 Describe the term "contagion." How does it apply to Latin America?

11 Suppose that an RCILA adopted limits on the inflows and outflows of portfolio capital. What might be the effect on the exchange rate? Why would a capital-scarce country in Latin America decide to do this?

12 Using the formula for relative PPP, show how high inflation in Latin America could lead to depreciation of currencies in the region.

13 Suppose that an RCILA had relatively high inflation. How would this affect PPP?

14 Describe how a fixed nominal exchange rate could be associated with the appreciation of the real exchange rate. Why would this distinction matter for Latin America?

15 Which is the most common type of exchange-rate regime in Latin America? Why?

16 Describe "fear of floating." How does it apply to Latin America?

Notes

1   It is normal for high-income countries to have a surplus in trade in services and for middle-income countries to have deficits in services.

2   For convenience, we are not including transactions in the capital account. These transactions include changes in the holdings of nonfinancial assets, such as the purchase of a condominium in Miami by a resident of the region. However, the capital account does include debt forgiveness, which can be a significant factor in some cases.

3   In reality, they frequently do not exactly match, due to the difficulties of recording every transaction. The result is that balance-of-payments statements have another line for statistical discrepancy.

4   For a sense of this period, see Fuentes (1998).

5   Thomas Friedman has dubbed the community of international investors involved in the movements of portfolio capital "the electronic herd."

6   For a more detailed account of the Tequila crisis and its aftermath, see de Gregorio and Valdes (2001). The debt crisis of the early 1980s is a less clear case of contagion, as debt problems were affecting many of the countries in the region.

7   For a sense of this debate in the context of Latin America, see the results for Chile in Edwards and Rigobon (2009) versus the results for Colombia in Kamil and Clements (2009).

8   For a survey of the literature and a sense of the conflicting results, see Chanda (2005).

 9 As an example, in late 2009, Chile was the second country in Latin America to be invited to join the OECD.
10 In the case of PPP calculations, the Producer Price Index is normally used, as it contains fewer items that cannot be traded in international markets.
11 As one might guess, crawling pegs were much more common in Latin America during the high-inflation years of the Lost Decade.
12 IMF (2014) contains much more country-specific detail that is updated annually.
13 The situation is analogous to some of the smaller countries of Europe that have chosen to use the euro.
14 For an excellent history on this issue, see Frenkel and Rapetti (2010).
15 For an interesting description of the evolution of exchange rate policy in Chile, see de Gregorio and Tokman (2004).

References

Bank for International Settlements (2015) *Real Broad Effective Exchange Rate for Venezuela*. Available at FRED, Federal Reserve Bank of St. Louis, http://research.stlouisfed.org/fred2/series/RBVEBIS/ (accessed August 23, 2019).

Calvo, Guillermo A. and Carmen M. Reinert (2002) "Fear of Floating," *Quarterly Journal of Economics*, 117 (2): 379–408.

Chanda, Areendam (2005) "The Influence of Capital Controls on Long-Run Growth: Where and How Much?" *Journal of Development Economics*, 77 (2): 441–466.

de Gregorio, José and Andrea Tokman (2004) *Overcoming Fear of Floating: Exchange Rate Policies in Chile*, Central Bank of Chile Working Paper No. 302, Santiago: Central Bank of Chile.

de Gregorio, José and Rodrigo O. Valdes (2001) "Crisis Transmission: Evidence from the Debt, Tequila, and Asian Flu Crisis," *The World Bank Economic Review*, 15 (2): 289–314.

Edwards, Sebastian (1998) *Capital Flows, Real Exchange Rates, and Capital Controls: Some Latin American Experiences, NBER Working Paper No. 6800*, Cambridge, Mass.: National Bureau of Economic Research.

Edwards, Sebastian and Roberto Rigobon (2009) "Capital Controls on Inflows, Exchange Rate Volatility and External Vulnerability," *Journal of International Economics*, 78 (July): 256–267.

Forbes, Kristin J. (2007) "One Cost of the Chilean Capital Controls: Increased Financial Constraints for Smaller Traded Firms," *Journal of International Economics*, 71 (2): 294–323.

Frenkel, Roberto and Martín Rapetti (2010) *A Concise History of Exchange Rate Regimes in Latin America*, Washington, DC: Center for Economic Policy and Research.

Fuentes, Daniel Diaz (1998) "Latin America during the Interwar Period: The Rise and Fall of the Gold Standard in Argentina, Brazil, and Mexico," in John H. Coatsworth and Alan M. Taylor (eds.), *Latin America and the World Economy since 1800*, Cambridge, Mass.: Harvard University Press, pp. 443–470.

Fullerton, Thomas M. and Roberto Coronado (2001) "Restaurant Prices and the Mexican Peso," *Southern Economic Journal*, 68 (July): 145–155.

International Monetary Fund (2006) *De Facto Classification of Exchange Rate Regimes and Monetary Policy Framework*, Washington, DC: International Monetary Fund.

International Monetary Fund (2019) *Annual Report on Exchange Arrangements and Exchange Restrictions 2018*, Washington, DC: International Monetary Fund.

Kamil, Herman and Benedict J. Clements (2009) *Are Capital Controls Effective in the 21st Century? The Recent Experience of Colombia, International Monetary Fund Working Paper 9/30/2009*, Washington, DC: International Monetary Fund.

Quispe-Agnoli, Myriam (2001) *Dollarization: Will the Quick Fix Pay Off in the Long Run?* Atlanta, Ga.: Federal Reserve Board of Atlanta.

Recommended reading

Bahmini-Oskooee, Moshen and Scott W. Hagerty (2009) "The Effects of Exchange-Rate Volatility on Commodity Trade between the United States and Mexico," *Southern Economic Journal*, 75 (April): 1019–1044.

Blanco-Gonzalez, Lorenzo and Thomas M. Fullerton (2006) "Borderplex Menu Evidence for the Law of One Price," *Economics Letters*, 90 (January): 28–33.

Edwards, Sebastian (1989) "Exchange Controls, Devaluations, and Real Exchange Rates: The Latin American Experience," *Economic Development and Cultural Change*, 37 (April): 457–494.

Frenkel, Roberto and Martín Rapetti (2011) "Exchange Rate Regimes in Latin America," in José A. Ocampo and Jaime Ros (eds.), *The Oxford Handbook of Latin American Economics*, Oxford: Oxford University Press, pp. 185–213.

Fullerton, Thomas M. and David Torres (2005) "Milkshake Prices, International Reserves, and the Mexican Peso," *Frontera Norte*, 17 (January–June): 53–76.

10 Financing current-account deficits

Introduction

In the previous chapter, an important concept was introduced. This involves the relationship between the current account and the financial account. Over a period of time, such as a year, these two accounts should be equal in magnitude and opposite in sign. Another way of putting this is that the total amount of inflows into a country should match the total amount of outflows. If a country has a current-account deficit, it should have a financial-account surplus. The reverse is also true: A current-account surplus should be matched by a financial-account deficit. In the modern history of Latin America, the former has been much more common than the latter. Until recently, ISI combined with overvalued exchange rates tended to create a high demand for imports coupled with difficulties in exporting goods other than commodities. This has obvious implications for the financial account. The current-account deficits in the region created a relentless need for inflows into the financial account. The purpose of this chapter is to illustrate how countries at Latin America's level of economic development usually accomplish this.

As we will see, a financial-account surplus can be accomplished in a number of ways. In the previous chapter, we showed how a country could deal with current-account deficits by either using previously accumulated reserves or, less prudently, relying on a complex system of exchange controls. There are other mechanisms available. Middle-income countries can frequently manage financial-account surpluses with flows of capital from capital-abundant countries. These flows can take a variety of forms. In the first several sections of the chapter, we will cover these flows in the context of Latin America. In turn, these are FDI, portfolio capital, official development assistance (ODA), remittances, and government borrowing from foreign financial institutions. The last has been a source of continual problems in the region. This process has been crucial for Latin America, and problems with inflows into the financial account have the capacity to create serious problems for the economic stability of a country.

Debt vs. equity

When discussing borrowing, a critical distinction must be made between debt and equity. *Debt* is the situation in which the borrower must repay all or part of the loan plus interest at certain points in time. In this case, the ability to pay off the loan over time is critical. In the international capital markets, debt occurs in one of three forms. First, firms and governments in Latin America could issue bonds to raise capital. Usually, selling a bond involves a promise to make periodic interest payments to the bondholder, with payment of the value of the bond due at the date of maturity. Financing debt by issuing bonds in Latin America has historically been done through government borrowing, as most private-sector firms were not large enough to issue bonds in the global marketplace.[1] Second, governments may be able to borrow money from commercial banks in the developed countries. This form of lending is referred to as sovereign lending. Loans by banks to governments go back hundreds of years. As indicated in the quotes at the start of the chapter, sovereign lending may not always work out well for the lender. As indicated earlier in the book, this has been the case in a number of instances in Latin America. Finally, governments may borrow money for projects or to finance current-account deficits from governments or multilateral institutions such as the World Bank or the IMF.

Capital may also flow into a country in the form of *equity* financing. Equity is a situation in which the lender is also an owner in the company or project being financed. A common form of equity finance is FDI. The company providing all or part of the capital is, to one extent or another, involved in ownership or control of the project. A typical example would be an MNC building a production plant in Latin America. Another example would be a company purchasing all or part of an existing company in the region.[2] A second form of equity lending is the movement of portfolio capital between countries. The foreign investor owns a part of the domestic company through stock ownership but usually does not completely control the foreign firm. Equity finance is different from debt in one important respect. Debt payments have to be made no matter what the condition of the borrower is at the time the debt payment is due. Payments to the owners of equity are much more tied to current economic conditions. Owners of equity normally do not have a right to fixed payments in the form of a stream of income. Rather, they have a claim on all or part of the firm's assets. Notice that in the case of equity, property rights and the rule of law are crucial. Foreign investors need to feel that in the case of a dispute their partial ownership of a firm will be treated impartially under the country's laws. To the extent that these systems are weak in the region, the flow of portfolio capital will be diminished.[3]

The debt-versus-equity distinction has been critical for Latin America. Historically, capital flowing into the region has been in the form of debt. Optimism about the future of the region has led to periodic bursts of loans to governments in the region. However, as stated above, the timing of the repayment of debt is fixed. If economic conditions turn out to be worse than expected, then governments in the region could find themselves in an uncomfortable position. If the debt cannot be repaid in full, the result could be, and has been, a *default*. Breaking this pattern of high debt and potential defaults has been a critical issue. As we move through the various means of financing current-account deficits in the region, keeping the debt vs. equity distinction in mind is important.

FDI

As we saw in Chapter 4, of FDI into Latin America have been increasing over the past several decades. Table 4.3 showed that FDI as a percentage of GDP in the region was just 0.7 percent in 1990. For a region composed of middle-income countries, this is an exceptionally low level. By 2017, things had improved considerably. FDI as a percentage of GDP had risen to 3.0 percent. Figure 10.1 puts these flows into a longer

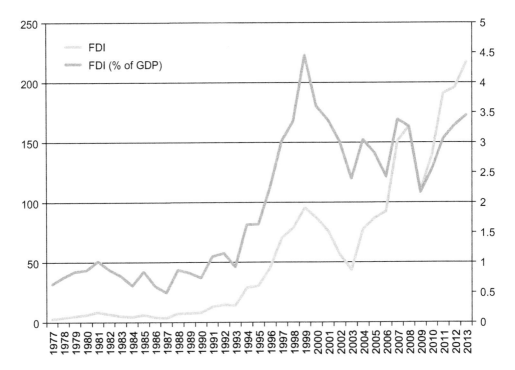

Figure 10.1 Flows of FDI into Latin America.

historical framework. Beginning in 1977, flows of FDI into the region were extremely small, accounting for around 1 percent of GDP. With a small amount of variation, these numbers were typical for the late 1970s through the early 1990s. They are also not surprising. Given the economic turmoil associated with the second oil shock, low FDI in the late 1970s and early 1980s is not unexpected. The low amount of FDI in the 1980s and early 1990s is also not surprising. The poor economic performance of the region during the Lost Decade would not be consistent with large inflows of FDI. Further, the Lost Decade also coincided with major political changes in Latin America. The authoritarian governments of the past were being transformed into new democracies. While this transition certainly was positive in the long run, such transitions may make foreign firms reluctant to invest in the short run until the political situation becomes more certain.

With stronger economic performance and increased confidence in the political situation, the 1990s saw a return of foreign investors to the region. While growth in Latin America may not be as high as growth in some other regions, the data given in Table 1.1 cannot be ignored. Over 600 million consumers with rising GDP per capita is simply too big a market for MNCs to ignore for an extended period of time. By the late 1990s, FDI had risen to over $80 billion. At the peak, FDI accounted for over 4 percent of GDP in the region. These are numbers much more consistent with healthy middle-income countries. The abrupt drop in FDI in the late 1990s had less to do with Latin America and more to do with the state of the world economy. Financial turmoil in Asia and elsewhere, followed by political violence in other parts of the world, drastically reduced FDI on a global basis. Fear, uncertainty, and doubt are normally negatively correlated with FDI. Unlike many episodes in the past, the decline in FDI in the region did not originate there. This decline was followed by a rapid recovery of FDI in the region. In 2007, total FDI reached $120 billion, and it is now over $200 billion. Now think of what has been accomplished in less than twenty years. Total FDI has risen by $100 billion per year from the early 1990s. Since most of these investments are long-run in nature, the numbers represent a very large positive bet on the future of the region. Note also that the trend in the ratio of FDI to GDP is not nearly as positive. This is because the rate of increase in the denominator (GDP) is rising faster than was true in the recent past. As per our discussion of growth in Chapter 4, FDI tends to be positively correlated with increases in the rate of growth of real GDP.

These inflows of FDI also make financing current-account deficits much easier. In a well-managed middle-income country, current-account deficits may be normal. Such countries may be exporting inexpensive, labor-intensive goods in line with their compara-tive advantage. At that stage of development, imports of expensive capital goods may be essential to develop both industry and infrastructure. On the other hand, such a country should be attracting a substantial amount of FDI. Middle-income countries are normally still relatively capital-scarce, and the rate of return to capital should be high. If a middle-income country is well managed, capital should be flowing into the country from high-income countries in search of a better rate of return. The result is that if a country in Latin America has a current-account deficit of 3 percent of GDP, and this is matched by a similar amount of FDI, then the current-account deficit should not be viewed as a problem. This allows us to further analyze Figure 10.1. In the 1970s and 1980s, something was clearly "wrong" with Latin America. For a region full of middle-income countries, there was little or no FDI. Foreign investors simply are not going to invest large sums of money in an uncertain economic environment combined with an uncertain political situation. Once growth and political stability had returned to the region, foreign investors quickly responded to that change. At this point, not all of the advantages of this increase in FDI are obvious. What is obvious at this point is the positive impact on the financial account coupled with the positive effects on growth shown in Chapter 4.

Portfolio capital

As was shown in the previous chapter, the other part of the financial account comprises flows of portfolio capital. This represents the flow of money to purchase financial assets such as stocks and bonds. Figure 10.2 shows these flows into Latin America from 1977 to 2013. In the mid 1990s, portfolio capital flows into Latin America amounted to $50 billion per year and accounted for over 2.5 percent of GDP. The problem is that these flows are inherently more volatile. International investors in financial markets are attempting to maximize returns over a shorter period of time than is true for FDI. As returns in various countries and regions change, flows of portfolio capital change as well. Turmoil in the world financial markets in the late 1990s and early in the past decade reduced portfolio capital flows into Latin America and other emerging markets. Note that for several years, there were small portfolio capital outflows from the region. A strong recovery in these flows was followed by a collapse caused by the global finan-cial crisis of 2008.

The data for Latin America in Figure 10.2 is not untypical. Portfolio capital can move from one country or region to another with startling speed. In part, this reflects the need for investors to find the highest rate of return. Not infrequently, high returns will

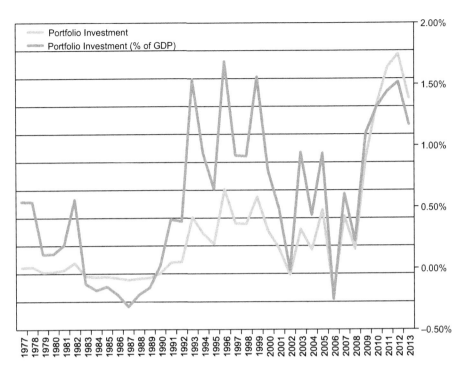

Figure 10.2 Flows of portfolio capital into Latin America.

be found in the middle-income countries that are capital-scarce. Unfortunately, high returns tend to be correlated with higher risk. As perceptions of potential returns and risk change, the flows of portfolio capital will also change. As the economic environment in Latin America has improved, flows of portfolio capital are positive, but only in the long run. As shown below, in the short run, capital outflows are possible. Portfolio capital flows are essential for the economic development of a country and especially for the development of modern financial markets. However, both large inflows and outflows can be destabilizing in terms of the exchange rate and possibly the economy as a whole. Controls on these flows have the benefit of insuring against such instability but at a cost of reducing the inflows in the long run. Uncontrolled flows optimize the inflows in the long run but have the potential to produce exchange-rate shocks. The example given for Chile in the previous chapter is instructive. The regulation or lack thereof of flows of portfolio capital is an economic problem for which there is no clear-cut optimal policy.

Box 10.1 Guano bonds

As we saw above, debt is one way a country can finance a current-account deficit. In Latin America, borrowing by governments has a long and troubled history. Most governments in the region were able to borrow in the international capital markets during an initial surge of enthusiasm for independence in the 1820s. The boom was short-lived, as most of the new countries defaulted on these debts. Peru was no exception. The government took out two loans in 1822 and 1825 and promptly defaulted in 1826. The debt was not resolved until 1849. The government reached an agreement with the creditors to issue new bonds for the principal. Twenty-five percent of the accumulated interest was written off, and the remainder was converted to new bonds that did not pay interest until 1852. Starting in 1853, the government was able to access the credit markets for more debt. Unfortunately, the government defaulted on its debts in 1875. However, for a twenty-five-year period Peru was able to borrow freely and made prompt payments on its existing debt. During this period, Peru had one of the largest stocks of total debt in Latin America, and its ratio of debt payments to government revenue was also quite large.

Peru was able to resolve its initial debt problems and even increase its borrowing because during this period of time its ability to pay its debts was credible. At the time of independence, Peru's economy was dominated by agriculture for domestic consumption and a mining industry that was a shadow of what it had once been. It had long been noted that the islands off the coast contained vast deposits of guano. Commercial development of these deposits began in the 1840s, with the resource being exported to the UK and the US. The mining, transportation, and sales in foreign markets were managed by British companies. Over half of the exports went to the UK market. Revenues from the export of guano flowed to the government, which maintained a monopoly on the trade. The boom in revenues from guano allowed the government to settle previous debts and take on new debt. This was possible only if the government could establish a *credible* commitment to pay the debts. As both the developer of the resource and the potential lenders were British, a credible solution was found. Guano was shipped from Peru to the UK and paid for in British pounds. The firm mining, transporting, and selling the guano was committed to make payments to the bondholders. Although the Peruvian government had taken on the debt, the debts were paid by a credible British firm. The fact that the markets supported this arrangement is evidenced by the relatively low interest rate that Peru could obtain. Predictably, the system began to fail as guano deposits were eventually exhausted. As one might expect, Peru defaulted on the debt in 1876.[4]

ODA

Capital may also flow into a region in the form of ODA. The primary purpose of these flows is to assist in the long-run economic development of the country. In many cases, the purpose is precisely the development of the sort of infrastructure that is essential for economic development. A well-known example of this was the partial funding for Itaipu Dam in Brazil provided by the World Bank. ODA flows take on two general forms. First, the money can move directly from government to government. This transfer can happen in two ways. First, the transfer may be what is known as a *grant*. The money is essentially a gift from the donor country to be used for economic development or national defense. The second type of transfer is in the form of a *loan*. Loans may be used either for economic development or for supporting current-account deficits. On occasion, loans end up being converted into grants. A problem with this sort of ODA is that the aid is frequently "tied" to the donor country. The donor may specify that the recipient country must use the money for a particular project. Further, there may be conditions that the money must be spent on goods and services produced in the donor country. The donor country has provided ODA, but the transfer of the money is not quite as generous as it appears. In some cases, the developing country may end up purchasing goods and services that are not completely appropriate due to the restriction on how the money must be spent. In practice, for Latin America, most of this ODA was a transfer of funds from the US to the region. In most cases, these transfers may have more to do with general foreign-policy objectives than with economic development. Capital flowing in from multilateral institutions such as the World Bank is more straightforward. Loan applications are made for specific projects, and capital flows in as the project is developed. Less recognized is the concomitant outflow. The money eventually has to be repaid. In this regard, the pre-dominantly middle-income countries of the region have a respectable repayment record. However, this middle-income status has some disadvantages. Many of the multilateral institutions have focused on loans and grants to low-income countries. This sort of ODA is not available to many of the countries of the region.

The data on ODA for Latin America is shown in Figure 10.3. From the mid 1960s to the late 1970s, ODA was never more than $1 billion. During the 1980s and 1990s, ODA increased to $6 billion and is now around $10 billion per year. As a percentage of GDP of the region, ODA has never been higher than 12 percent of GDP. It rose briefly during the Lost Decade. Understandably, the amount of ODA increased during that period in response to the economic hardship being experienced in the region, par-ticularly by the poor. This combination of rising ODA and stagnant GDP resulted in a temporary increase in the ODA to GDP ratio. Over the past decade, ODA received

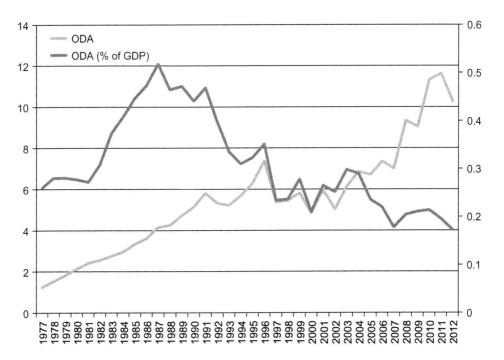

Figure 10.3 Flows of ODA into Latin America.

by Latin America has been relatively stable, and GDP has been increasing. The result is that ODA now represents only 4 percent of GDP in the region. The data indicates two things about ODA in Latin America. In the first place, the flow of ODA has never been a critical factor in terms of the balance of payments in the region. Dependence on ODA as a means of supporting a deficit on goods and services is generally not sound economic policy. Second, ODA has never been a major factor in the long-run economic development of the region. The sums have simply been too small to be a critical part of the development process. At times, such aid has been crucial for particular countries in the process of recovering from the frequent natural disasters outlined in Chapter 5 and for financing certain large infrastructure projects. As is shown in the data, ODA helped the region to weather the Lost Decade. However, overall ODA in Latin America has not been crucial. A far more important source of inflows is covered in the next section.

Box 10.2 The Inter-American Development Bank

One of the ODA success stories of the region is the Inter-American Development Bank (IDB). The IDB was set up in 1959 with the aim of providing loans for economic development in Latin America and the Caribbean. The institution is headquartered in Washington, DC. It currently has forty-eight member countries. Of this group, twenty-two of the countries are non-borrowing members that have contributed capital, and the remaining countries are eligible to borrow. Fifteen countries in western Europe, along with Israel and Japan, have contributed capital to the institution. The IDB has a unique organization. Unlike the World Bank, the developing-country members control most of the decision-making within the organization. The voting power of a country is determined by its subscription to the bank's capital. This gives the countries of Latin America and the Caribbean over 50 percent of the voting power, and the US controls 30 percent. Initially, this arrangement was considered risky. In effect, the borrowers control the IDB. However, the IDB has preferred-creditor status, which means that borrowers repay the institution before paying other creditors such as commercial banks. In this case, informal peer pressure has worked exceedingly well. In its history, only one country has ever defaulted on a loan from the IDB. This is essential, as the bulk of the funds for loans is raised by selling bonds in international markets. These bonds carry a sufficiently high rating to ensure that funds can be obtained at very favorable rates. In turn, this allows borrowers to obtain loans at rates that might not otherwise be possible.

The lending activities of the IDB are a guide to prudent practices in lending. Potential areas for loans are often identified by the institution in conjunction with governments in the region. Loan applications are reviewed for feasibility, and approved projects are monitored, with the disbursement of funds dependent on the execution of the project. In addition to specific project loans, loans are also made for sectoral adjustment and structural adjustment of the economy. Loans are evaluated for impacts on the environment and for their potential social impact. Finally, the IDB also provides funding for private-sector projects in the region. The amounts involved are not inconsequential. Since its inception, the IDB has made over $85 billion in loans. It is currently able to loan approximately $10 billion per year. For a variety of reasons, ODA does not have the best of reputations. However, criticisms of the activities of the IDB are few.

Remittances

A major source of inflows of money into Latin America in the twenty-first century is *remittances*. Remittances are flows of money back to the home country from workers who are employed in another country.[5] Remittances are hardly a new phenomenon, especially in the case of Latin America. Money has been flowing from the Latin American colonies back to Portugal and Spain for hundreds of years. In more recent times, remittances from the US to Mexico and other parts of Latin America have been occurring for a long time. What's new about remittances is the rapid increase in their absolute size. A global perspective might be useful at this point. In 1990, remittances in the world economy were approximately $30 billion. By 2014, they had ballooned to $584 billion. For Latin America, the figures are no less startling. In 1980, they were less than $2 billion. By 2014, they were approximately $55 billion. Table 10.1 shows the data for the countries of the region. In relation to GDP, remittances are a small fraction of the total GDP of the region. However, for some of the lower-income countries of Central America, remittances are between 10 and 20 percent of GDP. In addition, the countries for which remittances are large tend to be some of the poorest countries. Flows of remittances to the region are now far larger than ODA.[6] For many of the countries in the region, remittances represent a significant contribution to overall economic activity.

The sheer size of remittances now makes them important in terms of the balance of payments. Since they are accounted for under unilateral transfers, they work to offset outflows in other parts of the current account. By definition, their contribution to this balance affects the financial account. To the extent that they reduce current-account deficits, they reduce the size of the financial-account surplus. A logical extension of this is that remittances can lead to an appreciation of the exchange rate. Remittances also can lead to greater use of financial institutions and foster growth in that sector.

Table 10.1 Remittances in Latin America

	Remittances (US$ millions)	% of GDP
Argentina	540	0.1
Bolivia	1,201	3.9
Brazil	2,427	0.1
Chile	–	–
Colombia	4,233	1.1
Costa Rica	612	1.2
Ecuador	2,524	2.6
El Salvador	4,236	16.4
Guatemala	5,845	10.0
Honduras	3,329	16.9
Mexico	24,866	1.8
Nicaragua	1,140	9.6
Panama	760	1.1
Paraguay	591	2.0
Peru	2,639	1.3
Uruguay	124	0.2
Venezuela	121	0.0
Latin America	55,128	4.0

Source: World Bank (2015).

Overall, there is limited evidence that remittances enhance economic growth.[7] However, the growth of remittances has been so fast that research on the subject is still relatively new. Remittances are having obvious impacts on the region, but the exact extent of these impacts is still under study. However, their effects on the balance of payments are clearer.

Debt

The dismantling of the Bretton Woods system of fixed exchange rates had profound effects on Latin America. While the US abandoned fixed exchange rates, there were several attempts in the early 1970s to resurrect the system. Even outside Latin America, there was widespread reluctance to move to a global system of floating exchange rates. The first oil shock of 1973 ended any thoughts of returning to fixed exchange rates. For countries that were major oil importers, the demand for foreign exchange increased along with the price of oil. In this situation, countries could either devalue their currencies or borrow a sufficient amount of foreign exchange to continue to finance current-account deficits. This was precisely the choice faced by most of the countries of Latin America. Given the structure of the economies of the region, major depreciations of the exchange rate would have been devastating. It has already been mentioned that such an event can create a painful mix of inflation, low growth, and high unemployment. Major depreciations would also make it much more difficult to sustain ISI industries if necessary imports suddenly became more expensive. The decisions made by the governments of the region were not uniform. However, the region as a whole was slow to adopt floating exchange rates. Many countries continued with a system of fixed exchange rates. Others pursued more complicated systems of depreciating their currencies more slowly. Whatever the specific details for a country, the result was invariably the same. The current-account deficit could not be covered with inflows of ODA, FDI, and portfolio capital. For most countries, accumulated reserves had long since vanished. By the mid 1970s, this meant borrowing from international capital markets. For better or worse, the funds were available. The flow of money into the Organization of Petroleum Exporting Countries (OPEC) countries found its way into international financial institutions such as large commercial banks. With the world economy in recession, the need for borrowing for business investment was reduced. In turn, these institutions became willing to loan large amounts of money to developing countries to finance current-account deficits. The result was that many of these recycled "petrodollars" were loaned to countries in Latin America. The first surge of borrowing in the early to mid 1970s was moderate, in the sense that the countries of the region overall were able to manage the burden of debt. Unfortunately, the region's luck did not hold. The second oil shock produced another unprecedented surge of borrowing. Initially, the region was able to manage this debt and some of the worst effects of this event. By the early 1980s, the burden of debt had become unsustainable. At this point, increasing numbers of countries in the region were forced into major depreciations of their exchange rates as capital inflows decreased dramatically.

The data on debt in Latin America is shown in Figure 10.4. From 1970 to the late 1980s, the long-term debt of the region increased from a small amount to nearly $400 billion. As a percentage of GDP, the statistics are even more striking. Long-term debt rose from only 15 percent of GDP to nearly 50 percent. The difference over the past twenty years is instructive. Long-term debt has continued to rise to $700 billion.

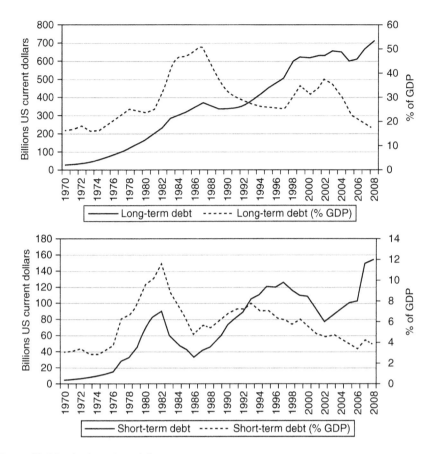

Figure 10.4 Latin American debt.

However, the ratio of debt to GDP has fallen back to under 20 percent. A similar story emerges from the data on short-term debt. For the region, it rose from a negligible amount in the early 1970s to over $80 billion in the early 1980s. As financial conditions became more difficult, short-term debt was cut to less than half that amount by the late 1980s. With an interruption early in this decade, short-term debt has climbed to $150 billion in 2008. As a percentage of GDP, short-term debt peaked at 12 percent of GDP in the early 1980s. As for long-term debt, the ratio is now back to where it began in the 1970s, at 3–4 percent of GDP. Putting long-term and short-term debt together gives an overall picture of debt in Latin America. At the start of the 1970s, total debt was comfortably less than 20 percent of GDP. At the peak in the 1980s, debt was over 50 percent of GDP. In approximately a decade, the region had taken on debt equivalent to 30 percent of GDP.

As the data above indicates, over the 1970s and early 1980s, the external debt of Latin America increased substantially. This is not necessarily a bad thing. If the money borrowed by the governments of the region had been invested in productive assets that enhance economic growth, then a rising level of debt could be a positive thing. On the other hand, if the debt is being used to intervene in the foreign-exchange market to support an overvalued exchange rate, that is not quite so positive. In this case, a rising level of debt was buying faster economic growth in the short run at the risk of a default on the debt or lower economic growth in the future caused by a major depreciation. Like all debt, money owed by citizens, firms, or the government has to be repaid. In this case, there is one important difference. For most countries, foreign debt cannot be repaid in domestic currency. Repayment of foreign debt must be made in an acceptable foreign currency. When debt payments come due, foreign exchange must be available. In order to make timely payments on foreign debt, two factors become critical.

As was covered in the previous chapter, countries have official reserve assets. These represent the stock of foreign exchange a country possesses at a point in time. In some time periods, inflows of foreign exchange will exceed outflows. In this circumstance, the stock of official reserve assets will rise. At other times, outflows may exceed inflows, and the stock will fall. Official reserve assets are important in that they represent a cushion of foreign exchange. If inflows of foreign exchange temporarily decrease or outflows increase, the country can still pay for imports or debt repayments if the level of official reserve assets is sufficiently high. However, if this level is extremely low, then a country may face the uncomfortable choice of imports versus debt repayments. There may not be enough foreign exchange for both.

The other critical factor is the *debt–export ratio*. This ratio expresses the amount of debt repayment a country must make in relation to its earnings from exports. Since foreign debt must be paid in foreign exchange, the ability to make these payments is critical. The lower this ratio, the easier it will be for a country to make debt repayments. However, if this ratio is high, the country may experience difficulties in repaying foreign debt. Putting these concepts together, one can get a picture of a country that can afford to take on more debt. A country with a high level of international reserves coupled with a low debt–export ratio should be able to comfortably repay foreign borrowing. On the other hand, a country with a low level of reserves and a high debt–export ratio may have difficulty handling more borrowing. Neither factor is a perfect predictor of a country's ability to repay debt. However, the level of both factors influences the probability that a country will be able to handle different levels of foreign borrowing.

The data in Figure 10.5 clearly shows the strain the region was under in servicing its debts. Debt service payments peaked in the early 1980s at 80 percent of exports. Aside from servicing debt, the region had little money left for necessary imports. At the same peak, debt service payments amounted to 8 percent of GDP. In effect, the region was transferring nearly 10 percent of GDP to creditors.

These concepts should give one a clearer picture of the situation of Latin America in the 1970s. The first oil shock coupled with current-account deficits increased the demand for foreign exchange in the region. This increase occurred so quickly that any stocks of official reserve assets soon fell to very low levels. Without major currency depreciations, a substantial amount of debt was acquired to support exchange rates that were not being adjusted fast enough. The result was a large increase in the numerator of the debt–export ratio. On the other hand, a combination of slow growth in the world economy, overvalued exchange rates, and reliance on commodity exports meant that the rate of growth of exports was slow. The denominator of the debt–export ratio could not keep up with increases in the numerator. A steadily rising debt–export ratio, coupled with low levels of official reserve assets, makes further borrowing difficult. If these numbers become increasingly problematical, then both domestic and foreign investors eventually may conclude that a major depreciation of the exchange rate is inevitable.

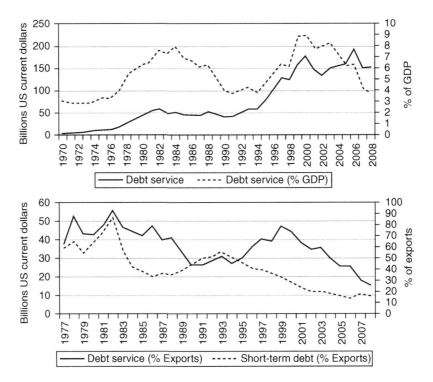

Figure 10.5 Debt service in Latin America.
Source: World Bank (2010).

The result may be capital flight, which simply hastens the inevitable depreciation. In the 1970s and early 1980s, such situations became depressingly common in the region. For the countries affected by this process, usually the only recourse was borrowing from the lender of last resort: the IMF.

Box 10.3 Argentina's currency board

One way of financing current-account deficits is for a country to adopt a currency board. On paper, a currency board will fix the value of the exchange rate, insure against current-account difficulties, and keep inflation under control. Also, it seems simple to do. A currency board is a system whereby the exchange rate is irrevocably fixed against a major currency. The domestic currency is also completely convertible. This means that domestic residents can always exchange domestic currency for the foreign currency. In order to do this, the central bank must keep reserves of currency equal to at least 100 percent of the amount of domestic currency that has been issued. In a well-managed currency board, this reserve is frequently 110 to 115 percent. After the inflationary problems experienced by many developing countries during the 1970s and 1980s, currency boards as a solution to inflation became fashionable in the 1980s and 1990s.[8] Given the history of inflation in Argentina, stretching back many decades, a currency board seemed to be an attractive solution to the country's problems. However, a currency board is not a magic bullet that insulates a country from economic mismanagement.

Argentina implemented a currency board in 1991. Initially, the effects were very positive. Inflation fell to low levels, and economic growth was high. There was a small crisis in the mid 1990s as the entire region was affected by an economic crisis in Mexico. Growth quickly resumed, with another small downturn in 1997 associated with the Asian economic crisis. Unfortunately, this recovery was short-lived. By the late 1990s, both private-sector lenders and the IMF became concerned about the large and growing amount of debt denominated in dollars. In effect, the currency board was working, but the reserves necessary to sustain it were being borrowed. Late in 2000, the IMF loaned Argentina $14 billion, supplemented by $6 billion from private lenders. The situation worsened in 2001 as the government swapped existing debt for new debt with longer maturities in the amount of $30 billion. The IMF provided a further $8 billion in funding later in the year. Not surprisingly, the country defaulted on its debt in 2002 and ended the currency board. The currency board eventually unraveled, as it was never a true currency board. The reserves necessary to support it came from borrowing in dollars from private lenders or the IMF. Without such borrowing, the system would have collapsed much sooner.[9] Freed from an onerous debt and high commodity prices, the economy of Argentina performed well in the first decade of the twenty-first century. More recently, a combination of fiscal deficits, inflation, and low commodity prices is having effects that are as predictable as the collapse of a currency board.

The role of the IMF

Many of those who negotiated the Fund programs with the countries, especially those in the geographic or area departments, had a purely accounting, short-term, and legalistic view of fiscal conditionality so that, if a fiscal deficit was contained within the agreed limits during a relevant period, no matter how, this was good enough.

(Vito Tanzi)

In the previous chapter, we described the role of the IMF under the Bretton Woods system of fixed exchange rates. In this section, we will go into more detail about the role of the IMF in that system and how this has evolved over time. Originally, the IMF was set up to assist countries that had temporary current-account deficits and lacked a sufficient quantity of official reserve assets to support a fixed exchange rate. A graph of this situation is shown in Figure 9.6. The supply and demand for foreign exchange are at an equilibrium that is higher than the fixed exchange rate. In this circumstance, the quantity demanded of foreign exchange (Q_1) is higher than the quantity supplied (Q_2). If the country cannot borrow the requisite amount of foreign exchange from other lenders, it could borrow it from the IMF. This would allow the country to shift the supply of foreign exchange to the right and maintain the official exchange rate. When the IMF was created in the 1940s, each member country was required to contribute a quota determined by the relative size of the country in the world economy. The total contributed created a pool of official reserve assets that could be loaned to countries with current-account deficits. Initially, countries could borrow up to 125 percent of their quota. The total was divided into five tranches. Borrowing in the first tranche carried no conditions. Borrowing in the higher tranches required that the country sign an agreement with the IMF to take policy steps that would correct the current-account deficit. The purpose of this *conditionality* was to correct the imbalance by reducing the demand for foreign exchange. Recall from the previous chapter that the demand for foreign exchange was influenced by domestic income and relative prices. To reduce the demand for foreign exchange, the IMF would request changes in domestic policy that decreased the rate of growth of GDP and reduced inflation. A commonly required change was a tightening of fiscal policy. The IMF would request some combination of lower government spending and higher taxes to reduce GDP and reduce the demand for foreign exchange. A tightening of fiscal policy in the form of a reduction in the rate of growth of the money supply and higher interest rates was also usually a part of conditionality. Collectively, these IMF-mandated conditions were usually referred to as an austerity program. In one sense, the programs would normally work. Declines in GDP and inflation would push the demand for foreign exchange to the left in Figure 9.6. External balance would be restored. However, the price of success was frequently a domestic recession, purposefully engineered by the government but designed by a foreign entity. In a high-income country, this might be considered a distasteful but temporary loss of sovereignty necessary to maintain a fixed exchange rate in a world where this was the norm.[10] The effects on developing countries such as those in Latin America were much more serious. In a low- or middle-income country without social safety nets, an austerity program could cause significant economic hardship. In most of the developing parts of the world, the IMF was not a popular institution. This was especially true in Latin America. During the 1960s and early 1970s, there was very little private capital flowing into the region. Countries in the region became regular "customers" of the IMF, the World Bank, and the IDB. The result was that for the average resident

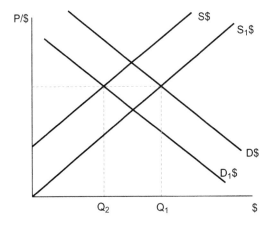

Figure 10.6 The effects of IMF austerity programs.

of the region, the phrases "IMF" and "austerity program" were all too well under-stood. Borrowing from the IMF became associated with potential economic hardship. Austerity programs engendered by borrowing in the higher tranches of a country's quota meant that the demand for foreign exchange would have to be reduced by a large amount. Such borrowing also meant even more stringent austerity programs.

The slow-motion collapse of the fixed exchange-rate system in the 1970s created an odd situation for the IMF. The system it was supposed to support was disappearing. At about the same time as the attempts to reconstruct the global system of fixed exchange rates were becoming futile, oil prices soared. Countries in Latin America and elsewhere increased their borrowing from the IMF. Conveniently, the IMF created a number of new "facilities" that allowed countries to borrow far more than 125 percent of their quota.[11] However, the countries of the region were well aware of the costs of borrowing from the IMF. At the same time, capital became available from large international banks, particularly in the US. The acquisition of debt from this source allowed the region to maintain fixed exchange rates or depreciate at a slower rate. Borrowing from the IMF continued during the decade, but at a slower pace because of the ability to borrow else-where. The second oil shock in 1979 dramatically increased the level of borrowing to finance the associated increase in current-account deficits. By the early 1980s, it was becoming clear that borrowing on this scale was not sustainable. Mexico's default in 1982 began a chain reaction in the region as lending from financial institutions was withdrawn. At this point, the only source of finance was the IMF. The second oil shock was accompanied by slow growth in the world economy, low commodity prices, rising payments on previously accumulated debts, and IMF austerity programs. The predict-able result was little or no growth in many of the countries of the region. The role of the IMF in this period is controversial. Its lending to countries of the region was a neces-sary cushion, but it came at the price of painful austerity programs. Its participation in the negotiations with commercial banks and the US government led to charges that it was overly concerned about the financial health of private-sector banks in high-income countries. Perhaps this is a reflection of the more general problem of the role of the IMF in a world of floating exchange rates.

The Brady Plan

While the IMF was created to finance temporary current-account deficits in a fixed exchange-rate system, it was increasingly lending large amounts of money to countries in the region that were already heavily indebted. It was also attempting to get other creditors to reschedule the existing debt to make the situation more manageable for the countries involved. By the late 1980s, it was clear that the institution could not continu-ally support current-account deficits on this scale. At this time, it was also clear that the region could not support the transfer of real economic resources necessary to fully pay off all accumulated debts. An initial plan to alleviate the problem involved new lending to the countries of the region in exchange for market-oriented reforms. The hope was that the reforms would produce enough economic growth to enable repayment of the debt. By the late 1980s, it was clear that this was not going to lead to a solution.[12] It was becoming increasingly clear that many of the countries of the region would not be able to repay the accumulated debt in total. While the IMF had provided needed foreign exchange in the early and mid 1980s, growth in the region had stagnated. With a large burden of accumulated debt and little growth, it was becoming increasingly unlikely that the total amount of debt could be repaid. Servicing this debt was still taking nearly half of export earnings. More importantly, servicing debt was requiring 5–6 percent of GDP in a region of middle-income countries. This situation could not continue. The pressing need was to combine the total amount of debt into a more manageable total and increase the maturity. In the end, a solution was brokered by the US government. Negotiations with Mexico provided a template for other countries in the region. Banks were offered a menu of choices. Debt could be swapped for thirty-year bonds at a discount of 35 percent of face value or thirty-year bonds at par with a below-market interest rate; or banks could offer new money for four years at up to 25 percent of their current loans. Banks could change their current exposure from 65 to 125 percent of the total. The results were interesting. Banks chose discount bonds, par bonds, or new money at 49, 41, and 10 percent, respectively. These bonds became marketable, as they were backed by US Treasury bonds.[13] With the template established, over the next several years most of the countries reached similar deals that differed mostly in the percentages of the different options banks chose. In total, approximately $190 billion in debts was rescheduled. In the end, $60 billion in debt was written off. The result was a reduction of the total amount of debt to a level consistent with a resumption of economic growth.

To put it mildly, the actions of the US government in Latin America are not usually seen in a favorable light. However, the actions of the US in resolving the debt crisis gripping the region worked. The debt of most of the countries of the region was reduced and replaced by thirty-year bonds. Growth resumed in the 1990s, and by the end of the decade much of the debt had been paid well in advance. The governments of the region borrowed far too much in the late 1970s and early 1980s. The penalty for this fiscal imprudence was a decade of lost economic growth. The commercial banks providing the loans were insufficiently attentive to the ability of the borrowers to repay their debts. Losing a substantial portion of the total loans was the penalty for a deficiency in analyzing sovereign risk. Given the size of the debt, whether or not IMF austerity programs would work was questionable. The problem was resolved by the US government putting public money at risk to back a solution. In a region not known for successful democratic rule, the US government took the not-inconsequential risk that the transition to democratic rule in the region would prove to be durable. In 1989, that was not clear.

Key terms and concepts

debt: borrowing by countries in the form of bonds or bank loans.
debt–export ratio: the ratio of a country's debt payments to its exports.
default: the inability of a country to repay all or part of its foreign debt when it is due.
equity: borrowing by countries in the form of FDI or portfolio capital.
remittances: flows of money back to the home country from workers who are employed in another country.

Questions for review and discussion

1   Describe the difference between financing a current-account deficit using debt and using equity.
2   Describe the importance of flows of FDI to Latin America.
3   How is the flow of portfolio capital different from FDI? Why does this matter?

4 What is ODA? Why is it important in the context of Latin America?
5 How did Peru use guano to finance debt in the nineteenth century?
6 Describe the activities of the IDB.
7 Because remittances are such a small part of the GDP of Latin America, they are not important to the region. Discuss this statement.
8 Describe the evolution of total debt in Latin America since the 1970s.
9 How has the composition of debt changed in Latin America from the 1960s to the present?
10 How has the debt–GDP ratio changed since 1970?
11 What contributes to a default on a country's debt? How does this apply to Latin America?
12 Why is the debt–export ratio important? Why did this ratio rise in Latin America in the 1970s and 1980s?
13 Describe the role of the IMF in a global system of fixed exchange rates.
14 What was the role of the IMF in Latin American debt?
15 Describe an IMF austerity program.
16 What was the role of commercial banks in the debt crisis of the 1980s?
17 Describe the Brady Plan. Did it work as planned?

Notes

1 One of the more encouraging signs in the region is the development of local bond markets and the ability of some firms in the region to raise capital in international markets. For more detail, see Borensztein et al. (2008).
2 The former type of FDI is known as greenfield investment. The latter is known as mergers and acquisitions (M&A).
3 For more on these issues, see Fajnzylber et al. (2009).
4 For complete details, see Vizcarra (2009).
5 Remittances are generally derived from balance-of-payments statistics. However, there is no universally accepted definition of remittances, and the data is not quite as reliable as other statistics, such as imports of goods.
6 See Acosta et al. (2008) for more detail.
7 For more details, see Fajnzylber and López (2008).
8 For more details on Argentina's currency board, see Hanke and Schuler (2002).
9 For detailed accounts of the collapse of the system, see Blustein (2005) or Tanzi (2007).
10 Under the Bretton Woods system, borrowing by high-income countries from the IMF was rare.
11 A list of the currently available facilities is available at www.imf.org.
12 This first program usually referred to as the Baker Plan.
13 For more detail see Vásquez (1996).

References

Blustein, Paul (2005) *And the Money Kept Rolling In (and Out)*, New York: Public Affairs.
Borensztein, Eduardo, Kevin Cowan, Barry Eichengreen, and Ugo Panizza (2008) *Bond Markets in Latin America: On the Verge of a Big Bang?* Cambridge, Mass.: MIT Press.
Fajnzylber, Pablo and J. Humberto López (2008) "The Development Impact of Remittances in Latin America," in Pablo Fajnzylber and J. Humberto López (eds.), *Remittances and Development: Lessons from Latin America*, Washington, DC: World Bank, pp. 1–19.

Fajnzylber, Pablo, J. Luis Guasch, and J. Humberto López (eds.) (2009) *Does the Investment Climate Matter? Microeconomic Foundations of Growth in Latin America*, Washington, DC: World Bank.

Hanke, Steve and Kurt Schuler (2002) "What Went Wrong in Argentina?" *Central Banking Journal*, 12 (February): 43–48.

Tanzi, Vito (2007) *Argentina: An Economic Chronicle*, New York: Pinto Books.

Vásquez, Ian (1996) "The Brady Plan and Market-Based Solutions to Debt Crises," *Cato Journal*, 16 (fall): 233–240.

Vizcarra, Catalina (2009) "Guano, Credible Commitments, and Sovereign Debt Repayment in Nineteenth-Century Peru," *Journal of Economic History*, 2 (June): 358–387.

World Bank (2015) *World Development Indicators*, Washington, DC: World Bank.

Recommended reading

Acosta, Pablo, Pablo Fajnzylber, and J. Humberto López (2008) "How Important Are Remittances in Latin America?" in Pablo Fajnzylber and J. Humberto López (eds.), *Remittances and Development: Lessons from Latin America*, Washington, DC: World Bank, pp. 21–49.

Barajas, Adolfo, Ralph Chami, Dalia Hakura, and Peter Montiel (2011) "Workers' Remittances and the Equilibrium Real Exchange Rate: Theory and Evidence," *Economía*, 11 (spring): 45–94.

Blustein, Paul (2003) *The Chastening*, New York: Public Affairs Press.

Della Paolera and Alan M. Taylor (2012) *Sovereign Debt in Latin America, 1820–1913*, *NBER Working Paper No. 18363*, Cambridge, Mass.: National Bureau of Economic Research.

Edwards, Sebastian (1998) *Capital Inflows into Latin America: A Stop-Go Story? NBER Working Paper No. 6800*, Cambridge, Mass.: National Bureau of Economic Research.

Edwards, Sebastian (ed.) (2007) *Capital Controls and Capital Flows in Emerging Economies*, Chicago, Ill.: University of Chicago Press.

Fajnzylber, Pablo and J. Humberto López (2008) *Remittances and Development: Lessons from Latin America*, Washington, DC: World Bank.

Gerardo della Paolera and Alan M. Taylor (2012) *Sovereign Debt in Latin America, 1820–1913*, *NBER Working Paper No. 18363*, Cambridge, Mass.: National Bureau of Economic Research.

Meyer, Carrie (2000) *The Economics and Politics of NGOs in Latin America*, Santa Barbara, Calif.: Praeger.

Ocampo, José A. (2017) "Latin America and the Global Financial Crisis," in W. Charles Sawyer (ed.), *Latin American Economics*, vol. III, London and New York: Routledge, pp. 234–260.

World Bank (2008) *Migration and Remittances Factbook 2013*, Washington, DC: World Bank.

World Bank (2010) *World Development Indicators*, Washington, DC: World Bank.

11 Macroeconomic policy in Latin America

Introduction

In several parts of the book, we have alluded to the effects of fiscal and monetary policy on the economies of Latin America. In addition, we have mentioned that some of the chronic economic instability in the region can be linked to inappropriate macroeconomic policies. In this chapter, we begin to explore these problems in more depth. However, one needs to be aware that with respect to macroeconomic policy, it is not possible to take the long historical view that was used in some previous chapters. Macroeconomic data is very incomplete prior to 1945. The result is that our discussion of macroeconomics for the region refers to the postwar world. In this case, this is less of a problem for Latin America. Macroeconomic imbalances developed in the region from the 1950s to 1970s that culminated in serious economic difficulties in the 1980s. These effects linger in the region in the twenty-first century. The result is that a more truncated history of macroeconomics is not as inappropriate as it would be for another subject such as commodities. Not accidentally, the time period under consideration is the same as was used for ISI. The two issues are not quite inseparable, but they are definitely related to one another.

The key to understanding macroeconomic policy in Latin America starts with a discussion of fiscal policy. In the first part of the chapter, we present the basic data on fiscal policy in the region over the past several decades. The combination of low tax revenues and high government spending combined to produce government budget deficits that were frequently large. The following section explains what these deficits would tend to do to GDP and the price level. Further, these deficits had to be financed. In most cases, this involved the creation of money to finance these deficits. As we will show, this process can produce serious macroeconomic consequences. Again, the effects of large changes in the money supply will be explained. The final section of the chapter outlines some of the factors that contributed to large fiscal deficits and large changes in the money supply that came to be typical for the region in the second half of the twentieth century.

Fiscal policy in Latin America

> [W]hat shouldn't be done is to ideologize economic policy. What matters is what works and what doesn't. A fiscal deficit is neither of the right nor the left, it's a problem of management.
>
> (Leonel Fernández)

In some of the previous chapters, we indicated that fiscal policy had been a persistently weak aspect of economic management in Latin America. In a well-managed economy, the government budget is essentially balanced when the economy is operating at *potential real GDP*. Potential real GDP is the amount of final goods and services an economy is producing at full employment.[1] To go further, such an economy may pursue countercyclical fiscal policy. As shown in Figure 11.1, at Y_p, the economy is in no need of stimulus from the government budget. If the economy is in danger of slipping into a recession, some combination of increased government spending and lower taxes may be appropriate. If there is a danger of the economy producing a level of output past Y_p, then lower government spending or higher taxes may contribute to economic stability. Another way of putting this is that a balanced government budget is prudent if the economy is at full employment. A government budget deficit is a reasonable response to a recession. Economic growth that is too fast may call for a fiscal policy that intentionally produces a surplus in the government's budget.

The situation described above is an ideal scenario, which assumes that fiscal policy in the country is being used in a prudent way to offset the effects of the business cycle in a free-market economy. Any government should at least make the attempt to align fiscal policy with macroeconomic conditions. To be honest, very few governments in the world are able to accomplish this. Even in OECD countries, democratically elected governments tend to produce perpetual government budget deficits. However, as we will see below, a government budget deficit will not create serious macroeconomic difficulties as long as it is relatively small. What is typical in these countries is a relatively small deficit if the economy is at Y_p and a larger deficit in recessions. "Relatively small" is an important term in this context. The size of the government budget deficit has to be measured relative to the size of GDP. In practice, this is the sum of government spending on goods and services (G) minus government revenues (T) divided by GDP. In most circumstances, a deficit of 1 or 2 percent of GDP would not be a cause for concern. Until the 1990s, the problem with fiscal policy in Latin America was twofold. First, governments in the region ran perpetual deficits. Government budget surpluses are rare under the best of circumstances. However, governments in well-managed countries understand that a surplus is a desirable policy goal under

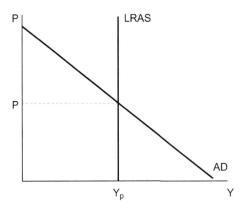

Figure 11.1 The equilibrium price level and real GDP.

Table 11.1 Fiscal deficits in Latin America

	1970s[a]	1980s[a]	1982[b]	1987[b]	1990s[c]	2000s[c]	2017[d]
Argentina	−3.86	−0.71	−7	−4	−0.81	0.11	−6.0
Bolivia	−4.2	−3.65	−16	1	−2.76	−3.6	−5.0
Brazil	−0.64	−14.61	−3	−12	−5.5	−3.89	−7.7
Chile	0	0	−1	0	1.46	2.55	−2.8
Colombia	0	0	−5	−1	−1.03	−1.83	−3.7
Costa Rica	−3.89	−1.76	−1	−3	−2.96	−2.11	−6.2
Ecuador	−1.4	−1.1	−4	−2	−1.72	1.53	−6.0
El Salvador	−0.88	−11.03	−8	1	−1.98	−1.88	0.0
Guatemala	−1.34	−2.96	−5	−1	−0.96	−1.71	−1.3
Honduras	−1.05	−5.34	–	–	−3.03	−3.11	−2.8
Mexico	–	−7.92	−15	−14	−0.4	−0.45	−1.0
Nicaragua	−5.56	−2.32	−20	−17	−1.73	−2.43	−0.6
Panama	−7.29	−5.02	−11	−4	−0.61	−1.01	−2.9
Paraguay	0	0	0	0	−0.65	−0.84	−1.1
Peru	−3.07	−5.29	−3	−6	−2.97	−0.74	−3.6
Uruguay	−0.95	−2.07	−9	−1	−3.3	−2.19	−3.0
Venezuela	−0.44	−1.19	−4	−4	−1.9	0.09	–
Latin America	−2.16	−3.82	−7	−4	−1.82	−1.27	−3.4

Notes: (a) Computed by authors using IMF GFSM database (1986); (b) Edwards (1995); (c) IDB Latin America and Caribbean Macro Watch Tool; (d) ECLA and the Caribbean CEPALSTAT.

certain circumstances. As we will show below, in the context of Latin America, even a relatively small fiscal deficit may be a problem. A more serious problem in Latin America has been the size of the deficits. If the deficit becomes a large percentage of GDP, then any prospect for macroeconomic stability has been lost. The situation for Latin America is shown in Table 11.1. In the 1970s, budget deficits in the region averaged slightly over 2 percent of GDP. In the 1980s, the situation deteriorated, and deficits averaged nearly 4 percent of GDP. However, the two columns for 1982 and 1987 are instructive. In 1982, deficits averaged an alarming 7 percent of GDP. By 1987, the deficits were back down to 4 percent of GDP. However, notice that some of the deficits during the decade for particular countries were astonishingly large. In the 1990s, deficits in the region were again below 2 percent. In this decade, they are approaching 1 percent.

An intriguing question emerges from the data presented above. Why were fiscal deficits so large and persistent in Latin America during the latter part of the twentieth century? While there is no definite answer to that question, there are some factors that contributed to the problem. The first factor has been alluded to before. The raising of tax revenue in the region has been historically problematical. During the colonial period, avoidance of paying taxes to the Spanish government made perfect sense. Much of the revenue would revert to Portugal or Spain as opposed to being spent in the region. Under these circumstances, tax evasion was understandable. One of the legacies of colonial rule was relatively weak government institutions, including the ability to levy taxes. This problem was accompanied by the concentration of income and assets that was partially a legacy of colonialism and partially the result of post-independence commodity booms. This concentration puts the higher-income groups in a good position to resist direct taxation of either income or assets. Thus, governments in the region have traditionally been in a poor position to raise revenue from the source with the highest ability to pay. Inequality also plays a part on the expenditure side. An unequal distribution of income increases the propensity of government to attempt to redress this problem through public expenditures. This may involve relatively high spending on social programs that are difficult for the government of a middle-income country to afford. While this sort of spending is understandable, in an environment where tax revenue is low, the result may be relatively large fiscal deficits. Financing these deficits may be difficult. This process, and its consequences, are the subject of the next section.

Financing deficits and the money supply

In the previous section it was shown that fiscal deficits have historically been a problem in Latin America. In this section, we will first assume that a fiscal deficit has become an intractable problem for an RCILA. Given a deficit, the country now has two options. The preferred option would be to borrow the money to cover the deficit. In developed countries, this is a routine transaction. The government would simply sell bonds to the public and use the proceeds of the sale to fund government expenditures. There is a critical assumption in this process. The sale of new government bonds assumes that there are willing buyers.[2] The only remaining question is how many. If the government has an excellent credit rating, then the bonds are perceived as being virtually risk-free. In this case, the government can raise the necessary funds at a low interest rate. Government debt that is perceived as being somewhat more risky can still be sold, but the interest rate will be higher. At the other end of the spectrum is a government that cannot sell bonds. If a country has a history of defaulting on its debts, then under-standably there may be no demand for its bonds. Latin America has been unfortunate in this regard. Since independence, defaults on debt by the governments of the region have been commonplace. The result was that through much of the latter part of the twentieth century, it was difficult for the governments of the region to finance deficit spending by borrowing.

In the frequent event of a government budget deficit in RCILA, that left the government in the position of financing the deficit via the creation of new money. Our task at this point is to demonstrate why this can cause significant economic problems. To do this, we will need to explain some of the relationships involved in determining the supply of money. First, consider the following relationship.

B = Cp + R where:

B is equal to the *monetary base*.

Cp is cash in the hands of the public.

R is the reserves of the banking system.

Cp is practically self-explanatory. It is the coins and paper money held by the public. The reserves of the banking system may need further explanation. If a deposit is made to a bank, the bank is legally obligated to hold a portion of this deposit in reserve (i.e. it cannot loan it out). The total of these reserves for all banks in a country is R.[3] From the monetary base, we can now proceed to the money supply.

Ms = B * 1/r

or

Ms = Cp + D where:

Ms is the *money supply* r is the percentage of deposits banks must keep in reserve.

D is the total amount of demand deposits in RCILA.

To keep things simple, assume that r is equal to 0.10. This would mean that if someone made a 100 peso deposit in a bank in RCILA, the bank would have to keep 10 pesos on deposit. The other 90 pesos could be loaned out. What happens next is interesting. The 90 pesos is new money. Whenever a bank makes a loan, new money is created. In a free banking market with fractional reserve banking, banks create money when they make loans. To see this more clearly, consider the balance sheet of a bank in RCILA.

Assets	Liabilities
R = 10	Deposit = 100
Loans = 90	

Notice what has occurred here. The bank is holding 10 pesos in reserve. It has made a loan of 90 pesos. Both the reserves and the loan are assets. The liability is that the depositor can still spend 100 pesos. The supply of money is now 190 pesos. The process does not stop here. The 90 pesos will eventually end up as a deposit. From here, a bank would have to hold 9 pesos and could make a loan of 81 pesos. The 81 pesos is also new money. One could continue to do the calculations from here, but fortunately there is a simpler way of accomplishing the same thing. This is the meaning of 1/r or the banking *money multiplier*. The banking money multiplier is the multiple by which a change in B translates into a change in the money supply. If we assume that r is equal to 0.1, then the money multiplier is 10. This may seem like innocuous arithmetic, but this relationship is crucial. If B changes by 1 peso, then the money supply of RCILA increases by 10 pesos. This is why the monetary base is sometimes referred to as high-powered money. Any change in B will have a large effect on the money supply.

We are now in a position to examine how a fiscal deficit can affect the money supply. Again, assume that the government cannot borrow the necessary funds. If it could, the effect of the deficit on the money supply would be neutral. The government would be borrowing the money instead of another entity (firms or individuals). This might push up interest rates, but there would be no effect on the money supply.[4] However, if the government has to print money to cover the deficit, the effect on the money supply can be dramatic. To illustrate this, let's assume some data for RCILA, which is shown in Table 11.2.

Table 11.2 Change in the money supply in a RCILA

GDP	B	Ms	Deficit	ΔB	ΔMs
1 trillion	10 billion	100 billion	50 billion	50 billion	500 billion

First, note that GDP is equal to 1 trillion pesos. Now, suppose that government spending is 200 billion pesos or 20 percent of GDP. Next, assume that tax revenues are 150 billion pesos or 15 percent of GDP. The resulting fiscal deficit is 50 billion pesos or 5 percent of GDP. In a 1-trillion-peso economy, this wouldn't seem to be a problem. If the government has to print the money in order to cover the deficit, then the monetary base increases by 50 billion pesos. The next step is crucial. If B increases by 50 billion, then the money supply increases by *500 billion*. As we will see in the next section, such a dramatic increase in the money supply will have large impacts on the economy of RCILA.

A reasonable question at this point is the role of the central bank. In any economy, the central bank is in charge of managing the supply of money. It does this by having the right to loan money to the government. In a high-income country, this would be rare. If the government runs a fiscal deficit, it would normally cover this by borrowing from the financial markets. It would not usually borrow from the central bank, as the effects on the monetary base and the money supply would be too dramatic. In most cases, the central bank is under no obligation to loan money to the government. It can if it chooses to, but this would normally be imprudent. Institutional arrangements have been set up to insure that the central bank is independent of the government. With this independence, the central bank can manage the supply of money without regard for the finances of the government. Unfortunately, until recently central banks in Latin America were not independent. If the government ran a fiscal deficit, the central bank was obliged to loan the government money. Technically, the books of the central bank balance. It has acquired an asset, a loan to the government. The corresponding liability is the new money created to finance the deficit. This new money increases the monetary base by an identical amount. Eventually, the money supply will increase by a multiple of that amount. Under these circumstances, the central bank is not really managing the money supply. In reality, the supply of money is being determined by whoever is running the government. In a sense, fiscal policy is determining monetary policy. The experience of most countries has been that allowing the government to determine the money supply does not work very well. The nonindependent central banks of Latin America were classic examples of this. In the latter half of the twentieth century, fiscal deficits in the region were the norm. What was also the norm was the central bank loaning the money to the government to cover the deficit. In the next section, the effects of this will become clearer.

The money supply, prices, and GDP

> Perhaps Latin America would have done better in terms of economic stability had the printing press never crossed the Atlantic.
>
> (Carmen Reinhart and Kenneth Rogoff)

In the previous section, we showed how a relatively small fiscal deficit can lead to an extremely large change in the money supply. In this section, the effects of this change in the money supply will be examined more closely. A change in the money supply has one of the most powerful influences on the state of the economy. Both real GDP and the price level are influenced by changes in the supply of money. In the first part of this section, some basic relationships between the money supply, the price level, and real GDP will be developed. In the second part of this section, we will examine how the money supply affects these variables using a basic macroeconomic model.

The equation of exchange

The simplest way to look at how the money supply affects the economy is by examining the equation of exchange. The equation of exchange is a basic framework for analyzing the interactions among the money supply, the price level, and real GDP. More formally, the equation is

$M\,V = P\,Q$ where:

M is the money supply.

V is the velocity of money.

P is the price level.

Q is real GDP.

All the terms in the equation of exchange should be familiar, with the exception of the velocity of money. The velocity of money is simply an expression of the fact that the money supply, if spent only once a year, would not buy nominal GDP. On average, money is spent more than once a year. For example, consider the data in Table 10.2. The nominal GDP of RCILA is 1 trillion pesos, and the money supply is 100 billion pesos. The velocity of money in this case is 10. This can be determined by dividing nominal GDP (PQ) by the money supply (M). On average, each peso is being spent ten times during a year. To summarize, the money supply multiplied by the velocity has to be identical to the price level multiplied by real GDP.

   The relationship given above is an identity. Now, let's make some assumptions about the movements of these variables over time. First, let's assume that the velocity of money is constant. In the short run, this is not an unrealistic assumption. From one year to the next, V is not likely to change by a large amount.[5] Second, assume that Q grows by a certain amount every year. In effect, this is the growth rate of potential real GDP. In the case of RCILA, this might amount to 6 percent per year under favorable circumstances.[6] Now, assume that the government desires price stability. The goal is to limit increases in P. In order for this to occur, changes in M need to be roughly equivalent to changes in Q. In other words, price stability requires that money supply growth is similar to the rate of growth of potential real GDP.[7] In practice, for the middle-income countries, maintaining this equality is not easy. If there is no local bond market, then the central bank has to use changes in the *discount rate* or changes in the reserve requirement to influence the monetary base. When the central bank makes a loan to a private-sector bank, the monetary base expands. When the loan is paid off, it contracts. By lowering or raising the discount rate, the central bank can increase or decrease the monetary base and the money supply. Likewise, changes in the legal reserve requirement (r) change both the monetary base and the money multiplier. An increase in r reduces the money supply, and a decrease in r increases it. Under the best circumstances, obtaining a growth rate of the money supply that will insure price stability requires very talented people at the central bank. For most middle-income countries, this isn't possible. What is possible is keeping inflation at a low enough level to prevent the disruption of normal economic activity. In this context, a rate of inflation of 5 percent or less is sufficient. Given the institutional difficulties of controlling the money supply in a developing country, this is no mean feat. The equation of exchange is a very useful device for thinking about these issues. Keeping inflation at acceptably low levels ultimately means keeping the rate of growth of the money supply at levels consistent with something like price stability.

One should now be able to see more clearly what the data presented in the previous section means. Suppose that a country is running a fiscal deficit and is unable to borrow to cover the deficit. If the central bank is obliged to loan the government money, the monetary base will expand. This expansion of the monetary base leads to a multiple expansion of the supply of money. A deficit that is even a small percentage of GDP can quickly lead to an enormous increase in the monetary base and the supply of money. This expansion can quickly outstrip the increase in potential real GDP. Once the economy is at full employment, the logic of the equation of exchange becomes inexorable. A large increase in the money supply leads to a large increase in the price level. In effect, fiscal policy becomes monetary policy. The deficits in the region in the 1970s and 1980s turned into large increases in the money supply. This can be seen in Table 11.3.

The data shown in Table 11.3 are consistent with Table 11.2. As fiscal deficits in the region increased, the growth rates of the money supply also increased. In the 1960s, money supply growth in the region was under 20 percent. This is high, but not potentially ruinous. By the 1970s, money supply growth had more than doubled as budget deficits became larger.

The fiscal deficits of the 1980s shown above set the stage for enormously rapid growth in the money supply. Even ignoring some of the larger numbers in the column, money supply growth in the region was rapid. By the 1990s, the situation had improved dramatically. Money supply growth was still too high, but the rate of growth had been noticeably reduced. In this decade, the rate of growth of the money supply for the region now looks "normal" for a collection of middle-income countries. A sure sign of progress is

Table 11.3 Changes in the money supply in Latin America (average annual percentage change)

	1960s	*1970s*	*1980s*	*1990s*	*2000s*	*2017*
Argentina	26.7	117.7	657.8	129.2	22.7	30.1
Bolivia	14	22.5	605.9	19.7	29	10
Brazil	52.7	40.6	311.8	803.8	15.5	4.2
Chile	40.4	169.5	25.6	20.3	17.1	0.6
Colombia	19.1	24.1	22.9	23.4	15.1	6.8
Costa Rica	9.6	20.9	28.3	25.4	24.5	1.5
Ecuador	10.2	20.2	−5.1	6	17.9	−20.6
El Salvador	4.8	16.9	3.6	6.8	7.6	11
Guatemala	5.1	16.1	14.2	20.8	15	7.3
Honduras	10.4	14.1	10.9	22.5	13.1	13.9
Mexico	11.8	23	56.9	34.2	14.9	11.1
Nicaragua	8.2	22.7	1553.6	778.5	20.7	16
Panama	8.6	14.4	1	14.6	2.9	–
Paraguay	9.6	23.4	25.8	18	22.7	10.7
Peru	16.5	33.8	300.2	717.6	9	9.3
Uruguay	48.9	58.5	53.6	47.9	26.7	1.9
Venezuela	7.2	22.4	13.1	52.8	43.7	58.8
Latin America	17.9	38.9	215.3	161.3	18.7	10.7875

Source: World Bank (2019).

Note: 2017 data for Venezuela from 2013.

Table 11.4 Changes in the rate of inflation in Latin America

	1960s	*1970s*	*1980s*	*1990s*	*2000s*	*2017*
Argentina	22.4	132.9	565.7	252.9	8.9	–
Bolivia	5.7	15.9	1383.2	10.4	5.1	2.8
Brazil	–	–	354.5	843.3	6.9	3.4
Chile	26.6	174.6	21.4	11.8	3.7	2.2
Colombia	11.5	19.7	23.5	22.2	6.3	4.3
Costa Rica	2.1	9.8	27.1	16.9	10.9	1.6
Ecuador	4.4	11.9	34	39	17.8	0.4
El Salvador	0.4	9.3	18.5	10.6	3.6	1
Guatemala	0.7	8.9	12.1	14.8	7	4.4
Honduras	2.3	6.6	7.4	19.7	8.2	3.9
Mexico	2.5	14.7	69	20.4	5.2	6
Nicaragua	–	–	–	–	8.4	3.9
Panama	1.1	6	3.2	1.1	2.4	0.9
Paraguay	3.8	11.1	20.2	16.4	8.3	3.6
Peru	9.9	26.5	481.3	807.9	2.6	2.8
Uruguay	51.4	59.3	57.6	48.9	8.6	6.2
Venezuela	1	6.6	23	47.4	27.1	254.9
Latin America	3.2	11.3	10.6	10.6	4.7	2.3

Source: World Bank (2019).

Notes: Venezuela 2017 data from 2016.

that the highest number by far in the column would have looked like a "good" number in the 1980s.

As per the equation of exchange, the changes in the money supply in Latin America translated into changes in inflation. These changes are shown in Table 11.4. Again, starting in the 1960s, rates of inflation in Latin America were fairly typical of middle-income countries. The average rate of inflation in the region was less than 10 percent. As fiscal deficits and money supply growth accelerated during the 1970s, the rate of inflation increased dramatically. While a regional average of 34.3 percent isn't good, the situation grew far worse during the 1980s. The *average* rate of inflation in the region was nearly 200 percent. This is such a devastating rate of inflation that normal economic activity becomes difficult. Also, the effects of this on the welfare of the poor are hard to imagine. As one might have guessed from Tables 11.1 and 11.3, the situation improved in the 1990s. Inflation moderated to a regional average of 136.5 percent. This was still far too high, but represented a dramatic improvement from the Lost Decade. The fiscal restraint of the past decade has worked in the usual way. As governments in the region have learned to achieve a better balance in the government finances, the rate of growth of the money supply has moderated. In turn, this has accomplished far lower rates of inflation. The progress that has been made in the region is remarkable but technically predictable. In a middle-income country, it is essential for fiscal policy to be prudent in order to keep inflation from devastating the economy. As we will see in the next section, these gains in lowering inflation came at a heavy cost in the short run.

The inflationary process

The *equation of exchange* is an exceptionally useful framework for thinking about how changes in the money supply affect the price level. However, it has some important limitations. First, it is a long-run concept. In the context of macroeconomics, the long run is usually a time period of more than two years. Second, since the equation of exchange is a long-run concept, changes in the money supply have no influence on either real GDP or the level of employment. In this section, the process of inflation will be covered using a more flexible model. This will allow us to show how changes in the money supply affect the economy over shorter periods of time. The model can also be linked to the previous analysis shown with the equation of exchange.

Analyzing changes in the economy caused by changes in the money supply can be shown most easily using a macroeconomic model that incorporates changes in both *aggregate demand* and *aggregate supply*. To begin our analysis, we will consider the model for the long run, as it is just a different way of reaching the same conclusions as were obtained in the previous section. In Figure 11.1, the price level (P) is shown on the vertical axis.[8] The horizontal axis is real GDP. Note already that we have graphed the two variables that form the right-hand side of the equation of exchange in the previous section. Note that in Figure 11.1, the aggregate-demand curve slopes downward and to the right. As the overall price level increases, the overall demand for goods and services declines, and vice versa. If the only thing that changes is the price level, then there are only movements from one point to another along an existing aggregate-demand curve. Recalling the components of GDP, if any of these components changes, then the aggregate-demand curve will shift. If consumption, investment, government spending, or the trade balance increases or decreases, then the aggregate-demand curve will increase or decrease, respectively. A change in the money supply can cause a change in aggregate demand. An increase in the money supply could increase consumption by the public. Such an increase could cause an increase in both nominal income and consumption. Second, an increase in the money supply could reduce interest rates and stimulate both business investment and residential investment.

In order to find a macroeconomic equilibrium, Figure 11.1 includes a long-run aggregate supply curve. This supply curve has two important characteristics. First, in the long run, aggregate supply (LRAS) is perfectly inelastic (i.e. a vertical line). This is because in the long run there is no relationship between the price level and real GDP. An example may illustrate the point. Suppose that in RCILA the price level doubled over the next five years. What else would occur? As the price level doubled, all other prices in the economy, such as wages, interest rates, asset prices, and so on, would also roughly double. The result would be that in the long run, the price level has no effect on the level of economic output. Second, the point at which the LRAS curve crosses the horizontal axis has meaning. This point coincides with potential real GDP (Y_p). This is the point where in the long run the economy is producing, assuming normal utilization of capital and labor. In Figure 11.1, the long-run equilibrium for RCILA occurs at Y_p and P.

We are now in a position to link Figure 11.1 with the earlier material on the equation of exchange. Assume that the supply of money increased dramatically, as shown in Table 11.5. As previously explained, such an increase would cause a large increase in aggregate demand. This is shown as an increase from AD to AD_1. Over several years, this would not change the output of the economy overall. It would still be producing an output consistent with Y_p. Consumption, investment, and government spending would all be increasing. Over a period of several years, this increase in aggregate demand would only influence the price level as wages and other prices adjusted to the higher price level. What is occurring in the long run is a little more complicated, but it is worth looking at it in the context of Latin America. This is shown in Figure 11.2. As was

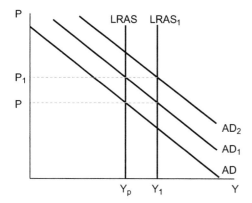

Figure 11.2 The price level and changes in aggregate demand.

shown in Chapter 3, the central problem of Latin America has been slow economic growth. Economic growth can be shown in the figure as a movement of the LRAS curve to the right over time. As the LRAS curve shifts, Y_p also shifts along with it. However, if economic growth is slow, then the movement of both LRAS and Y_p will likewise be slow. Now, think of this in combination with the macroeconomic policy goal of having a stable price level. In order to accomplish this, the aggregate-demand curve must be shifting to the right at approximately the same rate as the LRAS curve or the rate of growth of Y_p. This situation is shown in Figure 11.2 with the new equilibrium of AD_1 and $LRAS_1$. In this case, real GDP has grown over time, but the price level has stabilized. For this outcome to occur, the *central bank* must be very careful. If the LRAS curve is not shifting to the right quickly, then the central bank cannot let the money supply grow too rapidly. In a well-managed country, an independent central bank that is technically competent can accomplish this. The problem in Latin America is that the combination of a nonindependent central bank and a large fiscal deficit would push the growth of the money supply far higher than the growth of Y_p. In this case, the aggregate-demand curve might increase to AD_2. Since the growth of aggregate demand far exceeds the growth of Y_p, the price level can rise substantially. This result may seem puzzling at first. Why would a government engage in policies that would lead to substantial inflation that damages almost everyone's economic welfare? In the next section, at least a partial answer to that question will be provided.

Economic populism

In order to answer the question posed at the end of the previous section, we need to go a little further in our analysis of how the money supply affects the economy. Both the equation of exchange and the aggregate demand and aggregate supply model shown in the previous section give valid results for the long run. In this case, the long run means something like three to five years. At this point, our attention is turning to the more usual time frame for macroeconomic analysis, which is less than two years. This is convenient in a discussion of *economic populism*. The term refers to the tendency of governments to pursue policies that will produce the most favorable economic outcomes

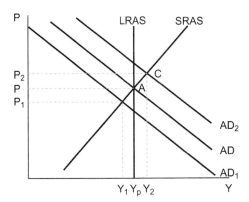

Figure 11.3 Changes in aggregate demand and changes in the price level and real GDP.

in the short run.[9] As we will see, such policies can have extremely unfortunate macroeconomic consequences in the long run.[10]

To begin our discussion, consider Figure 11.3. As before, the figure contains both the LRAS curve and the aggregate-demand curve that we used above to analyze changes in the price level and real GDP. The critical difference here is that the figure includes the short-run aggregate supply (SRAS) curve. The SRAS curve slopes upward and to the right, indicating that in the short run there is a positive relationship between the price level and real GDP. The optimal point for the economy is labeled point A in the figure. This is where LRAS, aggregate demand, and SRAS all intersect. Any points to the left of point A are undesirable. Suppose that aggregate demand fell from AD to AD_1. Real GDP would fall from Y_p to Y_1, and the price level would fall from P to P_1. This is a classic recession in which GDP is below potential, unemployment rises, and inflation is not a problem. In the context of Latin America, a more common problem is illustrated by Point C. In this case, aggregate demand has shifted from AD to AD_2. This increase in aggregate demand produces a higher price level. However, it also produces output greater than Y_p and low unemployment. As one can imagine, a government budget deficit mixed with an expansion of the money supply can produce this sort of outcome.

Box 11.1 Inflation and structuralist economics

The material in the preceding section implies that inflation is always caused by increases in the money supply that are larger than changes in LRAS. This simple explanation of inflation has roots stretching back hundreds of years. In the context of Latin America, this excessive creation of money is easily traced to fiscal deficits. A reasonable question is why governments in the region unleashed massive inflation when its causes are not exactly an economic mystery. Part of the answer can be attributed to the concept of structuralist economics, which was mentioned in Chapter 7. To briefly summarize, structuralist economics is the idea that the structure of an economy can have important effects on economic outcomes, in this case inflation. The basic idea is undeniably true. Even in Latin America, the structure of the economy of Guatemala is quite different from that of Mexico or Brazil. It is unlikely that an identical set of policies would have exactly the same effects in all countries of the region.

In the structuralist view of the economy, the story that inflation occurs as a result of the money supply increasing aggregate demand to too high a level is only part of the story, and perhaps not the most important part. Rather than focusing on aggregate demand, the structuralist approach to inflation emphasizes problems with aggregate supply. In this vision, the economies of Latin America were more prone to inflation because they tended to have supply problems that pushed up SRAS. Such an increase in the price level caused by a decrease in SRAS is usually referred to as cost–push inflation. Some of the factors that could cause such decreases in the short run included exchange-rate depreciations and the 1970s oil shocks. As we will see in the next chapter, these factors can push the SRAS curve to the left. The structuralists also emphasized other factors that tended to make inflation more prevalent in the region. As a result of ISI, many product markets in the region were less than perfectly competitive, which makes it more difficult for prices to adjust. On the production side of the market, trade restrictions and rigid labor markets make controlling costs of production more difficult. Further, if inflation becomes an economic fact of life, producers and consumers adjust their actions accordingly, and inflationary expectations become deeply embedded in the system.

It is a short step from emphasizing supply constraints as a cause of inflation to downplaying the role of the money supply in creating the problem. What this meant was that there was a tendency in the middle decades of the twentieth century to emphasize these supply factors as a cause of inflation, which conveniently shifted the focus from excessive money supply growth driven by lax fiscal policy. This was enhanced by the academic debate raging in the developed countries over the importance of the money supply in macroeconomic activity.[11] In terms of macroeconomic policy, for a time it was possible to blame inflation in the region on structural rigidities in the economies of the region as a primary cause of inflation. As the inflation problem worsened in the 1970s and 1980s, and the economic debate over the cause of high inflation became more settled, the structuralist approach to inflation faded in importance. This is perhaps unfortunate. In most cases, excessive money supply growth is the cause of inflation. However, structural problems in the economy can exacerbate the problem. To this extent, some of the problems the structuralists identified may not be the cause of inflation, but they can make it more difficult to control. If these factors are prevalent in an economy, then the government will need to be exceptionally vigilant concerning the deficit, and the central bank may need to be even more wary of inflation. In this sense, the recent tendency to dismiss the structuralist approach to inflation as irrelevant economic history is on a par with the earlier view that the money supply is not very important.

If this were the end of the macroeconomic story, then the effects of a fiscal deficit and the expansion of the money supply could seem rather benign. Point C involves more GDP and lower unemployment. The cost is a higher price level. In the context

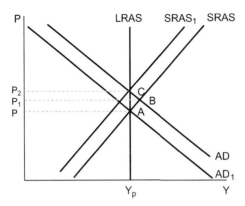

Figure 11.4 The effects of changes in inflationary expectations.

of the developing countries of Latin America, this may not be a suboptimal outcome. Unfortunately, point C is not a stable equilibrium. As the price level increases,
workers, consumers, and businesses will start expecting higher prices. As their inflationary expectations change, the SRAS curve will begin to shift to the left.[12] This
movement is shown in Figure 11.4. As inflationary expectations adjust, a new stable
equilibrium will be established at point C, or the intersection of LRAS, SRAS, and
aggregate demand occurs. The level of real GDP returns to Y_p, and unemployment
will rise as the economy moves from point B to point C. The expansionary fiscal
and monetary policies have created the following scenario. For a period of time, the
expansionary policies raised real GDP and lowered unemployment. The cost was a
moderate increase in the price level. As inflationary expectations increase, the SRAS
curve eventually shifts to the left and the price level rises further. The increase in real
GDP and the decline in unemployment were temporary. Unfortunately, the increase
in the price level was permanent. The policy bought temporary growth and employment at the cost of permanently higher prices. The graph illustrates the logic of economic populism. Policies can be pursued because they render short-run economic
benefits that may be politically popular. It is frequently the case that such policies
produce undesirable economic outcomes in the long run. If such a scenario were an
occasional random event, the damage to an individual economy in the region might
be tolerable.

Unfortunately, the situation described above is frequently not an idiosyncratic
event but, rather, the beginning of an unfortunate pattern shown in Figure 11.5.
As before, the initial expansionary fiscal and monetary policies led the economy
from point A to point B and eventually to point C. For any number of reasons,
policy-makers may want to increase real GDP again to a level higher than Y_p. In
Figure 11.1, this is shown as a movement along $SRAS_1$ from point C to point D. Real
GDP increases again, and the level of unemployment decreases. The price level again
begins to increase. However, after a lag, the SRAS will begin to shift upward once
more to $SRAS_2$. A new long-run equilibrium is established at point E. Real GDP and
the unemployment rate have returned to their initial levels with a new, permanently
higher price level.

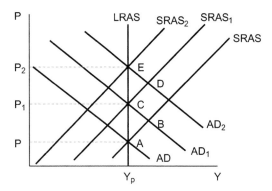

Figure 11.5 Long-run increases in the price level.

Box 11.2 Economic populism in the twenty-first century

The main feature of populism is the institutional underdevelopment it provokes. Populism hates limits to the ruler's power that sound institutions would otherwise bring about. As a consequence, the countries that experience populism do not have strong institutions, like an independent Central Bank, an active Supreme Court, or a democratically elected Congress.

(Paulo Rabello de Castro and Marcio Ronci)

As has been shown in this chapter, most countries in Latin America have managed to obtain either small fiscal deficits or surpluses. In turn, this has allowed countries to more easily moderate money supply growth and rates of inflation. This is not universally the case. The data in Table 11.5 is for a country in the region that is having increasing difficulties maintaining a balanced budget. Not surprisingly, the rate of inflation is increasing. Since inflation is high, the nominal exchange rate is depreciating. For some countries, the learning curve is flatter than it is for others.

Table 11.5 Fiscal deficits, inflation, and the exchange rate

	Budget deficit (% GDP)	*Inflation rate (annual)*	*Nominal exchange rate*
2000	1.7	16	0.754
2005	1.9	16	0.522
2014	11.5	62	0.848

This can be an understandably easy pattern for economic policy to slip into. Let's go back to a previous section of the chapter and consider the genesis of this problem. For Latin America, the difficulty begins with fiscal policy. Gathering tax revenue in the region has long historical roots. It has never been easy for governments in the region to collect substantial amounts of tax revenue. Moving into the twentieth century, spending on education and infrastructure, other forms of social spending, and spending associated with ISI increased dramatically in many countries of the region. In many cases, financing these deficits required increases in the money supply described earlier. The initial effects of these deficits were benign. GDP growth increased, unemployment fell, and the cost in terms of higher prices was modest. The continual application of these expansionary policies did not work nearly as well. As the public becomes increasingly accustomed to higher prices, the effects of the expansionary policies become ever more short-lived. The movements of the SRAS curve become increasingly rapid, and the stimulative effects on real GDP and unemployment become shorter. As a result, the movements of the economy become more like the long-run situation described earlier in the chapter, in which the economy is practically moving straight up the LRAS curve with shorter and briefer deviations to the right of Y_p. In effect, the expansionary policies are imposing ever larger costs in terms of the price level coupled with ever smaller benefits. In the end, the price level may have increased to a point where normal economic activity becomes difficult. Such situations require a different set of macroeconomic policies, designed to reduce the price level to tolerable values and maintain real GDP at a level close to potential real GDP. As we will see, this can be a very painful process, which is described in the next chapter.

Appendix: basic macroeconomics

The purpose of this appendix is to review the basic macroeconomic model commonly used in principles of economics courses. To build the model that is used in the next several chapters, we will proceed in two steps. First, we will need to construct a model of the economy that works over a longer time frame such as three to five years. Using this basic model, we will then add some detail that makes it more usable for a more traditional macroeconomic time frame such as six to eighteen months. As you will see, both versions are useful for the discussion of macroeconomic problems in Latin America.

To begin, consider Figure 11.6 below. The variable on the vertical axis, P, is some measure of the overall price level. Since all of the various types of price indexes are highly correlated, it is sufficient to say that this is some general type of macroeconomic price index. Y on the horizontal axis represents the real output of the economy which is normally some measure of real GDP. At the start, let's consider the relationship between P and Y in the long run or a period something like up to five years. To start, we will insert some measure of potential real GDP (Y_p) which is what the economy is

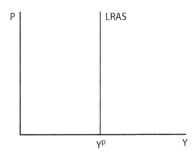

Figure 11.6 Long-run aggregate supply.

capable of producing if it is operating at full employment. At this point, we will draw a vertical line at Y_p. Y_p is related to the concept of GDP that we considered in Chapter 3. It is what the economy is capable of producing with the full employment of capital and labor with the existing level of technology. We label this line LRAS. It becomes the target rate of output that the economy should be operating at. Such a line implies that in the long run there is no relationship between the price level (P) and potential real GDP (Y_p).

To complete the simple model, we now need some measure of the overall demand in the economy. In Figure 11.6, this is the downward-sloping curve representing aggregate demand. Using the expenditure approach to GDP, aggregate demand represents the total demand from all sectors of the economy including consumption by the public (C); residential and nonresidential investment (I); government spending on goods and ser-vices (G); and the trade balance (exports minus imports). The curve slopes downwards and to the right for several reasons. First, with wages constant, consumption would increase with lower prices. Second, lower prices may cause a fall in interest rates which would increase investment. Finally, lower prices may increase exports as domestic prices become lower than foreign prices. The more critical point is that the aggregate-demand curve frequently shifts. Any change in one of the components of GDP could cause such a shift. Increases or decreases in C, I, G, or XM could cause the aggregate-demand curve to shift to the right or the left, respectively. Such shift are hardly uncommon and at times they can be rather large. This is particularly true for many of the small, open economies that are common in Latin America.

Given the two curves in Figure 11.6, the economy will be in long-run equilibrium where aggregate demand intersects LRAS. For any given level of aggregate demand, the economy will produce Y_p at a price level of P_e. An increase in aggregate demand, shown by a shift from AD to AD_1, would not increase output but would only increase the price level. A shift from AD to AD_2 would have the opposite effect. Overall, Figure 11.6 is indicating that in the long run changes in aggregate demand have no effect on real GDP and only influence the price level. Normally, aggregate demand will slowly shift to the right over a period of years as will LRAS for the reasons shown in Chapter 3. If the two shifts are roughly equivalent, then the price level would be relatively stable. Prices would tend to rise in the event that aggregate demand is systematically growing faster than LRAS. While a falling price level, deflation, is a technical possibility, it is rarely seen in Latin America.

While the long-run model shown in Figure 11.6 is a useful representation of reality over a period of years, it misses the key short-run dynamics that are at the heart of macroeconomic policy. In order to deal with the short run, we will need to add an SRAS to the long-run model shown in Figure 11.6. In the equilibrium shown in Figure 11.7, SRAS intersects LRAS at the same point that aggregate demand does. SRAS slopes upwards to reflect the fact that as the price level increases both wages and other input costs may rise. Also, firms may be in a better position to raise prices if the overall price level is rising. Like the aggregate-demand curve, the SRAS curve may shift. There are three things that could cause such a shift. First, a large increase in the price of oil could increase the overall cost of production in any economy. If the increase is both large and happens in a short period of time, then SRAS can shift to the left. The same type of effect can occur if the exchange rate depreciates by a large amount in a short period of time. Finally, if the inflationary expectations of the public and business should increase quickly, then workers and firms will attempt

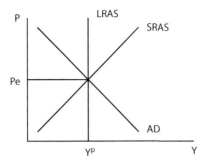

Figure 11.7 Macroeconomic equilibrium.

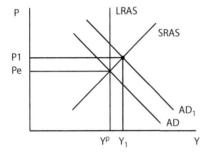

Figure 11.8 An increase in aggregate demand.

to raise wages and prices. Such a change in expectations could shift the supply curve to the left. In both the short and the long run, point A represents full employment coupled with stable prices. Any shift in the aggregate-demand or SRAS curves would lead to a new short-run equilibrium.

It is important to keep in mind that any equilibrium that is not at the intersection of the three curves is not stable. We will use two examples to illustrate this. In Figure 11.8, aggregate demand has risen from AD to AD_1. Output is now above Y_p at Y_1. An economy can produce more than Y_p in the short run as both labor and capital can temporarily be utilized at higher than normal levels. However, notice that P rises to P_1 as a reflection of higher wages and other input costs. While this can occur in the short run, over time there will be a change in inflationary expectations. As a result, SRAS will shift to the left to $SRAS_1$. The economy will move to a new stable, long-run equilibrium at point C. In the text, this situation will be covered as it is frequently the result of imprudent macroeconomic policy.

A final situation is shown in Figure 11.9. A common occurrence in Latin America is a sharp depreciation of the currency in a short period of time. The result of this is the movement of the SRAS curve to $SRAS_1$. This creates a truly unfortunate combination of lower output (Y_1) and a higher price level (P_1) at point B. In the long run, the economy would adjust to the new exchange rate and move back to point A. However, the short-run combination of both a recession and a higher price level is a difficult situation for the policy-makers to deal with. With the basics of aggregate demand and

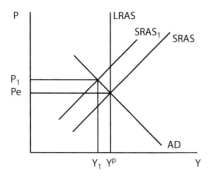

Figure 11.9 A decrease in aggregate supply.

aggregate supply in mind, one should now be better equipped to understand the macro-economic policy environment and the choices, both good and bad, that governments may make.

Key terms and concepts

aggregate demand: the relationship between the total quantity of goods and services demanded by all sectors of the economy and the price level.
aggregate supply: the relationship between the total quantity of goods and services that an economy produces and the price level.
central bank: the financial institution in a country that is in charge of managing the supply of money.
discount rate: the interest rate charged by the central bank on loans to private-sector banks.
economic populism: the tendency of governments to pursue policies that will produce the most favorable economic outcomes in the short run.
equation of exchange: a basic framework for analyzing the interactions among the money supply, the price level, and real GDP.
monetary base: the sum of cash in the hands of the public and the reserves of the banking system.
money multiplier: the multiple by which a change in the monetary base (B) translates into a change in the money supply.
money supply: the sum of cash in the hands of the public (Cp) and demand deposits (D) in an economy.
potential real GDP: the amount of final goods and services an economy is producing at full employment.

Questions for review and discussion

1 Describe the problems with fiscal policy in Latin America before the 1990s.
2 Describe the evolution of government budget deficits in Latin America from the 1970s.

3 If a government runs a budget deficit and cannot borrow, the deficit translates into an increase in the monetary base. Explain why this is true.
4 Show how a budget deficit of 5 percent of GDP could produce a large expansion in the supply of money.
5 Describe why having an independent central bank is important in maintaining a low rate of inflation.
6 Using the equation of exchange, show how the data in Tables 11.3 and 11.4 is related.
7 Draw a graph showing the inflationary process in the long run.
8 What is economic populism? How can it be related to aggregate demand?
9 Describe the structuralist view of the inflationary process. Does it have any relevance in the twenty-first century?
10 Show how short-run policies that reduce unemployment can lead to inflation in the long run.
11 Using the data in Table 11.4, describe the likely evolution of inflationary expectations in Latin America from the 1970s.
12 Why has inflation in Venezuela reached such high levels?

Notes

1 Potential real GDP is a constructed number assuming a normal level of unemployment of the labor force. As a result, it should be considered more of a constructed policy target than a precise number.
2 What is being described is known as a primary market for government bonds.
3 Coins and paper money held by the banks are counted as part of reserves.
4 This process is frequently referred to as *crowding out*. If the economy is at full employment, government borrowing may increase interest rates and reduce borrowing by the private sector. If the economy is at less than full employment, this is less of a problem.
5 In the long run, V will usually slowly increase as the financial system of a country becomes more developed. There is little knowledge about financial development in Latin America, as the study of this aspect of economic development is rather new.
6 Note that the change in Y_p was the subject of Chapter 3.
7 In this discussion, we are avoiding the problem of the relevant money supply. In practice, the money supply may be defined in different ways depending on which assets are included.
8 In this case, the price level is a price index and not the single price of a good or service.
9 This is but one definition of populism. Its virtue is brevity, but there are more complete definitions available. For more on this, see Dornbusch and Edwards (1991).
10 Our definition of economic populism follows the more recent tendency to use the term with respect to macroeconomic policies. However, this has not always been the case. For an outstanding discussion of these changes, see Cardoso and Helwege (1992).
11 This is a reference to the old Keynesian vs. monetarist debate in macroeconomics, which was common in the 1960s and 1970s.
12 We are implicitly assuming either adaptive expectations or rational expectations with institutional rigidities. The assumption is that the movement of the SRAS curve would not occur quickly.

References

Cardoso, Eliana and Ann Helwege (1992) *Latin America's Economy: Diversity, Trends, and Conflicts*, Cambridge, Mass.: MIT Press.

Dornbusch, Rudiger and Sebastian Edwards (eds.) (1991) *The Macroeconomics of Populism in Latin America*, Chicago, Ill.: University of Chicago Press.

World Bank (2015) *World Development Indicators*, Washington, DC: World Bank.

Recommended reading

Baer, Werner (2008) *The Brazilian Economy*, 6th edn, Boulder, Col.: Lynne Rienner.

Chong, Alberto and Carmen Pagés (2010) "Taxes and Productivity: A Game of Hide and Seek," in Carmen Pagés (ed.), *The Age of Productivity: Transforming Economies from the Bottom Up*, New York: Palgrave Macmillan, pp. 153–180.

Edwards, Sebastian (1995) *Crisis and Reform in Latin America: From Despair to Hope*, Washington, DC: World Bank.

García-Silva, Pablo and Manuel Marfán (2011) "Monetary Policy in Latin America: Performance under Crisis and the Challenges of Exuberance," in José A. Ocampo and Jaime Ros (eds.), *The Oxford Handbook of Latin American Economics*, Oxford: Oxford University Press, pp. 214–240.

Rabello de Castro, Paulo and Marcio Ronci (1991) "Sixty Years of Populism in Brazil," in Rudiger Dornbusch and Sebastian Edwards (eds.), *The Macroeconomics of Populism in Latin America*, Chicago, Ill.: University of Chicago Press, pp. 151–169.

Tanzi, Vito (2007) *Argentina: An Economic Chronicle—How One of the Richest Countries in the World Lost Its Wealth*, New York: Jorge Pinto.

Wiesner, Eduardo (2008) *The Political Economy of Macroeconomic Policy Reform in Latin America: The Distributive and Institutional Context*, Northampton, Mass.: Edward Elgar.

12   Macroeconomic stability

Introduction

In the previous chapter, the effects of fiscal and monetary policy in the context of the economies of Latin America were explained. In general, the goal of macroeconomic policy is to obtain a level of real GDP consistent with potential real GDP and a stable price level. Even for a developed country, this is not an easy task. Until recently, macroeconomic outcomes in Latin America were rarely even close to this ideal outcome. Unemployment and underemployment have been persistent problems in the region. As we saw in the previous chapter, controlling inflation has been particularly difficult. In the main, these problems are the result of the structure of the economies of the region and poor policy choices. By the late 1970s, a combination of factors made the continuation of the policies of the postwar era increasingly unsustainable. This led to a painful and protracted period of macroeconomic stabilization. By this, we mean the process of introducing macroeconomic policies that would reduce inflation and other economic imbalances and provide the basis for more sustainable growth in the region.

Unfortunately, these imbalances were so numerous that it will be necessary to consider them in stages. The first section of this chapter more fully covers a problem that was briefly covered in Chapter 6. Exporting commodities can complicate macroeconomic policy for any country. For Latin America as a region, this is especially true. In this section, we consider these problems in isolation from any other macroeconomic difficulties. The same is true for large changes in the price of oil. Most of the countries of Latin America are oil importers. The oil shocks of the 1970s created problems for much of the world economy. Countries can react to these shocks in different ways, and the reaction of the region to the two oil shocks tended to exacerbate existing macroeconomic problems. More specifically, the oil shocks of the 1970s contributed to inflation. As we saw in Chapter 9, high inflation is inconsistent with fixed exchange rates. The movement from fixed to flexible exchange rates was frequently not a smooth process and created yet another source of macroeconomic instability. In addition, the debt taken on by many countries of the region in the 1970s and 1980s eventually led to problems necessitating the assistance of the IMF. The austerity programs that accompanied borrowing from this source tended to make a poor macroeconomic environment even worse. The culmination of the above factors goes a long way toward explaining the "Lost Decade" of the 1980s. Sometimes the whole is even worse than the sum of the parts. The final section of the chapter details the substantial progress the countries of the region have made toward macroeconomic stability.

Commodity price shocks

> That which does not kill us makes us stronger.
>
> (Friedrich Nietzsche)

In Chapter 6, we covered the impact of commodities on the economies of Latin America. The initial focus of the chapter was on how commodities had influenced the historical evolution of the economies of the region. The chapter went on to cover the sometimes problematic relationship between commodities and economic development in the long run. In Chapter 9 and 10, it was mentioned that changes in commodity prices can have an influence on the exchange rate, the current account, and the economy at large. From the basic model that was developed in the previous chapter, we can now examine in more detail the effects of changes in commodity prices on the rate of growth of GDP, unemployment, and inflation. From this analysis, the response of macroeconomic policy to these changes will easier to analyze. As before, these changes will be analyzed with respect to an RCILA. While this is convenient, the importance of commodities to the economies of Latin America is not uniform. Before beginning, it might be a good idea to go back to Table 6.3 and review the information in the table on the ratio of commodity exports to total exports and the ratio of exports to GDP. This would give a better sense of the relative importance of commodities to the overall economy of various countries in the region. This section begins with a brief review of the microeconomics of commodity prices and their effects on exchange rates. This is followed by the analysis of how these changes in prices and exchange rates can affect the overall economy. The section concludes with a discussion of the difficulties that these changes can cause for macroeconomic policy in a country.

At this point, let's briefly review the fundamental problem with commodities. Recall that the demand for commodities is typically inelastic. This means that changes in price have very little influence on the quantity demanded. For example, very large changes in the price of oil do not affect the consumption of oil by very much in the short run. The same is true for the supply curve. Relatively large changes in the price do not influence the quantity supplied in the short run by a large amount. Under these conditions, small changes in either the demand curve or the supply curve can produce substantial changes in the price of a commodity. As was shown in Figure 6.2, changes in demand can be the source of these price changes. Likewise, price instability can be caused by changes in supply, as shown in Figure 6.3. Price changes can be truly extreme under the right set of circumstances. Increases in demand coupled with decreases in supply can create rapidly rising prices for a commodity, much as in the example on oil in the next section. Conversely, decreases in demand accompanied by increases in supply can cause a collapse in prices. It is not uncommon for these exaggerated changes in prices to occur over a relatively short period of time, such as six months.

For Latin America, these large changes in commodity prices can affect the macroeconomic performance of the economies in the short run. To consider this in more detail, we can combine the information contained in the expenditure approach to GDP and the model of aggregate demand and aggregate supply developed in the previous chapter. Recall that the expenditure approach to GDP can be represented by

$Y = C + I + G + (X - M)$ where:

C is consumption by the public.

I is investment.

G is government spending on goods and services.

$(X - M)$ is the balance on goods and services.

Now, if the ratio of exports to GDP (X/Y) is high, then rapid changes in exports can have a substantial effect on macroeconomic performance in the short run. Commodities now come into the picture. If X/Y is relatively high, and commodities are a high percentage of total exports, then changes in commodity prices have the potential to influence the overall economy.

Now consider what can occur if there is a large change in commodity prices that occurs in a very short period of time. Assuming that commodities are a large percentage of exports and the ratio of X/Y is high, large changes in the price of commodities can have a substantial impact on the aggregate-demand curve for a country. This is what we mean by a *commodity price shock*. The effects of a commodity price shock are outlined in Figure 12.1. In the figure, the economy is initially in equilibrium at point A. Now assume that there is a large increase in the price of one or more of a country's commodities that occurs in a short period of time, such as six months. Further assuming that commodity exports are a nontrivial percentage of GDP, the effect would be to increase aggregate demand from AD to AD_1. In the short run, the economy would end up at a new equilibrium at point B. Real GDP is now past Y_p, and the price level has risen. Neither of these undesirable outcomes was the result of policy decisions, and they may easily have been unanticipated. The problem is now with the evolution of fiscal and

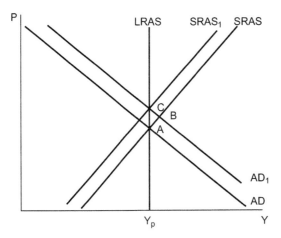

Figure 12.1 Macroeconomic effects of a commodity price shock.

monetary policy. Both policies had been set for a level of aggregate demand consistent with AD and point A. With the unanticipated upward pressure on aggregate demand, macroeconomic policy is now effectively too loose. With no change in fiscal or monetary policy, the rise in the price level will begin to increase inflationary expectations. Rising inflationary expectations would eventually start shifting the SRAS curve to the left. With no change in macroeconomic policy, the economy could end up at point C. This would be consistent with potential real GDP, but with a higher price level. With no change in policy, the commodity price shock has left its mark on the economy, a higher price level. To prevent this outcome, policy-makers will need to move rather quickly in response to a movement of aggregate demand from AD to AD_1. A combination of somewhat tighter fiscal and monetary policy would tend to reduce the movement of the economy from point A to point B. At a minimum, such a move would diminish the possibility of the even more undesirable movement of the economy from point B to point C. While this is easy to do in theory, in practice it would be much harder, for two reasons. First, forecasting large changes in commodity prices is always difficult. By their nature, such changes are normally unpredictable. Second, the initial stages of a com-modity boom can seem rather benign in a macroeconomic sense. Real GDP is rising, which increases employment, profits, and government tax revenues. The price level is increasing, but initially this increase may seem to be a small price to pay for the initial burst of prosperity. It is up to the policy-makers to adjust fiscal and monetary policy to prevent the later effects of the boom, which are not so benign, from setting in. With regard to fiscal policy, this involves some combination of cuts in government spending and increases in taxes to restrain the increase in aggregate demand. If these changes are made quickly, the necessity may not be apparent to the public at large, and they may well not be popular. An appropriate monetary policy would involve decreasing the rate of growth of the money supply. Invariably, this would involve increases in interest rates. Again, the necessity of these changes may not be fully apparent. The timing and magnitude of these changes may be excruciatingly difficult to get right. Effectively, the policy-makers are trying to calibrate the timing and magnitude of changes in fiscal and monetary policy to offset changes in aggregate demand caused by volatile com-modity prices that are difficult to forecast. A response that is too small and too late runs the risk of failing to stop an inflationary boom. A response that is premature or too severe would run the risk of triggering an unnecessary recession. If the economy is well managed, the policy-makers may prefer the latter mistake to the former. Acting too aggressively may trigger a recession, but such a mistake can be reversed more easily, as the SRAS curve will remain stable. Changing policy by an insufficient amount is a harder mistake to compensate for once inflationary expectations begin to rise.

Box 12.1 Copper prices and the Chilean economy

Being very conservative, Chile is considered to be one of the best-managed econ-omies in Latin America. A substantial part of this opinion is due to Chilean macroeconomic policy, in particular fiscal policy. As indicated in the preceding section, macroeconomic policy is crucial for a country where commodities are an important part of exports and GDP. Over the period 1996–2003, mining accounted for 46 percent of the country's exports. Copper alone accounted for 39 percent of exports.[1] The effect of exports on GDP is potentially high. From 2003 to 2008, mining accounted for 18 percent of GDP on average. Copper mining is dominated by COLDECO (Corporación Nacional del Cobre de Chile), supplemented by the production of a number of foreign-owned firms. All profits from COLDECO are returned to the government, and foreign companies pay taxes on their operations in Chile. Copper prices are extremely volatile, and the percentages above indicate that the entire economy can be influenced by changes in these prices. Further, it is anticipated that commodity prices will continue to be an important factor for the economy in the long run, as copper continues to be important and other minerals, especially lithium, become more important.

The primary device Chile has developed for dealing with commodity-related macroeconomic instability has been a "rule" for fiscal policy. The goal of fiscal policy is to generate a structural surplus of 0.5 percent of GDP annually.[2] In this context, *structural* refers to government spending and tax revenue that would occur if the economy were at full employment. For a country without significant commodity exports, this is equivalent to government spending and tax revenue at potential real GDP (Y_p). For a commodity exporter such as Chile, the calculation is slightly more complicated. One now has to factor in the price of one or more commodities and the changes in revenues coming from the mining companies. All of these estimates are subject to political manipulation. Chile avoids this by using independent panels of experts to estimate the trend rate of growth of the economy and the long-run price of copper. The structural surplus has been used to recapitalize the central bank, finance contingent liabilities for the social-security system, and create a buffer for changes in the exchange rate and capital flows. Surpluses in excess of the target have been placed in various sovereign wealth funds. These assets have grown to more than 13 percent of GDP. While the fiscal rule has not succeeded in completely insulating the economy from effects of changes in commodity prices, it has clearly made the economy more stable than would otherwise have been the case. Moreover, the economy is now more stable than it was in the 1990s. The fiscal rule was designed for macroeconomic stability and to provide revenues from commodities for future generations. However, in a disaster-prone region, the existence of sovereign wealth funds may provide a buffer against unexpected events such as the recent earthquake in Chile.[3]

Oil shocks

A fundamental reality of the world economy until the 1970s was that oil was a relatively cheap commodity. OPEC was formed in 1960 to mitigate relatively low oil prices. In Chapter 6 we showed that low commodity prices contain the seeds of their own destruction. Low prices engender insufficient development of new sources of supply. If demand for the commodity is increasing over time, then eventually prices will rise, sometimes dramatically. This turned out to be the case with oil. Although a political event triggered a spectacular rise in the price of oil in late 1973, the combination of low supply coupled with high global demand had set the stage for rising prices. The large increase in the price of oil over a short period of time defines the term "oil shock." The stabilization of oil prices after the first oil shock was short-lived. The world economy suffered a second oil shock in 1979 that drove prices to unprecedented levels in real terms.[4] In a sense, an *oil shock* is just a special case of a commodity price shock. For Ecuador, Mexico, and Venezuela, this rise in oil prices produced the effects on aggregate demand that were described in the preceding section. For the rest of the region, the price increases created macroeconomic difficulties.

For many of the countries of the region, macroeconomic conditions in 1973 left them ill prepared to deal with rising oil prices. While Latin America is a commodity-rich region in general, most of the countries of the region are oil-importers. ISI, coupled with loose fiscal and monetary policies, meant that the economies of the region began the decade of the 1970s at or close to potential real GDP. This policy mix, described in the preceding chapter, was already causing difficulties with respect to price stability. An oil shock simply compounds that problem. In order to see this more clearly, the effects of an oil shock are shown in Figure 12.2. In the figure, the economy of RCILA is shown in equilibrium at point A, where the economy is also at Y_p. The effect of an oil shock is to shift the SRAS curve backward and to the left. An oil shock tends to increase the costs of production for most goods and services. This is particularly true for an economy that must import virtually all of its oil. This pervasive increase in the cost of production is what gives rise to the leftward shift of the SRAS curve. Given aggregate demand, the new short-run equilibrium for the economy is now at point B. This point illustrates the twin macroeconomic difficulties of an oil shock. First, real GDP has fallen from Y_p to Y_1. The economy is now in a recession, and unemployment and underemployment will rise. To make matters even worse, the price level is rising. In the context of Latin America, this upward pressure

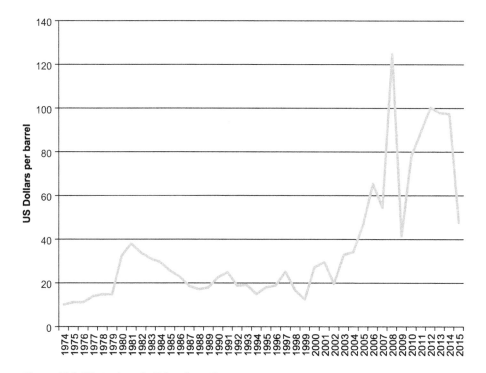

Figure 12.2 The price of oil (per barrel).

on prices was occurring at the same time as the countries of the region were struggling with inflation.

Point B presents policy-makers with three unpalatable choices. Since point B is not at Y_p, this is a short-run equilibrium. A more stable long-run equilibrium will eventually be established somewhere along the LRAS curve. There are three possible outcomes. The first possibility is in some senses the most difficult. Over time, consumers and firms in the economies of the region will learn to adjust to higher oil prices by using the now expensive resource more efficiently. The countless small and large adjustments will allow the economy's SRAS curve to move back to its original position at point A. Inflationary pressures will eventually subside, and real GDP will return to its previous level (Y_p). Unfortunately, this process could take years and involves tolerating higher prices and lower real GDP. In the context of a middle-income country, choosing this option could mean an extended period of both higher prices and higher unemployment among a population that was not affluent to begin with. The public might be patient in a high-income country, but patience might understandably be in shorter supply in different circumstances. Much the same can be said of the second option. If social preferences for low inflation are strong, then the optimal policy response might be reducing aggregate demand to keep the price level constant. This would be accomplished by some combination of tighter fiscal and monetary policy. In the case of the former, this would mean either higher taxes or lower government spending. Raising tax revenue in Latin America has always been problematic. Cutting government spending in this situation might well mean cutting social services during a recession in a poor country. Tighter monetary policy would involve reducing the rate of growth of the money supply with the attendant higher interest rates. The reduction in business activity would mean both lower profits and higher unemployment. In a high-income country with an aversion to inflation, such a policy response is not uncommon. In Latin America, the recession induced by the oil shock made this response unlikely.

Box 12.2 The price of oil: a brief history

Figure 12.3 shows changes in the price of oil from the early 1970s to the present. In 1973, oil prices rose dramatically in response to an oil embargo by Saudi Arabia. Oil prices had been extremely low for decades, and a price of $10 per barrel was a shock to the world economy. OPEC was formed in the 1960s as an attempt to increase oil prices. It took a war in the Middle East and an embargo to accomplish what OPEC was unable to do. The slowing of the world economy in the 1970s led to moderate oil prices until 1979. A political crisis in Iran led to the suspension of oil exports and a rapid increase in prices. This price increase was so large that demand growth was dampened for many years. Prices fell back into the $10–$20 per barrel range for much of the remainder of the century. The low prices caused low investment in new oil supplies. As is frequently the case, strong world demand coupled with low supply led to a surge in prices in the 2000s. Prices have fallen from their peak but are still high by modern standards.

For the oil-producing countries of Latin America, surges in prices can lead to destabilizing changes in aggregate demand. On the other hand, prolonged periods of low prices may lead to extended periods of slow economic growth. For the majority of the countries of the region that import oil, the long period of relatively low prices enhanced growth. The price spikes of the 1970s contributed to macroeconomic policies that led to the Lost Decade. While the most recent price increase lowered growth in the region, it was not nearly as devastating as the increases of the 1970s. The majority of the oil importers now have economies much better structured than the ISI-dominated economies of the 1970s.[5] Also, most countries of the region now have much more prudent macroeconomic policies, which makes it easier for them to weather oil shocks.

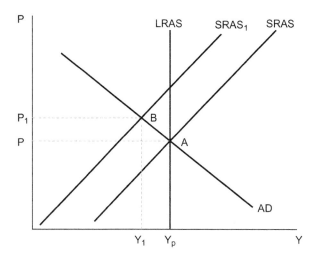

Figure 12.3 Macroeconomic effects of an oil shock.

As in many parts of the world, the policy response in much of Latin America to the two major oil shocks was to attempt to stabilize real GDP and unemployment. A policy mix that would accomplish this involves an expansionary fiscal policy composed of lower taxes and higher government spending. This fiscal policy in Latin America had the usual effect of producing an expansion of the money supply, as outlined in the previous chapter. As before, the effects of these policies combined with an oil shock are shown in Figure 12.4. Again, the oil shock has the effect of shifting the SRAS curve to the left. The economy of RCILA moves from point A to point B. Real GDP falls, and the price level increases. This time, the policy response is different. Expansionary fiscal and monetary policies serve to shift the aggregate-demand curve to the right. The economy establishes a new equilibrium at point C. Real GDP and employment have been stabilized but at the cost of a higher price level. In the context of Latin America, this policy choice makes some sense, as higher unemployment in a middle-income country with limited social safety nets would be difficult to tolerate. On the other hand, the price level has risen. Inflation is a particular burden for the poor, so the benefits of the stabilization of real GDP and unemployment are tempered by the costs imposed by inflation. Since this policy mix was common in the region in response to the oil shocks,

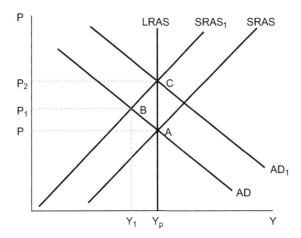

Figure 12.4 Policy responses to an oil shock.

one must presume that policy-makers considered the lower GDP and higher unemployment to be more costly to the population than the higher price level. However, the cost in terms of inflation was quite high.

Debt and exchange-rate shocks

> Each time a crisis related to capital inflows hits a country, it typically goes through the wringer.
>
> (Jagdish Bhagwati)

The oil shocks of the 1970s left Latin America in an uncomfortable position. As was covered in Chapter 9, the countries of the region preferred to maintain fixed exchange rates. Fixed exchange rates were essential to continue ISI as a development policy in the region. Unfortunately, the rising price of oil imports was putting a serious strain on the economic systems of the countries of the region. As we saw in the previous section, rising oil prices tended to reduce real GDP and raise the price level. Stimulative fiscal and monetary policies were adding to inflationary pressures. Severe balance of payments problems compounded these problems. In the first part of this section, we will review some previous material to set the stage for what occurred later in the decade and in the early part of the 1980s.

First, let's go back and consider the effects of rising oil prices on the economies of the region. By the 1970s, current-account deficits in the region were already common. The supply of foreign exchange earned from commodity exports was frequently insufficient to meet the demand for foreign exchange at the fixed exchange rate. This situation is shown in Figure 12.5. At the fixed exchange rate, the demand for foreign exchange is higher than the supply. As was shown earlier, this shortage of foreign exchange could be covered by measures such as exchange controls and restrictive trade policies that reduced the demand for foreign exchange. While this perpetual shortage of foreign exchange was not an optimal situation, it was in some sense manageable at the time.

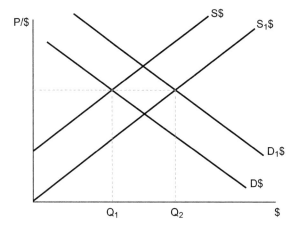

Figure 12.5 Maintaining a fixed exchange rate.

With the first oil shock of 1973, the situation became much more difficult. Rising oil prices had the effect of shifting the demand for foreign exchange from D to D_1. With the exchange rate still fixed, the current-account deficit increased dramatically. The usual mixture of exchange controls and restrictive trade policies could not close this gap. The solution was to borrow foreign exchange from banks in developed countries and use the proceeds of the loans to intervene in the foreign-exchange market and stabilize the exchange rate. In Figure 12.5, this is shown by the shift of the supply curve from S to S_1. In the aftermath of the first oil shock, the borrowing seemed to be on a reasonable scale, in the sense that most of the countries were able to service the debt. The process was aided by a decline in oil prices during the mid and late 1970s. The subsequent macroeconomic equilibrium was not optimal, as inflation was high in much of the region. Further, current-account deficits were putting downward pressure on real GDP. However, some of the harsher consequences of higher oil prices had been averted. Unfortunately, the situation was worse than it appeared on the surface. As inflation increased with a fixed exchange rate, the real exchange rates in the region began appreciating. This appreciation tended to increase imports and make a problematic situation with respect to exports even worse. Current-account deficits during the 1970s tended to widen even with a moderation in oil prices.

The second oil shock made the policy responses of the 1970s unsustainable. Expansionary fiscal and monetary policies were driving inflation to crippling levels. Again, the higher oil prices necessitated borrowing, which drove the total amounts of sovereign debt to unsustainable levels. The ratios of debt to GDP and the debt payments to exports eventually could not support further borrowing. Without the foreign exchange to intervene in the foreign-exchange markets, exchange-rate shocks now became a common occurrence. This situation is shown in Figures 11.4 and 12.6. Because exchange rates in the region were frequently overvalued, the size of the depreciations were sometimes large. Such large exchange-rate shocks can have traumatic macroeconomic consequences. This situation is shown in Figure 12.5. As with an oil shock, the large depreciation of the exchange rate increases the price of all imported goods. This includes commodities, imported inputs, and finished products. The effect of this is an

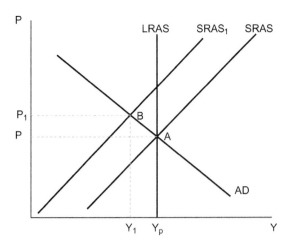

Figure 12.6 Macroeconomic effects of an exchange-rate shock.

enormous shift of the SRAS curve to the left. If the economy started out in equilibrium at point A, the exchange-rate shock quickly moves it to point B. Real GDP falls dramatically, and the price level rises. This creates both an unfortunate increase in the level of unemployment and rising inflation. In this case, inflation was already a problem in the region, and the depreciations made this situation even worse. The main thing to note at this point is that the economies of the region were now to the left of Y_p. Eventually, some sort of long-run equilibrium was going to be established along the LRAS curve. However, in this case, the policy responses were limited and not always determined by the governments of the region. This painful readjustment to a stable, long-run equilibrium is described in the next section.

The Lost Decade

Much of the point of the earlier material in this chapter was to prepare for a discussion of the Lost Decade of the 1980s in Latin America. The exceedingly bad economic conditions in the region had their roots in the previous decades. As the oil shocks affected the region, governments responded by pursuing expansionary fiscal and monetary policies in an attempt to stabilize GDP and employment. In order to maintain some exchange-rate stability, increasing amounts of debt were accumulated. By the early 1980s, the region was burdened with high inflation, slow economic growth, and increasing debt. This situation is summarized in Figure 12.7. The oil shocks and increases in inflationary expectations were putting continual pressure on the SRAS curve. Unfortunately, this pressure was all toward the left. The result of this pressure was slower growth, higher unemployment, and an ever higher price level. Macroeconomic policy in the region was geared toward offsetting the effects on real GDP and unemployment. This created some upward pressure on aggregate demand. However, counteracting this was the downward pressure being exerted by the current account balance. Overvalued exchange rates, coupled with the export of little more than commodities, suppressed exports. On the other hand, imports other than oil became increasingly cheap. The ability to purchase

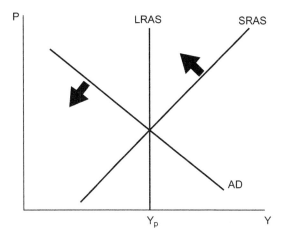

Figure 12.7 Macroeconomic effects of oil shocks, inflationary expectations and current-account deficits.

imports was being supported by the intervention in the foreign-exchange market that prevented the usual adjustment of exchange rates to this situation, that is, depreciation. The result was that rising trade deficits were exerting downward pressure on aggregate demand. The situation created something akin to a macroeconomic treadmill, where increasingly stimulative macroeconomic policies could barely keep pace with external factors limiting growth. Both were exerting upward pressure on prices and increasingly overvalued currencies.

As described in a previous chapter, the buildup of debt during the 1970s proved to be unsustainable. Ratios of debt to GDP and the ratio of debt payments to exports could not be maintained. In many countries, the sudden cessation of borrowing forced the withdrawal of intervention in the foreign-exchange markets. Without intervention, the supply of foreign exchange shifted quickly to the right, and the depreciation of currencies was rapid. This set the stage for classic exchange-rate shocks. The rising price of imports inexorably fed its way into the prices for commodities, intermediate goods, and final goods. The effect on domestic price levels was pronounced. Adding exchange-rate shocks to the preexisting oil shocks and rising inflationary expectations put extreme leftward pressure on the SRAS curve of the economies of the region. All else being equal, the predictable effects were lower output and a rising price level. In this environment, stimulative fiscal and monetary policy was like adding gasoline to a fire.

One might be tempted to think that the depreciations of the currency would have reduced the pressure on the current account by increasing exports and sharply reducing imports. Somewhat counterintuitively, depreciations have a tendency to worsen the current account in the short run. The *volume* of exports does not increase immediately due to the depreciation, and foreign-exchange earnings may not increase. On the other hand, the volume of imports may not decrease quickly, and the amount of foreign exchange needed to purchase imports increases immediately. This phenomenon is commonly known as the "J-curve", shown in Figure 12.8. After a depreciation, the current account has a tendency to become more negative initially and then improve.[6] For a country that has had to depreciate the currency as a result of losing the ability

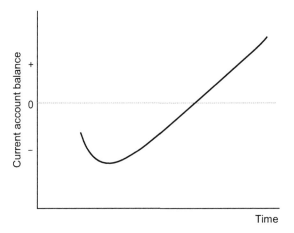

Figure 12.8 The J-curve.

to borrow, the situation can become desperate. The depreciation initially causes a deterioration in the current account. A steady flow of imports may be essential for the functioning of the economy even if GDP is below Y_p. Finding a short-term source of foreign exchange in this situation may be critical to prevent even further losses of real GDP. Hsing (2008) has found strong evidence of this effect for the largest economies in Latin America. In a policy context, a large depreciation of the currency due to current-account imbalances may be accompanied by a more difficult process of adjustment for the domestic economy.

In the 1970s and 1980s, this source of funding was the IMF. This was virtually the only institution in the world economy that was set up to loan foreign exchange to countries in need of short-run financing of current-account deficits. As described earlier, the IMF imposes conditions for this lending. This is not so much a preference by the institution as a legacy of Bretton Woods. Initially, the IMF was set up to provide short-run loans under a fixed exchange-rate system. In this situation, a brief period of austerity would produce a sufficient drop in the demand for foreign exchange to balance the current account. The institution had even developed models that would produce an "answer" in terms of the amount of austerity required for a country to obtain a current account balance and repay the lending. The term "short run" becomes important at this point. The drop in the demand for foreign exchange necessary to obtain this result could only be accomplished with a concomitant drop in aggregate demand. The magnitude of the austerity programs needed to obtain this drop in aggregate demand was large. This meant that extremely contractionary fiscal and monetary policies were mandated by the IMF for several years in exchange for short-run loans of foreign exchange. While the austerity programs that accompanied these loans would inevitably be associated with serious recessions, the alternative for the countries was even worse. Without adequate supplies of foreign exchange, much of the industry that had been developed over the preceding several decades could not function. The short-run macroeconomic equilibrium combining an exchange-rate shock with the reductions in aggregate demand necessary to obtain IMF loans is shown in Figure 12.9. The exchange-rate shock has shifted the SRAS supply curve a long way to the left, moving

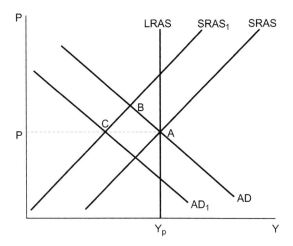

Figure 12.9 An exchange-rate shock combined with an austerity program.

the economy from point A to point B. Since the shift was so large, point B represents both a recession and a higher price level. While point B is an uncomfortable macro-economic equilibrium, the IMF was requiring reductions in aggregate demand in this situation. Putting the austerity programs on top of the exchange-rate shock is shown by a fall from AD to AD_1. This drop in aggregate demand produces a new equilibrium at point C. While the pressure on the price level has been reduced, the drop in real GDP becomes even more severe.[7]

To a greater or lesser extent, point C is reflective of the 1980s in Latin America. It is useful to think about what was occurring in terms of the expenditure approach to GDP. Inevitably, a large drop in aggregate demand is accompanied by a large drop in consumption by the public. In a high-income country, such a drop is troublesome. Consumers may buy fewer houses, cars, and durable goods, and social safety nets pro-tect the incomes of those at the bottom of the income distribution. In the middle-income countries of Latin America, drops in consumption are much more likely to entail drops in expenditures for basic necessities such as food, housing, and health care. In addition, both residential and nonresidential investment usually fall dramat-ically in such circumstances. Residential construction slows, as even the upper reaches of the income distribution are going to be adversely affected by a serious recession. Nonresidential investment will typically fall dramatically with a large decline in GDP.[8] A classic Keynesian policy response to decreases in consumption and investment would be an increase in government spending. In this case, the imposed austerity programs prevented this response. Indeed, government spending in many cases was being cut in order to obtain fiscal balance. The same logic was applied to the reduction of taxes to increase consumption.[9] Despite the economic hardships, the focus of policy was the reduction of imports and an increase in exports necessary to produce a current account surplus. This surplus was necessary for the countries of the region to continue to repay previously accumulated debt. In effect, intertemporal consumption had hit the region with a vengeance. Borrowing in the 1970s had allowed the region to avoid some of the painful drops in real GDP that would have occurred because of the oil shocks. Unfortunately, the accumulated debts of that decade necessitated the painful adjustments of the Lost Decade.

These problems were compounded by the decline of ISI in the region. During the preceding decades, the support of SOEs had made fiscal policy difficult. SOEs made it extremely hard for governments in many countries to achieve a fiscal balance. The imposition of fiscal austerity meant the end of government subsidies to many SOEs. The withdrawal of subsidies led to a wave of privatizations of firms in the region. Changes in trade policy, such as the elimination of quotas as a means of protection, left industries in a much more competitive environment than had previously been the case. The same is true for the exchange controls that came with the switch from an untenable fixed exchange rate to more flexible exchange rates. These changes in industrial policy would have been difficult for many industries in the region in a period of normal economic growth. Adding negative economic growth to these policy changes meant that many of the newly privatized firms had little chance of survival. Effectively, this meant the demise of much of the industrial base of the region. In theory, the resources being released from the ISI industries would have been briskly reallocated to more efficient sectors of the economy. Again, without the reductions in real GDP, more of this would have occurred. Under the circumstances, labor and capital formerly employed in these industries languished in the short run due to the poor economic climate. The effect of this restructuring on the rate of growth of real GDP is unclear. It clearly did not enhance economic growth in the decade, but the magnitude of the effect is uncertain.

Box 12.3 Macroeconomic instability in Brazil

Almost no other country in Latin America has had to work as hard to achieve macroeconomic stability as Brazil. In a sense, this is odd, as Brazil is the largest and most diverse economy in the region. A large internal market frequently makes it easier to achieve stability, as the economy may be less susceptible to external shocks. Further, macroeconomic stability in Brazil is important not only for the country but also for the region. Stability in Latin America overall coupled with instability in Brazil is hard to imagine. For Brazil, serious problems began with the oil shocks of the 1970s, particularly the second. Brazil was a textbook case of the situation shown in Figure 11.4. By 1980, the rate of inflation was over 100 percent. By 1983, the country had defaulted on its debt, producing a serious exchange-rate shock. Figure 11.5 shows the results. A new policy, the Cruzado Plan, involved issuing a new currency. Such a move may create the illusion of stability, but unless the underlying policies change, inflation will return. Despite two other "plans" aimed at reducing inflation, by 1990 prices were rising by 70 percent *per month*. The response was the Collor Plan, which included freezing wages, freezing bank deposits, and the taxation of financial transactions. It failed. All of these plans had a common thread. They were attempts to reduce inflation without resorting to fiscal and monetary policies that are consistent with price stability. Dealing with the effects of inflation, rather than the causes, is likely to be ineffective. By the mid 1990s, policy had changed. Inflation was subsiding, but the government was still reluctant to allow the exchange rate to float: so reluctant that in the aftermath of the Tequila crisis of 1994 and the Asian crisis of 1997, the central bank was willing to risk recession to prevent a depreciation of the currency. The macro-economic problems of the late 1990s finally forced the government to allow the exchange rate to float. Fast forward to 2008 and consider the response of the Brazilian government to the global economic crisis. Government spending was raised, monetary policy was loosened, and the exchange rate was not much of an issue: a far cry from the ill-founded "plans" of the 1980s, and virtually identical to the reaction of any high-income country.

The recovery from the Lost Decade

The recovery from the Lost Decade of the 1980s involved a protracted period of poor economic conditions, shown in Figure 12.7. Recovery was a long, involved process that is still a work in progress. The necessary, but hardly sufficient, condition for recovery was restoring some balance to fiscal policy. As we described in an earlier chapter, persistent fiscal deficits were one of the main drivers of excessive money supply growth. In turn, this was making it virtually impossible to control inflation. During the 1980s and 1990s, the majority of governments in the region were able to reduce or eliminate fiscal deficits. In hindsight, this is a rather incredible accomplishment. It was not always a smooth or continuous process, but, with exceptions, Latin America has become a region where balanced government budgets have become the norm. This has allowed central banks in the region to pursue monetary policies more in line with price stability. As inflation subsided, inflationary expectations in the region began to fall. Once this process sets in, macroeconomic outcomes begin to improve dramatically. This can be seen in Figure 12.10. Point C in the graph corresponds to point C in Figure 12.7. As inflationary expectations begin to fall, the SRAS curve begins to shift to the right. This shift produces two positive effects. First, real GDP begins moving back toward potential real GDP (Y_p).

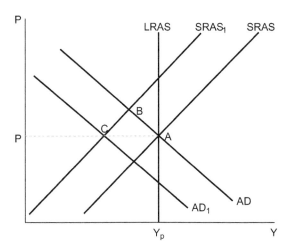

Figure 12.10 The effects of falling inflationary expectations.

As Y increases, a positive feedback loop begins to occur. With increased output, the level of unemployment falls. As both increase, the government finances improve. Tax revenues increase, and the level of spending on some social programs decreases. Less pressure is put on the government budget, which in turn makes the conduct of monetary policy less difficult. Second, the price level begins to fall. As the population experiences a reduction in inflation, inflationary expectations start to fall. Unfortunately, since inflation had been so high for so long, this was not a quick process. As economic conditions improved, consumption and investment began to increase aggregate demand. A combination of rightward shifts in both aggregate demand and SRAS eventually produces an equilibrium at point A. It took years of real GDP below Y_p to obtain a new stable equilibrium at this point. With variations by country, most of the countries of the region were at this point by the start of the twenty-first century. The importance of this achievement is hard to describe. If one had made the statement that in 2010 that the majority of the countries of Latin America would have balanced budgets, low inflation, and real GDP close to potential real GDP, the statement would have been met with some degree of skepticism. What was once difficult to imagine has now become the "norm."

However, it is a little too easy to overemphasize the accomplishment of macroeconomic stability. Recall the problem that we outlined in Chapter 2. The problem with Latin America historically has been that it has not grown as fast as was possible. Much of Chapter 3 was devoted to an analysis of this problem. However, one of the neglected factors in that analysis was macroeconomic instability as an impediment to growth. If inappropriate fiscal and monetary policies are creating high inflation, then this becomes a drag on economic growth.[10] With inflation as a problem, producers and consumers waste resources dealing with inflation rather than producing more goods and services. With a return to sound fiscal and monetary policies and the accompanying low levels of inflation, potential real GDP can grow more quickly. Economic growth in Latin America over the past twenty years is a case in point. Unfortunately, macroeconomic stability is a necessary, but hardly sufficient, condition for achieving a rate of growth in line with the best case scenario. The host of institutional factors outlined in that chapter still exist. Progress on these issues is being made, but it is hard to say that this is occurring quickly for the region. As a result, optimism over the economic future of the region has to be tempered. The hard-won macroeconomic stability will only increase growth to a certain extent. Faster growth in the future is more dependent on stronger institutions, better infrastructure, and increasing the stock of human capital. At this point, rapid improvement in these areas seems implausible. Perhaps this is the case, but one would have had similar reservations in 1985 about macroeconomic stability.[11]

Key terms and concepts

commodity price shock: a large change in commodity prices that affects the overall performance of the economy.
J-curve: the tendency for the trade balance to deteriorate in the short run following a depreciation of the exchange rate.
oil shock: a large increase in the price of oil over a short period of time.

Questions for review and discussion

1 Using the expenditure approach to GDP, show how a change in commodity prices can influence real GDP.
2 Graphically show the effects of a commodity boom and bust on real GDP and the price level. Explain the appropriate macroeconomic policies needed to offset these effects.
3 Describe the effects of copper prices on the Chilean economy.
4 Describe the macroeconomic effects of an oil shock on an oil-importing country.
5 In response to an oil shock, the countries of Latin America tended to respond with expansionary fiscal and monetary policies. What factors led to this policy choice?
6 For an oil-exporting country, an oil shock is just a special case of a commodity price shock. Explain why this statement is true.
7 Describe how the oil shocks of the 1970s led to a buildup of debt by the countries of the region.
8 How is the existence of a substantial amount of debt related to the probability of an exchange-rate shock?
9 Compare the macroeconomic effects of a commodity price shock and an exchange-rate shock. What are the differences in the factors influencing the probability of the two events?
10 List and describe the factors that accounted for large drops in real GDP in Latin America during the 1980s.
11 Describe the recovery of Latin America from the economic problems of the 1980s.
12 Describe the history of macroeconomic instability in Brazil.
13 Suppose that a country in Latin America experienced a rapid depreciation of the currency. What would happen to the current account balance in both the short run and the long run?

Notes

1 Other mining exports are molybdenum and, more recently, lithium.
2 The original target was 1 percent of GDP, but this was reduced in 2008.
3 For more on the Chilean economy, see OECD (2013).
4 See Box 12.2 for more data on real oil prices.
5 For more on this, see Fajnzylber (1990).
6 If the initial condition were a surplus, the same effect would occur.
7 Notice the different context from the Bretton Woods system of fixed exchange rates. In that system, austerity programs did not occur along with exchange-rate shocks. Unfortunately, IMF policy never really accounted for that difference.
8 Nonresidential investment responds to changes in the *rate of growth* of real GDP, i.e. the accelerator. Thus, a dramatic drop in real GDP can induce a very large drop in nonresidential investment.
9 However, the reduction of taxes was a less viable option in Latin America due to the historically low percentage of taxes collected in relation to GDP.
10 We are intentionally neglecting the effects of political instability on growth.
11 For the classic description of this period, see Edwards (1995).

References

Edwards, Sebastian (1995) *Crisis and Reform in Latin America: From Despair to Hope*, Washington, DC: World Bank.

Fajnzylber, Fernando (1990) *Unavoidable Industrial Restructuring in Latin America*, Durham, NC: Duke University Press.

Hsing, Yu (2008) "A Study of the J-Curve for Seven Selected Latin American Countries," *Global Economy Journal*, 8 (December): 1–14.

Organisation for Economic Co-operation and Development (2013) *OECD Economic Surveys: Chile*, Paris: OECD.

Recommended reading

Catão, Luis A. (2017) "Sudden Stops and Currency Drops: A Historical Look," in W. Charles Sawyer (ed.), *Latin American Economics*, vol. III, London and New York: Routledge, pp. 138–185.

The Economist (2007) "Adios to Poverty, Hola to Consumption," August 18, pp. 21–23.

The Economist (2007) "Dreaming of Glory: A Special Report on Brazil," April 14, S1–16.

Edwards, Sebastian (1989) "The Debt Crisis and Macroeconomic Adjustment in Latin America," *Latin American Research Review*, 24 (3): 172–186.

Edwards, Sebastian (2010) *Left Behind: Latin America and the False Promise of Populism*, Chicago, Ill.: University of Chicago Press.

Kaaminsky, Graciela L., Carmen M. Reinhart, and Carlos A. Végh (2017) "When It Rains, It Pours: Procyclical Capital Flows and Macroeconomic Policy," in W. Charles Sawyer (ed.), *Latin American Economics*, vol. III, London and New York: Routledge, pp. 186–233.

13 Poverty and inequality

Introduction

At a number of points in the book, we have mentioned or briefly discussed the issues of poverty and inequality in Latin America. Poverty has an obvious connection to the region. Only a small group of countries in the region have any realistic hope of joining the ranks of the high-income countries in the near future. Most of the countries of the region are middle-income countries. While Latin America is relatively well-off by global standards, poverty is still a daily fact of life for hundreds of millions of people. Income inequality exacerbates this problem. The average income data for the region masks the reality that income in Latin America is the most unevenly distributed among the world's regions. In the first two sections of the chapter, we consider the data and consequences of poverty and inequality in the region. In the third part of the chapter, the more commonly understood causes of poverty and inequality in Latin America are covered. A final section covers the list of public-policy changes that have been used and are evolving to address these issues in the region.

Poverty in Latin America

We begin this chapter by reviewing some information that was reported in Chapter 1. As was indicated in that chapter, for the most part Latin America is solidly middle class by global standards. The less encouraging side of the data is that only a few countries in the region could possibly be thought of as high-income. Table 13.1 reviews this data. GDP per capita in the region is $9,272. While this is lower than the world average, it is more than double the average for middle-income countries. However, the differences within the region are wide. Two of the poorest countries have GDP per capita under $3,000. At the other extreme, there are six countries with GDP per capita above $10,000. While adequate by global standards, the region is far from the affluence of the developed countries, where GDP per capita averages over $40,000. On the surface, Latin America seems relatively well-off by global standards.

As is frequently the case with Latin America, only looking superficially at the overall data can be quite misleading. One global standard of poverty is an income of $2.50 per day. For comparison purposes, we could use a higher standard of $4 per day. Table 13.2 presents the data for Latin America relative to the other developing regions of the world from 1990 to 2018. Relative to much of the rest of the world, poverty rates in Latin America are low. Further, they have fallen dramatically over the past two decades. On the other hand, there is still substantial progress to be made. Over a quarter of the

Table 13.1 Population, GDP, and GDP per capita for Latin America, low-, middle-, and high-income countries

	Population (millions)	GDP (billions)	GDP per capita
Argentina	44.3	637.4	14,398.4
Bolivia	11.1	37.5	3,394.0
Brazil	209.3	2,053.6	9,812.3
Chile	18.1	277.1	15,346.4
Colombia	49.1	314.5	6,408.9
Costa Rica	4.9	57.3	11,677.3
Ecuador	16.6	104.3	6,273.5
El Salvador	6.4	24.8	3,889.3
Guatemala	16.9	75.6	4,471.0
Honduras	9.3	23.0	2,480.1
Mexico	129.2	1,150.9	8,910.3
Nicaragua	6.2	13.8	2,221.8
Panama	4.1	62.3	15,196.4
Paraguay	6.8	39.7	5,823.8
Peru	32.2	211.4	6,571.9
Uruguay	3.5	56.2	16,245.6
Venezuela, RB	32	482.4	15,692.4
Latin America	644.1	5,972.1	9,271.6
Low income	732.4	576.9	787.7
Middle income	5,548.8	28,758.6	5,182.8
High income	1,248.4	51,625.9	41,352.4
World	7,529.7	80,934.8	10,748.7

Source: World Bank (2019).

Notes: Venezuela's GDP and GDP per capita data from 2014. Data in current US dollars.

Table 13.2 Poverty in Latin America and the world, 1990–2018

Region	Poverty rates (US$2.50 per day)		Poverty rates (US$4 per day)	
	1990	2018	1990	2018
Latin America	29.4	10.6	46.5	26.3
East Asia and the Pacific	88.6	12.4	95.9	34.8
Eastern Europe and Central Asia	11.1	5.4	28.3	14
Middle East and North Africa	36.1	15.6	63.3	42.1
South Asia	90.8	–	97.2	–
Sub-Saharan Africa	82.6	66.3	91.6	84.5

Source: World Bank (2019).

population are living on $4 per day, and over 10 percent on $2 per day. The decreases in poverty have been better than in any region of the world except East Asia. The improvement in poverty since 1990 has been impressive. However, this data indicates that even larger decreases might have been possible.

While instructive, Table 13.2 masks some useful information. As with other issues, poverty in Latin America is hardly homogeneous. Further, the data given in the table is based on global standards of poverty. These standards are based on the concept

Table 13.3 Relative poverty in Latin America (2017)

	$2.50 per day	*$4 per day*	*Poverty percentage (year)*
Argentina	2	7.1	–
Bolivia	11.8	24.7	32.7
Brazil	9.6	21	16.5
Chile	1.8	6.4	7.8
Colombia	10.8	27.6	28.6
Costa Rica	2.7	9.7	18.6
Ecuador	8.7	23.2	29.8
El Salvador	8.5	29	41.6
Guatemala	24.2	48.8	67.7
Honduras	31.6	52.6	74.3
Mexico	11.2	34.8	41.2
Nicaragua	12.8	34.8	58.3
Panama	6.3	14.1	21.4
Paraguay	5.6	18.6	42.3
Peru	9.8	23.9	22.7
Uruguay	0.4	2.9	4.4
Venezuela	–	–	32.1
Latin America	9.9	23.7	33.8

Source: World Bank (2019) and ECLAC (2019).

Notes: Data for Nicaragua and Guatemala from 2014; data for Mexico from 2016. Poverty percentages from 2014 except Bolivia, Chile, Honduras, Nicaragua, and Venezuela from 2013.

of *absolute poverty*. Absolute poverty is defined as lack of the amount of money necessary to meet certain basic thresholds of human existence. Outside the definition of absolute poverty, what constitutes "poor" becomes more specific to individual countries. For example, poverty in a high-income country is a standard of living that most people in the world would aspire to. The same is true even within Latin America. Someone considered poor in Chile might well be considered to be relatively well-off in some of the lower-income parts of the region. These differences give rise to the concept of *relative poverty*. Relative poverty is a standard of living that an individual country constructs to measure the number of citizens it wishes to define as poor. Table 13.3 is designed to illustrate this point. Using the lower standard of $2.50, 10 percent of the population falls below it. At $4, the percentage for the region jumps to nearly 25 percent. However, there is substantial variation in the region. For the higher-income countries, the poverty percentages have become quite low using either standard. More troublingly, poverty still afflicts over 10 percent of the population in six countries using the lower standard. The regional average is 10 percent. Likewise, the percentages are still depressingly high for the higher global standard of around $4 per day. There are only three countries in the region where this figure is less than 10 percent of the population. The average for the region is 23.7 percent. Taken together, nearly *25 percent* of the population of Latin America is poor, or poor by global standards. Again, comparisons with the poorer regions of the world are not encouraging. A substantial portion of the population of the region is existing on incomes more typical of East Asia or Africa than of a region of the world normally considered to be middle-income. Further, the problem is not wholly confined to the poorer countries of Central America. While substantial progress has been made, poverty is still a serious problem.

Income inequality

> To whom much is given, much is expected.
>
> (Luke 12:48)

The data in the previous two sections forms the basis for a discussion of income inequality in Latin America. In terms of GDP per capita, much of Latin America is solidly middle-class by global standards. From a superficial look at the overall data, the region seems relatively well-off. The second section of the chapter showed that the overall data on GDP per capita for the region is deceptive. A shockingly high percentage of the population of Latin America is poor by global standards. By the standards each country sets for itself, the picture is even bleaker. Under the best of circumstances, countries of the region are reporting poverty rates of 20–50 percent or even higher. Combining relatively high average incomes with high rates of poverty leads to an inescapable conclusion: the distribution of income is highly unequal. To anyone with a passing familiarity with the region, this is hardly surprising. The problem has been noted for centuries. While impressions and anecdotal information are not to be dismissed offhand, economists like to express things in a more numerical way. That is the purpose of this section. First, we need to define how economists measure income inequality. With this measurement in mind, we can then see more precisely just how unequal the distribution of income is in the region.

To measure income inequality, one needs some benchmark to measure inequality against. To begin, imagine a world where the total available income was perfectly distributed. In this case, each 10 percent of the population would receive exactly 10 percent of the income. Now, imagine the world as it is. In this case, some deciles would receive more than 10 percent and some less. Economists use a single statistic to express the extent to which the actual distribution of income deviates from perfect equality. This statistic is known as the *Gini coefficient*. The Gini coefficient is a measure of the deviation of the actual income distribution from perfect equality. The statistic ranges from 0 to 1. Perfect equality is 0: When this is the case, actual inequality is the same as perfect equality. At the other end of the spectrum, perfect inequality is 1. No economy in the world conforms to either extreme. For reference, a Gini coefficient below 0.3 would be considered a low level of inequality. On the other hand, a value of 0.70 or above would be considered high. For many of the world's countries, the Gini coefficient tends to be in the 0.30–0.40 range. With the concept of the Gini coefficient in mind and some sense of what constitutes low, high, and average, it now becomes easier to analyze the relative position of Latin America with respect to income inequality.

As one can see in Table 13.4, the position of Latin America with respect to income inequality is not favorable. The Gini coefficients shown in the table confirm the conventional wisdom that the distribution of income for the region is the most unequal among the world's major regions. The average for Latin America is 0.46. For comparative purposes, the US has one of the most unequal distributions of income among high-income countries. The Gini coefficient for the US is 0.42. Canada, Portugal, and Spain are more typical of high-income countries, with Gini coefficients of 0.34, 0.36, and 0.35, respectively.[1] As in virtually all of the regional economic data that we have studied in this book, the degree of income inequality for Latin America is not homogeneous. However, in this case, the degree of variance is less than is usually the case. The lowest Gini coefficients are 0.4 for Uruguay and El Salvador and the highest is 0.51 for Brazil and Colombia. The range around the average for the region is only 0.11. Even the lowest coefficients are high by global standards. On the other hand, even the

Table 13.4 Income inequality in Latin America, 2017

	Gini coefficient
Argentina	0.42
Bolivia	0.45
Brazil	0.51
Chile	0.48
Colombia	0.51
Costa Rica	0.49
Ecuador	0.45
El Salvador	0.40
Guatemala	0.48
Honduras	0.50
Mexico	0.43
Nicaragua	0.46
Panama	0.50
Paraguay	0.48
Peru	0.44
Uruguay	0.40
Venezuela, RB	0.47
Latin America	0.46
Portugal	0.36
Spain	0.35
Canada	0.34
US	0.42

Source: UN Development Programme (2019).

Notes: Venezuela Gini Index estimated by source.

highest coefficients are less than a very high coefficient of 0.70. For Latin America, the striking thing about the data is its relative *uniformity*. Every country in the region has a high Gini coefficient; some are just a little higher than others. This commonality is more striking than the differences. The data simply reflects what seemed to be the case from the previous section. The existence of high levels of poverty in middle-income countries strongly implies a high level of income inequality. However, since the 1990s, the average Gini coefficient has been falling in most countries.[2] While the current degree of inequality is still high, the situation is improving. As this high degree of inequality is pervasive for the region, perhaps the roots of this problem can be traced to similarities in the economic history of the region and, more recently, similarities in economic policies.

Box 13.1 The Human Opportunity Index

The results shown in Table 13.4 for the Gini coefficient for Latin America represent an outcome. The table shows a snapshot of the distribution of income for a particular year. However, this outcome is the result of the opportunities the population had at earlier points in time to make economic progress. In order to reduce the Gini coefficient in the future, it is important to provide more opportunities for a larger part of the population to improve their standard of living. As a result, it would be desirable to have some measure of the availability of economic opportunities now so that poverty and inequality could be reduced in the future.

Paes de Barros et al. (2008) have made an attempt at quantifying equality of opportunity in Latin America by constructing the Human Opportunity Index. This is a measure of the average access and inequities in access to basic services for children. Education is measured by the number of children completing sixth grade on time and school attendance from ages ten to fourteen. Housing is measured by access to clean water, sanitation, and electricity. The overall index is a composite of the education and housing indicators. The focus on children is sensible, as increasing their opportunities increases their chances for success later in life, with the potential to reduce poverty and inequality in the future.

The results of this exercise are shown in Table 13.5. As is usual, the range in the region is large in all cases. The averages for education, housing, and overall are 83.2, 72.0, and 77.6, respectively. These averages mask ranges from 69.0 to 93.3 for education; 42.4 to 98.1 for housing; and 57.3 to 94.5 overall. The best results are for education, but the ranges for access to clean water, sanitation, and electricity seem to be considerably worse. Obviously, this data is not a perfect exercise in measuring the degree of opportunity for children. However, it is a useful start for policy purposes. All the measures used in the index are based on the average access (supply) and inequalities in that access. It is quite possible for average access to improve over time, which may reduce poverty, but if inequalities in access persist, the effects on the distribution of income may be muted. Further, the gaps between education and housing vary enormously among countries. For example, Uruguay has the highest degree of opportunity in education but is not at the top in housing. For Bolivia, the situation is reversed. Education and housing are general problems in the region but to varying degrees. The implication is that policies to increase economic opportunity will vary considerably by country.

Table 13.5 Human Opportunity Index, 2016

	Education	*Housing*	*Overall*
Argentina	93.3	83.7	88.5
Bolivia	86.4	49.2	67.8
Brazil	81.6	92.5	87.0
Chile	88.6	96.0	92.3
Colombia	75.3	81.6	78.4
Costa Rica	85.2	96.7	91.0
Ecuador	85.2	82.4	83.8
El Salvador	72.2	42.4	57.3
Guatemala	69.0	47.4	58.2
Honduras	70.4	51.3	60.9
Mexico	92.8	79.4	86.1
Nicaragua	80.3	44.9	62.6
Panama	87.2	60.0	73.6
Paraguay	82.2	72.3	77.2
Peru	91.0	74.0	82.5
Uruguay	90.9	98.1	94.5
Venezuela, RB	–	–	–
Latin America	83.2	72.0	77.6

Source: World Bank (2019).

Causes of poverty and inequality

At a number of points in the book, we have pointed out that a certain characteristic or economic policy has had an adverse impact on either poverty or inequality, or both, in Latin America. In this section, we will review a number of these points and expand on some of them. Be aware that the topic is fraught with difficulties. Poverty and inequality in Latin America, or anywhere else for that matter, is not a simple thing to explain. As was seen above, both poverty and inequality are relative concepts. Further, the normal workings of a society operating under democratic capitalism are naturally going to produce some degree of inequality. There is no single, simple explanation such as capitalism, historical factors, or government policy. Rather, there are a number of factors that to a greater or lesser extent *contribute* to the existence of poverty and high levels of inequality. What follows is a list of factors that tend to worsen these problems in Latin America.

Historical roots

It is not too much of an exaggeration to say that modern Latin America was born with poverty and inequality literally baked into the economic system. The initial conditions in the late fifteenth and early sixteenth centuries involved the wresting of land and assets from the indigenous people of the region. The initial mineral wealth of the region and the later development of commodities for export created incentives for particular institutions to develop. More specifically, the rents generated from the production of commodities were, to the greatest extent possible, transferred to the governments of Portugal and Spain. These transfers were aided by concentrating land and resource holdings into a small part of the population. While convenient for the transfer of resources to the colonial powers, the institutional environment led to serious inequality. There was little or no incentive to provide land, education, or political power to the large mass of the people of the region. The indigenous population, and later the African slaves, benefited little from the abundance of resources. The result was a highly stratified economy with extremely high levels of income inequality.[3]

The independence movements of the early nineteenth century had the potential for reducing the level of inequality. Fewer resources were being transferred to the colonial powers, which held the potential for the new governments of the region to improve the incomes of the poor. Instead, independence in many cases was followed by decades of political violence. Such internal instability will reduce economic growth in any country, and Latin America was no exception. Under such circumstances, the poorer members of society not only do not progress but are the most vulnerable to the economic hardships produced by political instability. The end of this instability in the mid nineteenth century ushered in an era of relative prosperity. This "Golden Age" improved the average income of the population of the region. Unfortunately, the progress was not evenly spread. The end of political instability did not lead to widespread participation in the political system, that is, democracy. Rather, political power in the region became concentrated in the hands of the owners of land and other resources. Such a situation is not conducive to concerns about either poverty or inequality. To a greater or lesser extent, this situation persisted until the late nineteenth century. Growth was being fostered by the exports of commodities as Latin America became more integrated into the world economy. However, if the earnings from these exports are very concentrated in a small part of the population, then growth, in and of itself, may not reduce inequality.[4] From the forgoing discussion, note that the initial inequality created by colonial rule persisted for nearly 500 years. Such long-entrenched inequality is not going to be easily reduced in a short period of time even under the best of circumstances.

ISI

> Yes, there are oligarchies in Latin America. They are no longer oligarchies of land-owners and ranchers; instead they are industrial oligarchies and business groups that have prospered under protectionist power. To eliminate these oligarchies one doesn't have to eradicate their external manifestations – their money – but rather the system that made them possible.
>
> (Plinio A. Mendoza, Carlos A. Montaner, and Alvaro V. Llosa)

As we have seen in the previous section, the export of commodities tended to make the distribution of income in Latin America more unequal. The concentrated holdings of land and other resources became a primary driver of inequality. In the late nineteenth and early twentieth centuries, the region began to develop a small manufacturing sector. As noted on p. 35, the advent of the Great Depression and the subsequent global trade war made exporting from this small base difficult. Latin America already had high tariffs at this point, and the global trade war exacerbated this trend. The existing level of protectionism also found justification in popular policy prescriptions of the time. It was argued that due to declining terms of trade for Latin America, it would be advantageous to reduce imports by replacing them with domestic production in the form of ISI. The ultimately catastrophic effects of the collection of policies associated with ISI contributed to income inequality in the region in several ways.

First, the system encouraged the development of either private-sector firms or SOEs to produce products to replace imports. Most of these firms were operating with explicit or implicit government subsidies. These subsidies came in the form of loans on attractive terms, various forms of protectionism, and an overvalued exchange rate. In addition, many of these firms were operating in markets where the degree of competition was low. This mix of policies has the potential to increase inequality. The owners of such firms could reasonably be expected to make relatively high profits. On the other hand, consumers are likely to be paying relatively high prices for lower-quality goods. The vast majority are being made worse off while the gains from this arrangement are concentrated.

Second, the trade policy associated with ISI had the potential to increase inequality. Free trade has a tendency to increase the price of the abundant factor of production. In the case of Latin America, this would have meant the development of industry that intensively used cheap semiskilled labor. However, it would have reduced the returns to capital in the region. This sort of development has the potential to reduce the level of inequality. Wages might have risen for a large number of workers, and the returns to the owners of capital would have been smaller.[5] The protectionism associated with ISI worked in the opposite direction. High tariffs and quotas artificially encouraged the development of capital-intensive industries. The subsidies mentioned above added to this tendency. The result was the development of a profitable capital-intensive industrial base. Perversely, trade policy was increasing the return to the *scarce* factor of production as opposed to the abundant factor, labor. The policy favored the relatively well-off

at the expense of the larger group of semiskilled workers. Further, workers in ISI industries benefited indirectly from the profitability of the sector. The existence of these
profits and the ability to form unions helped a minority of workers in ISI industries to
earn wages in excess of what were available in the rest of the economy. The benefits of
ISI were spread a little more widely, but much of the population lost income as a result.
Wages were lower outside the protected sector, and the prices paid by most consumers
for domestically produced products were high. International trade has the potential to
reduce income inequality in a labor-abundant country. This outcome can be negated
if a country persists in developing industry based on comparative disadvantage. The
adverse implications for the distribution of income are just another in a long list of
problems associated with ISI.

Business and labor-market regulation

For any country, excessive regulation of markets can create adverse consequences.
While there is no perfect set of business or labor-market regulations, there are trade-
offs, which, if ignored, can cause significant problems. In Latin America, the combination of a difficult business environment coupled with the extensive regulation
of labor markets is both slowing economic growth and contributing to inequality.
While there is some debate over the effects of economic growth on the distribution
of income, it is rarely argued that slower growth makes the poor worse off in absolute terms. A thriving private sector is normally seen as a prerequisite for the reduction of poverty and perhaps eventually lowering the degree of inequality. As was
mentioned earlier in the book, Latin America is not an easy place to do business.
Business is always more difficult in a developing country. Inadequate infrastructure and other inherent difficulties make running a firm in Mexico City somewhat
different from operating in a large city in a high-income country. In a well-managed
developing country, the government is careful not to make these disadvantages even
more onerous through thoughtless taxation and regulation. Unfortunately, for Latin
America, this situation is common. The general perception of the region, now backed
up by a growing amount of research, is that the tax and regulatory environment is a
significant drag on growth. Further, this sort of environment favors the development
of large enterprises that have the resources to deal with complicated and at times
overlapping levels of regulation. This tends to drive smaller firms into the informal
sector and reduces the chances of these firms to grow to an optimal size. A business
environment favoring large firms over SMEs is not likely to contribute to the reduction of income inequality.

This problem is reinforced by labor-market regulation. In labor markets, there is
always a trade-off between the security of existing workers and the creation of new
jobs. For example, making it more difficult for firms to shed workers makes firms more
reluctant to create new jobs. Among the world's regions, Latin America has some of the
most generous levels of support for existing workers. This is so much the case that many
SMEs would not be able to operate profitably and comply with all relevant labor market
regulations. Again, the result is a large number of SMEs operating outside the formal
sector of the economy. Frequently, SMEs must be able to adjust their use of labor
quickly in order to survive in the long run. Firms that are unable to do this face a choice
between not doing business and operating outside the legal framework of business, in
the informal sector. In turn, this has created a dual labor market in much of Latin

America. Workers in the formal sector receive higher wages and other protections from the normal operation of the labor market. Workers who are not so fortunate typically find work in the informal sector, operating with lower wages and little job security. The effects on the distribution of income are obvious.

Educational inequality

One of the most common relationships in economics is between productivity and wages. In real terms, wages can only increase to the extent that *productivity* increases. The productivity of labor can be influenced by a number of factors, such as the institutional quality of the society in which workers are functioning. Productivity is also closely tied to the amount of human capital that workers possess. In turn, the amount of human capital embodied in a worker is partially a function of education. First, a higher level of education directly increases human capital. Second, education levels influence the ability of workers to continue to acquire human capital during the course of their careers.[6] As a result of these relationships, the distribution of income in a country can be influenced by the returns to and the distribution of human capital. In turn, the distribution of human capital is influenced by the distribution of educational opportunities. Not surprisingly, educational inequality in Latin America is high.

The data on educational inequality is shown in Table 13.6. At first glance, the data seems to be reasonable. Expressed as Gini coefficients, education is not as unequally distributed in the region as income. While this is the case for Latin America, it is also true for the world. The global average is 0.433. Still, this is encouraging, as education is not as unequally distributed in Latin America as it is in the world as a whole. Educational inequality is far worse in Africa and Asia, with Gini coefficients for these regions of 0.618 and 0.479, respectively. This is encouraging until one considers that the Gini coefficient for the high-income countries is 0.275. Relative to some of the other data on inequality for the region, in terms of education, the situation is better. Moreover, educational inequality has been falling since the 1960s.[7] However, this data is based on the distribution of the number of *years* of education obtained. Thus, the data is based on the quantity of schooling but says little about the quality of education. An educational system may well be successful at increasing the amount of time students spend in formal schooling but somewhat less successful at providing the basic human capital needed to succeed in a modern economy.

Unfortunately, the limited data on the quality of education overall in Latin America indicates that the quality of schooling is a problem. The measurement of educational outcomes on an international basis is relatively recent. The OECD has created the Program for International Student Assessment (PISA) to try to gain a better understanding of educational outcomes around the world. Data is available for all OECD countries and a limited number of developing countries.[8] At this point, only six countries in the region are participating in the project. The data for these countries and Canada, Portugal, Spain, and the US is given in Table 13.7. To better understand the data, a score of over 500 in the table puts a country in a very high position. For example, Canada is highly ranked in all categories. On the other hand, Portugal, Spain, and the US have PISA scores in the middle of the distribution for the sample of countries available. For Latin America, data is only available for eight countries. From this limited sample, students in Latin America are well behind students in Portugal, Spain,

Table 13.6 Educational inequality in Latin America

	Gini coefficients
Argentina	0.205
Bolivia	0.399
Brazil	0.349
Chile	0.195
Colombia	0.357
Costa Rica	0.283
Ecuador	0.323
El Salvador	0.418
Guatemala	0.560
Honduras	0.425
Mexico	0.324
Nicaragua	0.473
Panama	0.270
Paraguay	0.317
Peru	0.330
Uruguay	0.237
Venezuela	0.284
Latin America	0.338

Source: Cruces et al. (2014).

Table 13.7 Educational outcomes in Latin America, PISA scores for 2015

	Reading	Mathematics	Science
Argentina	425	409	432
Brazil	407	377	401
Chile	459	423	447
Colombia	425	390	416
Costa Rica	427	400	420
Mexico	423	408	416
Peru	398	387	397
Uruguay	437	418	435
Latin America	425	402	421
Portugal	498	492	501
Spain	496	486	493
Canada	527	516	528
US	497	470	496

Source: World Bank (2019).

and the US, and far behind a highly-rated country such as Canada. Note also that this sample is skewed. The countries of Latin America included in the sample are among the higher-income countries of the region. If the results for these countries are relatively poor, then it is difficult to imagine that the scores for some of the poorer countries of the region would be better. Unfortunately, this data makes sense when put together with the data on educational inequality. Inequality in educational opportunity will tend to lead to lower student performance. Large numbers of students in Latin America have some schooling, but the percentage attending is lower with each level of education. The situation also contributes to poverty as real wages are negatively influenced by a lack of educational achievement.

Reducing poverty and inequality

Given the long history of poverty and inequality in the region, reducing either of these problems is not going to be an easy task. In view of the troubling amount of *absolute poverty* that still lingers in the region, the reduction of poverty is a priority. Inequality in the distribution of income is obviously still a problem. Fortunately, policies to reduce poverty will usually also work to reduce inequality. In this section, we cover some of the more general themes involved in reducing both poverty and inequality. In doing so, we revisit some of the material from the previous section and add some other material on addressing these issues. These general themes are economic growth, the regulation of business and labor, educational inequality, and the role of the state.

Economic growth

The reduction of poverty in Latin America is dependent on maintaining or improving economic growth. As we saw in Chapter 2, the central economic problem of the region is that growth has been relatively slow. Over time, relatively slow growth makes it much more difficult to improve the welfare of those at the bottom of the income distribution. The dramatic reduction of the number of people living in absolute poverty in Asia over the past fifty years is a dramatic example of what economic growth can accomplish. As was also outlined in Chapter 4, increasing economic growth is not a simple formula, but the broad outlines of increasing growth in Latin America are understood. The easiest factor to address is increasing the stock of capital by increasing the historically low savings rates in the region and through more effective use of this capital. Further, the reduction of barriers to FDI accomplishes much the same thing. In any country, an increase in the K–L ratio increases productivity and real wages. In the long run, this increase in real wages tends to reduce the level of absolute poverty. In addition, FDI normally increases the level of TFP, which further increases growth and incomes. A more difficult factor for Latin America is the improvement of institutional quality. Modern research on economic growth has identified institutional quality as one of the most important factors for economic growth. While Latin America does not suffer from the deficiencies in institutional quality prevalent in low-income countries, there is a substantial room for improvement that would enhance growth. Unfortunately, institutional quality is a multifaceted term, and knowing precisely how to proceed on this front is still difficult to determine with any degree of precision. To the extent that poor institutional quality is hindering growth, it is also hindering the reduction of poverty and possibly contributing to greater inequality in the distribution of income.

Regulation of business and labor

Every country needs a framework to regulate the activities of business and the relationship between employers and employees. However, it is also important to construct regulation that will accomplish its goals without reducing economic growth. The general consensus, recently backed up with data, is that Latin America hasn't been able to accomplish this. Doing business in the region usually involves a large amount of time and cost that does not seem to be contributing much in the way of improving social welfare. Such a poor regulatory climate reduces growth and increases poverty. There are similar problems with the taxation of business. Taxes on businesses are a fact of life in any country. It serves no useful purpose for taxes to be so high that they are widely evaded or to be so complex that compliance costs reduce the ability of firms to grow. Likewise, this constraint also reduces overall economic growth and hinders the reduction of poverty. This degree of regulation may also exacerbate inequality. Needlessly complex business regulations and tax-compliance costs contribute to the development of a large informal business sector in the region. Small firms that cannot deal with compliance costs are consigned to the informal sector and may not grow to an optimum size. Such constraints on a significant portion of a country's business community reduce growth and inhibit the reduction of both poverty and inequality.

Much the same can be said about excessive regulation of conditions of employment. There is always a trade-off between protecting the conditions of employment for existing workers and the creation of new jobs. For example, making it difficult or expensive to reduce the workforce of a firm makes the firm more reluctant to hire new workers. In the case of Latin America, such regulations increase the unit cost of labor in the region for semiskilled and skilled workers. In turn, this reduces the ability of the region to trade on one of its sources of comparative advantage, an abundance of semiskilled labor. The effects on economic growth are not positive, as slower growth once again reduces the ability to mitigate poverty. This sort of labor-market regulation contributes to inequality. For workers in the formal sector of the economy, wages may be high by local standards, and job security may be high. For those workers who are less productive, jobs are still available. However, these jobs may only be plentiful in the informal sector, where wages are lower and labor-market regulations are not observed. Such a dualistic labor market cannot be expected to contribute to the reduction of income inequality.

Box 13.2 Reforming labor law in Latin America

In Chapter 4, we indicated that rigid labor laws were one factor that was inhibiting economic growth in Latin America. It also was pointed out that such laws can contribute to inequality. Thus, there is a powerful argument for reforming the labor laws that are prevalent in the region. To understand why it is difficult to reform these laws, it is necessary to understand some fundamental aspects of labor laws. These laws exist to protect workers from the risks associated with unemployment. In many developed countries, there is a system of unemployment insurance which is a way of pooling the risk of unemployment for workers. If a worker is laid off, there are payments made from a pool of funds created by taxes on workers and employers. Another way of solving this problem is to transfer the risk to the employer. In this case, the compensation to a laid-off worker is in the form of a severance payment. The problem with this system is that it creates disincentives for employers to hire workers in the first place. An optimal system combines the labor-market flexibility of a free market with substantial payments to workers who are laid off as a result of the normal workings of the market. The system Latin America uses was not original to the region. It was imported from Spain and Portugal. In many countries of the region, these laws were introduced or even strengthened during the movement to democracy during the 1980s. After that point, countries of the region moved toward a system of unemployment insurance. The seven countries are Argentina, Brazil, Chile, Colombia, Ecuador, Uruguay, and Venezuela. For several reasons, Latin American unemployment-insurance systems have not worked well. First, they only cover workers in the formal sector so the coverage is limited. Second, the benefit-replacement rates are low which is particularly problematic in middle-income countries. Finally, there is the usual problem of bureaucratic quality in the sense of monitoring and enforcement of the law. The result has been that most countries are still relying on rigid labor laws to protect workers from the costs of unemployment. There have been attempts at reform, but this has been a partisan issue. Some left-of-center governments have strengthened these laws while the other side of the political spectrum has tried to introduce more flexibility in the labor markets. More typically, the result has been the maintenance of the status quo. As is frequently the case in Latin America, the overriding issue is money. With money in short supply for such basics as education and infrastructure, money for a comprehensive unemployment-insurance system is simply not there. Since an unemployment-insurance system does not address the problems of workers in the informal sector, some countries have opted for spending the limited amount of money they have on conditional cash transfers to the poor. While this is an understandable choice, it still leaves the region hobbled by labor laws that restrain growth. Both the money and the political will to reform seem to be in short supply.

Educational reform

In a modern economy, the accumulation of human capital is a critical component of economic growth. All else being equal, the rapid accumulation of human capital increases the rate of economic growth. The accumulation of human capital is critically dependent on the quality of a country's educational system. The productivity of the labor force and the real wages that they can earn are positively correlated with the possession of human capital. The human capital a worker possesses and their ability to acquire more over the course of a working life determine both initial wages and the ability to increase income in the future. In this regard, the educational system of Latin America is considered to be deficient. In the first place, overall spending on education is not high. The region spends about 4 percent of GDP on all levels of education. This level of spending has been sufficient to reduce illiteracy rates in most countries to relatively low levels. Unfortunately, this level of spending has not changed significantly for decades.[9] In such a case, improvements in education become dependent on increasing the productivity of the educational system. The limited data on educational attainment given in a previous section indicates that students in the region lag behind the level of education obtained in OECD countries as well as other middle-income countries. Also, as shown above, part of the problem is the degree of inequality in educational opportunities. Education is very unequally distributed in the region. The result is that human capital accumulation is lower than it could be, and the distribution of human capital becomes unequal. Such a situation contributes to both poverty and the perpetuation of high levels of income inequality. Despite what has been accomplished in the twentieth century, reform of the educational system in much of Latin America to make it more effective and equitable is a pressing need.

The role of the state

> Except Max guessed what the change in Mexico would consist of: from a bourgeoisie dependent on the state to a state dependent on the bourgeoisie.
>
> (Carlos Fuentes)

The changes outlined above that would reduce poverty and inequality in Latin America would be desirable but would not work quickly. Improving institutional quality, reforming business and labor regulation, and reforming educational systems are the work of years, at best. The time lag between reforms and positive effects on poverty and income inequality would involve similar periods. For such reasons, governments wishing to reduce poverty or income inequality frequently pursue more short-run measures to mitigate these problems. To a greater or lesser extent, most high- and middle-income countries pursue a variety of policies designed to reduce poverty and income inequality. In general, these involve progressive tax systems, direct transfers of resources, or other programs designed to more directly address such problems in the short run. The countries of Latin America are no different in this regard. Each country has its own set of policies that are at least superficially aimed at the improving the welfare of the poor and addressing income inequality. It is beyond the scope of the discussion to study such systems for even one country, let alone the entire region. However, there is one way to capture the workings of the state with regard to poverty and the distribution of income. To do this, we will refer back to the concept of the Gini coefficient.

The Gini coefficients reported in Table 13.4 refer to the distribution of disposable income. This refers to income after taxes and transfer payments. To get an idea of the role of the state in reducing inequality, it would be useful to compare this measure of income inequality with a Gini coefficient based solely on *market* incomes. Fortunately, recent research makes this comparison possible.[10] The results show that the role of the state in changing the distribution of income in Latin America is modest at best. The Gini coefficient for market income is only 0.02 above the Gini coefficient disposable income. What this means is that the operation of taxes and transfer payments in the region has very little impact on the distribution of disposable income. Theoretically, progressive taxation should be working to reduce income inequality. This is true in Latin America. However, taxes change the Gini coefficient by approximately 0.01. The effect of transfer payments is slightly larger but still in the 0.01–0.02 range. The latter is important, as transfer payments tend to have the most dramatic effects on lowering the level of poverty and inequality. A comparison with Europe is useful to illustrate the point. The market Gini coefficient for Europe is 0.46. However, in Europe, transfer payments change the Gini coefficient by 0.10. The lowest level of transfers in Europe, in Portugal, changes the Gini coefficient by 0.06. The role of taxes is smaller. In Europe, taxes change the Gini coefficient by 0.05. In Latin America, market incomes are more unevenly distributed than in Europe. A key difference for Latin America is that the role of government in reducing inequality is modest.

Overall, the government's role in reducing poverty and reducing inequality could be improved. The endless complications of doing business in the region lower growth and impede the reduction of poverty. Likewise, the effects of labor-market regulation reduce growth and contribute to poverty. Further, they may work to increase inequality by encouraging the growth of the informal sector, where wages are lower. For the most part, education in Latin America is provided by the state. Low educational quality reduces the accumulation of human capital and depresses wages for the vast majority of the workers of the region. High levels of inequality in education tend to perpetuate already high levels of inequality. Governments have the ability to mitigate high levels of income inequality produced by the market through taxes and transfer payments. As shown above, these effects are small in Latin America. In the end, we will leave it to the reader to decide whether Latin America's primary economic problem is due to the poor quality of firms and workers in the region or to the poor quality of government. One may now hope that the spread of democracy in Latin America will give the people of the region the chance to obtain policies that are more likely to improve the welfare of the average citizen.

Box 13.3 Bolsa Familia

It is unusual for a program that distributes cash to the poor to be widely hailed as a model for reducing poverty and inequality. If not carefully designed, direct transfers of income can work to reduce poverty in the present but create negative incentives, which may perpetuate poverty and inequality in the future. The Bolsa Familia program in Brazil is seen as a model program in the sense that it reduces current levels of poverty while at the same time creating incentives to reduce poverty and inequality in the future. The basic benefit of the program is a cash transfer to families living in extreme poverty, with no conditions for receiving the money. The interesting part of the program is the cash transfers to higher-income families who fall below the poverty line. This program provides a cash transfer per child *conditional* on the children receiving vaccinations and school attendance. As a result, the program attacks poverty immediately by transferring cash to the poorest Brazilians. Family income increases immediately, and income inequality is reduced. The interesting effects will occur in the future. Vaccinations are a cost-effective means of improving the health of children now and in the future. Regular school attendance increases human capital and the ability to accumulate human capital over the course of a working life. Giving immediate incentives to improve school attendance has potentially large benefits for the children of the poor by increasing productivity and real wages in the future. The overall Brazilian economy may benefit going forward if this enhances economic growth. The effects of the program are potentially large, as it covers over 11 million families or 44 million individuals. The overall cost of the program is also interesting. It currently accounts for 0.5 percent of Brazil's GDP—only 2.5 percent of total government spending. At this level, the program would not have to produce enormous benefits in order to cover its costs. Because the program was only initiated in 2003, rigorous assessment of the benefits will be necessary before firm conclusions can be drawn. However, the modest cost, coupled with large potential benefits, makes the program an unusually promising policy.

Key terms and concepts

absolute poverty: lack of the amount of money necessary to meet certain basic thresholds of human existence.
Gini coefficient: a measure of the deviation of the actual income distribution from perfect equality.
productivity: the amount of output produced in a given period of time by a unit of labor.
relative poverty: a standard of living that an individual country constructs to measure the number of citizens it wishes to define as poor.

Questions for review and discussion

1 By global standards, Latin America is neither desperately poor nor rich. Using the data in Table 13.1, explain this statement.
2 Describe the percentage of the population of Latin America living on less than $2.50 per day. Relate this to the data on per-capita GDP in Table 13.3.
3 Define the terms "absolute poverty" and "relative poverty." How do these terms apply to Latin America?
4 What is the Gini coefficient? How does it apply to Latin America?
5 How does the Human Development Index apply to Latin America?
6 Describe how commodities and colonial rule interacted to increase income inequality in Latin America.
7 What is the relationship between ISI and poverty and inequality in Latin America?
8 How can trade policy contribute to income inequality in a labor-abundant country?
9 Describe the relationship between wages and productivity, and put this relationship into the context of Latin America.
10 How does inequality in education contribute to income inequality in Latin America?
11 How well are students in Latin America educated, based on global standards?
12 How are economic growth and poverty related?
13 What is the relationship between informality and poverty and inequality in Latin America?
14 Describe the difference between income inequality based on market incomes and overall income inequality.
15 To what extent have government actions changed income inequality in the region?

Notes

1 For more on Latin American income inequality versus the rest of the world, see Perry and López (2008).
2 See Gasparini et al. (2017) or López-Calvo and Lustig (2010) for more details.
3 For a dissenting view of this description, see Williamson (2009).
4 For a more detailed treatment of this period, see Arroyo Abad (2009).
5 This is just the usual comparison of economic development in Latin America versus East Asia.
6 As was pointed out in Chapter 3, the amount of human capital in an economy is also an important determinant of economic growth.
7 See Ferranti et al. (2004) for details.
8 See OECD (2007) for further details.
9 For more on this, see Damon and Glewwe (2009).
10 See Goni et al. (2008) or Lopez and Perry (2008).

References

Arroyo Abad, Leiticia (2009) *Inequality in Republican Latin America: Assessing the Effects of Factor Endowments and Trade, Global Prices and Income History Group Working Papers, no. 12*, Davis, Calif.: University of California at Davis.

Cruces, Guillermo, C. García Domenech, and Leonardo Gasparini (2014) "Inequality in Education: Evidence for Latin America" in Giovanni A. Cornia (ed.), *Falling Inequality in Latin America: Policy Changes and Lessons*, Oxford: Oxford University Press.

Damon, Amy and Paul Glewwe (2009) "Three Proposals to Improve Education in the LAC Region: Estimates of the Costs and Benefits of Each Strategy," in Bjorn Lomberg (ed.), *Latin American Development Priorities: Costs and Benefits*, Cambridge: Cambridge University Press, pp. 45–91.

Economic Commission for Latin America and the Caribbean (2019) *Social Panorama of Latin America 2018*, Santiago: Economic Commission for Latin America and the Caribbean.

Ferranti, David, Guillermo E. Perry, and Francisco Ferreira (2004) *Inequality in Latin America: Breaking with History?* Washington, DC: World Bank.

Gasparini, Leonardo, Guillermo Cruces, and Leopoldo Tomarolli (2011) "Recent Trends in Income Inequality in Latin America," in W. Charles Sawyer (ed.), *Latin American Economics*, vol. IV, London and New York: Routledge, pp. 192–235.

Goni, Edwin, J. Humberto López, and Luis Servén (2008) *Fiscal Redistribution and Income Inequality in Latin America, World Bank Policy Research Working Paper No. 4487*, Washington, DC: World Bank.

López, J. Humberto and Guillermo Perry (2008) Inequality in Latin America: Determinants and Consequences, *World Bank Policy Research Working Paper No. 4504*, Washington, DC: World Bank.

López-Calva, Luis F. and Nora Lustig (2010) *Declining Inequality in Latin America: A Decade of Progress?* New York: United Nations Development Programme.

Organisation for Economic Co-operation and Development (2007) *PISA, 2006: Science Competencies for Tomorrow's World*, Paris: Organisation for Economic Co-operation and Development.

Paes de Barros, Ricardo, Francisco H. G. Ferreira, José R. Molinas Vega, and Jaime S. Chanduvi (2008), *Measuring Inequality of Opportunities in Latin America and the Caribbean*, Washington, DC: World Bank.

United Nations Development Programme (2019) *Human Development Report, 2019*, New York: United Nations.

Williamson, Jeffrey G. (2009) *History without Evidence: Latin American Inequality since 1491, NBER Working Paper No. 14766*, Cambridge, Mass.: National Bureau of Economic Research.

World Bank (2019) *World Development Indicators*, Washington, DC: World Bank.

Recommended reading

Breceda, Karla, Jamele Rigolini, and Jaime Saavedra (2009) "Latin America and the Social Contract: Patterns of Social Spending and Taxation," *Population and Development Review*, 35 (December): 721–748.

Chen, Shaohua and Martin Ravallion (2007) *Absolute Poverty Measures for the Developing World, 1981–2004, World Bank Policy Research Working Paper No. 4211*, Washington, DC: World Bank.

Cook, Lorena M. (2007) *The Politics of Labor Reform in Latin America: Between Flexibility and Rights*, University Park, Pa.: Pennsylvania State University Press.

Galiani, Sebastian (2009) "Reducing Poverty in the LAC Region," in Bjorn Lomberg (ed.), *Latin American Development Priorities: Costs and Benefits*, Cambridge: Cambridge University Press.

Heckman, James J. and Carmen Pagés (2004) *Law and Employment: Lessons from Latin America and the Caribbean*, Chicago, Ill.: University of Chicago Press.

Loayza, Norman V. and Luis Servén (2010) *Business Regulation and Economic Performance*, Washington, DC: World Bank.

McEwan, Patrick J., Miguel Urquiola, and Emiliana Vegas (2007) "School Choice, Stratification, and Information on School Performance: Evidence from Chile," *Economia*, 8 (spring): 1–27.

Paes de Barros, Ricardo, Francisco H. G. Ferreira, José R. Molinas Vega, and Jaime Aaavedra Chanduvi (2009) *Measuring Inequality of Opportunities in Latin America and the Caribbean*, Washington, DC: World Bank.

Thorbecke, Erik and Machiko Nissanke (2008) "The Impact of Globalization on the Poor in Latin America," *Economia*, 9 (fall): 153–186.

Urquiola, Miguel (2011) "Education," in José A. Ocampo and Jaime Ros (eds.), *The Oxford Handbook of Latin American Economics*, Oxford: Oxford University Press, pp. 813–835.

14 Economic policy debates in Latin America

Introduction

In the countries of Latin America, there usually is a fair amount of debate about economic policy. This is nothing unique, but in each country or region of the world such debates take on some slightly different characteristics. Debates over economic policy in Brazil are somewhat different than in Italy, India, the US, or South Africa. In the case of Latin America, these region-specific characteristics come from the history of the region and the tumultuous economic conditions Latin America experienced in the past half century. The purpose of this chapter is to put these debates into a framework that will make them easier to understand. To do this, we start with the legacy of ISI and its effects lingering into the twenty-first century. The collapse of ISI ushered in a period of economic restructuring that was successful in many respects. However, economic growth in the region since 1990 has not been as high as in some of the more successful developing countries. This restructuring and the disappointing record of growth have spawned a cottage industry of critics, primarily outside economics. As we will see, this debate over economic policy is more apparent than real. As usual, economic policy debates end up being about government intervention, economic growth, and the distribution of income. The only difference here is that they are occurring in a uniquely Latin American context.

The end of ISI

The relatively slow growth of the economies of the region has naturally raised the question of its causes. The debate has tended to center on a set of policy choices made by most of the governments of Latin America during the Great Depression or in the following decade. In general, governments can allow the economy to develop using some mix of market forces coupled with a variety of government policies. Latin America in the second half of the twentieth century is a classic example. With the notable exception of Cuba, most governments in Latin America developed by relying on the actions of individuals and private-sector firms. However, there was heavy intervention by the state in the form of ISI. In reality, ISI is not a policy but a collection of policies designed to develop industries that, in many cases, might not even have existed in a free market. From the 1930s to the 1970s, the use of ISI was extensively pursued in Latin America. Although this set of policies was gradually abandoned in the 1980s, its impact on economic growth in the region and its lingering effects are still the subject of debate.

By the late 1970s, ISI had led to an unsustainable situation in the region. Supporting ISI industries required heavy direct and indirect subsidies by the government. These costs were fueling government spending that was not matched by tax revenues. With an inability to borrow, government budget deficits were causing increases in the money supply that were fueling inflation in most countries of the region. High rates of inflation, coupled with fixed exchange rates, were creating current-account deficits that could only be financed with increasing amounts of debt.[1] The inability to pay these debts eventually led to the collapse of the system. The Lost Decade of the 1980s was the direct result of this transition from ISI to a more market-oriented system. Unfortunately, the economic fallout of macroeconomic mismanagement, the burden of debt, and economies that have to be restructured is never a pleasant situation. As ISI collapsed, the difficult economic situation that followed was unavoidable. There is a legitimate debate among economists about the timing and severity of the austerity programs that accompanied the restructuring of the economies of the region during the 1980s. However, the restructuring was inevitable, and the effects would have been prolonged under any set of circumstances.

While the macroeconomic fallout of ending ISI was accomplished by the 1990s, the economies of the region are still affected by decades of ISI. ISI started out as a well-intentioned but flawed form of economic development policy. It involved heavy protection of capital-intensive industries that took on a variety of forms. In an international context, industries were heavily protected from foreign competition. They were subsidized in the form of overvalued exchange rates and with access to cheap credit from development banks. Because many of the internal markets in the region were small, domestic industries were composed of only one or a small number of firms. Subsidies and the lack of competition resulted in the ability of inefficient firms to earn abnormally large profits. In effect, ISI led to a form of crony capitalism. The abnormal profits of ISI industries were directly tied to economic policy decisions made by the government.[2] Unfortunately, before 1980, the majority of these governments were authoritarian in nature. The economic goal of such governments is to stay in power by satisfying the needs of groups within societies with the potential power to displace them.[3] As we saw in Chapter 2, these groups have deep historical roots stretching back to the colonial period. This causes two problems the region still struggles with in the twenty-first century. First, the dismantling of ISI is an ongoing process. Second, Latin America has always had a problem with the distribution of income. As was outlined in previous chapters, ISI exacerbated an existing problem.

Unfortunately, ISI is not just history. Its effects can be easily seen in the economies of Latin America. It can also be seen in policy debates within the region. The groups that benefited from ISI and the policies that are still in place are going to work to preserve these policies. This is understandable, as rent-seeking is hardly peculiar to Latin America. Instead, these groups will work to preserve their benefits derived from government policy by advocating them as being in the national interest. A few specific examples can serve as illustrations. First, removing protectionism in most countries is still difficult. As shown in Chapter 7, most countries in the region are still moving slowly toward becoming more open. Second, while most of the countries of the region have flexible exchange rates, they are being managed. With respect to exchange-rate flexibility, most countries are moving in the right direction, but there is still the fear of floating. Third, state-owned development banks are still common. In Brazil, they are still an important part of the financial markets. In all these cases, there is still a legacy of state management of the economy left over from ISI and a political battle to be fought in moving to freer markets. Hopefully, at this point, the reader now has a better understanding of policies that enhance economic growth and development as opposed to policies that benefit groups within the economy but tend to lower economic growth.

The Washington Consensus

The growing realization that ISI was not a sustainable policy for economic development in the region logically led to the search for an alternative set of policies. In determining economic policy, there is a common trade-off between the amount of decision-making that is left to the private sector and how much is done by the government. ISI was heavily tilted toward government intervention in the economy. As the performance of this set of policies was not as successful as was hoped, there has been an inevitable tilt of policy in Latin America toward greater reliance on market forces. A somewhat more precise way of describing the policy changes that have occurred in Latin America since the 1980s is to refer to the *Washington Consensus*. The Washington Consensus refers to a loose collection of economic policies that has been promoted by multilateral institutions in Washington, DC, such as the World Bank, the IMF, and a number of think tanks. John Williamson has summarized the main points of the Washington Consensus into a short list of general economic policies:

- a fiscal policy appropriate for macroeconomic conditions;
- a focus on improving the welfare of the poor by improving basic services that promote economic growth, such as education and infrastructure;
- a tax system featuring lower marginal tax rates levied on a larger base of taxation market-determined interest rates realistic exchange rates liberalization of trade barriers;
- relatively free flows of FDI privatization of inefficient state enterprises government regulation that does not restrict competition protection of property rights.

This list is a useful way to think about economic policy in Latin America. It is a loose description of economic policies that are commonplace in most high-income countries or faster-growth middle-income countries. They are the source of some controversy in Latin America, partially because economic policy in many countries of the region prior to the 1980s was so far from these sorts of policies. The controversy is also partially a result of the movement away from ISI and toward more market-based economies. As we will see, this movement has caused a substantial amount of economic dislocation and not a small amount of short- to medium-term economic discomfort. Not surprisingly, the failures of ISI, coupled with the economic dislocations of changing economic policies, have led to the consideration or, in some cases, the adoption of policies that do not neatly fit into either the older ISI or mainstream molds. At times, these policies are referred to as being associated with *heterodox economics*. However, this term refers to a number of different schools of economic thought that are outside the mainstream of modern economic thought. Part of the problem with policy debates in Latin America has to do with how one defines economics in the twenty-first century.

The Washington Consensus is just a list of general economic policies that successful countries tend to follow. It has also become a phrase used to characterize these policies as being extremely free market or associated with right-wing politics.

There is a negative connotation associated with the Washington Consensus that is closer to the sort of policy analysis that economists engage in, and is important to consider. The Washington Consensus came out of policy advice that was being given to the countries of Latin America during the 1980s. By 1980, economic policy in the region was frequently so far from the norm that implementing the Washington Consensus required wrenching changes in economic policy. Not surprisingly, such changes led to a long period of very poor economic performance. Unfortunately for many, the Lost Decade and the Washington Consensus became inextricably linked in a negative way.

On the other hand, there was a tendency to oversell the benefits of the policy agenda. It was assumed by some that a strict adherence to the Washington Consensus would quickly produce East Asian-style economic growth. Sadly, that has not been the case. While economic growth in the region over the past twenty-five years has been good, it has fallen short of what was hoped for in the early 1990s. Part of the problem has been that the set of policies has not been completely implemented. For example, trade barriers in the region are still high, and tax systems are needlessly complex. This set of policy recommendations will definitely improve the prospects for growth, but in a different way than is usually supposed. The Washington Consensus can be thought of as a necessary condition for rapid growth, but not a sufficient condition. The example of Chile is instructive. It is the country in the region that has probably followed the Washington Consensus most closely. It is also the country with the fastest economic growth. However, it has been unable to match the growth of the countries of East Asia, as there is more to rapid growth than the basics. What the set of policies is capable of producing is the drastic lowering of the probability of serious economic trouble, especially macroeconomic trouble. It is perhaps not accidental that countries such as Argentina and Venezuela are experiencing economic problems that the other countries of the region are not struggling with. In a sense, it might be reasonable to say that the Washington Consensus is a damaged brand because it could not automatically deliver rapid economic growth. However, given the long history of economic turmoil in the region, if it can deliver a measure of stability, then the set of policies has substantial value.[4] Looking at the list above, the reforms suggested by the Washington Consensus can be divided into two broad categories: (1) macroeconomic reform and (2) structural reform. As we will see in the next two sections, the process of macroeconomic reform in the region has been very successful, while the process of structural reform has been more gradual.

Box 14.1 The Chicago Boys

I am not a politician, Marucho. I am a technocrat and believe in technocracy, and technicians are politically neutral.

(Raúl Prebisch)

The Chicago Boys is a term used to refer to a group of economists in Chile who were instrumental in moving economic policy in the country to the position one can see in Table 14.1. The usual story is that the group trained under Milton Friedman at the University of Chicago and implemented an extreme "right-wing" set of policies under the dictatorship of Augusto Pinochet during the 1970s and 1980s. A standard part of the story involves a visit Friedman made to Chile in

1975 and his controversial meeting with Pinochet. This linking of economic policy in Chile with Friedman is in reality only a small part of the story. The actual story is much longer, more complicated, and more interesting. In the 1950s, the US government and some private foundations began sponsoring Latin American students to study economics in the US. The economics department at the University of Chicago began participating in the program through the efforts of Theodore Schulz and especially Arnold Harberger. Harberger was married to a Chilean and spoke fluent Spanish. Through his efforts, a "pipeline" was developed between the Catholic University of Chile and the economics department at Chicago. All through the 1950s, 1960s, and 1970s, a large number of Chilean students studied at Chicago and went back to Chile. The result was a substantial number of Chilean economists who were uncomfortable with the economic policies of the times and who were committed to the sort of mainstream economic policies associated with high-income countries. Their influence first surfaced in a set of policy reforms for Chile known as "el ladrillo" (the brick). This in turn became the beginning of economic policy in modern Chile. Following the military coup in 1970, Pinochet gave the Chicago Boys a free hand in shaping the economic policy of the country. The country quickly recovered from the economic difficulties of the 1970s and went on to become the best-performing economy in Latin America. These policies are frequently described as "right-wing," but this criticism is odd. Since the beginning of democracy in Chile in 1990, the elected government has usually been a left-wing coalition. Through twenty-five years of democracy, the basic economic policy of the country has not changed. The reader is left to consider whether economic policy in Chile is, in fact, extremely free market or whether it simply reflects the fact that Chile is now a developed country whose voters tend to vote for economic policies that are prevalent in developed countries. However, it is an inescapable reality that the Chicago Boys were working for an authoritarian regime in which human-rights abuses were common. This creates a dilemma facing economists in any authoritarian country, of either the left or the right, for which there are no quick and easy answers. The quote at the beginning of this box illustrates that the dilemma is neither new nor unique. The most famous economist in the history of Latin America faced a similar dilemma in the 1930s as Argentina moved from a democracy to a military dictatorship.

Macroeconomic reform

> Brazil is like a drug addict, once you get started living with inflation you can't stop.
> (Luis Ewald)

One of the hardest lessons learned in the region during the period of ISI and the Lost Decade was the importance of sound macroeconomics. Macroeconomic instability creates two very important economic problems. First, it impedes economic growth. Inflation is akin to throwing sand into the gears of the economic system. Economic agents make their most efficient decisions in an environment where changes in real prices can be easily seen because prices are stable. With high and fluctuating inflation, both consumers and investors make mistakes due to an inability to determine exact changes in real prices. These mistakes detract from economic growth, as resources are not being put to their most efficient use. The second serious problem is that inflation has asymmetric effects on different levels within the distribution of income. Higher-income consumers may be better able to purchase assets such as land or financial assets whose value will not be seriously eroded by inflation. With few assets and wages that may lag behind changes in prices, high inflation can have devastating impacts on the economic welfare of the poor. Extreme fluctuations in real GDP also slow down economic growth as investors become more reluctant to make long-term commitments to invest. As investment is an important contributor to long-run growth, short-run instability in real GDP growth can have long-run negative effects. It obviously increases unemployment, which negatively impacts the lower part of the income distribution more than the upper levels. In a Latin American context, it may also drive some workers from the formal to the informal part of the economy.

The Lost Decade was an extreme example of the damage that macroeconomic instability can do. As we saw in Chapter 11, inflation rose to exceptionally high levels. In addition, real GDP growth during the decade was extremely low. The poor macroeconomic environment of the 1980s paved the way for the macroeconomic stability that has characterized Latin America for the past twenty-five years. The fiscal prudence prevalent in the region is a remarkable turnaround. Prior to the 1990s, large government budget deficits were a constant problem. With an inability to borrow, financing these deficits via printing money was also common. Not surprisingly, high inflation was a frequent problem. After more than two decades of fiscal prudence, balanced budgets or small deficits have become the norm for the region.[5]

The establishment of sound fiscal policy has led to much more prudent monetary policy. With government budgets at, or near, balance, the central bank is under considerably less pressure to increase the money supply at an inappropriate rate. However, fiscal prudence can change as rapidly as the political situation in a country can change. Over time, countries have found that it is important for the central bank to be insulated from short-run changes in the government. In general, this is known as *central-bank independence*. Unfortunately, central-bank independence is not a binary variable. Rather, it is measured in degrees along a scale from a totally nonindependent central bank to one that is very free from interference from the government in the short run. The traditional solution for measuring central-bank independence is to create an index number, which is a weighted average of factors that affect the insulation of the central bank from the government. A simple example of an important factor is whether or not the CEO of the central bank can be removed from office by elected politicians due to a disagreement over the course of monetary policy. The problem in Latin America is that while monetary policy in general has been prudent, central banks in the region are, on average, not as independent as they are in the developed countries. This leaves many countries in the region vulnerable to a reemergence of inflation. If economic conditions worsen and fiscal deficits become larger, there is the uncomfortable possibility of the return of inflation as a problem. A related issue is central-bank transparency. Even if a central bank is independent, it may not effectively communicate information on the current and future course of monetary policy. This is a problem for reasons that are not immediately obvious. Market participants must frequently make long-run decisions. They can do this more effectively when the central bank does a good job of communicating its current policy and provides information on possible future changes in policy. In the absence of such information, market participants will have to make decisions based on some assumed conduct of monetary policy. Having official guidance from the central bank allows them to spend less time trying to determine what the central bank will do and to make better decisions in the process. Transparency does not imply that either the central bank or market participants will not make mistakes. However, transparency allows some interaction between the two, which should improve the decision making of both.

Over the past two decades, better fiscal and monetary policy have led to relatively low inflation in Latin America. It is a measure of the improvement in the situation that Argentina and Venezuela are now just reminders of the adverse effects of bad macroeconomic policy. Despite these improvements, central-bank independence is still a reform that has not been fully implemented. Central-bank independence and its relation to economic outcomes has been an active area of research. As a general rule, it makes inflation less likely. Central-bank independence is usually measured as an index number incorporating a number of factors that influence it: For example, can the CEO of the central bank be removed because the government disagrees with the conduct of monetary policy? As a result, it is now possible to rank the central banks of the world on their degree of independence. Recent research indicates that the central banks of the region have become slightly more independent over the past twenty years. However, many of the central banks in the region are not as independent as they are in developed countries.[6] In terms of macroeconomic policy, the lack of central-bank independence means that many of the central banks of the region lack proper insulation from the political process. While this is currently only a problem in Argentina and Venezuela, the risk is still there for much of the rest of the region. For whatever reason, governments in the region seem uncomfortable with delegating monetary policy completely to an independent central bank. Until this is accomplished, the region is still vulnerable to the return of an inflationary past.[7]

Structural reform

Enhancing TFP and economic growth in any country or region usually involves a complex set of reforms to economic policy that are generically referred to as structural reforms. One frequently hears this phrase with respect to the efforts of the EU to enhance the low rate of growth that has been common in the region since the 1980s. Structural reform is less commonly mentioned in the context of Latin America, but it is a problem for this region as well. One of the difficulties associated with structural reform is assigning some type of precise meaning to the term. It refers to the reform of economic policy, but exactly which policies and to what extent the relevant policies need to be changed normally is not clear. To an extent, we have already covered part of the problem with Latin America in the discussion above of business regulation and labor-market distortions. However, reforms of these specific policies would still leave considerable scope for structural reform in the region. The research on structural reform in Latin America gives us a general idea of the types of reforms that can be plausibly related to TFP and economic growth. Lora (2012) has constructed an index of structural reform for Latin America. As in any such exercise, the components of the index are not necessarily comprehensive, especially for any one country. However, the components of the index and its changes over time can help one to get a feel for both the breadth of the problem and the progress that has been achieved.

The index of structural reforms contains five categories: (1) trade policy; (2) financial policy; (3) tax policy; (4) privatizations; and (5) labor legislation. Each of these categories contains indicators used to show the degree of reform for each one. An advantage of this index is that the indicators are actual measures of policy as opposed to measures of the outcomes of policy. Trade policy represents the average tariff and the degree of dispersion around the average. Financial policy consists of four indicators:

(1) bank reserve ratios; (2) the ability of interest rates to fluctuate; (3) taxes on financial transactions; and (4) the quality of banking supervision. There are five indicators of tax policy, reflecting the complexity of the issue: (1) the maximum corporate tax rate; (2) the maximum rate of personal income tax; (3) the productivity of income taxes; (4) the basic rate of value added tax (VAT); and (5) the productivity of the VAT.[8] Privatizations are measured as the cumulative amount of privatizations, net of nationalizations, as a percentage of GDP. Labor legislation contains five components: (1) ease of hiring; (2) ease of firing; (3) flexibility of working hours; (4) social-security taxes (as a percentage of wages); and (5) the minimum wage expressed as a percentage of income per capita. These policy variables are not comprehensive. However, virtually any list of structural reforms would contain all or most of the indicators listed above. Further, structural reforms in these areas would tend to improve TFP over time.

The overall index of structural reform can vary from 0 to 1. A lower number indicates economic policy that tends to distort economic activity. A higher number represents policies that are more neutral for different types of economic activity and would enhance TFP. The absolute values for the overall index over time are given in Table 14.1. Values are given for the initial year of 1985, 2000, and 2009 for every country in the region and the regional average. Over the time span of nearly twenty-five years, the index has risen from 0.38 to 0.65. Starting in 1985, there were only five countries in the region with an index of 0.4 or above. By 2000, the regional index was nearly 0.6.

In the 2000s, the pace of reform had slowed. The regional average in 2009 was 0.65, and only four countries had an index below 0.6. Over the time span, the average change in the index was 0.27. Clearly, there have been substantial changes in economic policy for the region. Unfortunately, there is no perfect correlation between the depth of reforms and economic growth. The index can only show the potential for reform that changes in the law can allow. Whether or not these reforms translate into higher TFP and growth may be dependent on the overall environment of the country in which the reforms are occurring. In any country, structural reforms are difficult. As was covered

Table 14.1 Structural reform in Latin America

	1985	*2000*	*2009*	*Change*
Argentina	0.4	0.63	0.65	0.25
Bolivia	0.41	0.71	0.78	0.37
Brazil	0.3	0.57	0.66	0.36
Chile	0.54	0.73	0.8	0.26
Colombia	0.35	0.59	0.63	0.28
Costa Rica	0.38	0.56	0.56	0.18
Edcuador	0.34	0.52	0.59	0.25
El Salvador	0.37	0.61	0.64	0.27
Guatemala	0.38	0.59	0.66	0.28
Honduras	0.38	0.6	0.67	0.29
Mexico	0.35	0.52	0.53	0.18
Nicaragua	0.3	0.6	0.67	0.37
Paraguay	0.42	0.57	0.68	0.26
Peru	0.28	0.64	0.69	0.41
Uruguay	0.47	0.54	0.56	0.09
Venezuela	0.34	0.56	0.62	0.28
Latin America	0.38	0.60	0.65	0.27

Source: Lora (2012).

above and in Chapter 7, trade-policy reform is always hard, as there are identifiable losers from liberalizing trade. Structural reform in banking is difficult in most countries, as the banking industry is important and influential. Liberalization of banking frequently means more competition and lower profits for the domestic industry. In Latin America, the problem is heightened by the fact that liberalization is frequently accompanied by the movement of foreign banks into the domestic market. The need to reform tax systems in the region has been mentioned in a number of places. It is in this area that reform is both critical and probably easiest to accomplish. Governments in the region have critical needs for funds for infrastructure, education, and transfer payments. While reform of the tax systems will not automatically produce the necessary revenue, it is implausible to suppose that it could reduce it. The potentially positive effects on economic growth simply make reform both more attractive as a policy and more urgent. Privatizations are more a part of the economic history of the region than of the future. While there is still a need to reform or privatize some of the existing SOEs, the majority of that work has been accomplished. Finally, labor-market reform is critical and will also be politically difficult. It is critical, as the development of the labor-intensive industries the region needs to provide employment will be very difficult under existing labor laws. It will also be difficult, as many groups receive protection from these laws, and there will understandably be great resistance to change.

Neoliberalism and its critics

> And, of course, to my left-wing friends, whose ideas I share, in the hope that we may also agree on ways to achieve them.
>
> (Hernando de Soto)

For better or worse, this general drift in the direction of market forces has come to be known as *neoliberalism*. This movement from ISI to more market-based economic policies has been highly contentious, so much so that the term "neoliberalism" is most frequently used by its critics. Indeed, the debate has reached the point where it is somewhat hard to define exactly what the term means. Fortunately for economists, it doesn't really matter. One hardly ever hears the term "neoliberal" used by economists. The term is primarily used by noneconomists who are critical of capitalism in general. If one reads the critics closely, the debate, if one can call it that, is the assertion that capitalism creates poverty, inequality, pollution, the destruction of the environment, and a host of other social problems too numerous to mention. Only rarely does one hear any mention of what sort of system should replace capitalism in any sort of detail.

The Washington Consensus outlined above is just a set of statements representing the mainstream view of economic policy in a well-managed economy. To a certain extent, the same can be said of neoliberalism. However, in the policy debates concerning Latin America, there has been a tendency to define both the Washington Consensus and neoliberalism as being extremely rigid and dogmatic extensions of free-market economics. While both are relatively free-market-oriented, the Washington Consensus is hardly a "pure" free-market list. Indeed, one could just as easily call the list above the Madrid or Lisbon Consensus, as the Washington Consensus could be used to characterize virtually any high-income country, such as Spain or Portugal.[9]

Table 14.2 is designed to show where Latin America fits in terms of overall economic policy. The Fraser Institute puts out an annual report with an index number representing many of the points contained in the Washington Consensus. The index number varies

Table 14.2 Economic Freedom Indexes (2018)

	Index	Rank
Singapore	8.94	2
New Zealand	8.44	3
Australia	8.09	5
Ireland	8.05	6
UK	7.89	7
Canada	7.77	8
US	7.68	12
Chile	7.54	18
Sweden	7.52	19
Finland	7.49	20
Germany	7.35	24
Uruguay	6.86	40
Peru	6.78	45
Colombia	6.73	49
Panama	6.72	50
Spain	6.57	57
Costa Rica	6.53	61
Portugal	6.53	62
Mexico	6.47	66
France	6.38	71
Guatemala	6.26	77
Italy	6.22	80
El Salvador	6.18	84
Paraguay	6.18	85
Honduras	6.02	93
Nicaragua	5.77	107
Argentina	5.22	149
Brazil	5.19	150
Ecuador	4.69	170
Bolivia	4.23	173
Venezuela	2.59	179
Latin America	5.96	–

Source: Gwartney et al. (2019).

from 10 to 0, with the former being closer to market-oriented government policies and the latter representing more government action relative to market forces. The first and second columns show the index number and world rank, respectively, of a number of high-income countries. As an economist would expect, the differences among high-income countries are not extreme. On the other hand, the differences in Latin America have become large. Over half of the region is pursuing economic policy that is similar to that found in high-income countries. This is precisely where economists have trouble understanding the term "neoliberal." The country with the most neoliberal policy in the region is Chile, which has an index identical to that of Finland. The rest of the region is pursuing policies in which the role of government is still large. Obviously, there is plenty of room in the region for debates on economic policy. However, the characterization of economic policy in countries such as Chile, Peru, or Costa Rica as being extremely free-market relative to the rest of the world does not look credible. Countries moving in this direction are moving in the direction of the high-income countries of Asia, Europe, and North America.

Box 14.2 The two lefts in Latin America

From the above, it is clear that the criticism of the Washington Consensus over-whelmingly comes from the political left. In Latin America, as in most demo-cratic countries, the left is not a monolithic part of the political spectrum. Rather, the left in Latin America is represented by a variety of views on eco-nomic and political issues. While it is difficult to be precise, political scientists studying the left in Latin America typically divide it into two broad categories. The first is the moderate left. The distinguishing feature of the moderate left is the willingness of this group to work within the constraints of democratic cap-italism. Politically, this means a willingness to work within existing institutions and engage in compromise to achieve their goals. With respect to economic policy, a similar situation applies. The moderate left basically accepts the broad outlines of the Washington Consensus. The necessity of sound fiscal and mon-etary policy is no longer seriously questioned. In most countries, structural reforms are ongoing at a slow pace. This is understandable, as issues such as clean water and paved roads are somewhat difficult to turn into political issues. The debates on economic issues are now occurring in the narrow space that you would find in most developed countries, partially because the moderate left has accepted the proposition that economic development is difficult outside some form of capitalism.

The second group is referred to as the contestatory left. This group may reject the existing political framework. Their political goals are aimed at overhauling the existing political systems of their countries. In some cases, they may support the weakening of democratic institutions as a vehicle of change. The economics of the contestatory left are interesting. Watching the movements of governments at the bottom of the list in Table 14.2 is like watching a return to the past. Fiscal deficits become larger and are financed by increases in the money supply. Exchange rates are fixed or heavily managed. The resulting current-account deficits are financed by borrowing or exchange controls. Private-sector firms are nationalized or put under state control. Price controls and other interventions in the workings of the market become common.[10] The fiercest critics of neoliberalism have seemingly embraced the economic policies of the pre-1980 authoritarian regimes usually associated with the political right.

Growth versus equity

In assessing economic policy, it is important to understand the effects of policy changes on the welfare of those at the bottom of the income distribution. As noted in the pre-vious chapter, there is a difference between absolute and relative poverty. The distinc-tion is especially important in a developing country. In a developed country, only a very small percentage of the population is experiencing absolute poverty using a global standard. However, in developing countries, the problem of absolute poverty is perva-sive. In the middle-income countries of Latin America, the problem is still quite serious.

In these situations, economic growth is critical. However, how the increase in GDP is distributed can also be important. If high growth is positively correlated with a higher Gini coefficient, then the possibility of an unfortunate trade-off between growth and the welfare of the bottom of the income distribution could exist. In this section, we will discuss this trade-off in general and look at the case of Latin America in more detail.

The possibility of a trade-off between growth and income inequality has been discussed in the literature since the 1960s.[11] The trade-off for developing countries is a special case of a more general trade-off for all countries. As we saw in Chapter 3 and other places in the text, the possibility exists that government policy to accomplish a social goal may reduce economic growth. The question then becomes: do the costs and benefits work in favor of the policy? An example is pollution control. In the case of the distribution of income, the policy decisions are more difficult. In this case, to what extent is a society willing to sacrifice economic growth in order to achieve a more equitable distribution of income?[12] This is not an easy question to answer. In a developed country, the answer, given through the political process, may well be: to quite a large extent. In the absence of high levels of absolute poverty, the population of a high-income country may prefer a lower Gini coefficient coupled with a relatively low level of growth. The trade-off is different for a developing country. In the presence of high levels of absolute poverty coupled with a high Gini coefficient, an understandable government policy would be to quickly reduce the level of inequality via progressive taxes and large government transfer payment programs. However, if pushed too aggressively, this policy mix may have unfortunate consequences for economic growth. On the other hand, a mix of policies that maximizes growth could produce small gains for the bottom of the income distribution. This is especially problematical if absolute poverty is much more prevalent in rural areas that may be bypassed by the overall growth of the economy. The policy mix in China is a current example of high growth producing gains for society as a whole but with a rising Gini coefficient. The result is that in a middle-income country, finding the policy mix that balances growth with equity considerations can be extremely difficult.

In Latin America, this policy problem had the potential to be very serious indeed. The region has a long history of a very unequal distribution of income. The twentieth century did not improve the situation. However well intentioned, ISI had a tendency to increase the Gini coefficient. In this case, the policy mix was designed to produce rapid industrialization. A by-product of the policy mix was favoring groups in society that were already relatively well-off. The new industrialists did not spring from the ranks of the poor. Policies such as protectionism, access to cheap credit, and access to foreign exchange virtually guaranteed private-sector firms abnormal profits. Even in the SOEs, wages and benefits were frequently much higher than would have prevailed in a free market. The union movement also provided wages that were high by local standards. The policies were accompanied by implicit discrimination against the agricultural sector. Overvalued exchange rates reduced the profitability of the sector. Poor transportation infrastructure and other infrastructure such as electricity reduced the ability of rural areas to participate in economic growth. The lack of educational opportunities in rural areas contributed to both absolute and relative poverty. ISI proved to be almost the worst of all possible development strategies. It tended to slow down growth, which hindered the reduction of absolute poverty. In addition, it produced a very high Gini coefficient.

The slow dismantling of ISI during the Lost Decade was inevitable, but initially had unfortunate consequences. Growth in GDP per capita stagnated as the region struggled to find a macroeconomic equilibrium. The Gini coefficient continued to rise all through the Lost Decade. An initial reaction was that moving from ISI to a more free-market form of capitalism was going to end up making the poor in the region even worse off. In the 1990s, growth returned in the region, accompanied by an overall improvement in wages and living standards. However, the gains were still spread unevenly, as the Gini coefficient continued to rise at a slower rate. The situation changed dramatically at the end of the twentieth century. The percentage of the population of the region defined as poor began to fall. Both absolute poverty and the Gini coefficient have declined dramatically. At least for now, Latin America has been able to beat the uncomfortable choices associated with economic growth and equity. This situation has been created by a number of factors. First, the dismantling of ISI is improving both growth and the distribution of income. As distortions to economic activity are removed, both capital and labor are moving to more productive activities. This has a tendency to favor labor, as ISI tended to favor capital-intensive industries. This movement produces increases in growth along with reductions in the Gini coefficient. In addition, government transfer payments have risen, which primarily benefits the poor. A final factor is that the flow of remittances from the developed countries to Latin America has risen dramatically. As these funds tend to be concentrated among the poor, both the absolute and relative incomes of the poor increase.

Going forward, there is the possibility that this favorable trend could continue. The dismantling of ISI is an ongoing process that is far from complete. Tariffs in the region are still high by global standards. In many countries, the allocation of capital is still distorted by state-owned financial institutions. As market forces come more into play in the economies of the region and economic growth improves, both absolute and relative poverty could continue to improve. As was shown in Chapter 3, economic growth in the region is still slower than is possible. In the current environ-ment, more of this growth seems to be reaching the poor than is typically the case. It is also clear that policies to improve growth would also increase the welfare of the poor. Improvements in infrastructure would increase the ability of the rural poor to participate in economic growth. In a world where wages are increasingly a function of human capital, improvements in education would have a disproportionately positive impact on the poor. The same would be true of improvements in institutional quality. Corruption and poor government services adversely impact the poor much more than the rich or middle class. These positive trends can be supplemented by government transfer payments. The ability to provide such payments may be contingent on the countries of the region being able to generate sufficient tax revenues. This has proven to be difficult so far. In this case, as in many others, the legacy of colonial Latin America is still apparent.

Key terms and concepts

heterodox economics: a term describing the collection of schools of thought in
economics that are currently outside the mainstream of the economics profession.
neoliberalism: in a Latin American context, the tendency to shift government
economic policy from a heavy reliance on government intervention in the economy
to more market-based economic policies.

Washington Consensus: a term referring to a loose collection of primarily market-based economic policies.

Questions for review and discussion

1 Why did ISI become unsustainable?
2 What is crony capitalism? How is it related to ISI?
3 How does ISI still affect Latin America in the twenty-first century?
4 Describe the Washington Consensus.
5 How was the Washington Consensus related to ISI?
6 Describe the Chicago Boys.
7 What is the proper role of an economist in an authoritarian government? Is it acceptable for an economist to work for an authoritarian government?
8 Why is sound fiscal policy so important in Latin America?
9 What does the term "structural reform" mean? Why is structural reform important?
10 How is the Washington Consensus related to neoliberalism?
11 Could economic policy in Latin America be considered extremely free market?
12 What are the two types of the left in Latin America?
13 How are growth and equity related in Latin America?

Notes

1 The current situation in Venezuela is very similar to past problems common to the region.
2 For more on this, see the essays in Haber (2002).
3 For an outstanding treatment of the economics of authoritarian regimes, see Wintrobe (1998).
4 For a more complete analysis of the Washington Consensus, see Birdsall et al. (2011).
5 A sign of this turnaround occurred in (2009) with the report of the president of a country in Latin America lecturing a prime minister in Europe on fiscal prudence. For details, see *The Telegraph* (2009).
6 For more detail, see Dincer and Eichengreen (2014).
7 Central bank independence was an issue in the (2014) Brazilian elections.
8 The productivity of taxes refers to which taxes are neutral with respect to different economic activities.
9 For a description of how this occurred, see Williamson (2004).
10 For a more complete discussion of these issues, see Kingstone (2011).
11 For an example, see Adelman and Morris (1973). For a recent review of this issue for Latin America, see Ffrench-Davis and Machinea (2007).
12 For the classic statement of the problem, see Okun (1975).

References

Adelman, Irma and Cynthia T. Morris (1973) *Economic Growth and Social Equity in Developing Countries*, Palo Alto, Calif.: Stanford University Press.
Birdsall, Nancy, Augusto de la Torre, and Felipe Valencia Caicedo (2011) "The Washington Consensus: Assessing a Damaged Brand," in José A. Ocampo and Jaime Ros (eds.), *The Oxford Handbook of Latin American Economics*, Oxford: Oxford University Press, pp. 79–107.
Dincer, Nergiz N. and Barry Eichengreen (2014) "Central Bank Transparency and Independence: Updates and Measures," *International Journal of Central Banking*, 10 (March): 189–253.

Ffrench-Davis, Ricardo and José L. Machinea (eds.) (2007) *Economic Growth with Equity: Challenges for Latin America*, New York: Palgrave Macmillan.

Gwartney, James, Robert Hall, and Joshua Lawson (2019) *Economic Freedom of the World: 2018 Annual Report*, Vancouver: Fraser Institute.

Haber, Stephen (ed.) (2002) *Crony Capitalism and Economic Growth in Latin America: Theory and Evidence*, Washington, DC: Hoover Institute.

Kingstone, Peter (2018) *The Political Economy of Latin America: Reflections on Neoliberalism and Development*, 2nd edn, London and New York: Routledge.

Lora, Eduardo (2012) "Structural Reforms in Latin America: What Has Been Reformed and How to Measure It," *IDB Working Paper Series No. IDB-WP-346*, Washington, DC: Inter-American Development Bank.

Okun, Arthur (1975) *Equality and Efficiency: The Big Tradeoff*, Washington, DC: Brookings Institute.

The Telegraph (2009) "Gordon Brown Embarrassed by Chile President on Economy," March 27.

Williamson, John (2004) "The Strange History of the Washington Consensus," *Journal of Post Keynesian Economics*, 27 (winter): 195–206.

Wintrobe, Ronald (1998) *The Political Economy of Dictatorship*, Cambridge: Cambridge University Press.

World Bank (2012) "Shifting Gears to Accelerate Prosperity in LAC: Ending Extreme Poverty and Promoting Shared Prosperity in Latin America and the Caribbean," *Poverty and Labor Brief*, Washington, DC: World Bank.

Recommended reading

Cook, Maria L. (2007) *The Politics of Labor Market Reform in Latin America: Between Flexibility and Rights*, University Park, Pa.: Pennsylvania State University Press.

Edwards, Sebastian (2010) *Left Behind: Latin America and the False Promise of Populism*, Chicago, Ill.: University of Chicago Press.

Inter-American Development Bank (2006) *The Politics of Policies*, Washington, DC: Inter-American Development Bank.

Lopez-Calva, Luis F. and Nora Lustig (eds.) (2010) *Declining Inequality in Latin America: A Decade of Progress?* Washington, DC: Brookings Institution.

Mendoza, Apuleyo M., Carlos A. Montaner, and Alvaro V. Llosa (2000) *Guide to the Perfect Latin American Idiot*, New York: Madison.

Reid, Michael (2007) *Forgotten Continent: The Battle for Latin America's Soul*, New Haven, Conn.: Yale University Press.

Index

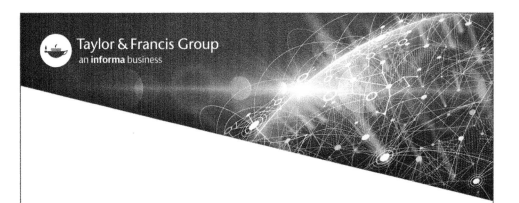